Book of Tasty and Healthy Food

Ministry of the Food Industry, USSR

CONTENTS

INTRODUCTION

"Book of Tasty and Healthy Food" - Iconic Cookbook of the USSR

"Book of Tasty and Healthy Food" is a soviet collection of culinary recipes and food-preparation hints, curated by the USSR Ministry of Food and by people's commissar Anastas Mikoyan himself. It was first published in 1939.

This book discusses the basics of healthy eating, provides information about food products made in USSR and gives recipes of various dishes.

Updated editions of the book were coming out almost every year. There were about 8 million copies of the book printed since 1952.

Currently the "Book of Tasty and Healthy Food" is viewed as one of canonic symbols of Soviet propaganda: the assortment of ingredients described in the book was almost never available in stores to an average Soviet citizen.

History and Background

The idea to create a modernized and universal culinary book first appeared in mid-1930s, after food ration cards were done away with. It was first envisioned as a scientific work, emphasizing the importance of healthy nutrition. It was written by experienced chefs, doctors and prominent scientists. First edition was published in 1939.

SELECTING DISHES FOR BREAKFAST, LUNCH AND DINNER

Correct distribution of nutrients and selection of dishes during the day is one of the most important requirements of rational nutrition.

While selecting ingredients for breakfast, lunch, and dinner, you have to consider which particular foods and their quantities are required for different members of the family, depending on their age and occupation.

A person who leaves their home in the morning without having breakfast will quickly tire at work and will experience loss of energy far ahead of lunch. Overabundant lunch on the other hand will result in drowsiness and loss of productivity.

Adults should eat three to four times a day, while children and adolescents should eat four to five times.

All these circumstances require us to consider how to plan our meals, how to allocate food products throughout the day, what to cook for breakfast, lunch, and dinner.

Московский
ордена Ленина
Мясокомбинат
им.А.И.Микояна

Сибирские
ПЕЛЬМЕНИ

Breakfast first of all has to be nourishing, it could consist of boiled or fried meat or fish, eggs, cheese, bread, tea, coffee, or milk. It's advisable to eat porridge (oatmeal, buckwheat, millet) with milk or butter, and fruits.

Lunch - about three to four hours after start of work - should include one hot dish, preferably vegetarian (casserole, ragout, burgers), sandwiches with tea (or milk or coffee). It can also include hot dogs or bratwurst.

It is recommended to have dinner sometime after finishing work, when a person had some rest and managed to work up an appetite. Dinner could have up to three courses. First course – meat, vegetable, or fish soup, second course – roasted or fried meat, fish, or vegetable dish, and dessert - compote, pastry and fruits. To improve the appetite before the beginning of dinner it is recommended to serve an appetizer or a salad.

If a meat-based soup (shchi, borscht, pickle soup) is served for the first course, then the second course should be light – cooked from vegetables, grain, or fish; and conversely, if the first course is light (broth with vegetables or soup-puree), then the second course should be more substantial – dishes with meat or fish with garnish.

Supper is always assumed to be light, and should be eaten no later than two to three hours before sleep. Recommendations include salads, yogurt, eggs, sandwiches, vegetable casseroles, milk, tea, vegetable and fruit juices.

If work schedule or other circumstances do not permit to eat four meals per day, three meals can be eaten instead - a big breakfast before work, another meal during a break and dinner after work.

Cumulative amount of food per day (or daily ration) depends on height, weight, age, climate, type of work and season. It is not advisable to eat too much meat. It is recommended that plenty of plant-based foods are included - vegetables, fruits and berries.

The menu must have variety. Oftentimes, this is overlooked. Not all housewives take the time and effort to make a plan for food preparation in advance. Mostly they only have around 10 or 12 dishes that they alternate throughout the years, and the family receives monotonous meals.

Seasons should also be taken into

consideration. In the fall and winter hot meat and fish soups should be consumed, and in the spring and summer many prefer cold soups - cold borscht, fruit and berry soups. Fish products are more plentiful in the spring and fall, and during spring and summer dairy, eggs, fowl and vegetables are abundant.

Very important for menu selection is the frequency with which different dishes and ingredients are consumed. Borscht, shchi, cutlets will taste more delicious if they appear on the menu once every ten days, or every week, at most. Therefore it is important to think of daily menu for ten days in advance and stick to it, if possible. Combining foods is also important - for example, if potatoes or porridge were eaten for breakfast, it is better not to eat these foods again for lunch - it is better to eat a vegetable casserole instead.

If there are small children or ill people in the family, it is important to account for that. Also, people who are engaged in physically demanding labor need to eat more than those who have sedentary lifestyles.

Housewives should keep in mind that some foods take longer to prepare then others, and plan accordingly for meals such as breakfast, when everyone is in a rush, and quick preparation is essential.

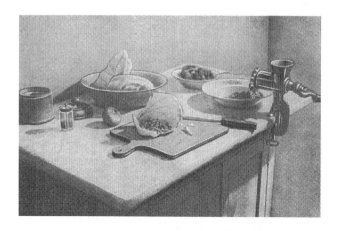

ORDER OF DINNER PREPARATION

Before starting to cook lunch, breakfast, or dinner, it is necessary to decide what time it needs to be ready by, and determine how much time will be needed to prepare this meal. Also keep in mind that as soon as lunch, breakfast, or dinner is ready, it is best to serve it immediately, otherwise it will get cold and will no longer taste great.

It is important to be punctual when serving breakfast, lunch or dinner. Each dish should be delicious and have a visual appeal.

If there is too little time remaining before lunch you should select ingredients that can be cooked fast. In this case, it is better to use meat or fish-based ready-to-cook foods. You can buy different kinds of vegetables - fresh, canned, frozen - already cleaned, washed, and peeled.

Ready-to-cook foods used can be of different types and varieties - cutlets, steaks, shish kebabs, fish fillets, etc. Different types of sauces can be purchased and used for these dishes.

Dinner can be quickly made from canned food - mean or fish soups, stewed meat, fish with different sauces, corn with butter. Canned fruits and berries make excellent desserts.

Dinner preparation can be sped up by combining ready-to-cook foods with canned foods. For example, cutlets can be served with garnish of canned corn, beans or green peas. Fish fillet can prepared with canned beans. Different salads can be complemented by canned fish, crab meat, crayfish, etc. Mayonnaise can be used as dressing for these types of salads.

Finally, a wide assortment of already-made products such as sausages, smoked goods, meat pates, hot dogs, bratwurst, dairy, etc., allows preparing and serving lunch or breakfast in 10 to 15 minutes.

Using ready-to-cook foods saves a tremendous amount to time and frees the housewife from the most labor-intensive and unpleasant work in the kitchen - cleaning fish, vegetables and meat. It makes cleaning the kitchen easier and there are not that many dishes to be washed afterwards.

Besides ready-to-make and canned foods, there are other options available in stores, such as bouillon concentrates and powdered soups that can be used when meal preparation time is limited. In this case preparation time will be as quick as boiling a pot of water.

The recipes in this book contain the amount of ingredients needed to prepare a dish for approximately 4-5 people. It is understood that that if there are more or less people, the amount of ingredients must be adjusted, but proportions should remain the same. For 500 grams of meat that's used for borscht it is recommended to take around 800 grams of different vegetables; if there is more meat, for example 750 grams, then 1,200 grams of vegetables should be used, and more water as well. Incorrect proportion of water and vegetables will made borscht either to thick or too watery. For cutlets, incorrect amounts of bread or liquid added to ground meat can make the cutlets less juicy and shapely then they otherwise could have been.

The amount of garnish should also correspond to the amount of the main product. For example, if each person is served 100 grams of meat or fish, garnish should be 150-200 grams of potatoes or 100-150 grams of macaroni or porridge.

When starting to make dinner, in order to save time it is first recommended to start on ingredients that need longer cooking, or those that need to be served cool.

Let's take for example a three-course dinner with an appetizer of herring. First course is meat-based shchi, second course is cutlets with fried potatoes and third is kissel. Preparing this meal would begin with cooking meat and boiling broth. Part of the washed meat, placed on a board, should be put aside in a bowl for cutlets, and the rest of meat and bones should be placed in a pot with water and put on a stove. Herring that previously has been soaked in water can be cleaned, cut and served on a plate, shaped as one whole fish. Boil the potatoes, which will be needed as garnish for cutlets and herring. Then, after thoroughly washing hands, boil kissel, which must cool off before lunch. While kissel is being made, broth will start to boil. Fire underneath the pot needs to be reduced. Now it is time to take care about onions and cabbage for shchi - clean, wash them and cut them, and fry them if desired.

By this time the broth is almost ready, it needs to be strained into a soup pan, put the meat there, add cabbage, salt, pepper, bay leaf and continue to boil.

While shchi is boiling, prepare ground meat and cutlets, cover them in breadcrumbs, put them before frying on a board or on a plate and cover with a towel. Boiled potatoes need to be peeled, cut and fried (part of boiled potatoes can be used as garnish for herring), and start frying cutlets on another frying pan.

In 15 to 20 minutes after this dinner will be ready. Remove meat from shchi, cut it, put it on plates, pour shchi into them, add sour cream and parsley.

Ready cutlets and garnish (fried potatoes) are placed on a plate. Pour some broth into the frying pan where cutlets were frying, boil it, strain and use as sauce for cutlets. Sprinkle potatoes with parsley.

Some lunch dishes can be prepared so that leftovers might be used for dinner or breakfast. For example, potatoes can be boiled in such amounts so that there is enough to use some for dinner's salad. Some of leftover cutlets can be eaten during dinner or breakfast.

Finally, broth can also be made for two days. In this case, half of the broth can be used for shchi, and another half can be used the next day to make a different kind of soup.

Food storage is very important, even for short periods of time, like one or two days. Meat, fish, dairy, fresh vegetables and fruits deteriorate rapidly, losing their smell, taste and color. Cold is the best way of keeping these products fresh.

After finishing your meal, wash all dishes

and silverware with hot water and soda or soap, rinse with cold water, dry it and store away. Leaving dishes unwashed is unacceptable, because food remains rot, smell and attract flies. It also makes dishes turn dark over time.

SETTING UP THE TABLE

Cover the table with white, well-pressed tablecloth. Middle fold of the tablecloth should be at the center of the table. It is recommended to place flannel or some other type of heavy, soft cloth underneath - tablecloth will be resting straight and the noise of plates and silverware will be reduced.

Depending on the number of people at the table, put two or three plates of thinly sliced black and white bread, positioning them in such a way so that they are close to each set of silverware. Wine (except champagne) needs to be served in bottles that have already been opened. Same goes for mineral water. Vodka should be served in decanter. Open champagne immediately before pouring it into glasses. Appetizers should be positioned throughout the table.

Quantity of containers with pepper, vinegar, sauces, mustard and salt would depend on the number of meal participants. It is desirable to place containers with seasonings closer to the middle line of the table. Silverware and plates should preferably be from the matching set for the whole table.

Each guest and family member will have a shallow plate with appetizer plate on top of it, and a dessert plate on the left side of it. To the right of the plate put a spoon and a knife (knife's cutting edge should be facing the plate), and to the left put a fork. Spoon and fork should lie with their concave side on the top. Ideally, a small salt shaker should be placed next to each person or be shared between two people. Napkins, folded into a triangle or cap shape is placed on top of the appetizer plate.

Usually there is a limited variety of wine during a home meal. Therefore, there is no need for extra glasses on the table. If you are having a celebration, put a shot glass for vodka, a glass for wine, and a tall glass for mineral water or fruit/tomato juice next to each person.

Flowers will add beauty to the table. Place them in the middle of the table in vases that are not too tall.

Next to the dining table, next to the hostess' seat, you may put a small table where a soup bowl, clean soup plates, etc., can be placed.

If there are 5 or 6 people sitting at the table, the host or hostess may easily pass the dishes around the table. If there are more people, it might be more convenient to carry the dishes around. Keep the following rule in mind - if the food is already placed on the plate for the guest to eat, give it to them from the right side; if the food is given on a serving plate for each guest to take it into their individual plates and then come to the guest from the left.

If dinner consists mostly of cold foods, they may be placed on the table right away, if the size of the table allows that, of course.

Approximately in the middle of the table, place a plate with stew, to the right and to the left of it put plates with fish and appetizers. Between the plates put wine bottles and pitchers with tomato and fruit juices. Sauceboats should be placed in different locations, depending on the size of the table and the number of guests.

Place only knife and fork, since soups are rarely served for supper. If broth has been prepared, serve it in broth bowls and place a dessert spoon on little plates.

Evening tea (which sometimes can replace supper) is served somewhat differently. Put tablecloth on the table, preferably multi-colored. Samovar or kettle with hot water is placed on a little table next to the main one, by the hostess, who will pour tea.

In the middle of the table put vases with candy and jams, next to them - bowls with cookies covered with napkins, little plates with thinly sliced lemon, decanters with fruit and berry juices, cognac, cream or milk, sugar. It would also be nice to serve one or two bottles of dessert wine for this table.

If tea is replacing a light supper, then have some butter, ham, cheese, cold beef and other sandwich meats on the table. Distribute decanters with fruit and berry juices, wine or cognac evenly around the table. Each family member or guest will have a dessert plate with a tea napkin placed on top of it. To the left of the plate put a dessert fork, and to the right - dessert knife.

Main goal of setting up the table is comfort, neatness and pleasant look of the dinner or tea table. Here is a sample set of tableware for 6 people:

Deep Plates 6
Shallow Plates 6
Appetizer Plates 6
Dessert Plates 6
Plate for Herring 1
Salad Bowls 2
Soup Bowl 1
Sauceboat 1
Round Dish 1
Oval Dish 1
Dish for Bread 1
Broth Bowls with Saucers 6
Containers for pepper, mustard and vinegar 1
Decanter for Water 1
Decanter for Fruit Juice 1
Decanter for Vodka 1
Wine Glasses 6
Shot Glasses 6
Champagne Glasses 6
Knives, forks, desert forks 6

Children should be taught how to behave properly while eating and how to use spoon, knife and fork. They need to be taught to sit up straight and not lean on the table, as it disturbs their neighbors. Unacceptable behaviors include rocking in the chair, playing with tablecloth - it is possible to drag the tablecloth off the table and burn yourself with hot broth. Children should never be allowed to put knives in their mouth - it is possible to cut lips and tongue. This is where the rule of not eating off the knife comes from. Another categorical rule is never to pick your teeth with anything other than a toothpick. After eating it is advised to rinse the mouth with warm water that has been boiled and baking soda.

Cutlets, meatballs, fish, boiled vegetables and similar foods are not cut with a knife, but rather just divided into smaller pieces with a fork. Fork is held in the right hand in this particular case. If the second course includes food that needs to be cut with a knife, then the fork needs to be held in left hand, and knife in right hand, since it is easier to cut with right hand.

While cutting food with knife, fork is to be held in a tilted position. If fork is held perpendicular to the plate, it might slip and throw the contents of the plate onto the table.

When children are done eating, they should put their fork and spoon not on the tablecloth, but on the plate instead.

Meat and other foods should not be cut into small pieces immediately on your plate, they should instead be cut gradually, as you're consuming them during the course of the meal. Small pieces get cold very quickly and eating them might affect digestion negatively.

Children should know that they should not use their own individual knife, fork and spoon to take food from common plates and dishes that are used to serve everyone at the table.

For common plates and dishes their own utensils are used. Most of the time these utensils are of different shape and size than individual ones. Only these utensils are to be used to put food on your plate. It is also unacceptable to cut bread with your own knife. This rule is dictated by common sense concepts of personal hygiene.

In addition, children should be taught to chew their food well, not rush and be neat. Bad table habits of eating loud and messy should not be allowed to form - this will become a burden to them and those around them.

SAMPLE MENUS FOR ALL SEASONS

Sample Spring Menu (Three Course Dinner and Appetizer)

Sunday
Salad "Spring"
Whitefish appetizer

Meat broth with pirozhki
Sour-cress soup

Fried spring chickens
Roast-beef
Vareniki with farmers cheese

Rhubarb kissel
Airy cake

Monday
Radish with oil

Herring with garnish

Pureed lettuce soup
Potato soup

Chopped beef sausage
Fried bream
Vegetable ragout

Berry preserves jelly
Compote of preserved fruits

Tuesday
Salad with ham
Smoked salmon

Beef broth with omelet

Shchi

Fried veal
Potato and beef casserole
Curd cake with sour cream

Kissel with dried apples
Sweet pie

Wednesday
Squash puree
Poltavskaya sausage

Chicken broth
Noodles in milk soup

Chicken pilaf
Stuffed fish sausage
Rice casserole

Frozen fruit compote
Sponge roll with jam

Thursday
Radish salad with sour cream dressing
Marinated walleye

Beef broth with toasts
Liver soup

Fried lamb
Schnitzel with sour cream sauce
Crepes with curd

Sour cherry kissel
Guriev porridge

Friday
Salad with game
Liverwurst

Shurpa
Ukha with pirozhki

Beef, stewed with onions
Fish stuffed with porridge
Millet casserole

Cranberry mousse
Ice cream

Saturday
Canned vegetables
Salmon caviar

Noodles with chicken

Potato soup-puree

Boiled beef
Beef Stroganoff
Noodle pie with curd

Prune compote
Chocolate cream

Sample Summer Menu (Three Course Dinner and Appetizer)

Sunday
Salad with fresh tomatoes and cucumbers
Smoked whitefish (balik)

Green shchi
Botvinya with fish

Breaded and fried spring chickens
Schnitzel
Eggplant stewed with sour cream

Fresh berries ice cream
Sour cherry kissel

Monday
Vinaigrette with fruits and vegetables
Liver pate

Rassolnik with kidneys
Cauliflower soup

Boiled fish with potatoes
Veal schnitzel
Stuffed squash

Strawberry kissel
Apricot compote

Tuesday
Fried eggplant
Semi-smoked sausage

Vegetable soup
Okroshka with meat

Fried fish in breadcrumbs
Sausage patties with milk sauce
Buckwheat porridge with milk

Raspberry mousse
Vanilla breadcrumbs pudding

Wednesday
Salad with greens and game
Gravlax

Potato soup with fresh mushrooms
Milk soup with oatmeal

Shish-kebab
Beefsteak with onions
Young potatoes with sour cream

Peach compote
Blini with apples

Thursday
Fruit salad
Boiled tongue

Broth with root vegetables and greens
Ukrainian borscht

Canned sturgeon with sour cream
Fried brains
Potato roll with vegetables

Vanilla ice-cream
Berry pie

Friday
Cod salad with mayonnaise
Eggplant caviar

Summer shchi with potatoes
Fish soup with potatoes

Meatballs in tomato sauce
Omelet with tomatoes
Cauliflower with breadcrumbs

Currant kissel
Watermelon

Saturday
Tomato salad
Chopped herring

Broth with root vegetables and rice
Vegetable okroshka

Lamb ragout
Rice porridge with milk
Stuffed cabbage

Apple and plum compote
Red wine jelly

Sample Fall Menu (Three Course Dinner and

Appetizer)

Sunday
Baskets with salad
Mushrooms in sour cream

Cauliflower soup
Chicken soup-puree

Fried duck with apples
Cutlets natural
Stuffed eggplant

Apple and pear compote
White bread and apple pudding

Monday
Vinaigrette
Canned fish

Potato and meat soup
Pea soup

Sturgeon in tomato and mushroom sauce
Macaroni roll
Vegetarian holubtsi

Apple kissel
Rice pudding

Tuesday
Fish and tomato salad
Beet caviar

Bozbash
Tomato soup

Rabbit in white sauce
Fish cutlets
Vegetable and bean ragout

Grapes
Blini with jam

Wednesday
Sprats with potatoes
Mushrooms in sour cream

Shchi with white cabbage
Fish soup with grains

Chopped schnitzel
Stuffed peppers
Curd dumplings

Apple mousse
Melon with sugar

Thursday
Salad "Health"
Sardines

Clear broth with dumplings
Assembled meat solyanka

Offal ragout
Liver in sour cream
Cabbage cutlets

Milk kissel
Apples in puff pastry

Friday
Lamprey with onions

Forshmak (Chopped herring salad)

Brussels sprouts soup
Mushroom soup with prunes

Fried pork
Buckwheat patties
Potato pirozhki with mushrooms

Fresh fruit compote
Pastries with cream

Saturday
Salad with sausage
Stuffed peppers

Broth with meatballs
Pumpkin soup

Beef kidneys in onion sauce
Noodle pie with eggs
Blini with meat

Angel cake with apples
Sour cream mousse

Sample Winter Menu (Three Course Dinner and Appetizer)

Sunday
Suckling pig in aspic
Baskets with eggs and salad

Broth with pelmeni
Fish solyanka

Fried goose with apples

Entrecote with potatoes
Blini with curd

Orange jelly
Compote with oranges and liquor

Monday
Meat salad
Smoked sturgeon

Shchi with sauerkraut
Apple soup

Walleye fried in dough
Lamb stew with vegetables
Bean patties with mushroom sauce

Berry syrup kissel
Mandarin oranges

Tuesday
Vinaigrette with stuffed peppers
Beef aspic with horseradish

Meat soup with barley
Bean soup

Rump steak
Fried veal liver
Curd casserole

Apple and mandarin orange compote
Guriev porridge

Wednesday
Mushroom caviar
Bean spread

Mushroom soup with pirozhki
Chihirtma with lamb (Georgian soup)

Chicken with white sauce
Hot dogs with cabbage
Pilaf with raisins

Lemon jelly
Dried fruit compote

Thursday
Sour cabbage salad with apples
Smoked salmon

Meat soup with noodles
Green pea soup

Goulash with potatoes
Hare in sour cream
Stuffed turnip

Oranges
Blini with jam

Friday
Crab salad
Roast pork

Broth with toasts
Kharcho

Fried meat in sour cream and onions
Breaded fried brains
Krupenik (grain casserole)

Prune and dried apricots compote

Apples baked with jam

Saturday
Cod and horseradish salad
Blini with sour cream

Bean soup
Borscht with prunes
Fried blackcock

Pelmeni in butter
Barley casserole

Cranberry kissel
Walnut pudding

COLD DISHES
AND
APPETIZERS

COLD DISHES AND APPETIZERS

SALADS

Green Salad with Sour Cream and Eggs

Ingredients:
300 g salad greens
1 medium cucumber
1 egg, hard boiled
1/2 cup sour cream and vinegar dressing

Cut washed and dried salad greens into bite-sized pieces and put them into a bowl. Cut egg into slices and mix with dressing made from sour cream and vinegar. Dress salad right before serving, lay it into a salad bowl and surround with sliced cucumber. Top with finely chopped dill or parsley leaves. This salad goes well with all meat and fish dishes.

Salad with Oil and Vinegar

Ingredients:
300 g salad greens

1/4 cup dressing (salad oil mixed with vinegar)

Cut washed and dried salad greens into bite-sized pieces. Just before serving dress salad with oil mixed with vinegar, top with finely chopped dill or parsley leaves. You can also add thinly sliced cucumbers or croutons made from white bread rubbed with garlic and cut into decorative shapes. This salad could be served with any fried or boiled meat, or with fried fish.

Salad "Health"

Ingredients:
2 medium cucumbers
2 medium carrots
2 medium apples
2 medium tomatoes
100 g salad greens
1/2 cup sour cream
Juice of 1/4 lemon

Julienne washed cucumbers, carrots, and apples. Cut salad greens into bite-sized pieces. Mix it all together and dress with sour cream mixed with lemon juice, salt, and sugar. Decorate the salad with slices of tomatoes. Due to raw fruits and vegetables in this salad, it contains a significant amount of vitamins.

Fresh Cucumber Salad with Sour Cream Dressing

Ingredients:
3 medium cucumbers
1/4 cup sour cream
1/2 tbsp vinegar

Put washed and thinly sliced crosswise cucumbers into a salad bowl. Just before serving lightly season with salt and pepper, and add dressing made from sour cream mixed with vinegar and salt. Top with finely chopped dill. This salad is served with meat and fish sausage patties, fried meat and fish, or by itself.

Radish Salad with Sour Cream Dressing

Ingredients:
2-3 bunches of radishes
1 egg, hard-boiled
1/2 cup sour cream

Thinly slice washed radishes and egg white. Mash egg yolk in a bowl together with sour cream and some salt. Put radishes with egg white into a bowl and mix it with dressing.
Popular variations of this salad include finely-chopped dill or scallions.

Salad with Fresh Tomatoes and Cucumbers

Ingredients:
5-6 medium tomatoes
2-3 medium cucumbers
3-4 tbsp vinegar
2 tbsp salad oil

Slice washed tomatoes and cucumbers into circles, season with salt and pepper and arrange in a salad bowl. Dress with oil and vinegar right before serving and top with finely chopped dill or parsley leaves.
This salad could be made with only cucumbers or

tomatoes. Fresh tomatoes could also be replaced with canned ones. You can also add thinly sliced onions or scallions. This salad is served with meat of fish sausage patties, boiled or fried meat or fish, or by itself.

Beet Salad

Ingredients:
2-3 medium beets
1/4 cup vinegar
2 tbsp salad oil

Boil or bake beets in the oven until cooked through. Once cooled, peel and julienne beets, season with salt and pepper and add oil and vinegar. Top with finely-chopped dill or parsley leaves. This salad goes well with fried or boiled meat. You can also make this salad with potatoes. If using potatoes - use equal quantities of beets to potatoes.

Potato Salad

Ingredients:
500 g potatoes
50 g scallions, thinly sliced
1/4 cup vinegar
2 tbsp salad oil

Wash and boil potatoes in their skins. Once potatoes are cooked through, peel and slice them. Season with salt and pepper, mix with dressing. Pile seasoned potatoes on a plate and top with scallions. You can also add finely chopped dill or parsley leaves. This salad is served with hot or cold fried mean, veal, lamb, pork, or fish, or could be eaten by itself. It is especially delicious when made from freshly-cooked warm potatoes.

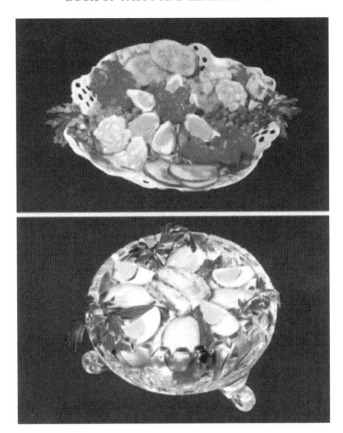

Red Cabbage Salad

Ingredients:
500 g red cabbage
1/4 cup vinegar
1/2 tbsp sugar

Remove the outer leaves from a head of red cabbage and wash it well. Cut cabbage into quarters and remove the core. Finely shred cabbage with a very sharp knife or a mandoline. Put shredded cabbage into a pot and cover with boiling water. Let it stand for 20 to 30 minutes, drain and rinse with cold water, then squeeze dry. Put squeezed cabbage into a salad bowl and mix with sugar and vinegar, let stand another 20 to 30 minutes. You can also add a tablespoon of salad oil to this salad.

Another version of this salad could be made by rubbing shredded cabbage with salt between your palms until it becomes soft and releases its juice. Once the juice is released the cabbage should be squeezed and then mixed with sugar and vinegar. After a couple of minutes the cabbage will become bright red. This salad could be served with meat, poultry, and fish.

White Cabbage Salad

Ingredients:
500 g white cabbage
1/4 cup vinegar
1/2 tbsp sugar

Remove outer leaves and wash a head of white cabbage. Cut it into quarters, remove the core and shred finely. Salt shredded cabbage lightly and rub it between your palms until is becomes soft and releases its juice. Squeeze the cabbage dry and put it into a salad bowl together with vinegar and sugar. Let it stand for 30 to 40 minutes. If desired - you can add 1 tablespoon of salad oil into this salad.

The salad could also be prepared by lightly heating shredded cabbage, together with salt and vinegar, in a pot on a stove top, mixing all the time until the cabbage settles down and becomes soft. Cool the cabbage and dress with sugar and a little bit of oil.

White Cabbage, Apple, and Celery Salad

Ingredients:
500 g white cabbage
1 stick celery
1 apple
1/4 cup vinegar
1/2 tbsp sugar

Peel and core apple and slice it thinly. Wash and cut celery into 4-5 cm matchsticks. Prepare cabbage as described in "White cabbage salad" recipe. Mix apple, celery, and cabbage together, put it into a salad bowl and season with sugar and vinegar. This salad goes well with all fried or boiled meat or fish dishes, as a garnish to cold meat or fish, or by itself.

Sour Cabbage Salad

Ingredients:
500 g sour cabbage
1 tbsp salad oil
1-2 tbsp sugar

Mix sour cabbage with sugar and oil (ed. note - Russian sour cabbage differs from sauerkraut, see recipe. Most of the time, however, sauerkraut can be used instead and the names will be used interchangeably). If desired - add thinly sliced fresh or fermented apples, celery, or fresh or pickled cranberries. This salad goes well with frankfurters, brats, fried pork, or boiled poultry.

"Spring" Salad

Ingredients:
100 g salad greens
2 eggs
2 medium cucumbers
1 bunch radishes
1 medium carrot, boiled
2-3 medium potatoes, boiled

2 medium tomatoes
50 g scallions
3/4 cup sour cream
1 tbsp vinegar
1/2 tsp powdered sugar

Cut washed and dried salad greens into a bite sized pieces. Pile greens into a salad bowl. Around the pile of greens accurately lay cut into rounds carrot, tomatoes, potatoes, radishes, cucumbers, and scallions. Put cut into rounds eggs on top of the pile. Make a dressing by mixing sour cream, vinegar, and sugar powder. Right before the serving, salt the salad lightly. Serve dressing separately.

Fruit Salad

Ingredients:
3 medium apples
1 pear
1 orange
1 mandarin orange
1/4 cup mayonnaise
juice of 1/4 lemon
1 tsp powdered sugar

Peel and core washed fruits - apples, pears, oranges, and mandarin oranges - and slice into thin slices. (ed. note - To prevent darkening of the fruit dip them into a water with some lemon juice). Just before serving pile the fruit into a salad bowl, season with powdered sugar and a little bit of salt and mix with dressing made from mayonnaise mixed with lemon juice. Decorate with julienned orange zest.
The salad could also be decorated with the

same fruits, or with cooked prunes, grapes, or berries. Depending on a season you can also use different fruits, such as peaches, apricots, cooked quince, or berries like strawberries, but always combined with apples. This salad should be served with cold fried or boiled meat, veal, lamb, poultry or game, or it could be served by itself.

Meat Salad

200 g fried or boiled meat
100 g salad greens
4-5 medium potatoes, boiled
2 medium cucumbers
1/2 cup mayonnaise

Slice the meat, potatoes, and cucumbers and put most of it into a mixing bowl. Season with salt and dress with mayonnaise and vinegar (ed. note - Vinegar is not mentioned as an ingredient, but it is mentioned in the recipe. Use 1 tbsp or less). Mound the mix in the middle of a salad bowl and decorate with salad greens, and remaining slices of cucumbers and meat.

Salad with Sausage or Ham

Ingredients:
200 g smoked sausage (kielbasa) or ham
3-4 medium potatoes, boiled and peeled
75 g salad greens
75 g gherkins
50 g celery
1 medium apple, peeled
1/2 cup mayonnaise

Cut washed and dried salad greens into a

bite-sized pieces. Dice ham, potatoes, apple, celery, and gherkins into a mixing bowl. Mix mayonnaise with a small quantity of mustard, finely chopped parsley leaves and tarragon, add vinegar and salt to taste. Dress diced ingredients mixed with salad greens with this sauce, put into a salad bowl. If desired, decorate with slices of boiled beets, apples, or onions.

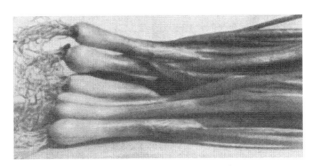

Salad with Game

Ingredients:
grouse or partridge
100 g salad greens
4-5 medium potatoes, boiled and peeled
2 medium cucumbers or 2 pickles
2 large eggs, hardboiled
1 medium apple, peeled
1/2 cup mayonnaise
1 tbsp vinegar (or lemon juice)
1/2 tbsp "Southern" sauce
1/2 tsp powdered sugar

Cut washed and dried salad greens into bite-sized pieces. Slice thinly filets of boiled (or fried) grouse or partridge, potatoes, eggs, and apple. Mix all the ingredients with mayonnaise, salt, vinegar, and powdered sugar. Pile dressed salad into a salad bowl. Decorate with lettuce leaves, hardboiled egg slices, or slices of tomatoes and cucumbers.

Salad with Greens and Game

Ingredients:
grouse (boiled or fried)
2-3 medium potatoes, boiled and peeled
100 g asparagus (or cauliflower)
100 g green beans (or peas)
100 g salad greens
1 medium cucumber
1 medium tomato
1/2 cup dressing made with vegetable oil and vinegar

Pile salad greens cut into bite-sized pieces in a middle of a salad bowl. Around the pile of greens decoratively place thinly sliced vegetables (just like in the "Spring" Salad). Cut filet of grouse into a thin wide slices and set it on top of mound of greens in a shape of a pyramid, in a middle of which set a branch of parsley. Just before serving lightly season the salad with salt and dress with oil and vinegar.

This salad could also be made with a meat of poultry, and instead of fresh vegetables you can use canned ones (asparagus, cauliflower, peas, green beans, and tomatoes).

Fish and Tomato Salad

Ingredients:
200 g fish, boiled and cooled (sturgeon, walleye, salmon)
1 medium tomato

1 medium cucumber
3 medium potatoes, boiled and peeled
75 g salad greens
75 g gherkins (or 1 pickle)
1/2 cup mayonnaise
1 tbsp vinegar

Cut fish filet into small pieces. Thinly slice potatoes, cucumber, gherkins, and tomato. Combine all ingredients in a bowl together with salad greens. Just before serving season the salad with salt and dress with mayonnaise and vinegar. Pile the salad in the middle of a salad bowl on top of leaves of lettuce and surround with slices of tomatoes and cucumbers. You can decorate this salad with caviar, sturgeon or salmon, slices of smoked salmon or sturgeon, and with olives. You can also add some sliced onions or scallions (50 g).

Cod and Horseradish Salad

Ingredients:
250 g cod fillet
100 g horseradish, grated
50 g scallions
4-5 medium potatoes, boiled and peeled
2 medium cucumbers
1/2 cup mayonnaise
2 tsp vinegar

Dice boiled and cooled cod fillet. Thinly slice potatoes and cucumbers. In a mixing bowl mix grated horseradish with mayonnaise, vinegar, and salt, and then add fish, potatoes, and cucumbers. Put salad into a salad bowl and decorate with slices of cucumbers, finely-sliced scallions, grated horseradish and a sprig of parsley.

Cod Salad with Mayonnaise

Ingredients:
200 g cod filet
100 g salad greens
50 g celery
1 medium apple,
1 bunch radishes
1 medium cucumber
1/2 cup mayonnaise
1 tbsp vinegar

Cut celery, cucumber, apple, and radishes into matchsticks and keep it in cool place. Cut cooked and cooled skinless fish fillet into a number of servings, dress with vinegar, and keep in a cool place. Just before serving season vegetables with salt and mix with 2-3 tablespoons of mayonnaise. Set seasoned vegetables on top of salad greens in a salad bowl, lay pieces of fish on top of vegetables and cover with remaining mayonnaise.

Crab Salad

Ingredients:
1 can crab meat
100 g green peas (or green beans)
100 g salad greens
2-3 medium potatoes, boiled
1 turnip, boiled
1 medium carrot, boiled
1 medium cucumber
1 medium tomato
1/3 cup mayonnaise
2 tbsp vinegar
1 tbsp salad oil

Slice tomato into circles, dice all other prepared vegetables. Just before serving, slice salad greens into bite-sized pieces, leaving a couple of leaves for decoration, and pile in a middle of a salad bowl. Around the mound of greens pile all other vegetables in separate mounds. Drain the crab meat (keep the juice) and set it on top of the pile of greens. Season vegetables with salt and dress with a mix of salad oil, vinegar, and juice from the can. Top crab meat with mayonnaise and decorate with remaining leaves of greens. This salad can also be made by substituting crab meat with meat of crayfish.

Herring Salad

Ingredients:
1 medium herring
2 medium potatoes, boiled
1 medium apple, peeled and cored
1 pickle
1 onion
1 beet, boiled
1-2 eggs, hard-boiled
3 tbsp salad oil
2 tbsp vinegar
1 tsp mustard

Cut cleaned herring into small pieces. Slice vegetables and apples into thin slices. Make a sauce by mashing egg yolk with salt, mustard, and salad oil. Make sure to add oil slowly for better emulsification. Once all the oil was incorporated, add vinegar. Just before serving mix all vegetables with sauce, diced onion, and finely-chopped dill or parsley leaves. Put salad into a salad bowl and top slices of beet, pieces of herring, and sliced egg whites.

Bean Salad

Ingredients:
1 cup dry beans
200 g salad greens
2-3 medium carrots, boiled
75 g celery
2 tbsp salad oil
mustard, vinegar, sugar to taste

(ed. note - This recipe does not give instructions how to cook beans, which was not required at the time when the book was published, since every cook knew how to do it.)
    Cook previously soaked beans until ready, drain and let cool. Dice carrots, julienne celery, cut washed and dried green into a bite-sized pieces, and mix together with beans in a mixing bowl. In another bowl make a dressing by mixing mustard, salt, sugar, and then slowly adding oil. Mix dressing with vinegar once all the oil was incorporated.
        Dress mixed vegetables and put into a salad bowl. Decorate the salad with leaves of greens, or, if desired, slices of apples.

Vegetable Vinaigrette

Ingredients:
4-5 medium potatoes, boiled and peeled
100 g sauerkraut
1 beet, boiled and peeled
1 carrot, boiled
2 pickles

1 fresh or pickled apple
50 g green onions
2-3 tbsp salad oil
1/4 cup vinegar (ed. note - might be a bit too much)
1 tsp mustard
salt, sugar to taste

Slice, dice, or julienne potatoes, apple, pickles, carrot, and mix with the sauerkraut in a mixing bowl (ed. note - The most common way to prepare this salad is to dice vegetables). Mash mustard, salt, pepper, and sugar with oil, then mix with vinegar. Just before serving dress mixed vegetables with dressing and put into a salad bowl. Decorate with slices of boiled beets, sliced green onions, and finely-chopped dill. You can also decorate the salad with slices of fresh cucumbers and tomatoes. Vinaigrette will also taste great if dressed with mayonnaise.

Vinaigrette with pickled mushrooms is prepared the same way - just use 25 g of pickled mushrooms per serving.

Fruit and Vegetable Vinaigrette

Ingredients:
1 medium apple
1 pear
1 mandarin
1 orange
3-4 potatoes, boiled and peeled
1 carrot, boiled
1 cucumber
50 g celery
50 g salad greens
50 g green peas

1/2 cup mayonnaise
lemon juice, salt, sugar to taste

Thinly slice peeled apple, pear, potatoes, carrot, cucumber, celery, and mix in a mixing bowl with peas and bite-size pieces of salad greens. Just before serving season the mix with salt and sugar and dress with mayonnaise and lemon juice. Set the salad in a salad bowl and decorate it with slices of oranges, mandarins, and some salad leaves.

Vinaigrette with Stuffed Peppers and Potatoes

Ingredients:
1 can (500 g) stuffed peppers
5-6 medium potatoes, boiled and peeled
1 egg, hard-boiled
100 g scallions

Thinly slice potatoes and egg, mix in a mixing bowl with peppers, cut into pieces, season and move into a salad bowl. Surround the salad with thinly sliced scallions, decorate with slices of hard-boiled eggs and finely-chopped dill.

Vinaigrette with Corned Beef

Ingredients:
1 can (338 g) canned corned beef
5-6 medium potatoes, boiled and peeled
100 g scallions
3 pickles
1 beet, boiled and peeled
1-2 eggs, hard-boiled
1/2 cup mayonnaise
1 tbsp vinegar

1 tsp mustard

Thinly slice potatoes, pickles and scallions, dice meat, and mix all of this in a mixing bowl. Season to taste with salt, pepper, and dress the mix with mayonnaise and mustard.

Pile vinaigrette in a salad bowl and decorate with slices of beet, hard-boiled eggs, and, if desired, with leaves of salad greens. Top with finely-chopped dill.

COLD APPETIZERS

Sandwiches

For sandwiches (ed. note - Usual sandwiches in Soviet Union where open-face sandwiches. This section, dealing primarily with appetizers mostly talks about canapés), a variety of products may be used: cold boiled or fried meat, boiled or smoked tongue, ham, different types of sausage, cheese, sturgeon, salmon, sardines, black or salmon caviar, etc.

Any kind of bread, cut into pieces of about 1 cm thick, is spread with butter (if butter is cold and hard, cut it into thin pieces and put them on the bread). On top of the layer of the butter put any of the above mentioned ingredients, same size as the bread. Fish for sandwiches should be free of bones and served on bread together with pieces of hard-boiled eggs.

Besides regular sandwiches, it is possible to make small sandwiches with fried bread, as well as closed sandwiches (ed. note - The usual kind of sandwiches in United States).

Canapés with Toasted Bread

To make canapés cut 1 cm thin slices of wheat or rye bread and toast it. Cut different shapes no more than 6 cm/2 in from the toasts - stars, diamonds, moon, ovals, or squares.

Butter the toasts and garnish with different ingredients - finely-chopped hard-boiled eggs, slices of tomatoes, boiled beets. A number of examples of different canapés are included below.

Canapés with tomatoes and cucumbers. On a round piece of toast put half-circle slice of tomato and the same size slice of cucumber. Two semi-circles should create a full circle. Dab a little mayonnaise in the middle of the canapé and decorate with a thin slice of radish. (ed. note - Remember to butter the toast to preserve its crispiness.)

Canapés with caviar. Lay a round slice of hard-boiled egg on a toast made with white bread. In the middle of the slice mound a little bit of sturgeon or salmon caviar. Pipe a little border with butter around the mound of caviar.

Canapés with cheese. Cover a crusty star-shaped toast with a thin star-shaped slice of cheese. Spread some butter mixed with tomato paste on top of the cheese and top with grated cheese.

Canapés with sprats, anchovies, or herring. Top round piece of rye toast with a circle slice of tomato. Lay a round slice of hard-boiled egg on top of tomato and put a sprat, anchovy, or a slice of herring on top for the egg. Pipe a thin border of mayonnaise around the fish and a small dot right no the fish and decorate with salad greens, small piece of tomato, or capers. If herring is used the canapé can be covered in lattice pattern.

Canapés with sardines or salmon. To make a

canapé with sardines lay a boneless fillet of fish on an oval-shaped toast and spread a thin layer of mayonnaise by itself or mixed with either 1/2 tbsp spinach, boiled and mashed, or tomato paste. Top with a half-circle slice of lemon without pits or skin.

Canapé with salmon is made as follows. Lay a thin slice of smoked salmon on an oval-shaped piece of toast and fold one of the corners of the fish. Decorate with butter, sturgeon caviar, parsley leaves and slice of a cucumber.

Tea Sandwiches

Sandwiches are made with the same ingredients that are used for canapés.

Cut white bread into long slices about 5 cm wide and 1/2 cm thick and butter it. For some topping butter is mixed with different flavorings -- mustard (for sausage or ham), grated cheese (for liverwurst), horseradish (for sturgeon), sauce "Southern" (for boiled meat or tongue). For smoked salmon, sturgeon caviar, or cheese no flavorings are used in the butter.

Lay thin slices of topping on the prepared slice of bread, cover with another slice of bread, and cut across to get small tea sandwiches 3 1/2 cm wide. Serve sandwiches on a plate covered with a napkin.

Cheese

Any types of cheese, except the soft ones, should be served already sliced and placed on a plate. Slice cheese into thin, equal size slices. To make sure that cheese does not dry wrap the plate with a clean towel (ed. note - Plastic wrap would work just as well) and keep it in a cool place.

Cream cheese should be spread on toasts.

Butter for Appetizers

Unsalted butter is served with appetizers such as caviar, cheese, pirozhki, kulebyaka, herring. The butter should be served in a butter dish, decorated on top with shape of flowers with help of a teaspoon, a knife, or a fork. Butter can also be served on a small plate in a shape of a log, also decorated with different patterns and sprigs of parsley.

COLD FISH DISHES AND APPETIZERS

Herring with Garnish

Soak herring for 3-4 hours in water or weak tea if it is too salty. Filet of herring cleaned from bones and skin could be soaked in milk to give it a more refined flavor.

Start cleaning herring by cutting off its tail, head, and the lower part of the belly. Remove all the innards and wash it. Make a shallow cut in the spine area and remove skin from both sides. Separate meat from the backbone and then slice off area of rib bones. Put both fillets together and cut into uniform pieces.

Transfer pieces of herring on a serving plate and position washed head (gills already removed) and tail to "recreate" the fish.

Herring prepared this way could be garnished with fresh cucumbers, tomatoes, gherkins, marinated mushrooms, boiled beets, potatoes, carrots, onions, or scallions, capers, and boiled eggs. Garnishes have to be cut uniformly into either circles, slices, or cubes. Garnish should be set symmetrically on both sides of the herring. Thin slices of onions should be set on top of the herring. Just before serving, herring should be dressed with sauce.

Oil and vinegar sauce. Mix 2 to 3 tbsp of vinegar with salt, sugar, and pepper to taste. Add 1 to 1 1/2 tbsp of sunflower oil.

Mustard sauce. Mash 1 hard-boiled egg yolk with 1 tsp of prepared mustard and 1 tsp of sugar. Add 1 tbsp of sunflower oil, 2-3 tbsp of vinegar, and salt to taste. Mix well.

Chopped Herring

Ingredients:
1 herring
2 tbsp unsalted butter
1 large apple

Take a well-washed and cleaned herring filet, cut it into small pieces, mix with butter and mash through a sieve. Then put it in a cup and whip with a spoon. You may add nutmeg for flavor. Place the prepared herring on a serving plate, shape it as a fish, attach head and tail, and then put sliced apples and parsley leaves around it. Herring that has been mashed through a sieve with butter and apple is delicious. Herring prepared in this manner can be served in a butter-dish or put on sliced bread fried in oil.

Herring with Potatoes and Butter

Ingredients:
1 large herring
500 g potatoes
50 g butter
2 cucumbers

Place prepared herring on a plate, put fresh cucumber slices and parsley around it. Serve freshly boiled peeled potatoes and butter separately.

Anchovies or Sprats with Potatoes

Ingredients:
1 can of anchovies
5-6 potatoes
1 tbsp oil
2 tbsp vinegar

Freshly boiled and peeled potatoes are mashed through a sieve and mounded in the middle of a salad bowl. Right next to the mound, place anchovies, rolled into rings or sprats, cleaned and without bones. Put sliced scallions in between them. Pour sauce made of oil, vinegar, salt and pepper on potatoes.

Smoked Salmon with Garnish

Remove skin and bones from smoked salmon, cut into thin slices, put in straight rows on a plate, decorate with parsley and lettuce. Serve sliced lemon as garnish. If salmon happens to be very salty, soak it in cold water for 3-4 hours. After removing it from water, dry it with towel, put oil on it, keep in cold place or on ice for 1 - 1 1/2 hours and cut into thin slices.

Lampreys

Cooked lampreys are cut across into pieces of 3 - 4 cm and placed into a salad bowl. Put thinly sliced rings of onions on top, and pour dressing made of oil and vinegar, which has been prepared the same way as dressing for herring. Add 1-2 teaspoons of dry grated horseradish.

Sturgeon and Salmon Caviar

Salmon caviar should be served in small crystal salad bowls or vases. Serve thinly sliced scallions on the side. Sturgeon caviar should be formed into a log on a plate, and decorated with sprigs of parsley, garnished with slices of lemon. Serve unsalted butter on the side.

The usual accompaniments to caviar are rasstegai (open-top fish-stiffed pirozhki).

Sturgeon or Catfish with Garnish

Cool boiled fish, remove all the bones, cut into uniform pieces and lay on a serving plate. Garnish could be set all around the fish, or just on one side. Choice of garnish depends on season and personal preferences (tomatoes and cucumbers sliced thinly, gherkins, green or red cabbage, green or potato salad). You can use diced boiled carrots or green peas dressed with oil and vinegar. Garnish should be dressed just before serving the fish. Separately serve horseradish with vinegar, mayonnaise, green sauce, and pickles.

Marinated Fish

Ingredients:
2-3 carrots
1 parsnip
2-3 onions
3-4 tbsp vegetable oil
1 cup tomato puree
3-5 cloves
bay leaf
ground black pepper
piece of cinnamon
1/2 cup vinegar
1 - 1 1/2 cups stock or water

You can marinate any fish - sturgeon, pikeperch, pike, smelts. Fish should be prepared as described in the section "Herring with Garnish". Large fish (like sturgeon or walleye) should be cut into pieces, while small one (like smelts) should be left whole. Season prepared fish with salt and pepper, coat with flour and fry in vegetable oil. Cover fish with marinade once it cools down.

To prepare marinade - thinly slice carrots, parsnip, and onions and fry in a pan until soft - 10 to 15 minutes. Add tomato puree and spices - bay leaf, black pepper, cloves, cinnamon, cover the pot and braise 15 to 20 minutes. Add vinegar and stock or water and bring to simmer. Taste for seasoning - add salt and sugar and let it cool.

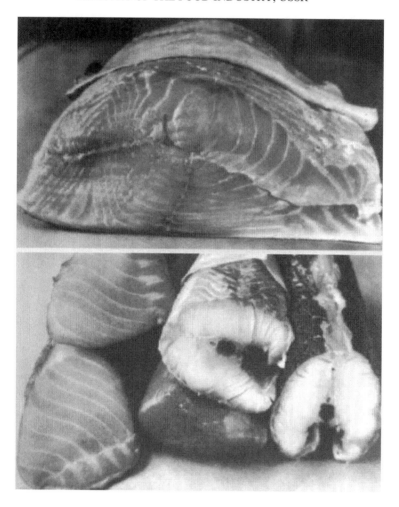

Fish in Aspic with Mayonnaise

Ingredients:
500 g fish
1 cup mayonnaise
10 g gelatin

Skin fillet of walleye, salmon, trout, or any
other fish and cut it into pieces of about 50-60 g,
set into an oiled pot and add enough water or fish

stock so that fillets would be half-submerged, cover the pot and poach fish until cooked. Remove fish and set it on serving plates. Make aspic from the poaching liquid - bloom gelatin in 1/3 cup of cooled poaching liquid. Mix 2/3 cups mayonnaise with 1/3 cup of aspic, add vinegar and salt to taste. To prevent sauce from setting you should stir it frequently. You can also warm it up on a water bath until it reaches pourable consistency. Once the aspic is ready - pour it over fish. Once set, decorate with crayfish meat or crab meat, salad leaves, capers, or thin cucumber slices. This aspic should be served with either remaining mayonnaise or mustard and capers sauce.

Sturgeon in Aspic with Mayonnaise

Sturgeon in aspic with mayonnaise is prepared almost just as the previous recipe of fish in aspic. The only difference being that fish should be cooked whole, and the aspic is cooked from the broth.

Cut the cooked fish into pieces 1 cm thick, or, if the dish is mean as an appetizer, into smaller uniform pieces. Lay fish on a plate and cover it with mayonnaise aspic (2/3 cups of mayonnaise mixed with 1/3 cup of aspic). Decorate each slice of fish with parsley leaves, decorations from carrots. Affix decorations to the fish adding a thin layer of aspic on the top - from a spoon. Trim the finished pieces of fish and set them on a serving plate. Serve this dish with a mustard and capers sauce, or mayonnaise.

Canned Fish

Canned fish should not be served out of the

can. It is very awkward and uncomfortable to do so: the contents break and crumble - and most of the sauce or oil is not used. It is necessary to place canned fish in a salad bowl or regular bowl before serving. For garnish, slices of fresh cucumbers, tomatoes, scallions, quarters or halves of hard-boiled eggs may be used. Decorating can be done with parsley or lettuce.

Sardines. Take out of the can, put on the plate, cover with slices of lemon or pour on lemon juice, sprinkle with finely chopped parsley.

Sprats. Serve on a plate with slices of lemon, cover the fish with a rim of finely chopped onions.

Fish in tomato sauce. Cut large pieces of fish (sturgeon, etc.) into small pieces, put them on a plate and pour sauce over it. Sprinkle with finely chopped parsley and cover with slices of fresh cucumbers, tomatoes and pitted olives.

Crabs and crayfish tails. Take them out of the can, place in a salad bowl, put slices of fresh cucumbers, tomatoes, peeled apples around. Serve mayonnaise separately.

Oysters

Wash shells of oyster in a cold water. Just

before serving opens shells with an oyster knife, remove the smaller side, leaving oyster in the deep portion of the shell which should be instantly dipped into a cold salted water (preferably with ice), since and set on a serving tray with a layer of finely-crushed ice. Serve slices of lemon or lemon juice on a side.

COLD MEAT DISHES AND APPETIZERS

Many products for these dishes could be purchased already cooked, such as bacon, roast beef, ham, veal, fried poultry or game.

Meat for cold dishes cooked exactly the same way as for hot dishes.

In the following section we will provide instructions how to correctly cut and serve the meat, how to garnish and decorate the dishes, and which sauces should be served along.

Assorted Meat Appetizer

This dish may consist of different prepared meat products: ham, sausage, boiled tongue, fried veal, lamb, fried beef, fowl, game, etc.

Put slices of meat on the plate in specific order, for example piece of chicken in the middle of the plate, with slices of ham, sausage, lamb and veal around it. Use fresh cucumbers, tomatoes, fresh or pickled apples, lettuce leaves or parsley branches. Serve tomato sauce, herring sauce or mayonnaise separately.

Sausages and Kielbasa

(ed. note - Boiled, dry-cured, and smoked sausages are an integral part of any celebration table).

Make a thin cut with a tip of a knife along the loaf of boiled sausage (such as bologna, mortadella) and peel it. Thin sausage should be sliced on a bias to form thin oval slices. Thick sausage should be cut into circles across, and then each circle should be cut into smaller sections. Lay sliced sausage on a serving plate and decorate with sprigs of parsley or salad leaves. Serve sliced cucumbers, gherkins, red, or green cabbage, mustard, or "Southern" sauce.

Smoked or dry-cured sausages should be prepared as follows - peel the loaf and slice it thinly on a bias. Lay it on a serving plate and decorate with sprigs of garnish. Serve with butter and mustard on the side.

Liverwurst and Pates

Peel liverwurst and slice into equal slices frequently dipping knife into hot water to ensure that slices are smooth. Serve pate in a small salad dish, butter dish, or a on a small plate, decorated with parsley. Serve butter on a side.

Liver Pate

Ingredients:
500 g liver (beef or veal)
100 g bacon
100 g unsalted butter
1 carrot
1 parsnip
1 onion
Bay leaf
3-5 whole black pepper

Wash and clean liver removing film and bile ducts and cut it into small pieces. Cut bacon into small pieces. Thinly slice carrot, parsnip, and onion. Fry all of the ingredients together with bay leaf and a black pepper. It is very important not to overcook liver; otherwise the pate would not be as smooth as it should be. Pass the mixture through a small plate in a meat grinder two to three times (ed. note - Or just use a food processor). You can also rub it though a sieve to improve texture of pate.

Move prepared live into a pot, season with salt, paper, and nutmeg to taste, and whip with a mixing spoon while adding butter, little bit at a time.

Move finished pate into a glass or ceramic dish and cool.

Pate, garnished with hard-boiled eggs, could be served as an appetizer, or, spread on toasts for breakfast.

Cooked Veal, Beef, Lamb, or Pork

Select lean meat for fried or roasted dishes to be served as an appetizer. Cooked meat should be cut across the grain on a bias, into wide thin slices. If serving a whole roasted leg of lamb or veal - cut the meat off the bone, lay the bone on a serving tray or plate, and arrange the meat to form the whole leg. Cold meat appetizers should be garnished with gherkins, tomatoes, as well as some salads (green, potato, tomato, or mixed vegetables). Serve "Ostry", "Kubansky", "Yuzny" sauces, or mayonnaise.

COLD VEGETABLE DISHES AND APPETIZERS

Fried Beans

Ingredients:
1 cup dried beans
1 onion
2 tbsp vegetable oil

Cook beans until ready, drain, and fry in a frying pan until some beans form a crust. Mix with fried onion, season with salt and pepper, and let cool. Top with chopped herbs right before serving.

Bean Spread

Ingredients:
1 cup dried beans
1 onion
2-3 tbsp vegetable oil

Cook beans until ready, drain and mash them. Mix well with fried onions and vegetable oil. Season with salt and pepper. Cool before serving.

Mushroom Caviar

Ingredients:
250 g marinated mushrooms or 50 g dried mushrooms
1 onion
1-2 tbsp vegetable oil

Mushroom caviar could be made with either marinated mushrooms or cooked dried mushrooms. Rinse and drain marinated mushrooms. Once the mushrooms are drained -

finely chop them. Dice onion and fry it in vegetable oil, then cool and mix with chopped mushrooms. Season with pepper to taste.

To make this dish with dried mushrooms - follow the same procedure. Soak and cook mushrooms until ready, then drain and chop them. Once drained, mix with fried onion and season with salt and pepper. For spicier flavor add lemon juice or vinegar. Top with sliced scallions before serving.

Eggplant Caviar

Ingredients:
300 g eggplant
1-2 onions
1 tomato
2 tbsp vegetable oil

Bake or boil eggplant until ready, then peel and finely chop. Add slightly fried onions and tomato, season with salt and pepper, and add vegetable oil and a little bit of vinegar. Mix well and simmer the mixture on a low heat to remove excess moisture. Cool before serving.

Beet Caviar

Ingredients:
500 g beets
2-3 tbsp sugar
2 tbsp vegetable oil
1/2 lemon

Wash and cook beets until ready (boil or roast), peel and pass through a meat grinder. Mix the puree with sugar, vegetable oil, lemon zest and juice of 1/2 lemon. Heat the mixture in a pot on a low heat for 5 to 10 minutes frequently stirring to prevent burning. Cool and serve in a salad bowl.

Appetizer with Canned Vegetables

Peppers, eggplants, stuffed zucchini, and other canned vegetables are served in a salad bowl, dressed, if desired, with lemon juice or distilled vinegar, and topped with chopped parsley leaves. Decorate with apple slices.

Puff Pastry Baskets with Salad

Thinly roll a sheet of puff pastry dough and cut out small shapes, slightly bigger than the molds they will be baked in. Line molds about 5-6 cm in diameter with rolled dough, set them on a baking sheet, and fill with dry peas or buckwheat. Bake in a preheated oven until ready. Take the baskets out of the molds and pour out peas or buckwheat. Once cooled - fill with meat or game salad, set on a serving tray or plate covered with clean linen napkin. You can also line serving plate with leaves of lettuce and set basket on top of the leaves.

Egg Baskets with Salad

Peel hard-boiled eggs and slice them across into halves. Remove yolks and fill with a desired salad. Decorate with chopped herbs and scallions.

Stuffed Tomatoes

Wash ripe, medium-sized tomatoes, and cut out the stem side. Remove seeds and flesh and season inside with salt and pepper. Fill with "Salad with Game".

DISHES IN ASPIC

Dishes with aspic could be made with fish, meat, or vegetables. For fish in aspic we recommend to use walleye, sturgeon or fillet of bream, carp or perch. For meat in aspic, use suckling pig, tongue, veal, ham, poultry, or game birds.

Wonderful aspic dishes could be made with stuffed fish or meat products (stuffed perch or liverwurst). These products should be thinly sliced, decorated with slices of hard-boiled eggs, lemons, tomatoes, cucumbers, apples, and herbs.

To make vegetables in aspic use carrots, turnips, cauliflower, asparagus, green peas. Fruits like apples, pears, or peaches can also be added to the vegetable aspics.

Stock or broth from cooking of fish, meat, or vegetables for aspic is used to prepare jelly. Quantity of gelatin required to add to stock depends on the strength of this stock. For example - it is enough to add just 1-2 g of gelatin into 1 cup of fish stock made from walleye. Stock made from poultry would require 4-5 grams of gelatin per 1 cup. To make a good vegetable jelly, use 6-7 g of gelatin per 1 cup of stock.

Gelatin has to be bloomed in cold water. Use 5 parts of water to 1 part of gelatin by weight. Simmer broth or stock on low heat for 3 to 5 minutes, add gelatin and mix until all gelatin is completely dissolved. Strain broth through a clean kitchen towel or cheese cloth, let cool slightly, pour over prepared fish, meat, or vegetables.

To clarify broth for more transparent jelly take 1 raw egg white for each 4-5 cups of broth, whip egg whites with fork or whisk. Add a cup of cooled broth and a tablespoon of vinegar or lemon juice to whipped egg whites. Mix well and add to simmering broth. Cover the pot and keep it on low heat until it starts boiling. Remove from heat the moment it start boiling and let it stand for 15-20 minutes. Accurately remove the crust formed on top of the broth and strain it.

Walleye in Aspic

Ingredients:
1 walleye (1000-1200 g)
10-12 g gelatin
1 onion
1 carrot
1 parsnip
Bay leaves

Fillet scaled and gutted walleye and cut fillets into uniform pieces. Put bones and head (remove gills) of the fish into a pot, together with onion, carrot, parsnip, 1-2 bay leaves, and salt. Bring to boil and simmer for 15 to 20 minutes. Add sliced fillets of fish to the pot and cook until cooked through. Remove pieces of fillets from the pot and arrange in a shape of fish on a plate, but leaving some space between pieces. Keep it in cool place. Strain the broth and make 2 - 2 1/2 cups of jelly as described in the section "Dishes in Aspic". Decorate each piece of the fish with a slice of lemon, star-shaped carrot, parsley leaves, and cover with jelly making sure that decorations are not disturbed. Keep in cool place until jelly sets. Serve with red cabbage salad,
potato salad, fresh cucumbers, or pickles, and mayonnaise.

Sturgeon in Aspic

Ingredients:
1 kg sturgeon
25-30 g gelatin
1 carrot
1 parsnip
1 onion

Boil fish will carrot, parsnip, and onion until ready, then cool. Make about 3-4 cups of clear jelly from fish broth. Strain and cool it.

Cut boiled fish into thin slices and lay on a baking tray or a large dish making sure to leave some space between pieces of fish. Decorate fish with leaves of parsley, slices of carrots or cucumbers, pieces of crab meat or crayfish, capers. Affix decorations to the fish by accurately pouring cooled jelly over the fish from a spoon, using about 2 to 3 tablespoons of jelly. Once the initial jelly is set, pour all the remaining jelly to make even layer. Once all the jelly is set, accurately cut out pieces of fish with a tip of a knife and set on a serving plate. Garnish on one or all sides with boiled carrots, parsnips, potatoes, green peas.

Just before serving dress garnish with oil and vinegar. Serve with horseradish with vinegar and mayonnaise.

Suckling Pig in Aspic

Ingredients:
1 suckling pig (2 – 2.5 kg)
30g gelatin
1 carrot
1 parsnip
1 onion

If the pig still has any hairs left, singe it, then wash and disembowel it.

Before boiling it, chop it into pieces: remove the head; cut the carcass across in the kidney area (each half can additionally be cut lengthwise along the backbone).

Put chopped pig in a pot, pour cold water, add salt, carrot, parsnip and onion, cover and bring to boil.
It is also possible to boil whole pig in a large pot. In this case chop the backbone by the neck across from the inside.

When water boils, remove the foam and continue to cook on slow fire for 40-50 minutes. Put cooked pig on a plate, cover with moist napkin and cool.

Bring broth to boil, add pepper, bay leaf,

clove. Once boiled, add gelatin which has been pre-soaked in cold water. Bring to boil while stirring, then strain through cloth.

Cooled pig is chopped into serving-sized pieces and lay out on a plate so that there are ½ cm spaces between pieces; decorate with hard boiled eggs cut in semi-circular shapes, parsley, slices of boiled carrot and lemon.

Cover pig with prepared gelatin the same way as walleye.

Horseradish sauce with sour cream or horseradish with vinegar are served separately.

Beef Tongue in Aspic

Ingredients:
1 beef tongue (about 1 kg)
20-25 g gelatin
1 carrot
1 parsnip
1 onion

(ed. note - This recipe assumes that cook knows how to cook the tongue and does not provide basic instructions)

Cool cooked fresh tongue, slice and follow the instructions from the recipe "Sturgeon in Aspic". Make jelly from the broth making sure to skim all the fat before using it. Decorate slices of tongue with circles of hard-boiled eggs, slices of cucumbers, gherkins, parsley leaves before covering them with jelly. Cut the tongues out with a tip of a knife once the jelly sets, lay on a serving plate and garnish with "White Cabbage Salad" or "Red Cabbage Salad", slices of tomatoes or cucumbers, pickled cherries, plums, or grapes. Serve with sauce "Ostry", mayonnaise, sauce with sour cream and horseradish, or horseradish with vinegar.

You can use lean ham instead of tongue in this dish.

Beef Studen

Ingredients:
1 kg cows feet
1-2 carrots
1-2 parsnips
1-2 onions
bay leaves
whole black pepper

Wash and clean cows feet and soak in cold water for 3-4 hours. Drain, put into a pot an cover with cold water. Layer of water should be 10 cm on top of the meat. Bring to boil over medium heat and remove all the scum. Add vegetables, bay leaves, and peppers, cover and simmer on low heat for 6 to 7 hours, until meat falls off the bones. Skim all the fat from the stock and remove bay leaves and peppers. Separate meat from bones, dice it or pass it through a meat grinder, and add it to strained broth. Season with salt and pepper, and pour it into deep bowls of forms. If you want to decorate studen with slices of boiled eggs - fill the forms one third of the way up, let it set, lay a row of egg slices on top and pour it another third of the way up. Repeat the procedure until all the broth has been used.

Dip a form into a bowl of hot water and invert onto a serving plate, decorate with parsley leaves. Serve with horseradish and vinegar, mustard, source cream and horseradish sauce, cucumbers and "White Cabbage Salad" or "Red

Cabbage Salad".

Veal Studen

Ingredients:
4 calves feet
5-6 eggs
2 carrots
2 onions
1 parsnip
bay leaves
whole black pepper

Pour boiling water over calves feet and dry them with clean kitchen towel, rub with flour and singe any bristles off. Separate meat from bones and cut bones into smaller pieces. Put meat and bones into a pot and cover with cold water to reach 5 cm on top of the meat. Bring to boil over medium heat and remove all the scum. Add vegetables, bay leaves, and whole black pepper, cover and simmer on low heat for 3 to 4 hours. Skim all the fat from the broth and remove bay leaves and pepper. Separate meat from bones, dice it or pass it through a meat grinder. Add bones back to the broth and simmer until 5-6 cups of broth is remaining. Strain the broth and mix with meat. Season with salt and pepper, and pour it into deep bowls of forms decorating with slices of hard-boiled eggs in the process (2-3 rows). Serve with sour cream and horseradish sauce, mustard, horseradish with vinegar, grated horseradish, green salad dressed with sour cream and vinegar, and cucumbers.

The same procedure could be used to cook studen from pig feet or pig head. If using pig head, then add 5-7 g of gelatin.

SAUCES AND DRESSINGS FOR SLADS AND OTHER COLD DISHES

Mayonnaise

Ingredients:
1 egg yolk
1/2 cup vegetable oil
1 tbsp vinegar

In a ceramic bowl beat egg yolk lightly and season with salt. Start adding vegetable oil, a teaspoon at a time, while whisking nonstop. Make sure that all the oil incorporated before adding more. Once all the oil had been mixed, add vinegar. If the sauce is too thick, add about a tablespoon of warm water into it. For spicier taste you can add a 1/4 tsp of mustard which could be mixed with egg yolk before addition of oil.

Mayonnaise is served with boiled and fried mead and fish cold appetizers. It is used as a base in making dishes in aspic with mayonnaise.

Mayonnaise with Sour Cream

Ingredients:
1/4 cup mayonnaise
1/4 cup sour cream
1 tbsp vinegar or 1 tsp lemon juice
parsley leaves

Mix mayonnaise with sour cream, vinegar (or lemon juice), and finely chopped parsley leaves. Serve with the same dishes as mayonnaise. You can you this sauce to dress salads, in which case do not add parsley.

Mayonnaise with Gherkins

Ingredients:
1/2 cup mayonnaise
5-6 gherkins

Add finely chopped gherkins to mayonnaise and mix well. Serve with cold roast beef, veal, lamb, boiled meat, and with breaded fried fish.

Green Sauce

Ingredients:
1/2 cup mayonnaise
1 tbsp cooked greens
1 tbsp vinegar

Blanch washed leaves of spinach, tarragon, or parsley, in boiling water for 2-3 minutes, drain well. Chop the greens finely and mash them through sieve. Mix with mayonnaise and season with vinegar and salt to taste. Serve with cold fish appetizers, or breaded fried fish.

Mustard and Capers Sauce

Ingredients:
2 eggs
2 tbsp vegetable oil
1/2 tbsp mustard
3-4 tbsp vinegar
1 tbsp small capers
1/2 tsp sugar

Mash egg yolks of hard boiled eggs through a sieve and mix with mustard, sugar, salt. Slowly add vegetable oil, and, once oil is fully incorporated, add vinegar. Add capers and finely chopped egg whites to the sauce. Serve with cold fish appetizers - sturgeon, pike, salmon, or canned fish.

Sauce Vinaigrette

Ingredients:
1 egg
2 tbsp vegetable oil
2-3 tbsp vinegar
1/2 tbsp capers
1/2 cucumber
1/2 onion
1/2 tbsp parsley and tarragon leaves
1/2 tsp sugar

Mash and rub hard-boiled egg yolk through a sieve, and mix with salt, pepper, and vegetable oil to make a thick paste, then add vinegar, finely chopped egg whites, onion, capers, and herbs. Mix well.

Serve this sauce with cold fish or pork appetizers, boiled pig or calves feet.

Fruit and Berry Sauce

Ingredients:
2 tbsp black currant jam
1/2 tsp mustard
1 tbsp port wine
1/2 tbsp lemon and orange zest
1/2 small onion

Mash black currant jam with mustard, add port wine, juice of lemon and orange, rub through a sieve (ed. note - Apparently editors missed lemon and orange juice on the list of ingredients). Julienne lemon and orange zest and blanch it for one minute in boiling water. Blanch thinly sliced onion the same way. Once zest and onion are cooled -mix it with the sauce. You can season the sauce with pepper. Serve this sauce with fried game or fowl.

Horseradish with Vinegar

Wash and peel a horseradish root and finely grate it into a ceramic bowl and cover with vinegar. Season with salt and sugar to taste. Serve with cold fish or fish in aspic, studen, ham, bacon.

Sour Cream and Vinegar Dressing

Ingredients:
1/4 cup sour cream
1/4 cup vinegar
1 tsp powdered sugar

salt, pepper
or
1/2 cup sour cream
1-1 1/2 tbsp vinegar
sugar, salt, pepper

Mix sour cream with vinegar, sugar. Season with salt and pepper to taste.

Vinegar and Oil Dressing

Ingredients:
1/4 cup vinegar
1-2 tbsp vegetable oil
1 tsp powdered sugar
or
2 tbsp vinegar
4-5 tbsp vegetable oil
1/2 tsp powdered sugar
salt and pepper

Just before dressing salad, mix vinegar with salt, pepper, sugar, and oil.

HOT APPETIZERS

Hot appetizers may include meat, fish, eggs, mushrooms in sour cream, pies with cabbage and other stuffing, pirozhki, etc.

In contrast with regular meals, pieces of fish or meat for appetizers are considerably smaller; same applies to cutlets; in addition, they are served with no garnish and they are prepared immediately prior to serving.

From the recipes included in this book, several can be used as hot appetizers - meat chops with spicy onion sauce (make chops 3-4 cm in diameter); meatballs in tomato sauce (diameter of each should be 1.5-2 cm); fried ham with mustard and tomatoes; fried kidneys with tomatoes; fish or mushroom solyanka on frying pan; fried walleye filet cut into pieces of 4-5 cm, and others.

Fried pirozhki for hot appetizers are also small (5-6 cm), kulebyakas are not wide, with a lot of ground meat.

Hot Dogs

Hot dogs are a very filling and tasty hot appetizer. They should be boiled in salty water and served with mustard or grated horseradish.

There is another way to prepare hot dogs: cut them across into 3 or 4 parts, fry them on a frying pan in oil for 2 to 3 minutes, then put tomato slices with salt and pepper on the frying pan and fry for another 2-3 minutes.

After this put hot dogs with tomatoes on a plate and sprinkle with finely chopped greens. It is also possible to add grated garlic. Fresh tomatoes can be replaced with canned tomatoes or tomato paste.

Fried Sausage with Cabbage

Take off the wrapper off boiled sausage, cut into slices of 5-6 mm and fry them before serving. At the same time, prepare braised cabbage, a little spicier than usual. Put cabbage on a plate, put sliced sausage on top, sprinkle with finely chopped parsley or dill. Thin sausage can be washed, dried and fried in lard so that there is a crunchy crust on it.

When serving cut sausage into portions, put on a hot plate and garnish with braised cabbage.

Meat Patties in Sour Cream

Ingredients:
500 g meat (beef, veal, lamb, or pork)
125 g crustless stale white bread
3/4 cup milk or water
2 tbsp butter
sour cream

Pass meat through a meat grinder, season with salt, mix with bread soaked in milk or water and pass it through a meat grinder again one or two times. Form patties 1 1/2 to 2 inches in diameter and coat with flour. Fry patties in melted butter on both sides, then add sour cream, cover the frying pan with a cover and braise for 5 to 7 minutes.

To serve set patties on a serving plate and cover with sauce. Top with finely chopped herbs.

Forshmak (Chopped Herring)

Ingredients:
250 g boiled or fried meat (beef, veal, lamb, poultry)
1/2 herring
2 tbsp flour
2-3 medium potatoes, boiled and peeled
2-3 tbsp sour cream
2-3 eggs, separated
1 tbsp grated cheese

Pass boiled or fried meat, and skinless and boneless filet of herring soaked to remove excess salt, through a fine plate of a meat grinder. Mash potatoes together with fried onion. Add mashed potatoes to ground meat, mix together, add flour, softened butter, and sour cream and once more pass everything through a meat grinder. Add egg yolks and season with salt and pepper. Whip egg whites until stiff peak form and carefully add to the mixture. Put the mixture on a well-oiled frying pan, smooth the top and cover with grated cheese, sprinkle with little bit of oil and bake in an oven for 30-40 minutes.

Forshmak is ready when it pulls away from the sides of the pan. Move it to a serving plate and season with small quantity of sour cream and tomato sauce. Serve the same sauce on the side.

SOUPS

SOUPS

Soups are based on stock - meat, fish, mushroom or broth made from water with potatoes, cabbage, beets, grains, legumes or flour, and also roots.

Vegetables for soups are cleaned and cut, and it is desirable that pieces are consistent in shape. For example, if you're making a potato soup with grain, roots are cut into dice, and if you're making noodle soup, roots are cut into julienne. Cabbage for shchi is usually chopped.

Tomato paste or fresh tomatoes may be added to soup, depending on the season. Tomatoes should not be used in rassolnik, green shchi, soup with spinach or sorrel.

When making soup, potatoes and cabbage should be placed in the pot while still fresh; root vegetables such as carrots, parsnips, celery) and onions are pre-fried, while beets and sauerkraut are braised.

You should not add raw root vegetables and onions because when boiled, their aroma and taste evaporates with water steam. In order to preserve them, chopped root vegetables and onions are placed on a frying pan that has been pre-heated with some cooking oil, and fried until a light film forms on them, but not until that film turns dark. This way, the aroma of the roots and onions are absorbed into the lard, from which they are released slowly and gradually. Due to this, the soup acquires the flavor associated with root vegetables and onions, as well as keeps it for a long time.

Additionally, carrots make fat appear orange in color. Fat looks even brighter then it would have been with tomato puree. Presence of colored tinsels of colored fat gives soup a more attractive look.

Beets for soup are braised in order to maintain their color. If beets are added raw then during prolonged boiling their color will change; whether as braising uses very little water and discoloration is not likely to occur. Added vinegar also helps.

Instead of braising, whole well-washed beets may be baked or boiled in a small quantity of water, then clean, chop and put into borscht.

Braising of sauerkraut improves its taste.

Grains (except for buckwheat and semolina), peas and beans are thoroughly washed before putting them into stock or broth. For quicker cooking, pearl barley and legumes (peas, beans, lentils) need to be pre-soaked. Soaking times are 2-3 hours for pearl barley, 4-6 hours for lentils. Hulled peas don't need to be pre-soaked.

Soup with barley sometimes acquires unpleasant bluish shade; in order to avoid this barley should be boiled separately almost until readiness, instead of being placed in the pot raw.

To preserve Vitamin C in vegetables they should be put into boiling water and boiled on slow flame. Placing vegetables in cold water and gradually heating them leads to severe destruction of Vitamin C. For the same reason, it is not desirable to overcook vegetables.

Putting vegetables in the soup should be timed in such a way that they all are ready just in time for the soup to be served. Sequence of putting the ingredients in the soup is described in individual soup recipes.

Pepper, bay leaf and roux can improve taste and aroma of the soup.

Prepare roux in the following manner: put butter in the pan (one spoon of butter per spoon of flower), pour flour, mix and fry for 5-10 minutes while stirring. When frying flour, moisture is evaporating from it along with substances that give flower its specific smell and taste. Fried flour is then added to stock and poured into the soup (10-15 minutes before soup is ready).

In some cases, for example when making green shchi, flour can be fried with root vegetables.

Sometimes milk, cream, sour cream and clabber can be added to vegetable soups to enhance their taste and nutritional value.

Sour cream can be placed directly into the soup bowl or served separately.

When soup is ready, you can sprinkle it with fresh parsley, dill, scallions. It improves taste and look of the soups and enriches them with Vitamin C.

Vegetable soups are made immediately before consuming them, since Vitamin C is destroyed if they are stored for a long time. For example, if shchi or potato soup are kept for three hours in warm state, about half of Vitamin C is left if compared to when soup was just prepared.

Therefore, soups should not be prepared to be eaten the next day. It might be advisable to prepare stock for the next day, and use that stock to prepare fresh soup. In addition to preserving vitamins, it will ensure taste and nutritional variety.

If the stock is made to last for today and tomorrow, half of it should be poured into a separate container, cover with gauze and placed in cool place on wood or metal stand. When there is no more steam coming out, replace gauze with lid.

In order to speed up the process of soup preparation, frozen mixes that are available for borscht, soups, etc. can be purchased. Pour some stock into this mix and braise until ready, then add tomato puree which has been warmed with fat and bring to boil.

There are also ready canned vegetable soups in glass jars available for sale in stores. Delicious soups are made after adding the required quantity of water. To prepare meat soups from them, use stock or canned meat.

Canned meat and fish might be used instead of fresh ones when there is not much time to prepare soup. Prepare soup with water and then add canned meat or fish and boil.

Meat Broth

Ingredients:
500 g meat
2-3 l water

Wash meat under cold running water, put into a stock pot, cover with cold water and bring to boil. Once the water stars boiling, bring the heat down to a simmer. Remove all the foam and scum that rises to the top. Skim the fat and use it to fry onions and root vegetables if using them to make the stock. If you will not remove the fat it will decompose after extensive exposure to heat and will negatively affect the taste of the stock. After an hour or an hour and a half of cooking season the stock with salt. From the beginning and almost to the end of cooking meat releases mineral salts and so-called extractive substances which give the stock its pleasant smell and flavor. Remove the meat from the broth once it is cooked, and strain the broth. Use a fork or a knife to test the meat for doneness - if it goes in without resistance - the meat is ready.

This broth is used in cooking meat shchi, borscht, and other soups. Meat that was used to cook this broth is served with a soup or used to cook other dishes. Meat broth could also be cooked with root vegetables. If using vegetables - add washed and peeled carrots, turnip, parsnip, and onion. After cooking these vegetables (except onion) could be used in a soup, salad, or vinaigrette.

Stock with Bones

Ingredients:

500 g meat bones
1 carrot
1 parsnip
1 onion
2-3 l water

Stock with bones is cooked when you want to use meat for some other dishes (cutlets, goulash and such). To make sure that the stock cooked faster and better, cut large bones into smaller pieces. Put cut and washed bones into a stock pot, cover with water and bring to boil. Stock from bones is cooked exactly like the stock from meat - at a simmer, periodically removing foam, scum, and fat. The time of cooking this stock is 2 1/2 to 3 hours. To improve the flavor of this stock, about an hour before the stock is done, add peeled vegetables and onion, and season with salt. Strain the finished stock.

Because the quality of this stock is not as good as the meat stock, we recommend to use this stock primarily for potato soup.

Quick Cooking Meat Broth

Ingredients:
500 g meat
1 carrot

1 parsnip or celery root
1 onion
1 1/2 - 2 l water

Wash the meat, separate meat from bones and pass it through a meat grinder. Cut bones into smaller pieces. Put meat and bones into a stock pot and cover with cold water. Leave to soak for 20 to 30 minutes, then, without changing water, bring to boil, lower the heat to maintain constant simmer. Add root vegetables (some of which could be lightly charred in a dry frying pan) and onion to the stock when the broth comes to boil. Season with salt 20 minutes after start of cooking. Simmer for 30-40 minutes, then strain and use as you would use regular meat stock. Meat from this broth could be used as stuffing for pirozhki or casseroles.

Fish Stock

Ingredients:
500-600 g fish
1 onion
1 parsnip
2-3 l water

To prepare fish for cooking scale it, then gut and remove all innards, wash inside and cut into pieces. Remove gills from heads. Put the fish into a stock pot, cover with cold water, add salt, diced parsnip and onion, bring to boil and cook on low heat for 25 to 30 minutes. Remove fish from the pot leaving only head and tail and continue to simmer for another 15 to 20 minutes. Fish from the stock could be used in a soup, or in some other dish.

Fish stock could also be cooked from bones, heads, and other remains of a filleted fish. When using only sub products, chop bones into smaller pieces, gills are removed from heads, and together with tails and fins all this is covered with water in a stock pot together with root vegetables, and simmered for an hour.

Finally, fish stock could be cooked with red fish. In this case we recommend to take fillet of fish, cover it with cold water, add salt, root vegetables, onions, and simmer for 30 to 40 minutes.

In all cases finished stock should be strained and used in further cooking of fish based soups.

Mushroom Stock

Ingredients:
50 g dry mushrooms
1 onion
2-3 l water

Wash mushrooms in warm water and put into a stock pot. Add cleaned and halved onion and cover with cold water. Bring to boil and cook a simmer for 2 to 2 1/2 hours. To shorten the cooking time soak mushrooms for 1 to 2 hours in cold water, then cook them in that same water.

Strain finished stock, rinse mushrooms with

cold water, dice them and add back to the stock.

Shchi with Cabbage

Ingredients:
500 g meat
500 g cabbage
200 g root vegetables and onion (carrot, parsnip)
200 g tomatoes
2 tbsp butter

Start by cooking meat broth. Peel and dice root vegetables and onion. Finely shred cabbage. Fry vegetables in butter until softened. After 1 1/2 - 2 hours after the start of cooking, take meat out of the broth, strain broth another pot, add sautéed root vegetables, meat, and cabbage, and cook for 30-40 minutes more. About 5-10 minutes before the end of cooking season the soup with salt and pepper and add bay leaf.

Shchi could be cooked with potatoes and tomatoes. If using these ingredients, add peeled and diced potatoes about 10-15 minutes after adding cabbage. Sliced tomatoes should be added at the same time when seasoning the soup.

Shchi without potatoes could be lightly thickened with fried flour (roux).

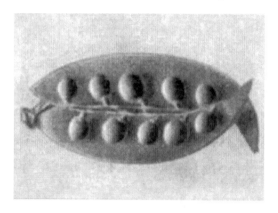

Shchi with Sauerkraut

Ingredients:
500 g meat
500 g sauerkraut
1 carrot
1 parsnip
1 onion
2 tbsp butter
2 tbsp tomato paste
1 tbsp flour

Cook meat broth. Add sauerkraut to a soup pot (if it is too sour - soak and drain it in advance), add 1-1 1/2 cups of water, a little bit of butter, cover the pot and braise it for approximately 1 hour.

Add beef broth to the sauerkraut, together with root vegetables sautéed with tomato paste and cook until ready. Just before the soup is done add salt, pepper, bay leaf, and thicken with roux. (ed. note - The usual proportion of butter to flour in roux is 1 to 1, so for 1 tbsp of flour, use 1 tbsp of butter.)

Another way of cooking this soup is to add sauerkraut to meat when cooking broth. Fry root vegetables with onion and tomato paste, and add them to the soup 20-30 minutes before it is done. Season with salt, pepper, bay leaf, and thicken with roux just before taking the soup off the heat.

Fish Head Shchi with Sauerkraut

Ingredients:
1 kg fish heads
500 g sauerkraut
200g root vegetables and onion
2 tbsp tomato paste
2 tbsp butter
1 tbsp flour
2-3 l water

Chop sturgeon or salmon fish heads into pieces (ed. note - not the most usual ingredient, but readily available in Asian markets, at least salmon heads), wash, and blanch by submerging for 1-2 minutes in boiling water, wash again and put into a stock pot. Cover with cold water, bring to boil, lower the heat and simmer for 3-4 hours. One hour after start of cooking take fish heads out of the stock with a skimmer, strain the stock to remove any bones. Separate meat and cartilage, and add cartilage back to the stock to continue cooking.

About an hour before finishing cooking, add sauerkraut braised according instructions in the "Shchi with Sauerkraut" recipe, and sautéed with tomato paste root vegetables.

Just before the soup is done -- season it with salt, pepper, bay leaf, and thicken with roux.

Shchi with Cabbage Sprouts

Ingredients:
500 g meat
800 g cabbage sprouts
200 g root vegetables and onion
2 tbsp butter

Cook meat broth. Dice peeled root vegetables and sauté them in butter in a soup pot until soft. Remove roots from cabbage sprouts, cut them into 2-3 parts each, wash, blanch, and douse with cold water to stop cooking. Once all the water is drained, add sprouts to the soup pot with root vegetables and cover with boiling broth. Season with salt, pepper, and bay leaf and cook for 25-30 minutes. Thicken with roux if desired. Serve with meat from broth and sour cream, top with finely chopped dill and parsley leaves.

Summer Shchi with Potatoes

Ingredients:
500 g meat
800 g cabbage sprouts
200 g root vegetables and onion
2 tbsp butter

    Cook meat broth. Dice peeled root vegetables and sauté them in butter in a soup pot until soft. Remove roots from cabbage sprouts, cut them into 2-3 parts each, wash, blanch, and douse with cold water to stop cooking. Once all the water is drained, add sprouts to the soup pot with root vegetables and cover with boiling broth. Season with salt, pepper, and bay leaf and cook for 25-30 minutes. Thicken with roux if desired. Serve with meat from broth and sour cream, top with finely chopped dill and parsley leaves.

Green Shchi

Ingredients:
500 g meat
500 g spinach
200 g sorrel
1 carrot
1 parsnip
1 onion
2 tbsp butter
1 tbsp flour

Cook meat broth. Cook washed spinach in boiling water until ready, drain, but keep the water. Rub cooked spinach through a sieve. Wash sorrel and cut big leaves into smaller pieces.

Peel and dice carrot, parsnip, and onion, and sauté them in butter in a soup pot until soft. Add flour to the pot and continue to sauté for 1-2 minutes more. Add spinach puree to the pot, mix well with sautéed vegetables, and then add strained beef broth and spinach-cooking water. Season with pepper and bay leaf, and cook for 15-20 minutes. About 5-10 minutes before the soup is done add leaves of sorrel and season with salt. Serve with sour cream and hard-boiled eggs.

Borscht

Ingredients:
500 g meat
300 g beets
200 g cabbage
200 g root vegetables and onion
2 tbsp tomato paste or 100 g tomatoes
1 tbsp vinegar
1 tbsp sugar

Cook meat broth. Peel and julienne beets, carrot, parsnip, and onion, put into a soup pot with tomatoes or tomato paste, vinegar, and sugar, and a little bit of broth with skimmed fat (or use 1-2 tbsp of butter or oil). Cover the pot and braise vegetables, mixing from time to time. To insure that vegetables do not burn, add more broth or water if needed.

After 15-20 minutes add finely shredded

cabbage to the braising vegetables and continue braising for 20 minutes more. Add prepared broth with meat, season with salt, pepper, and bay leaves, more vinegar to taste, and cook until vegetables are completely cooked. Serve with a dollop of sour cream.

Borscht could be cooked with potatoes - whole, or diced, and fresh tomatoes, slices of which are added about 5-10 minutes before the end of cooking. Besides the meat used to cook broth, boiled ham, frankfurters, or sausage can also be added to borscht.

To add more color to borscht, make an infusion from beets. To make this infusion slice one beet, cover with 1 cup of hot broth and 1 tsp of vinegar, and simmer for 10-15 minutes on low heat. Strain the infusion and add it to borscht right before serving.

Summer Borscht

Ingredients:
1 bunch beets
3-4 potatoes
1 carrot
1 stick celery
200 g squash
1-2 tomatoes
50-75 g scallions

Separate beets from stems. Slice or julienne peeled beets, cut stems into smaller pieces, add to pot together with carrots and cover with boiling water or mushroom stock. Cook for 10-15 minutes. Add blanched and shredded beet leaves, peeled squash, tomatoes, potatoes, scallions, celery, season with salt, pepper, cloves, bay leaf, and cooked until vegetables are done. Serve with sour cream, hot milk, or clabber.

Ukrainian borscht

Ingredients:
500 g meat
400 g cabbage
400 g potatoes
250 g beets
1/2 cup tomato paste
1/2 cup sour cream
1 carrot
1 parsnip
1 onion
20 g bacon
1 tbsp butter
1 tbsp vinegar
2 cloves garlic

Cook and strain meat broth. Julienne peeled carrot, parsnip, and beets. Braise beets with skimmed fat, tomato paste, vinegar, and some broth for 20-30 minutes (you can also add some beet or bread kvass to beets). Sauté onion, carrots, and parsnip in butter until softened. Add some broth to vegetables and bring to boil.

Add diced potatoes, shredded cabbage, braised beets to the remaining broth and season with salt. Bring to boil and cook 10-15 minutes, then add sautéed vegetables, bay leaves, whole black pepper, and continue cooking until potatoes and cabbage is done.

Season finished borscht with bacon minced with garlic, add slices of tomatoes, bring back to boil and then turn of the heat and let it infuse for 15-20 minutes.

Add sour cream to each serving of borscht and top with chopped parsley leaves.

Mushroom Borscht with Prunes

Mushroom borscht with prunes is cooked the same way as regular borsch, but instead of meat broth, use mushroom stock. Wash 200 g of prunes and add to vegetables at the end of braising, add mushroom stock and cook for 25-30 minutes.

Sorrel Soup

Ingredients:
500 g meat
400 g sorrel
200 g root vegetables and onion
2 tbsp butter
2 tbsp flour

Cook meat broth. Peel and dice root vegetables and onion, and sauté in butter or in skimmed fat. Add flour and sauté for 1-2 minutes more. Wash sorrel, add to pot with a small quantity of water, cover and braise for 10 minutes. Pass braised sorrel through a meat grinder or a sieve, mix with sautéed vegetables, add to meat broth and cook for 15-20 minutes.

When serving add sour cream and soft-boiled egg to a bowl, top with dill and parsley leaves.

Soup could be server with meat from meat broth, in which case put only half of a hard-boiled egg into a soup bowl.

Rassolnik

Ingredients:
500 g beef kidneys
2 pickles
2 parsnips
1 stick celery
1 onion
4 potatoes
2 tbsp butter
100 g sorrel or spinach

Remove fat and film from kidneys, cut each kidney into 3-4 parts, wash, put into a pot, cover with cold water and bring to boil. Drain and wash kidneys, cover with cold water and bring to boil again. Cook for 1-1 1/2 hours. Julienne peeled parsnips and onion and sauté in butter in a soup pan until soft. Off the heat add diced pickles and tomatoes, cover with strained broth. Bring to boil and cook for 25-30 minutes. About 10 minutes to completion add brine from pickles, cut greens, and season with salt.

Serve with kidneys, sour cream or heavy

cream, and finely chopped dill or parsley leaves.

Use finely cleaned and cut into pieces offal of poultry instead of beef kidneys if desired.

Rassolnik could be cooked with fish stock and served with fish from which this stock was made.

Fish Rassolnik with Quenelles

Ingredients:
For soup:
500 g small fish
2 pickles
1 carrot
1 parsnip
1 leek
3-4 potatoes
1/2 cup barley
2 tbsp butter

For quenelles:
200 g fish fillet (carp, walleye)
50 g crustless white bread
1/2 cup milk
1 tbsp butter

Start cooking fish stock and at the same time prepare barley - wash, cover with 1 1/4 cups of boiling water in a small pan and put into a water bath for soaking.

Strain finished fish stock, add barley, bring to boil and lower the heat to maintain constant simmer. Add diced pickles, potatoes, and, sautéed in butter until soft, diced carrot, parsnip, and leek. Season with salt.

Pass fish fillets though a meat grinder together with bread soaked in milk. Repeat 2 to 3 times. Mix with softened butter and seasoned with salt and pepper. Form quenelles and add them to the soup about 5 minutes before it is cooked.

Sliced fresh tomatoes could be added to this soup. It could also be seasoned to taste with brine from pickles.

Serve with finely chopped dill or parsley leaves.

Cauliflower Soup

Ingredients:
2 heads of cauliflower
1 bunch of carrots
1 stick celery
1-2 parsnips

Cook meat broth. Separate cauliflower into florets (cut large florets into smaller parts). Slice carrots and parsnips into rounds. Add vegetables to strained broth together with celery and cook at slow simmer for 20-30 minutes. About 2-3 minute before the soup is cooked remove celery and add finely chopped parsley leaves. If desired - add 2 tbsp of rice in the beginning of cooking.

Serve this soup with pirozhki or pie with beef or liver stuffing.

Soup with Brussels Sprouts

Ingredients:
600 g Brussels sprouts
3-4 potatoes
2 tbsp butter
1/2 cup sour cream

Clean and blanch Brussels sprouts in boiling water for 2 minutes. Drain blanched vegetables and sauté slightly in butter in a soup pan. Cover Brussels sprouts with 6-7 cups of mushroom stock (or hot water), add peeled and diced potatoes, season with salt and cook for 20-30 minutes at slow simmer. Add sour cream before serving.

Vegetable Soup

Ingredients:
500 g meat
500 g potatoes
200 g cabbage
200 g tomatoes
200 g root vegetables and onions
100 g spinach
2 tbsp butter

Cook meat broth. Was cabbage and cut it

into small squares. Dice root vegetables and onions. Melt butter or skimmed fat in a soup pan. Add diced vegetables and sauté until softened. Remove soup pan from heat and add cabbage. Cover everything with strained broth, return to the stove, bring to boil, add diced potatoes and cook for 30 minutes. Add spinach, sliced tomatoes, bay leaf, and season with salt 5-10 minutes before the soup is ready. Serve with sour cream.

Use mushroom or vegetable stock for vegetarian version of the soup.

Potato Soup

Ingredients:
500 g meat
800 g potatoes
200 g root vegetables and onion
2 tbsp butter

Cook meat broth. Dice peeled root vegetables and onion and sauté in a butter or skimmed fat until soft. Dice peeled potatoes and add to the boiling broth together with sautéed vegetables. Season with bay leaf, salt and pepper, and cook for 25-30 minutes. Add finely chopped dill or parsley leaves before serving.

This soup can be cooked with fish or mushroom stock. When serving soup made with mushroom stock -- add diced mushrooms to the plate. Add boiled fish into the soup made with fish stock.

Potato Soup with Fresh Mushrooms

Ingredients:
500 g mushrooms

800 g potatoes
200 g root vegetables and onions
2 tbsp butter

Clean and wash fresh mushrooms. Dice stems and sauté in butter. Separately sauté diced root vegetables and onions. Slice mushroom caps, blanch and drain. Put mushroom caps into a soup pot, cover with water and cook 40 minutes.

Add diced potatoes, sautéed mushroom stems, sautéed vegetables, bay leaf. Season with salt and pepper and cook 20-25 minutes more. Serve with sour cream and finely chopped dill and parsley leaves.

This soup could be cooked with meat broth. If desired the soup can be thickened with 40 g of farina.

Fish Head and Potato Soup

Ingredients:
1 kg fish heads
800 g potatoes
200 g root vegetables and onions
2 tbsp butter

Cook fish stock using fish heads just like in "Fish Head Shchi" recipe. Peel and dice root vegetables and onions. Sauté them in butter until softened. Peel and dice potatoes and add to the boiling strained stock together with sautéed vegetables. Season with salt, pepper, and bay leaf, and cook for 25-30 minutes. Top with finely chopped dill or parsley leaves before serving.

Potato Soup with Barley

Ingredients:
500 g meat or 50 g dried mushrooms
500 g potatoes
200 g root vegetables and onions
1/2 cup grains
2 tbsp butter

Cook meat broth. Wash and drain barley. Cover with 1 1/2 cups of cold water and leave to soak for 2 hours. Peel and dice root vegetables and onions. Sauté in butter until softened. Drain barley and add to meat broth, return to boil and lower the heat. 10-15 minutes after broth returns to boil add peeled and diced potatoes, sautéed vegetables. Season with salt, pepper, bay leaf. Cook until done. Top with finely chopped dill or parsley leaves before serving.

This soup can be cooked with fish stock. Barley could be replaced with rice, millet, or farina. Rice or millet has to be washed but not soaked before being added to the broth.

Noodle Soup

Ingredients:
500 g meat
150 g noodles or vermicelli
1 carrot
1 parsnip
1 onion
2 tbsp butter

Noodles:
1 cup all-purpose flour
1 egg
1/4 cup water

Cook beef or chicken broth. Julienne peeled carrot, parsnip, and onion. Sauté vegetables in butter or skimmed fat until soft. Add sautéed vegetables to the strained broth and bring to boil. Add noodles or vermicelli to the broth, season with salt, pepper, and bay leaf, and cook for 15-20 minutes. Add finely chopped dill or parsley leaves before serving.

Noodles or vermicelli could be replaced with any other pasta.

To make homemade noodles make a mound of the flour on a board with a well in the middle. Put lightly beaten egg and a pinch of salt into the well and mix dough, adding water as needed.

Roll the dough until thin and cut into strips of desired width. Hang the pasta dry; then, add to the soup when ready.

Potato Soup with Vermicelli

Ingredients:
500 g meat
500 g potatoes
200 g root vegetables and onions
100 g vermicelli
2 tbsp butter

Peel and julienne root vegetables and onions. Sauté in butter until soft. Peel and dice potatoes and add them to a boiling broth together with sautéed vegetables. Cook for 15 minutes. Add vermicelli, season with salt, pepper, and bay leaf, and cook for 12-15 minutes more.

If desired, use mushroom stock for this soup.

Pea Soup

Ingredients:
500 g meat
250 g dried peas
200g root vegetables and onions
2 tbsp butter

Cook meat broth. Add previously soaked peas and cook for 1 1/2 hours.

Dice washed and peeled root vegetables and onions and sauté them in butter until softened. Add sautéed vegetables to the soup 15-20 minutes before serving. Season with salt.

This soup could be cooked on a broth made from smoked ham. Serve with croutons made from white bread.

Bean Soup

Ingredients:
1 1/2 cups dried beans
1 carrot
1 parsnip
1 onion
2 tbsp butter
1 tbsp tomato paste

Cover previously soaked beans with water in a soup pan and bring to boil. Peel and dice root vegetables and onion. Sauté in butter with together with tomato paste. Add sautéed vegetables to beans 20-30 minutes from the time when water started boiling. Season with salt, pepper, and bay leaf. Cook until beans are cooked through.

Top with chopped dill or parsley leaves

before serving. Put sour cream into serving bowls.

Bean and Potato Soup

Ingredients:
1 cup dried bean
5-6 potatoes
1 carrot
1 onion
2 tbsp butter

Cook previously soaked beans until ready. Add sautéed carrot and onion together with peeled and diced potatoes. Season with salt, pepper, bay leaf, and continue cooking until potatoes are cooked.

Bean and Noodle Soup

Ingredients:
1 1/2 cup dried beans
1 onion
100 g noodles
2 tbsp butter

Soak washed bean for 3-4 hours in cold water. Drain beans, add 2 1/2 l of stock or cold water and cook until done. Add onion sautéed in butter, noodles, and season with salt and pepper.

Cook for 20 more minutes. Top with chopped herbs before serving.

Red Bean Soup

Ingredients:
1 1/2 cup red beans
1-2 onions
50 g walnuts
1/2 tbsp flour
2 tbsp butter
red pepper as needed

Wash the beans, put in the pot, pour 2 l of water, add 1 teaspoon of salt, cover with lid and bring to boil. Once water boils, remove the foam and simmer for 1 to 1 1/2 hours. Separately fry finely chopped onions, towards the end of frying add red peppers and flour, mix everything and fry for another 1-2 minutes. After this put onions into boiled beans, add grated or finely chopped walnuts, salt and boil for 15-20 minutes.

When serving, add some finely chopped parsley into the soup.

Assembled Meat Solyanka

Ingredients:
500 g meat (for stock)
300 g boiled or fried meat products
4 pickles
2 onions
2 tbsp tomato puree
3 tbsp butter
1 tbsp olives
1 tbsp capers

100 g sour cream
1/4 lemon

Shred onions, fry them a little and braise them with tomatoes and butter, adding some stock. Peel cucumbers, cut into halves and slice. Meat products (boiled and fried) used can be of many varieties: meat, ham, veal, kidneys, tongue, hot dogs, sausage, etc. Cut them into thin slices, out into a pan with prepared onions, add cucumbers, capers, salt, bay leaf, add stock and boil for 5-10 minutes. You can also add sliced tomatoes.

When serving solyanka, add sour cream, olives, lemon slices, finely chopped parsley or dill.

Fish Solyanka

Ingredients:
500 g fish
4-5 pickles
1-2 onions
2-3 tomatoes or 2 tbsp tomato paste
1 tbsp capers
1 tbsp olives
2 tbsp butter

Any fish can be used to cook solyanka, preferably not too small and not too bony. Sturgeon or salmon are the best for this soup.

Cut fish fillets into pieces, about 2-3 per serving, make fish stock from heads and bones.

Thinly slice peeled and washed onions and sauté in butter in a soup pan. Add tomato paste and braise 5-6 minutes. Add fish, sliced pickles, sliced tomatoes, capers, bay leaf, cover with hot fish stock, season with salt and pepper and cook

10-15 minutes. Just before serving add olives and finely chopped dill or parsley leaves. Decorate with peeled lemon slices.

Lamb Chihirtma

Ingredients:
500 g lamb
2 onions
2 eggs, separated
1 tbsp butter
1 tbsp flour
2 tbsp white wine vinegar
1/2 tsp saffron

Wash lamb with cold water and cut into small pieces (about 3-4 pieces per serving), put into a stock pot filled with cold water, bring to boil over high heat and then simmer, removing foam and scum. Remove cooked lamb from the pot and strain the broth.

Sauté finely diced onion in butter until soft, add flour, mix well and brown the mixture. To the strained broth add cooked lamb, browned onions, saffron, and season with salt and pepper and bring it to boil.

Separately boil vinegar and add to the soup, bring soup to boil yet again and remove from heat.

Just before serving beat eggs yolks, mix with a small quantity of broth, add back to the soup, mix and warm it up without letting it boil (otherwise eggs would curdle), then add chopped cilantro.

Kharcho

Ingredients:
500 g meat
2 onions
2-3 cloves garlic
2 tbsp tomato paste
or 100g tomatoes
1/2 cup rice
1/2 cup sour plums

Kharcho is cooked primarily from beef, but lamb can also be used.

Wash meat and cut it into small pieces (about 3-4 per serving). Put into a stock pot, cover with water and bring to boil. Cook at a simmer, removing foam and scum that rises to the top. After 1 1/2-2 hours add finely chopped onions, crushed garlic, rice, sour plums, season with salt and pepper, and continue cooking for 30 minutes more. Fry tomato paste in butter or in fat skimmed from the broth, and add it to the soup 5-10 minutes before it is cooked.

Add finely chopped dill, cilantro, or parsley leaves just before serving.

Shurpa

Ingredients:
500 g beef
750 g potatoes

2 onions
2 carrots
2 tbsp tomato paste
2 tbsp butter

Cook meat broth. Thinly slice onions and sauté them in butter until soft.

Cut meat into pieces about 25-30 g , brown it, add sautéed onions, diced carrots, tomato paste, mix well and continue frying for 5-6 minutes. Transfer meat with vegetables into a soup pot, cover with meat broth and bring to boil. Add sliced potatoes, season with salt and pepper, and cook for 15-20 minutes, until potatoes are cooked through.

Soup with Canned Meat

Ingredients:
1 can - canned meat (beef, pork, lamb, or venison)
500-600 g vegetables
1 1/2-2 l water
1 tbsp butter

Cook a vegetable soup (potato, shchi, borscht), add canned meat and bring to boil. Just before serving, sprinkle with finely chopped dill or parsley leaves.

Soup with Canned Fish

Ingredients:
1 can - canned fish (walleye, sturgeon, salmon, etc.)
500-600 g vegetables
1 1/2-2 l water
1 tbsp butter

Cook a vegetable soup (potato, rassolnik, shchi with sauerkraut), add canned fish and bring to boil.

Just before serving, sprinkle with finely chopped dill or parsley leaves.

CLEAR SOUPS

A base of all clear soups is a strong broth cooked from beef, game, or chicken.

Rice, eggs, dumplings, vermicelli and different vegetables are usually cooked separately, added to the bowls just before serving, and covered with hot broth. This method preserves clarity of the broth and gives soup its pleasant and appetizing appearance. Vegetables for clear soup should be julienned or diced.

Calorie content of clear soups primarily depends on ingredients added to it, not the broth itself; however, significant content of extractive substances in the broth causes increased secretion of stomach acid and, therefore, helps to increase appetite and improves digestion of the food consumed after soup.

Clear soups are especially recommended when they are followed by high-calorie meat or fish dishes.

Clear Meat Broth

Ingredients:
500 g meat
1 carrot
1 parsnip
1 celery root
1 onion

2-3 l water

Wash meat, put it into a stock pot, and cover with cold water. Bring the pot to boil and remove foam that rises to the top. Lower the heat and keep at simmer. Add root vegetables about 1-1 12/ hours after the water starts boiling. To improve flavor and color of the broth, char half of the carrot, parsnip, and onion on a hot cast-iron pan. Season broth with salt when adding vegetables.

Broth should be cooked anywhere from 2 to 2 1/2 hours. Remove cooked meat and use it in some other dishes. Skim all the fat from the broth and then strain it through a fine strainer or a clean kitchen towel.

To make even stronger and clearer broth you can do additional clarification. To clarify broth take 300 g of meat (same type as used to cook broth) and pass it through a meat grinder. Add one egg white and a cup of broth, mix and let it stand for 20-30 minutes. Add ground meat into a hot broth, cover the pot, and simmer on low heat for 30-40 minutes. When the mix curdles and settles on the bottom, strain the broth carefully. Finished clear broth can be served with toasts, pirozhki, corn flakes, or used in clear soups. Curdled mix can be used in a casserole.

Broth with Game Birds

Ingredients:
1 pheasant or 1 blackcock or 4 grouse
1 carrot
1 parsnip
1 onion
1-2 sticks celery
2-3 l water

Broth with game birds is usually made when cooking birds for salads, or if carcasses of the birds are available after meat has been removed for some other preparations. When using primarily carcasses - make sure to chop bones into smaller pieces before putting it into a stock pot. Add charred in a cast-iron pan carrot, parsnip, and onion. Add celery, cover everything with water, and bring it to boil.

Lower the heat and simmer broth for about an hour, removing all the scum and foam that rises to the top. Season with salt just before it is done. Turn of the heat and let it settle before straining.

Chicken Broth

Ingredients:
1 chicken (about 1 kg)
1 carrot
1 parsnip
1 onion
2 1/2-3 l water

Wipe the chicken dry and singe any remaining feathers. Cut off its neck and feet, gut and thoroughly wash inside and out.

Cut the stomach, clean it and remove film; cut the heart; scald its feet and peel, cut off the claws; pick feathers off its head; carefully separate gallbladder from liver. Wash all innards.

Put prepared chicken and its innards together with prepared roots into a stock pot and cover with water. Bring to boil and remove all foam and scum that rises to the top. It takes about 1 to 2 hours to cook chicken broth, depending on the size and age of the bird.

To check if chicken has been cooked poke it with fork in the thigh. If fork goes in easily - the chicken is done. Remove chicken and innards from the pot and save for another use. Strain the broth.

Broth "Borschtok"

Ingredients:
2-2 1/2 l clear broth (meat, chicken, or game birds)
250 g beets
2-3 tbsp vinegar
1 tbsp sugar

About 10-15 minutes before broth is done cooking add thinly sliced peeled beets, 2 tbsp of grape wine or vinegar and sugar.

Strain finished "borschtok" and serve in soup mugs. Serve cheese toasts on the side.

Broth with Pasta

Ingredients:
2 l clear broth
100-125 g pasta

Parboil noodles, vermicelli, or any other pasta for 2-3 minutes in boiling water. Strain pasta, add to boiling clear broth and cook 12-15 minutes until completely cooked. Pasta is parboiled to preserve clarity of the broth.

Broth with Dumplings

Prepare meat or chicken broth and at the same time prepare dough for dumplings from flour, semolina or potatoes. Cut the prepared dough with tablespoon and teaspoon. Take the dough from the pot with tablespoon and remove small oval-shaped pieces with teaspoon moistened with water. Place these pieces in hot broth and boil them in it. For 2 l of broth make dumplings from 1/2 cup of flower (semolina) or 3 potatoes.

Pate a choux for dumplings. Pour 1/3 cup of broth in pot, put butter, salt and bring to boil. Then pour flour or semolina, mix with a spoon and boil for 1-2 minutes (5-6 minutes for the semolina), after which remove from fire, put eggs and mix well. For 1/2 cup flour or semolina use 2 tbsp butter, 2 eggs.

Simple dough for dumplings. Pour 1/4 cup of broth into a bowl, put butter, egg, flour, salt and mix the dough. For 1/2 cup flour use 1 egg, 1/2 tbsp butter.

Potato dough for dumplings. Peel potatoes, boil and mash or rub through a sieve, add raw egg yolks and mix well. Then add whipped egg whites and mix again. For 3 potatoes, use 3-4 tbsp flour, 2 eggs.

Broth with Pelmeni

Ingredients:

2 l broth for pelmeni
300-400 g meat
1-2 onions
1 1/2 cup flour
1 egg

This dish can be quickly prepared by purchasing pre-made pelmeni. Put them into boiling broth and boil on slow fire, until they float on the surface, which should take around 10 minutes.

If pelmeni are not available for purchase, you may prepare them as follows. Meat (half beef, half pork is the best choice) mixed with onions is put through meat grinder twice. Add a little water, salt, pepper and mix well.

Dough is prepared separately. Whisk egg and mix into flour, pour 1/4 cup water, add salt, mix well and mix dough.

Roll the dough into thin layer, cut out circles with a glass and place small balls of prepared ground meat on top of each. The edges of dough circles should be pinched.

In order for broth with pelmeni to be clear, submerge pelmeni into hot water for a few seconds to wash off the dough, and then place into boiling broth.

When serving, sprinkle with finely chopped parsley or dill.

Broth with Puffs

Ingredients:
2-2 1/2 l clear broth
100 g flour
2-3 eggs
3 tbsp butter

Puffs for this broth are made from hazelnut-sized balls of pate a choux. To make the dough add 1/2 cup of water, butter, and salt to a pot, bring it to boil and add flour when the water starts boiling. Lower the heat and stir the mixture with a spoon for 1-2 minutes. Remove from heat and add eggs, one at a time, making sure that each one is well incorporated before adding the next one.

Put the dough into a piping bag with 1/4 inch diameter nozzle and pipe the small mounds of dough onto a parchment paper on a baking sheet. Bake in the heated oven for 10-15 minutes.

Ladle broth into bowls and add puff just before serving, or serve puffs on a side.

Broth with Farina

Ingredients:
2-2 1/2 l clear broth
4 tbsp farina

Add farina into a pot with boiling meat or chicken broth, and cook for 10 minutes stirring from time to time. Ladle finished soup into bowls and sprinkle with finely chopped parsley. If desired, add warmed green peas, or soft-boiled egg.

Broth with Sago

Ingredients:
2-2 1/2 l clear broth
1/2 cup sago

Add sago to a boiling meat broth, and cook

for 15-30 minutes. Ladle finished soup into bowl
and sprinkle with chopped parsley.

Broth with Rice

Ingredients:
2-2 1/2 l clear broth
1/2 cup rice

Wash rice in several changes of water and
put into a pot with hot water. Parboil rice for 3-5
minutes.

Drain parboiled rice in a strainer and wash
it again. Add drained rice to the boiling broth and
cook for 20-25 minutes, until it is fully cooked.
Ladle finished soup into bowls and sprinkle with
chopped parsley leaves.

Broth with Roots and Rice

Ingredients:
2-2 1/2 l clear broth
1 carrot
1 onion
1 parsnip
1 turnip
50 g sorrel
50 g peas or green beans
1 tbsp butter
3 tbsp rice

Dice peeled vegetables and sauté in butter,
add 2 cups of broth and cook on a low heat for 5-
10 minutes, add peas or green beans and cook 10
more minutes. Add cut sorrel and cook for 2-3
minutes.

Cook rise separately. Put cooked rice and

vegetables into bowls and add broth. Sprinkle with chopped parsley. This soup can be made with barley instead of rice.

Broth with Baked Rice

Ingredients:
2-2 1/2 l clear broth
1/2 cup rice
2 eggs
1 tbsp butter
1 tbsp breadcrumbs
50 g grated cheese

Cook rice, drain in a strainer, then put into a mixing bowl. Add eggs, butter, part of grated cheese, season salt, and mix well. Put this mix on a well-oiled and covered with crumbs frying pan. Smooth the top, put the remaining cheese on top, sprinkle with melted butter and put into a heated oven for 15-20 minutes. Slightly cool baked rice, flip onto a cutting board, cut into servings and put into bowls. Add hot meat or chicken broth.

Broth with Roots and Greens

Ingredients:
2-2 1/2 l clear broth
250-300 g different roots and vegetables
(carrots, turnips, parsnips, cauliflower or asparagus, green peas or string beans, spinach, parsley leaves)

Bring meat or chicken broth to boil and add prepared vegetables in the following order -- carrots, turnip and asparagus, cut into batonnets, cauliflower separated into florets, then green peas and string beans cut into smaller pieces. After 15-20 minutes of cooking add cut spinach leaves cut into smaller pieces. Let it cook for 2-3 minutes more.

Serve this soup with boiled chicken meat or soft-boiled eggs. Depending on a season different vegetables could be used to cook this soup. For example, use more carrots if asparagus is not available, peas or beans could be replaced by canned variety if fresh are not available.

Broth with Celery

Ingredients:
2-2 1/2 l clear broth
100 g celery root
1 carrot
1/2 parsnip

Cook clear meat broth. About an hour - hour and a half after it starts boiling add peeled roots - carrot, parsnip, celery - and continue cooking until vegetables are ready. Strained finished broth, ladle into soup mugs, and serve with toasts or pirozhki.

Broth with Eggs

Cook meat or chicken broth, ladle into bowls or soup mugs, and add soft boil eggs into broth.

Broth with Omelet

Ingredients:
2-2 1/2 l clear broth for omelet
1 cup milk

1 tbsp butter
4 eggs

Prepare meat or chicken broth, then prepare omelet.

To make omelet, whip eggs in a bowl, add salt. Keep whipping, add cold milk or broth.

Pour this paste into smooth molds or on a frying pan greased with butter, put it in a bigger frying pan with hot water, cover with lid and bring to boil until omelet thickens. For small bowls this should take 10-15 minutes, in a large frying pan around 30-40 minutes. In order for the surface of the omelet to be smooth, water should be almost boiling, but not quite.

Once omelet is ready, cool it (10-15 minutes), then remove it from molds and put into bowls with broth. Omelet that has been prepared in a frying pan needs to be cut into squares.

Omelet for broth can be prepared with spinach or tomatoes. Spinach might be either canned or fresh. Wash fresh spinach well, boil in a small amount of water and rub through a sieve. Prepared spinach or tomato paste is added to the egg mix before it is cooked. When serving, add parsley to the broth.

Broth with Meatballs

Ingredients:
2 - 2 1/2 l clear broth
200 g meat (lean with fat)

Pass raw meat through meat grinder twice; add salt, pepper and 2 tbsp of cold water. Mix well, form into meatballs and put them into boiling meat or chicken broth. Remove meatballs and place on plates, 8-10 per plate. Strain broth and pour it over meatballs, sprinkle with parsley.

Meatballs can also be made from beef or lamb. Lamb fat is best removed and replaced with butter.

Broth with Chicken Dumplings

Ingredients:
2 - 2 1/2 l clear broth
100g chicken filet
1 egg white
1/4 cup milk
1 slice white bread

To prepare chicken dumplings pass chicken meat through meat grinder, add egg white, bread that has been soaked in milk and salt. Mix well and pass through meat grinder again, then put into pot and mix. After this, while gradually adding milk (one tbsp at a time), whip and rub through a sieve in order to obtain a smooth uniform paste. Using two spoons, cut it (like dough dumplings) and put them in hot water. Once ready, remove from water, put on plates, pour chicken broth and sprinkle with parsley.

Ukha (Fish Soup)

Ingredients:
1 kg fish
1 onion
1 leek
1 parsnip
1 celery
2 1/2 -3 l water

The tastiest ukha is prepared from freshly caught fish (sterlet, bass). It can also be made from walleye or various small fish, with the exception of crucian carp and tench. In order for ukha to have desired adhesiveness, small fish - ruffe and bass - are boiled with scales intact, gutted and thoroughly washed. For bass, the gills will have to be removed as well, otherwise broth will have bitter taste.

Place prepared fish in a pot, pour cold water, add cleaned roots, leek, salt and simmer from 40 minutes to one hour. Strain the broth after.

In order for ukha to be clear and transparent, it is necessary to perform extrusion (clearing) with salmon or sturgeon caviar. Grind 50 g of caviar in a mortar, gradually adding water by a spoon, until a dough-like paste is formed. Dilute with a cup of cold water, add a cup of hot ukha, mix and pour into the pot with hot ukha in two steps. After you pour the first half, wait for ukha to boil, and then pour in the rest. Once it boils for the second time, remove the lid and simmer for 15-20 minutes.

When ukha is ready, remove from stove and let it cool for 10-15 minutes, so that the residue settles on the bottom of the pot. After that, carefully strain. Prepared ukha is usually served with kulebyaka or similar dish. You can also put a piece of boiled fish in a plate of ukha.

PUREED SOUPS

Pureed soup can be prepared from vegetables, grains and legumes, meat or fish products.

Vegetable pureed soup is made from one or

several kinds of vegetables, for example from cauliflower or carrots, or from potatoes, carrots and turnips.

Grains used in pureed soups are most often rice and pearl barley; legumes are usually beans and peas.

Meat pureed soups are best prepared from poultry and game.

For fish soups carp is recommended, as well as smelt, navaga, walleye, cod, etc.

Ingredients for pureed soup are rubbed through a sieve.

Pureed soups made from vegetables, grains, legumes can be prepared with broth that has been obtained by boiling these products, with added milk. The can also be cooked with meat or chicken broth, prepared the same way as regular meat soup. For pureed soups made from poultry, game or fish broth that has been obtained by boiling these products is used.

To prevent ingredients that have been rubbed through a sieve from depositing on the bottom, add some flour fried in oil and boil for 20-30 minutes.

Thickness of pureed soup should resemble cream.

Before serving, add a piece of butter into pureed soup and stir. Butter adds taste and visual appeal to the soup.

To increase nutritional value of the soup, in addition to butter, cream or egg condiment may be added. Egg condiment is prepared as follows: 2-3 egg yolks are whisked in a bowl, while gradually pouring in 3/4 cup of milk or cream, then strained through a sieve and added to the soup while stirring.

If pureed soup is not served immediately

after it is ready, it should be kept hot (while not boiling).

When serving, it is recommended to add a little (approximately 1 tbsp per plate) un-grated ingredients. For example, add slices of cabbage stalk that have been boiled in salty water or broth into cauliflower soup; add fresh or canned sweet peas into potato pureed soup, etc. For pureed soups made with poultry or game it is recommended to leave some filet as garnish, which should be julienned.

All pureed soups are served with croutons made from white bread, diced and dried in oat case or fried on a frying pan with oil. You can also serve pirozhki with different stuffing: for meat and vegetable soups - with meat or cabbage and eggs, for fish soups - with fish.

Potato Soup-Puree

Ingredients:
1 kg potatoes
2-3 cups milk
3 tbsp butter
3 leeks
2 egg yolks
3/4 cup milk

Slice washed and cleaned leeks, sauté in butter until soft. Add peeled, washed, and sliced potatoes, cover with 5 cups of water, season with salt and cook 20-25 minutes. Rub cooked potatoes together with its broth through a sieve (ed. note - Obviously at the time when this book was published blenders did not exist), add hot milk and mix well. Just before serving add a little bit of butter and egg yolks mixed with milk. Serve toasts or corn flakes on the side.

Pumpkin Soup-Puree

Ingredients:
800 g pumpkin
300 g potatoes
150 g croutons or 2 tbsp flour
4-5 cups milk
3 tbsp butter
2 tsp sugar

Peel, wash, and slice pumpkin and
potatoes. Add pumpkin and potatoes to a soup
pot together with 3-4 cups of water, add 1
tablespoon of butter, season with salt and sugar
and simmer for 25-30 minutes. Sauté croutons in
butter, add to the soup and bring to simmer.
Strain the soup and rub solids though a sieve (or
blend in a blender), mix with hot milk and add
butter.
This soup could also be cooked differently.
Cook sliced pumpkin with 2 cups of water.
Make roux by sautéing 2 tablespoons of flour in 2
tablespoons of butter, then add 4 cups of hot milk
and 2 cups of water, bring to simmer, add to
pumpkin and cook for 15-20 minutes. Rub
everything through a sieve (or blend until
smooth), season with salt, add 1-2 cups of hot milk
and butter, mix well. Serve croutons or toasts on a
side.

Carrot Soup-Puree

Ingredients:
800 g carrots
1/2 cup rice

3 tbsp butter
2 cups milk
1 tsp sugar

Thinly slice peeled and washed carrots, put into a soup pot together with 1/4 cup water, 1 tbsp of butter, 1 tsp of salt and 1 tsp of sugar, and stew for 5-10 minutes. Add 1/2 cup of washed rice with 5 cups of water, cover the pot and cook for 40-50 minutes on low heat. Set aside 2 tbsp of cooked rice for garnish. Rub everything through sieve (or blend until smooth).

Add hot milk to the puree and season with salt. Just before serving add butter and remaining rice to the soup. Serve croutons or toasts on a side.

String Beans Soup-Puree

Ingredients:
600-700 g string beans
500 g potatoes
3 tbsp butter
2 cups milk

Wash and clean string beans. Slice one-fourth of beans on a bias and keep for garnish, pass remaining beans through a meat grinder. Slice peeled and washed potatoes and add to a soup pot together with ground beans, salt, 1-2 tbsp of butter, and 4-5 cups of hot water. Cover the pot and cook until the potatoes are cooked through. Rub the soup through a sieve (or blend until smooth). Add hot milk to the puree and season with more butter. Just before serving add separately cooked sliced string beans. Serve with croutons or toasts on a side.

This soup can be cooked with canned string

beans. Just like in the main recipe - take some of the beans for garnish, add the rest, together with liquid from the can, to potatoes and follow the recipe above.

Cauliflower Soup-Puree

Ingredients:
600 g cauliflower or 750 g white cabbage
500 g potatoes
2 cups milk
3 tbsp butter

Cook 1/4 of small cauliflower florets in salted water and set aside for garnish. Peel and wash potatoes and add to a soup pot together with remaining cauliflower. Cover with 4 cups of water, add 2 tsp of salt and cook for 25-30 minutes. Rub everything though a sieve (or blend until smooth) and mix with hot milk. Add cream or butter just before serving, mix well and add separately cooked florets. Serve with croutons or toasts on the side.

Canned cauliflower can be used instead of fresh one. Decrease cooking time by 10-15 minutes if using canned variety.

This soup can be cooked with green cabbage. Remove outer leaves and core, and wash cabbage, add to a soup pot, cover with water and bring to simmer. Add potatoes to cabbage 15-20 minutes after the start of cooking, and cook until done. Follow main recipe after that.

Asparagus Soup-Puree

Ingredients:
800 g asparagus

4 cups milk
4 tbsp butter
2 tbsp flour

Clean, cook, and set aside 20-25 head of asparagus for garnish. Wash remaining asparagus, cut it and cook in 2 cups of lightly-salted water for 15-20 minutes.

Sauté 2 tbsp of flour with 2 tbsp of butter in a soup pan, add 4 cups of milk and bring to simmer. Add asparagus together with its cooking water and continue to simmer for 10-15 minutes. Mash everything through a sieve (or blend until smooth), and season with salt to taste. Just before serving add butter and asparagus tips. Serve with croutons or toasts on a side.

Vegetable Soup-Puree

Ingredients:
150 g carrots
150 g turnips
200 g potatoes
100 g leeks
3/4 cups rice
100 g green peas
3 tbsp butter
2 cups milk

Thinly slice carrots, turnips, and white parts of leeks and sauté in a soup pot with 2 tbsp of butter for 10-15 minutes. Add 4 cups of water, potatoes, and washed rice, cover the pot, bring to boil, lower the heat, and simmer for 30-35 minutes. Mash vegetables and broth through a sieve (or blend until smooth), add 2 cups of hot milk, remaining butter, and season with salt to taste.

Just before serving add fresh or canned green peas. Serve croutons or toasts on a side.

Tomato Soup-Puree

Ingredients:
750 g tomatoes or 100 g tomato paste or 1 can tomatoes
4 tbsp butter
2 tbsp flour
4 cups milk
1 tsp sugar
2 tbsp rice

Lightly sauté flour in 2 tbsp of butter. Add hot milk and bring to simmer mixing all the time.

Cut fresh tomatoes into quarters and sauté with 1 tbsp of butter and sugar in a covered soup pot for 10-15 minutes. Add 3 cups of water, bring to boil, add milk sauce and simmer for 15-20 minutes. Mash everything through a sieve (or blend until smooth). Add cooked rice just before serving.

If using canned tomatoes - add full contents of a can into milk sauce together with 2 cups of vegetable stock and follow the above recipe.

If using tomato paste, add it to the milk sauce together with 2 cups of water or vegetable stock, bring to boil, lower the heat and simmer for 15-20 minutes. Mash everything through a sieve (or blend until smooth), add butter and season with salt.

Lettuce Soup-Puree

Ingredients:
800 g lettuce

3 tbsp butter
2 tbsp flour
5-6 cups milk
1 cup cream

Put washed lettuce leaves in boiling water for 1-2 minutes, put in a sieve, drain, pass through a meat grinder with fine mesh. In a separate pot, fry the dough with 2 tbsp butter, mix with 5-6 cups of mil, boil, mix with lettuce and cook for 15-20 minutes. Then add salt, butter, one more cup of hot milk or cream and mix. Serve with croutons or toasts on a side.

Champignon or Porcini Soup-Puree

Ingredients:
600 g fresh champignons or porcini (cepes)
2 tbsp flour
4 cups milk
4 tbsp butter
1 carrot
1 onion

For seasoning:
2 egg yolks
1 cup heavy cream or milk

Clean fresh champignons, wash them, pass through a meat grinder, put in a pan, add one tbsp of butter, one carrot that's been cut in half lengthwise, one onion, cover with lid and sauté 40-45 minutes, then add 1 cup of water bring to boil, then remove carrot and onion.

In a soup pan make roux from 2 tbsp of flour and 2 tbsp of butter, add 4 cups of hot milk and a cup of vegetable stock or water, bring to simmer and add to mushrooms. Cook for 15-20 minutes. Season finished soup with salt and add egg yolks blended with cream or milk. Serve croutons or toasts on a side.

This soup can be cooked with fresh porcini (cepes) or morels.

Sweet Peas Soup-Puree

Ingredients:
1 can (800 g) sweet peas
3 tbsp butter
2 tbsp flour
4 cups milk

This soup can be cooked with frozen or canned peas. Keep 2-3 tbsp of peas for garnish.

Mash canned or cooked in advance frozen peas through a sieve (or blend until smooth) and mix with milk sauce.

To make the sauce sauté 2 tbsp of flour in 2 tbsp of butter, then add hot milk and cook for 10-15 minutes. Strain the sauce through a sieve, thin with hot water to a desired consistency, and season with salt. Just before serving add remaining butter to the soup and garnish with whole peas. Serve croutons or toasts on a side.

Rice Soup-Puree

Ingredients:
1 cup rice
3-4 cups milk
3 tbsp butter

Wash rice in warm water, add to a pan with 4 cups of water, season with salt and cook 35-40 minutes. Mash rice with cooking liquid through a sieve, add hot milk, heat through and season with salt and butter. Garnish finished soup with rice - just add 1 tbsp of rice in each bowl. Serve with croutons or toasts on a side.

Bean Soup-Puree

Ingredients:
400 g dried beans (or peas)
1 carrot
1 onion
4 tbsp butter
2 cups milk

Wash and soak beans in cold water for 5-6 hours. Add soaked beans to a pot, cover with 4-5 cups of water, add sliced in half lengthwise carrot and onion with 2 cloves stuck into it. Cover the pot and cook beans on low heat 40-50 minutes. Remove carrot and onion from the pot and mash beans together with cooking liquid through a sieve (or blend until smooth). Add hot milk to mashed beans and season with salt. Just before serving add butter to the soup. Serve with croutons or toasts on a side.

Canned Corn Soup-Puree

Ingredients:
1 can corn
2 tbsp flour
4 tbsp butter
3 cups milk

Pass corn through a meat grinder, add to a pot with 3 cups of water and bring to boil. Saute flour in 2 tbsp of butter, add hot milk, bring to simmer, add this sauce to corn and cook 15-20 minutes. Mash the soup through a sieve (or blend until smooth), head through and season with salt and butter. Serve with croutons or corn flakes.

Liver Soup-Puree

Ingredients:
400 g beef or veal liver
500-600 g meat (for broth)
4 tbsp butter
2 tbsp flour
1 carrot
1 parsnip
1 leek

For seasoning:
2 egg yolks
1 cup heavy cream or milk

Wash liver well and remove outside membrane and ducts. Dice and sauté liver lightly together with cleaned a thinly sliced leek, then add 1/2 cup water, cover the pot and stew the contents for 30-40 minutes. Pass liver 2-3 times through a meat grinder, then rub it through a sieve. While the liver is stewing prepare white sauce. Sauté flour in 2 tbsp of butter, then add 4 cups of hot meat broth simmer 20-30 minutes. Strain the sauce, add prepared liver, mix well and bring to simmer. If soup is too thick - add some broth. Season with salt, add egg yolks mixed with cream or milk and butter. Serve with croutons or toasts on a side.

Chicken Soup-Puree

Ingredients:
1 chicken
4 tbsp butter
2 tbsp flour

For seasoning:
2 egg yolks
1 cup heavy cream or milk

Cook chicken and separate meat from bones. Leave one fillet for garnish, pass all the other meat two-three times through a meat grinder. Add 2-3 tbsp of broth to the meat and rub the mixture through a sieve.

Sauté flour with 2 tbsp of butter, add 4 cups of hot broth and simmer for 20-30 minutes. Strain the sauce, add ground chicken and bring to boil. Add more broth if soup is too thick. Turn off the heat, season with salt and butter, and add egg yolks mixed with cream or milk. Just before serving garnish with finely sliced fillet. Serve with croutons or toasts on a side.

Game Birds Soup-Puree

Ingredients:
1 pheasant or blackcock (or 2 partridges or 2 quails)
500-600 g meat (for broth)
4 tbsp butter
2 tbsp flour
1 carrot
1 parsnip
1 leek

For seasoning:

2 egg yolks
1 cup cream or milk

Brown prepared birds on all side, than cook
in meat broth 20-30 minutes together with carrot,
parsnip, and leek. This way of cooking will insure
that birds will keep their flavor and taste. Separate
meat from the bones and leave part of the fillet for
garnish. Pass remaining meat 2-3 times through a
meat grinder, mix with 2-3 tbsp of broth, and rub
through a sieve.

Finish cooking the soup following
instructions from recipe "Chicken Soup-Puree".

Fish Soup-Puree

Ingredients:
750 g fish
4 tbsp butter
2 tbsp flour
2 cups milk
1 carrot
1 parsnip
2 onions

Scale, wash, and fillet the fish. Make a stock
from bones, root vegetables, and 1 onion. Cut fish
fillets into small pieces and sauté in butter
together with diced onion. In a pot make a roux
with 2 tbsp of flour and 2 tbsp of butter, add 4
cups of strained hot fish stock and bring to
simmer. Add prepared fish and cook 15-20
minutes. Strain the soup and rub the fish through
a sieve, mix with hot milk and season with salt
and butter. If desired - add egg yolks mixed with
milk.

The soup could be served garnished with

pieces of fish or quenelles. To make quenelles set aside 100 g of fish fillets. Serve with croutons or toasts on a side.

Canned Crab Soup-Puree

Ingredients:
1 can crab meat
4 tbsp butter
2 tbsp flour
4 cups milk

For seasoning:
2 egg yolks
1 cup heavy cream or milk

Set aside a couple of larger pieces of crab meat for garnish, pass remaining meat through a meat grinder, put into a pit, add a cup of stock or water, cover the pot and simmer for 5-10 minutes. In a separate pot, sauté flour with 2 tbsp of butter, add hot milk, bring to simmer, add crab meat and cook 15-20 minutes longer. Strain the soup and rub solids through a sieve. , season with salt, butter, and egg yolks blended with cream or milk. Garnish with remaining crab meat. Serve with croutons or toasts on a side.

MILK SOUPS

Milk soups are very nutritious and easy to prepare. Milk soups can be prepared from regular or canned milk (powdered or condensed).

Powdered milk is placed in a pot, 1 - 1 1/2 tbsp per cup of water. Thoroughly mix the powdered milk, first in a small amount of warm water so that a thick, uniform paste is formed;

then gradually add more water of the same temperature into the pot, and stir until powdered milk is completely dissolved. Then bring to boil and begin cooking soup.

Condensed milk is usually made with a significant amount of added sugar. Dissolve the milk with hot water (1 tbsp per cup). Put noodles, rice or other ingredients in dissolved boiled milk and add salt (approximately 1/2 teaspoon per l of milk).

Milk soups should be made in thick-bottomed pots or on low heat, so that milk doesn't burn.

Milk Soup with Rice

Ingredients:
1 l milk
4 tbsp rice
1 tbsp butter
1 teaspoon sugar

Wash the rice well, strain, put rice in boiling milk, add salt, sugar and cook for 30 minutes. When serving, add butter.

Milk Soup with Noodles

Ingredients:
1 l milk
50 g noodles
1 tbsp butter
1 tea spoon sugar

Put noodles into boiling milk, add salt, sugar and cook for 20-25 minutes. When serving, add butter. If using vermicelli, decrease cooking time to 12-15 minutes. If using homemade noodles, cook for 15-20 minutes.

Milk Soup with Baked Rice

Ingredients:
1 l milk
3 tbsp rice
1 egg
1 tbsp butter
25 g cheese
2 tbsp breadcrumbs

Cook rice following instructions from the recipe "Broth with Baked Rice". Put slices of baked rice into bowls and cover with hot milk.

Milk Soup with Barley

Ingredients:
1 l milk
4-5 tbsp pearl barley
1 tbsp butter
1 tsp sugar

Wash barley, cover with cold water and let soak for 2 hours. Drain the grain, cover with hot water and parboil for 10 minutes. Drain barley yet again, add to a pot with boiling milk, lower the heat and simmer 40-50 minutes. Season with salt, sugar, and butter, and serve.

Milk Soup with Potato Dumplings

Ingredients:
1 l milk
3-4 potatoes

2 eggs
3-4 tbsp flour
1 tbsp butter

Mix boiled, grated potatoes, egg yolks and flour, season with salt and carefully fold in whipped egg whites. Take a tablespoon of mixture and, using a teaspoon dipped into a hot water, separate small portions of potato dough and put into simmering milk. Cook potato dumplings on low heat 10-12 minutes. Season soup with salt and butter.

Milk soul could be also cooked with simple dough dumplings or with farina dumplings -- as in recipe "Broth with Dumplings".

Milk Soup with Oats

Ingredients:
1 l milk
1 cup oats
1 tsp sugar
1 tbsp butter

Add oats (ed. note - Quick cooking oats are probably more appropriate for this recipe since steel-cut oats take longer to cook) to a pot with boiling milk, season with salt and sugar, and cook 20-25 minutes.

Put butter into the soup just before serving.

BERRY AND FRUIT SOUPS

Sour Cherry Soup with Dumplings

Ingredients:
600 g sour cherries

1 cup flour
1/2 cup sugar
2 eggs

Pit half of the cherries, mash the other half of the cherries. Add pits from the first half of the cherries to mashed cherries, cover with 4-5 cups of hot water, add sugar, bring to boil and strain.

Make dough. Mix eggs with flour and add water until it all comes together. Roll the dough thinly and cut out circle shapes. Put 1-2 pitted cherries in the middle of each circle and pinch the sides together.

Just before serving put cherry dumplings into hot cherry broth and cook 5-10 minutes.

Sour Cherry Soup with Rice

Ingredients:
300 g sour cherries
4-5 tbsp rice
1/2 cup sugar

Wash and pit sour cherries. Cover pits with hot water, add sugar, bring to boil and strain. Add rice to the broth and cook 30 minutes. Add pitted cherries to the soup 5 minutes before the end of cooking.

Cranberry and Apple Soup

Ingredients:
300 g cranberries
500 g apples
1 cup sugar
1 tbsp potato starch

Pick through, wash and mash cranberries in a pot. Cover with 5 cups of hot water, mix, cover the pot and let infuse for 10-15 minutes. Strain the infusion into a different pot, add sugar and sliced thinly peeled and cored apples. Bring to boil and add potato starch, mixed in small amount of water, to thicken.

Soup is served chilled. Add sour cream to bowls if desired.

Soup with Currants and Peaches

Ingredients:
300 g currants (black or red)
500 g peaches
1 cup sugar
1 tbsp potato starch

This soup is cooked just like "Cranberries and Apples Soup". Remove pits from the peaches before slicing them.

Apricot and Apple Soup

Ingredients:
500 g apricots
500 g apples
3 tbsp sugar
2 tsp potato starch

Wash and pit ripe apricots. Cook with 2 cups of water until soft, then rub through a sieve. Add 3 cups of hot water to the apricot puree, add sugar and peeled and cored apples, cut into slices or julienned. Bring the mixture to boil and add potato starch mixed with a small quantity of water. Bring to boil mixing constantly. Season with lemon acid to taste if desired.

Serve chilled. Add sour cream to bowls if desired. If fresh apricots are not available - use dried variety.

Fresh Berry Soup-Puree

Ingredients:
500 g berries
1/2 cup sugar
150 g vanilla rusks
1/2 cup sour cream

Pick through, wash, drain, and mash fresh berries (strawberries, raspberries) through a sieve. Add sugar to 2 cups of boiling water and mix until dissolved. Cool the syrup down and mix with berry puree. Serve chilled with sour cream and vanilla rusks.

Apricot or Peach Soup-Puree

Ingredients:
400 g apricots or peaches
1/2 cup sugar
1 tbsp potato starch
1/2 cup rice
4 tbsp sour cream

Wash ripe apricots or peaches, add to a pot with 6 cups of water and cook until soft. Mash cooked fruits through a sieve together with cooking liquid. Use canned apricot or peach puree if fresh fruits are not available.

Add sugar to prepared puree, bring to boil and add potato starch dissolved in 1/2 cups of cold water, bring to boil again, take off the heat and let it cool. Serve chilled. Add cooked rice and sour cream or heavy cream to the soup.

Dried Fruit Soup

Ingredients:
200 g dried fruits
50 g potato starch

For garnish:
1/2 cup sugar
100 g rice, sago, or pasta

Wash and pick over dried fruits. Separate dried apples and pears, cover with cold water in a pot, bring to boil and cook until done. Add remaining fruits, sugar, cinnamon and cook on low heat 10-15 minutes. Add potato starch mixed with small amount of water and bring to boil.

Soup could be served with cooked rice, sago, or pasta.

Fruit Soup with Pasta or Grain Garnish

Cook any fruit or fresh berry soup from the previous recipes. Separately cook one of the following garnishes for the soup:

1. Cook pasta (noodles, vermicelli) or rice in water, drain, and add to the soup once it it taken off the heat.

2. Small dumplings (potato, farina, or dough)are cooked in water, drained, and added to the soup when it is taken off the heat.

Soup should be served chilled. Serve sour cream if desired.

Apple Soup-Puree

Ingredients:
500 g apples
200 g crustless white bread
1/2 cup sugar
2 tbsp rice
lemon zest
cinnamon

Wash, core, slice apples, and add them to a pan together with bread, lemon zest and cinnamon (if using). Add 4 cups of hot water, cover and cook until apples are cooked through. Remove from the heat and take cinnamon and lemon zest out of the pan. Mash what remains in the pan through a sieve. Put apple puree into a pan together with sugar, thin to a desired consistency with hot water and bring to boil.

Add cooked rice to the bowls before serving the soup. If desired - serve with sour cream.

Currant or Cranberry Soup with Farina

Ingredients:
300 g currants or 200 g cranberries
2 tbsp farina
1 cup milk
1/2 cup sugar

Wash and pick berries over. Mash cleaned berries with a spoon, add 4-5 cups of water and sugar, bring to boil, strain and cool.

Cook farina in milk, put into a bowl moistened with water and let cool. Cut cooled farina into pieces (squares, diamonds), put into bowls and top with berry broth.

BREAD KVASS OR BEET BROTH BASED COLD SOUPS

Okroshka, botvinya, borscht and holodets are cooked with bread kvass or beet broth.

Ingredients for these recipes should be chilled and not exceed the temperature of 10-12 degrees centigrade. In addition to that it is also recommended to add clear ice made from drinking water to some of the soups (okroshka, botvinya) at a time of serving.

Cold soups - okroshka, botvinya, borscht, just like fruit and berry soups - are especially good in the summer. They are tasty, nutritious, refreshing, and improve appetite.

Vegetable Okroshka

Ingredients:
1 l bread kvass
1-2 potatoes, boiled
1 beet, boiled
1 carrot, boiled
1-2 cucumbers
50-75 g scallions
2 eggs
2 tbsp sour cream
1 tsp sugar

Dice boiled and cooled beet, carrot, and cucumbers. Peel and grate potatoes. Thinly slice scallions, add a little salt, and mash them until they become soft and release juice. Peel hardboiled eggs, separate whites from yolks, finely chop whites and mash yolks with mustard.

Add mashed scallions to grated potatoes,

mix in egg yolks, sour cream, sugar, salt, and pour in kvass. Add diced beet, carrot, cucumbers, and chopped egg whites.

Sprinkle with finely chopped dill just before serving.

Carrot and beet in this recipe could be replaced with other cooked vegetables, such as turnip or cauliflower.

Assembled Meat Okroshka

Ingredients:
1 l bread kvass
250 g cooked meat
2 cucumbers
75 g scallions
2 eggs, hard boiled
1/2 cup sour cream
1 tsp sugar

Dice boiled beef, ham, tongue, and peeled cucumbers. Thinly slice scallions and mash them in a bowl with a little salt until they become soft and release juice. Finely chop egg whites. Mash egg yolks in a pot with sour cream, sugar, salt, and a little bit of mustard, sugar, and salt. Add kvass and mix everything well. Add remaining ingredients. Just before serving sprinkle the soup with finely chopped dill.

Fish Botvinya

Ingredients:
1 l kvass
250 g spinach
250 g sorrel
2 cucumbers

75 g scallions
50 g horseradish
1 tsp sugar
250 g boiled fish (sturgeon, walleye)

Pick over spinach and sorrel and wash well. Cook spinach in boiling water, while sautéing sorrel in a covered pot. Once cooked, mash them through a sieve. Put greens puree into a pot, add sugar, salt, a little bit of mustard, and mix in kvass. Add diced cucumbers and thinly sliced scallions and dill. Just before serving add grated horseradish and pieces of fish into bowls.

Cold Borscht

Ingredients:
500 g beets
200 g potatoes
2 cucumbers
75 g scallions
2 eggs, hard boiled
2 tbsp sour cream
1 tsp sugar
1 tsp vinegar

Peel and dice beets, add to a pot, and cover with water (about 2 cups per serving), add vinegar and cook for 20-30 minutes. Strain finished beet broth and cool it down. Put beets into a pot, add diced potatoes and cucumbers, chopped eggs, and thinly sliced scallions. Add grated horseradish, salt, sugar, and mustard to the pot just before serving.
Add beet broth, sour cream, and mix well. Sprinkle chopped parsley or dill into bowls.

Soup-Holodets

Ingredients:
1 l bread kvass
500 g young beets with leaves
2 cucumbers
75 g scallions
2 eggs, hard boiled
2 tbsp sour cream
1 tsp sugar

Wash and peel beets, add to a pot, cover with water (2 cups per serving) and cook for 20-30 minutes. About 10 minutes before beets are cooked add beet leaves to the pot. Drain cooked beets and leaves, finely chop, put into a soup bowl together with diced cucumbers, eggs, thinly sliced scallions, sour cream, and sugar. Add kvass and cooled beet broth.

Sprinkle with finely chopped dill or parsley leaves just before serving.

FISH

Fish is just as nutritious as meat. Protein and fat that fish contains are well digested.

There are different types of fish available for purchase: live, steamed, frozen, salted and ready-to-eat fish products.

Live fish should be well-fed, agile, with scales intact and without spots.

Quality steamed fish has smooth, shiny, snug scales. The eyes should be transparent and convex, bright red gills and belly that is not swollen.

Fish that has been frozen while live, if unfrozen properly, is almost just as good as fresh.

Fillet of carp, walleye, cod, bream and other fish is also available for purchase, and it makes preparing fish dishes a lot easier and quicker. Fish fillet doesn't require any processing, except for defrosting.

Preparing fish for boiling or frying

Defrosting frozen fish. Frozen fish and fish fillet should be defrosted by placing it in cold water so that the fish defrosts faster and doesn't get dry. Using warm water is not recommended:

fish becomes flabby and tasteless. After defrosting fish and fish fillet are washed with clean water.

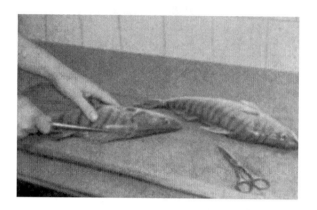

Soaking of salted fish. Salted fish (walleye, carp, bream, etc.) is soaked in cold water. Pour enough water to cover the fish completely and leave to soak for 30-40 minutes. Scale, cut, wash and again submerge in clean cold water to soak, this time for 4 to 6 hours, depending on how salty fish is. Every hour or two hours water needs to be changed.

Butchering fish. There are different ways of butchering fish, depending on the type and also depending on what type of dish is going to be prepared from it. Live fish should be killed before scaling; with sharp end of a small knife make a deep cut into the throat between head fins and let the blood drain.

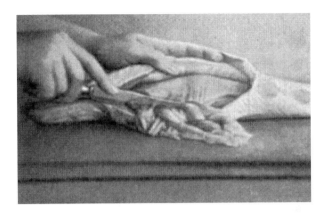

Butchering walleye, pike, carp, bream, other fish with scales. First of all, remove the back fin from walleye and bass. To do this, make shallow incisions on both sides of the fin. Grasping the fin with a towel (in order not to get pricked), pull it out from tail to head. Then scale the fish with a knife or a grater. Now it is time to gut the fish. Make a cut along the belly from head to the fin under the tail and carefully remove liver and gallbladder. If gallbladder is torn, the part of fish where gall has spilled needs to be removed and rubbed with salt immediately. Other insides are also removed along with gills and the film that covers the backbone is cut lengthwise. After gutting, wash fish thoroughly in cold water and clean the blood off the backbone.

Washed fish is cut into pieces, starting from the head. Cut the top part of the fish until the bone, then chop the backbone with a light strike and cut the bottom half.

Fish that weights 1 1/2 kg and more should be cut in half first, according to the following procedure. Cut the fish all the way to the ribs along the back, head to tail, then separate the filet. Each half is then cut into pieces across; some pieces end up with bone and some without.

If fillet is to be used for croquettes, rib bones should be removed.

For croquettes and roulades fish is butchered somewhat differently. It is gutted without scaling, then both filets are cut off and then the skin is removed together with scales from each one. Skin covered with scales is easier to remove.

Head, tail, fins and bones are used to make broth. They need to be thoroughly washed and gills should be removed.

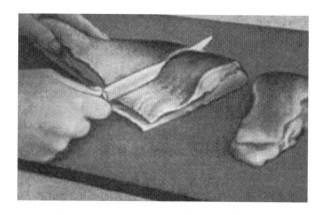

Catfish butchering. Catfish is butchered in the same manner as scaly fish; in instances where it is to be used for croquettes and roulades, skin is removed.

Navaga butchering. Cut skin along the back, cut off lower jaw, take a pinch of salt so that the hand doesn't slip, remove skin from both sides, beginning with upper jaw and to the tail, then remove fins, gut the fish without cutting the belly. Leave caviar inside. After gutting, wash navaga in cold water.

Flounder butchering. Cut off the head and remove insides, after which remove the dark skin off the fish. Wash and cut lengthwise in two equal halves along the lower, white side from tail to head. Then chop off back fins. Wash each half of the fish and cut along into two parts and across into serving slices.

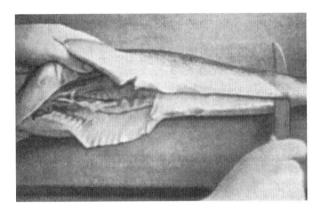

Burbot, eel butchering. Cut the skin around the head and remove from fish (as if a glove off hand), then cut the belly, remove the insides, cut off the head. Wash in cold water.

Tench butchering. Place fish in hot water for 15-30 seconds, so that the slime comes off and scaling is easier. From hot water, place into cold water. Scale with dull end of the knife, gut and wash.

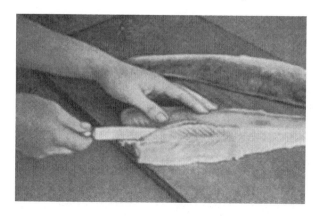

Sturgeon cleaning. Defrosted piece of fish is placed on the table. Remove the backbone with pin or fork and clean the blood. Wash in cold water and place in hot water for 2 minutes. Then thoroughly clean the bony scales off the skin. If they are not coming off easily, put the fish in hot water again. Cleaned fish is washed in cold water again.

Sterlet butchering. Clean the large scales off the back with a knife. Then clean the bony scales off sides and belly (from tail to head). Cut the belly, remove the insides and gills and remove the backbone, same as with sturgeon. Wash and dry with a towel.

POACHED FISH

The easiest way of cooking fish is poaching it in water. Any fish can be poached; however, smaller fish like crucian carp, navaga, smelts are better fried. The less water used for coking, the tastier fish; therefore, it is recommended to add enough water just to barely cover the fish.

Use 1 tsp of salt for each l of water when cooking fresh fish. To make fish taste even better, add 1/2 carrot, 1/2 parsnip, 1 onion, 1-2 bay leaves and a little bit of pepper to the cooking liquid. Roots and onion should be peeled and cut into small pieces.

When cooking cod, flounder, catfish, or pike, to get rid of the fishy smell in addition to roots and onion add 1/2 cup of pickle brine for each l of water.

Fish could be cooked in one piece or cut into smaller pieces - 75-100 g. Sturgeon varieties of fish should be cooked in one piece and cut into portions just before serving. Fish cooked this way is juicer and tastier. When adding pieces to water for cooking, large pieces of fish weighting from 500 g and more should be placed into cold water, while small pieces should be placed into boiling water.

From the moment water starts boiling to the end of cooking water should be at a constant simmer. All fish should be cooked through. Small pieces of sturgeon varieties should be cooked for 20-30 minutes, while pieces over 500 g - 1 hour 30 minutes from the moment the water comes to boil. Ordinary fish cooks faster than sturgeon. Walleye, carp, pike weighting 1-1 1/2 kg cook in 50-60 minutes, pieces of 100-150 g - 15-20 minutes.

To check if fish is done cooking use a

wooden toothpick. If it goes into fish easy - the fish is cooked.

Fish cooking liquid is used to make a sauce to serve with fish - white or tomato. The rest of liquid could be used to cook a soup. After salted fish has been soaked, cook it in fresh water without adding salt.

Poached fish is served cold or hot; hot with boiled potatoes, while cooled - with vinaigrette salad, potato or cabbage salad, picked beets, cucumbers, or with green salad.

Serve fish with horseradish in vinegar or other sauces.

Poached Fish with Potatoes

Ingredients:
500 g fish
800 g potatoes

Scale and gut fish (walleye, pike or cat fish). Cut prepared fish into pieces and boil it.

Separately cook whole peeled potatoes. To server - remove fish with a skimmer from the cooking liquid and put it on a serving dish, surround with potatoes and decorate with sprigs of parsley. In a sauce-boat serve egg-and-butter sauce or horseradish with vinegar. If desired, instead of sauce serve with butter, softened to sour cream consistency, mixed with finely chopped parsley leaves.

Poached Sturgeon

Ingredients:
500 g fish
800 g potatoes
1 tbsp butter

Any type of sturgeon, or large catfish should be cooked in one piece and cut into servings just before serving. Fish cooked this way is juicier and tastier.

Put prepared fish into a shallow pot, add water to top the fish by 2 cm, season with salt, cover the pot and bring to boil. The moment water starts boiling, lower the heat and cook at a slow simmer 30-40 minutes (pieces of fish over 1 kg are cooked 1-1 1/2 hours).

Cut fish into pieces before serving, set on a serving plate, garnish with boiled potatoes dressed with butter, and sprinkle with finely chopped parsley leaves. Serve horseradish with vinegar on a side.

Poached Walleye with Vegetable Garnish

Ingredients:
1 kg fish
1 carrot
1 beet
1 onion
800 g potatoes
1 tbsp butter
1/2 cup milk

Scale and clean walleye and cut it into pieces. Peel and wash carrot, beet, and onion, and cut them into thin slices. Cut peeled potatoes into halves or quarters. On a bottom of a pan put beet, carrot, and onion slices, then put potatoes, add 1 1/2 cups of water and salt. Salt fish and put it on top of the vegetables. Add pepper and bay leaf.

Cover the pot and cook on low heat for an hour, not mixing but shaking a pot every 10 minutes to make sure that vegetables do not burn. When vegetables and fish are almost cooked, add milk and butter to the pot and cook 15-20 more minutes. Take the pot off the heat and baste the fish with cooking liquid. Keep covered until ready to serve.

Fish Cooked in Parchment

Ingredients:
500 g fish
1 carrot
1 onion
1 tbsp lemon juice
2 tbsp butter

Cut fillet of bream into portions and cover with brine for 5 minutes (1 tbsp of salt to 1 cup of water). Take fish out of the brine and let it drain. Put fish on buttered parchment, top with butter mixed with pepper, grated carrot and onion, and sprinkle with finely chopped parsley or dill. Fold the sides of the parchment to form a packet and tie a kitchen twine around it. Put parchment into a pot filled with boiling water and cook for 15-20 minutes on low heat.

Take the fish out of the packet and put on a warm serving plate together with its sauce. Fish could be garnished with boiled potatoes dressed with butter and malosol cucumbers.

This method of cooking is suitable for walleye, bream, cod, or fillet of other fish.

Poached Fish with Fatback and Potatoes

Ingredients:
750 g fish
800 g potatoes
1-2 onions
100 g fatback

Cut fatback into small pieces and sauté it in a frying pan together with thinly sliced onions. Add peeled and sliced potatoes, season with salt and pepper, add 1 cup of water, cover and cook for 5 minutes on low heat. Add cleaned and cut fish to potatoes and cook until done.

To serve - put fish in a middle of a warm serving plate, surround with potatoes and sprinkle with finely chopped parsley leaves.

Poached Flounder with Butter

Ingredients:
500 g fish
800 g potatoes
2 tbsp butter

Poach fish that has been cleaned, washed and cut into pieces. When serving, remove from broth, put on plate, garnish with boiled potatoes and pour butter (fried on frying pan until it reaches golden color). Add parsley, washed and dried in napkin to the butter. Also add vinegar (1 tsp for 3-4 servings). Before pouring butter, drain the liquid from the plate with fish.

Canned Fish with Potatoes

Ingredients:
1 can fish (about 350 g)
800 g potatoes

Open can of fish, put the contents of the can into a pot and heat it up. To serve - put fish on a warm serving plate, garnish with boiled potatoes and decorate with sprigs of parsley. Serve with egg-and-butter sauce, cucumbers, or green salad on the side.

STEAMED FISH

To cook fish with steam use a small quantity of liquid. It is recommended to steam fillets of walleye, catfish, pike, burbot, salmon, or prepared pieces of sturgeon. Instead of water use fish stock to steam fish. To cook the stock use heads with gills removed, tails, and fins. Cook well-washed bones with onion and parsnip in water 40-50 minutes. Strain finished stock.

Use broth obtained while steaming fish as sauce when serving fish.

Prepared pieces of fish are placed in a shallow pot in one row or on the rack of the fish poacher, add salt and pepper, and cover with enough broth so that the fish is submerged in it by 2/3 of its thickness. Cook with lid closed.

Steam fish tastes better than boiled fish because a lot more taste substances are preserved.

Steamed Sturgeon

Ingredients:
500 g fish
200 g mushrooms
3 tbsp dry white wine
1 tbsp flour
2 tbsp butter

Put cleaned, scalded, washed, and cut fish into a shallow pan. Put cleaned, washed, and cut into pieces mushrooms (cepes, champignons) between pieces of fish.

Season fish with salt and pepper, add white wine, cup of stock (or water), cover the pot and cook for 15-20 minutes.

When the fish is done - pour the cooking liquid into a different pot and reduce to 1 cup. Add flour mixed with 1 tbsp of butter and continue to simmer 3-4 minutes, stirring frequently. Take the sauce off the heat and add remaining butter, season with salt, mix well, and strain.

If fish was cooked without wine - add 1 tsp of lemon juice or lemon acid dissolved in water to the finished sauce.

To serve - put fish on warmed serving plate, put mushrooms on top of the fish and pour the sauce on top. Garnish with boiled potatoes, cucumbers or salad, and slices of lemon.

Sturgeon in Brine

Ingredients:
500 g fish
2 pickles
200 g fresh cepes(porcini) mushrooms or 100 g
pickled mushrooms
1 tbsp cucumber brine
1 tbsp flour
2 tbsp butter

Cut prepared fish into portions. Peel
pickles, cut lengthwise, remove seeds, and cut
each half across into three pieces. Clean, wash,
and slice fresh mushrooms. Put fish into a shallow
pan. Lay pickles and mushrooms among pieces of
fish. Season with salt and pepper, add 1 1/2 cups
of stock (or water), add cucumber brine, cover the
pot and cook 15-25 minutes. Pour off cooking
liquid into a different pot and reduce. When about
1 cup of liquid remains, make sauce just like in
"Steamed Sturgeon" recipe, but without lemon
juice.

Serve fish on a warm serving plate. Top
pieces of fish with mushrooms, pickles, and
strained sauce. Garnish with boiled potatoes.

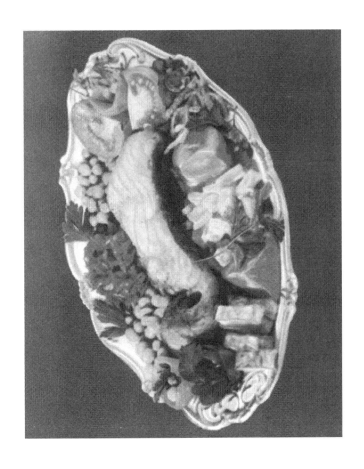

Sturgeon with Mushrooms and Tomato Sauce

Ingredients:
500 g fish
200 g champignons (or cepes)
3 tbsp white wine
3 tbsp tomato paste
1 tbsp flour
2 tbsp butter

Cut prepared fish into servings, scald, and
wash with cold water. Clean, wash, and cut

mushrooms. Put fish and mushrooms into a pot. Season with salt and pepper, add white wine, 1 cup of stock (or water) mixed with tomato paste, cover the pot and cook fish for 15-25 minutes. Pour off cooking liquid and make a sauce just like in "Steamed Sturgeon" recipe.

Serve fish with boiled potatoes and malosol cucumbers.

Walleye in White Wine

Ingredients:
750 g fish or 500 g fish fillet
1/2 cup dry white wine
200 g mushrooms
1 tbsp flour
1 egg
200 g white bread
4 tbsp butter

Put walleye fillet cut into pieces and sliced mushrooms (champignons or cepes) into a shallow pan, season with salt and pepper, add white wine and 3/4 cup stock (or water). Cook fish 15-25 minutes.

Make toasts. Remove crust from bread and cut into slices, one large and two smaller per each serving of fish. Sauté bread in 2 tbsp of butter.

Pour off cooking liquid and make sauce as described in "Steamed Sturgeon" recipe. Remove from heat and season sauce with salt, add egg yolk mixed with 1 tbsp of butter and stir well.

Cod with Potatoes and Onions

Ingredients:
750 g cod
2 onions
800 g potatoes
300 g tomatoes
1 tbsp vinegar
4 tbsp butter

Lightly fry in butter peeled, washed, thinly sliced onions. Add prepared, seasoned with salt pieces of fish to the frying pan, top with slices of tomatoes, add 3-4 tbsp of water, season tomatoes with salt and pepper. Put slices of fried potatoes around pieces of fish and sprinkle with melted butter. Cover the frying pan and put into a heated oven for 20-30 minutes. Sprinkle with finely chopped parsley leaves and vinegar just before serving.

Flounder, pike, or eel could be used instead of cod in this recipe.

Flounder in Red Wine

Ingredients:
500-750 g fish
1 cup dry red wine
1 tbsp flour
800 g potatoes
1 parsnip
1 onion
2 tbsp butter

Put peeled, washed, and sliced parsnip and onion on a bottom of a pan, add 4 cloves, little bit of pepper and bay leaf. Put prepared and cut into pieces fish, season with salt, add wine and 1 cup of stock (or water). Cover the pot and cook for 15-20 minutes. Once fish is cooked pour off cooking liquid and make sauce as described in "Steamed Sturgeon" recipe.

When serving put fish on heated serving plate, garnish with whole boiled potatoes, and top with strained sauce.

Walleye, pike, or eel could be used instead of flounder in this recipe.

Canned Sturgeon in Sour Cream with Potatoes

Ingredients:
1 can (350 g) sturgeon in tomato sauce
1/2 cup sour cream
2 tbsp butter
800 g potatoes

Take fish out of the can, cut into pieces, and put into a pan. Pour sauce from the can into the pan and add sour cream. Cover the pan and cook 5-6 minutes. To serve - put fish on a heated serving plate, garnish with boiled potatoes seasoned with butter, pour the sauce from the pan over fish and sprinkle finely chopped herbs. Serve cucumbers or pickles on a side.

Canned Salmon in White Wine

Ingredients:
1 can (350 g) salmon
1 cup dry white wine
200 g mushrooms
1 tbsp flour
200 g white bread

1 egg
4 tbsp butter

Put fish from the can into a pot, add cut into pieces boiled mushrooms (cepes or champignons), add liquid from the can and white wine, cover the pot and warm through for 5-6 minutes.

Put a fish on a heated serving plate. Bring broth to boil, add flour mixed with 1 tbsp of butter and stir until everything is mixed well. Simmer for 3-5 minutes. Take sauce off the heat and add egg yolk mashed with 1 1/2-2 tbsp of butter. Mix well, season with salt and strain the sauce through a sieve.

When serving pour the sauce over the fish and garnish with slices of bread sautéed in butter. If desired, garnish with boiled potatoes.

Steamed Fish Sausage Patties

Ingredients:
750 g fish or 500 g fish filet
300 g green beans
100 g crustless white bread
1/2 cup milk
200 g fresh mushrooms
1 cup white table wine
1 egg
4 tbsp butter

Prepare ground fish, same way as for rissole, and shape as patties. Put them in one row on the bottom on the pan greased with butter, and fill the gaps with cleaned, washed and cut mushrooms (porcini, champignons). Sprinkle with butter, pour white wine and broth made from fish bones so that patties are 3/4 submerged in liquid. Cover with lid and cook for 15-20 minutes.

When finished, pour broth into a pot and make sauce same way as in canned fish in white wine. Separately boil cleaned and washed green beans and add butter. When serving, put patties on a hot plate, and mushrooms on top of patties. Garnish with green beans and pour sauce.

Types of fish recommended for patties include walleye, pike, burbot, catfish and cod.

Stuffed Fish

Ingredients:
1 large fish 2-3 kg
100-200 g white bread
300 g onion
2 beets
3 carrots
1 tbsp sugar

2 eggs
1 tbsp vegetable oil

Scale fish, cut off the head, and without slicing the belly, remove the insides; remove gills from head, wash with cold water and cut fish into pieces across.

From each piece, remove the flesh without damaging skin. To make forcemeat, take the flesh removed together with onion and bread (soaked in water and drained) and pass through a meat grinder. Add raw eggs, sugar, oil, pepper, salt and mix well.

Stuff the fish pieces in those places where flesh has been removed with prepared forcemeat and even out with a wet knife.

Put thinly slices beets and carrots on the bottom of the pan, together with thoroughly washed onion peel.

Place stuffed fish pieces on top of vegetables, add another layer of vegetables on top, then another fish layer on top, and yet another layer of vegetables over it. Cover with water so that it just covers it, close the lid and put on low heat for 1 1/2 - 2 hours from the moment water starts boiling. During cooking make sure that fish or vegetables don't burn; top layer of fish should be poured with formed broth from time to time.

Before serving, put the fish and vegetables on a plate, strain the broth and pour over fish. If desired, broth can be used to boiled potatoes that might be used as garnish.

Pike, walleye, bream and carp can be prepared in this manner.

FRIED FISH

Fish can either be sautéed or deep-fried. To make sure that the fish is fried evenly, fish filet or large fish should be cut into pieces no thicker than 3 cm, since sides of a thick piece might be burned before the whole piece is ready. Small fish can be fried whole. Removing skin from fatty fish before frying is not recommended. Some varieties of fish taste better if fried with skin. Fish can be fried in oil, margarine or butter.

15 to 20 minutes prior to frying, soak

cleaned, washed and cut fish in milk mixed with salt and pepper (1/4 cup milk, 1/2 tsp salt), coat with flour or breadcrumbs.

While frying in cooking fat, use enough of it so that the fish is half-way covered in a shallow pot or flying pan. Submerge fish to fry first on one side, then on the other. When finished frying, drain cooking fat and pro in clean container with a lid.

It is best to fry fish on a cast iron skillet. Heat it well, then put in cooking fat, followed by fish. Fry fish until golden crust is formed - first one side, then another. If the fish is not yet ready, put the skillet, covered with lid into an oven or on low heat for 5 to 7 minutes.

Fried Fish with Garnish

Ingredients:
750 g fish or 500 g fish fillet
2 tbsp butter
2 tbsp flour

Season prepared fish with salt and pepper, coat with flour and fry in butter. Pour melted butter over the fish and sprinkle with finely chopped parsley leaves or dill before serving. Garnish with fried potatoes, buckwheat, barley, sauerkraut or red cabbage salad, pickles or fresh cucumbers, tomatoes.

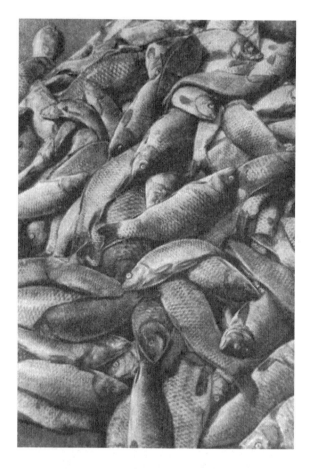

Fried Sturgeon with Tomatoes and Onions

Ingredients:
750 g fish or 500 g fish fillet
1/4 cup milk

4 tomatoes
1 onion
2 tbsp flour
3 tbsp butter

Dip prepared pieces of fish into milk seasoned with salt and pepper, coat with flower and fry until cooked. Separately fry in butter fresh or canned tomatoes, cut in half and seasoned with salt and pepper. Brown in butter peeled and thinly sliced onions.

When serving put pieces of fish on warmed serving plate, top each piece with onion slices, set tomato halves on the sides. Pour melted butter from frying pan over fish and sprinkle with finely chopped parsley leaves or dill. Garnish with boiled or fried potatoes.

Fried Breaded Fish

Ingredients:
750 g fish or 500 g fish fillet
1/4 cup milk1 lemon
1/2 cup bread crumbs
1 egg
2 tbsp flour
100 g vegetable oil

Wash and dry prepared fish, season with salt and pepper, coat with flour, then dip into a egg mixed with milk (1/4 cup milk to 1 egg), and coat with breadcrumbs. Fry fish in oil 10-15 minutes before serving. Serve on warmed serving plate, decorated with slices of lemon and parsley sprigs. If desired, serve with cold tartar sauce, or hot tomato sauce instead of lemons. Serve salad, pickled apples, or mashed potatoes on a side. Use walleye, bream, carp, crucian carp, sturgeon, or other fish for this recipe.

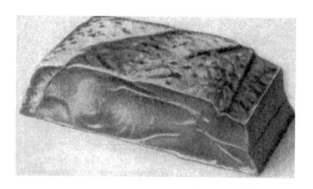

Fried Fish in Dough

Ingredients:
500 g fish filet
5 tbsp flour
3 tbsp oil
1/2 lemon
2 eggs
100 g cooking fat

Prepare the dough. Mix dough and salt with two tablespoons of oil or melted butter, add warm water (1/2 cup), making sure there are no clumps. Cover and let it rest. Cut fish filet into pieces 1 cm thick and 5 - 7 cm long, sprinkle with salt, pepper, chopped greens; squeeze half a lemon on fish, add a spoon of oil, mix and leave for 15-20 minutes.

10-15 minutes before serving, add two whipped egg whites to the dough; take each piece of fish with a fork, dip in dough and then submerge into very hot cooking fat prepared in a pot. When frying, rock the pan so that pieces of fish get covered with fat.

When serving, lay pieces of fish in a form of

a pyramid on heated plate, with paper napkin on top of it. Decorate with parsley. Serve mayonnaise with gherkins or hot tomato sauce separately.

For garnish serve lettuce and boiled potatoes with butter.

Fish Sausage Patties

Ingredients:
500 g fish fillet (walleye, pike, or cod)
100 g white bread
1/2 cup milk
3 tbsp breadcrumbs
2 tbsp butter

Pass skinless fish fillet through a meat grinder, add bread soaked in milk, season with salt and pepper, and pass the mixture through a meat grinder one-two more times. Add softened butter to the forcemeat, mix well and shape into patties. Fry patties in oil or butter in a heated skillet 10-15 minutes before serving. If needed - finish in a preheated oven for 5-7 minutes.

To serve put patties on a heated serving plate and pour melted butter on top. Garnish with green peas, bean, cauliflower, vegetables in milk sauce. Serve tomato sauce on a side.

Fish Telnoe (Stuffed Fish Sausage Patty)

Make stuffing. Brown thinly sliced onions in a frying pan, add boiled and sliced fresh or pickled cepes (porcini), stir, take off the heat, add chopped hard-boiled egg, parsley leaves, season with salt and pepper and mix well.

Make forcemeat from 500 g of fish fillet just like in "Fish Sausage Patty" recipe and form patties. Put a walnut-sized amount of stuffing on one half of patty, fold the other half over and pinch it into a half-moon shape. Use moistened cheese cloth or clean kitchen towel to help with folding.

Dip stuffed patty into egg wash and roll in bread crumbs. Cook just like Fish Sausage Patty about 10-15 minutes before serving, and serve with the same garnish. Serve tomato sauce on a side.

Sturgeon on Skewer

Take prepared for grilling pieces of

sturgeon weighting 40-50 g, wash in cold water, season with salt, pepper, thread on metal skewer, and grill over red-hot coals (no flames) for 6-10 minutes.

During grilling, keep greasing fish with butter and turning the skewer so that fish is fried uniformly.

When serving, remove from skewer, place on a heated plate and garnish with fresh tomatoes, grilled on a skewer, onions, scallions and parsley.

Fresh salmon is prepared the same way.

BAKED FISH

Fresh, as well as seared or boiled fish (with or without garnish) is baked in a well-heated oven. If the oven is not heated well enough, fish is not going to be baked properly, will get dry and lose taste.

Baked Bream or Carp

Ingredients:
500 g fish
1/4 cup milk
2 tbsp flour
2 tbsp butter

Cut cleaned and washed fish along the backbone, cut into slices across and submerge into salted milk for 2-3 minutes. Coat in flour or breadcrumbs and lay out on a greased frying pan skin side up. Brush with melted butter and put in an oven. After 5 minutes the skin will start to get browned/caramelized. Filet is ready in 6-7 minutes, pieces with bone - in 12 minutes.

Serve in frying pan or on heated plate,

pouring in butter from frying pan. Garnish with boiled or fried potatoes, cucumbers, lettuce.

Fish prepared in this fashion can be served cold with cucumbers, tomatoes, marinated fruit.

Walleye Baked with Potatoes

Ingredients:
750 g fish or 500 g fish fillet
800 g potatoes
1 tbsp flour
2 tbsp breadcrumbs
2-3 tbsp butter

Cut cleaned and washed fish along the spine, then cut each side across, season with salt and pepper and lay on a well-oiled skillet. Top with peeled, washed, and julienned potatoes. Set thin slices of potatoes on the sides of the skillet. Season potatoes with salt, sprinkle with flour, add fish stock or water, spread breadcrumbs and pour melted butter and put skillet into a heated oven. Depending on thickness of potatoes the dish will bake for 20-35 minutes.

If stock evaporates too quickly during baking - add more stock or boiled water. Sometimes lightly fried onions are added to the fish before potatoes.

When serving sprinkle fish with chopped herbs. Serve with green salad with vegetables or fruits, cucumbers, pickles, or sour cabbage.

Sturgeon Baked in One Piece

Ingredients:
500 g fish
1 tbsp sour cream

1 tbsp butter

Season scaled and washed fish with salt and pepper, put into a skillet, cover with sour cream, sprinkle with melted butter, add 1/2 cup of water to the skillet and put it into a preheated oven. Bake 25-30 minutes basting from time to time with pan juices. To serve cut the fish across into pieces, put on a warm serving plate and pour strained pan juices over the fish. Decorate with parsley sprigs. Serve boiled potatoes with butter or fried potatoes, green salad, vegetable salad, cucumbers, and slices of lemon on a side.

Fish Baked in Sour Cream

Ingredients:
750 g fish or 500 g fish fillet
800 g potatoes
1 cup sour cream
2 eggs, hardboiled
200 g mushrooms (cepes)
25 g cheese
2 tbsp flour

4 tbsp butter

Season pieces of fish with salt and pepper, coat with flour and sear on a skillet with butter. Fry washed, cleaned, and sliced mushrooms. Fry sliced 1/2 cm thick potatoes.

Put pieces of fish on a skillet. On top of each piece put slices of egg. Surround fish with slices of fried potatoes and pour strained sour cream sauce over everything. To make sauce bring sour cream to simmer in a small pan, add 1 tsp of flour mixed with 1 tsp of butter, cook for 1-2 minutes stirring all the time. Season with salt.

Sprinkle grated cheese on top of the fish covered with sauce, pour melted butter and put into a preheated oven to brown on top. Sprinkle with finely chopped parsley leaves just before serving.

Use sturgeon, sterlet, walleye, carp, pike, or other fish in this recipe.

Canned Fish in Sour Cream with Potatoes

Ingredients:
1 can (350 g) fish
800 g potatoes
2/3 cup sour cream
1 tsp flour
1 tbsp grated cheese
2 eggs
200 g mushrooms
3 tbsp butter

Take fish out of the can, cut into serving pieces and put into a skillet. Put slices of potatoes fried in butter around the fish. Put slices of hardboiled eggs and fried mushrooms on top of the fish. Pour the sauce over everything. To make sauce combine sour cream with liquid from the can in a pot and bring to boil and add flour mixed with 1 tsp of butter. Let boil for 1-2 minutes stirring all the time, season with salt. Sprinkle grated cheese and melted butter on top of the fish with sauce and bake in preheated oven 10-15 minutes. Add finely chopped parsley leaves before serving. Serve with cucumbers on a side.

Fish Stuffed with Buckwheat

Ingredients:
750 g fish (carp)
100 g buckwheat
2 eggs
1 cup sour cream
1 onion
1 tbsp flour
3 tbsp butter

Scale whole fish, cut head around fins and take innards out without cutting its belly. Wash well inside and wipe with towel, stuff with buckwheat mixed with caramelized onions and chopped hardboiled eggs. Season fish outside with pepper, coat with flour and sear in butter in a frying pan, and put into a preheated oven. After 5-6 minutes take pan out, pour (ed. note - Soviet sour cream frequently had pourable consistency) sour cream over fish and return to oven for 3-5 minutes, basting frequently with pan juices. Total time of baking depends on the baking temperature and size of the fish.

Serve the fish in the pan it was cooking in, or move carefully to a warm serving plate together with pan sauce. Serve with cucumbers, vegetable or fruit salads, or pickled apples.

Fish Solyanka in a Skillet

Ingredients:
500 g fish fillet
1 kg white cabbage or sauerkraut
2 tbsp butter
2 tbsp tomato paste
2 tbsp breadcrumbs
2 pickles
50 g capers
50 g olives
2 onions

For cabbage:
2 tbsp tomato paste
2 1/2 tbsp butter or lard
1 onion
1 tbsp sugar
1 tbsp flour

Braise green cabbage or sauerkraut.
prepared fish (sturgeon, sterlet) cut into pieces of
40-50g, put into a pit, season with salt and pepper,
add capers, peeled and deseeded and diced
pickles, tomato paste, slightly browned in butter
diced onions, cup of fish stock (or water), 2 bay
leaves, cover the pot , bring to boil and cook 15-20
minutes.

To the pot with fish add flour mixed with 1
tsp of butter, and cook stirring for 1-2 minutes.
Make sure not to break fish when stirring. Put one
third of braised cabbage on the bottom of a skillet,
level it, put fish with garnish from the pan and
pour all the sauce from pan over the fish, cover
with remaining cabbage, level it and sprinkle with

breadcrumbs and melted butter. Bake in a preheated oven for 8-10 minutes.

Just before serving, put olives on top of solyanka. Decorate with slices of lemon, pickled cherries, grapes, plums, or cranberries, and parsley sprigs.

CRAYFISH AND CRABS

Crayfish

Ingredients:
10 crayfish
1 carrot
1 onion
1 small bunch parsley
1 bunch dill
1 tbsp salt

Put washed crayfish into a pot, add peeled and sliced carrots, onion, chopped parsley leaves, dill, bay leaf, salt, and 4-5 cups boiled water and cook 10 minutes.

Serve crayfish in the pot with broth or put them in deep bowl and pour broth with roots over.

Canned Crayfish Tails with Potatoes

Ingredients:
1 can (340 g) crayfish tails in tomato sauce
800 g potatoes
2 tbsp butter

Open the can, put crayfish tails together with sauce into a pan and heat. Separately in salted water boil peeled potatoes, each cut into four pieces. When it is ready, drain and add melted butter. When serving, put on a round heated plate, with crayfish tails and sauce in the middle. Sprinkle with finely chopped parsley. Fresh cucumbers and lettuce can be served separately.

Crayfish in Beer

Crayfish in beer are prepared the same way as crayfish in water - the only difference is that less water is used - just 2 cups, and the rest of the water is replaced with beer.

Crayfish in White Wine

Ingredients:
10 crayfish
1 cup white wine
1 tsp flour
1/4 tsp cumin
2 tbsp butter

Melt one spoon of butter in a heated pot, put washed crayfish in, fry and turn with fork until crayfish turn pink. Sprinkle with salt, pepper, ground cumin, add 2 bay leaves, pour in white wine, cover and boil for 10 minutes.

When crayfish are ready, remove and put them on a plate and cover with lid. Make sauce from broth obtained by boiling crayfish. To do this, strain broth through a sieve in a pot, bring to boil, add flour mixed with a teaspoon of butter.

Boil for 1-2 minutes, remove from fire, add more butter while stirring, until it dissolves in sauce. When serving, decorate with parsley. Sauce served separately.

Crabs with Egg-Butter Sauce

Ingredients:
1 can (225 g) crabs
500 g potatoes
1/2 cup white table wine
3/4 cup egg-butter sauce

Open the can, remove crabs with juice, put in a pot, pour white wine, close lid and boil for 5 minutes.

When serving, put crabs in the middle of round heated plate, lay potatoes (baked in salted water, peeled and cut in halves) around the crabs. Pour broth over the crabs; serve egg-butter sauce separately. Decorate with parsley. You can also serve crabs with dill pickles or lettuce.

Crabs Baked in Milk Sauce

Ingredients:
1 can (225 g) crab meat
1 cup milk sauce
25 g grated cheese
200 g mushrooms
2 tbsp butter

Cut crab meat into pieces, put into a pan together with juices from the can, add boiled and chopped mushrooms (ceps, champignons) and a teaspoon of butter. Cover the pot and cook on low heat for 5 minutes. Transfer contents of the pan into a well buttered skillet and pour milk sauce mixed with grated cheese on top. Sprinkle with remaining cheese and melted butter. Put into a preheated oven to brown. (5-6 minutes) and serve.

Sauces for Fish Dishes

Sauces are one of the major components of dishes with fish; they diversify the taste and increase the nutritious value of the dishes. Sauces are made from fish stock from cooking of the fish, or the stock could be made from heads and bones left after the cleaning and butchering of the fish. Heads without gills, bones, and fins are washed thoroughly, added to a pot together with 2 1/2-3 cups of cold water and finely chopped 1 onion and 1 parsnip. Cook the stock and strain when finished.

Egg-Butter Sauce (For Poached Fish)

Peel and finely chop 2 hardboiled eggs. Melt 100 g of butter; mix with chopped egg, finely chopped parsley leaves, season with lemon juice, salt. Pour on top of the fish or serve on a side in a sauce boat.

White Sauce (For Steamed and Pickled Fish)

Sauté 1 tbsp of flour in the same quantity of butter, add 2 cups of fish stock and cook for 7-10 minutes. Season the sauce with salt, take off the heat, add lemon juice or dissolved lemon acid, a piece of butter, mix and strain.

For pickled fish use 1-2 tbsp of pickle juice instead of lemon juice.

White Wine Sauce (For Steamed Fish)

Peel 1 each medium parsnip and medium onion, wash, dice, and sauté in a pan with 1 tbsp of butter and same quantity of flour until brown.

Add 2 cups of fish stock to the pan, season with salt and cook for 7-10 minutes. Take sauce off the heat and incorporate 1 egg yolk mixed with 1 tbsp of butter. Mix sauce well and strain. Add 1-2 tbsp of dry white wine or lemon juice.

Tomato Sauce (For Poached and Steamed Fish)

Peel, wash, and dice 1/2 of each - carrot, parsnip, and onion and sauté in a pan with 1 tbsp of butter and same quantity of flour. Add 3 tbsp of tomato paste, mix, add 2 cups of fish stock, season with salt and cook 8-10 minutes on low heat. Remove the sauce from heat; add 1 tbsp of butter and mix to incorporate. Strain the sauce.

MEAT

MEAT

Meat - beef, pork, lamb - is one of the most important food products, with excellent culinary qualities. It is easy to combine with other food products - vegetables, grains, pasta that can serve as garnish. In addition to complete proteins and fat, meat contains so-called extractive substances which do not provide nutritional value but serve as strong stimulants for secretion of digestive juices, ensuring food is more efficiently absorbed.

The weight of the meat lost when boiled is 40% on average, due to the discharge of water from proteins. 1 kg of fresh meat ends up about 600 g once boiled. Together with water, extractive substances, salts and gelatin are also released from meat; gelatin is also released from bones and cartilage. All these substances are dissolved in the water where meat is being boiled, and the broth is formed. Nutrition value of the meat is essentially not reduced during boiling, because the most valuable component of it - proteins - is almost entirely preserved. Only a small fraction of the proteins are transformed into the broth and form foam.

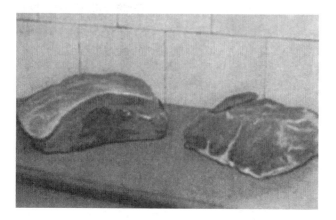

During frying meat also loses a lot of water which is released mostly as steam; therefore the extractive substances mostly stay in the meat. Considerable amounts of extractive substances present in fried meat, combined with the crust that forms during frying, make fried meat taste and smell delicious. Frying makes meat shrink by 35-38%. This means that 1 kg of fresh meat will end up 620-650 g fried meat. Juice that forms on the bottom of the frying pan during frying consists of water, fat and extractive substances.

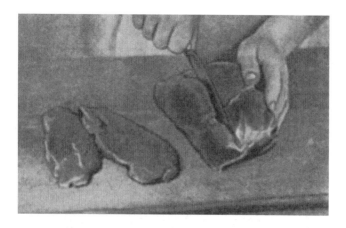

Fresh meat used for food preparation

should have normal color, smell and springy consistency. If a dimple is made in the meat with the finger, it should regain original shape fairly quickly if meat is of high quality.

Meat can be sold by weight, packaged or as semi-finished meat.

Meat sold by weight is available in pieces of different sizes, and from different parts of the carcass, depending on customers' preference.

Meat sold by weight is available fresh, refrigerated or frozen. Packaged and semi-finished meat are only sold refrigerated.

Packaged meat is prepared in a meat-packing

plant, in slabs of 250 g or 500 g. It is wrapped in cellophane or parchment with a label, stating packaging date, weight, cut and its culinary purpose.

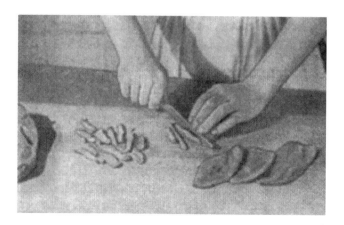

Packaged meat is made from cuts classified as first and second grade.

Semi-finished meat is especially useful for second-course dishes, which can be prepared from it literally within minutes. Semi-finished meat is portions of meat without bones, prepared mostly for frying.

Butchering of large and small animals for market sale is done according by the standards approved by the State.

BOILED MEAT

Meat products for second-course dishes should be boiled in such a way as to maximally preserve their taste qualities. Use enough water just to cover the meat. Use cold water only for salt beef and salt tongue. These products should be soaked prior to boiling for 5-8 hours; change water four times during the course of soaking.

Salted meat products can be boiled without soaking, but with large amount of water.

Broth from boiling can be used to prepare soups and sauces.

Boiled Beef with Horseradish Sauce

Ingredients:
500 g boneless meat
800 g potatoes
2 carrots
1 leek
1 turnip

Put prepared and washed meat (rump, shin, sirloin, brisket) in one piece into a pot and add enough boiling water to cover it. Cover the pot and put it on high heat. When water returns to boil, lower the heat and remove all the scum with a skimmer, cook for 2-2 1/2 hours. About 30 minutes before the end of cooking add peeled and sliced carrots, turnip, and leek (it is also good to add celery, parsley, or parsnip - 30-40 g), 2 bay leaves, 5-8 peppercorns (or 5-10g of red chili pepper) and salt. When meat and vegetables are cooked - strain meat broth to use in horseradish sauce and cover the pot with meat.

Cut meat into thin slices, put on a dish with vegetables, add boiled potatoes and pour the sauce over.

Boiled Salt Beef with Horseradish Sauce

Ingredients:
500 g salt beef
800 g potatoes
1 carrot
1 onion
1 parsnip
2 tbsp butter

Soak salt beef in couple of changes of water. Put salt beef into a pot, cover with cold water and bring to boil. Remove all foam and scum that rises to the top, then add roots, onion, and cook on low heat for 2-3 hours. Remove cooked beef from the pot, slice thinly, put on a serving plate and pour sauce on top.

Garnish with potato or pea puree, or boiled potatoes.

Boiled Lamb with White Sauce

Ingredients:
500 g lamb
600 g potatoes
1 turnip
2 onions
2 carrots

For sauce:
1 tbsp flour
1 tbsp butter

Wash lamb (leg, shoulder, fillet), put into a pot and add enough boiling water to cover the meat. Cover the pot and put it on low heat. When water returns to boil remove foam and scum and cook 1 - 1 1/2 hours. Add washed and peeled vegetables and salt 30-40 minutes after the start of cooking. Remove cooked lamb and vegetables from the broth, slice meat thinly and out it on a serving plate. Garnish with boiled potatoes, sliced vegetables and dress with white sauce made from the broth.

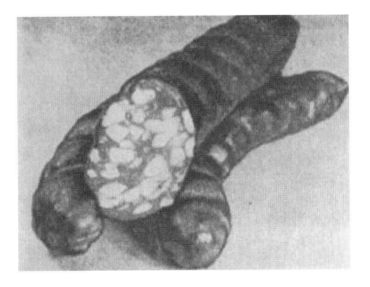

Lamb with Beans

Ingredients:
500 g lamb
1 cup beans
1 onion
200 g tomatoes
2 tbsp vegetable oil

Season lamb, cut into small pieces, with salt and pepper, and brown in oil. Put browned meat into a pot, add previously soaked beans, 2 1/2 - 3 cups of water and cook approximately 1 hour. Add slightly browned diced onions, chopped tomatoes, and continue braising for 30-40 minutes. Sprinkle with chopped parsley leaves before serving.

Beef Franks

Ingredients:
500 g beef franks
500 g potatoes
1 tbsp butter
1/2 cup milk (for potato puree)

Put beef franks into a pot with boiling water, bring water back to boil and simmer for 5-10 minutes. Take franks out of the water and put on a plate. Garnish with potato puree or braised cabbage.

Beef franks can be served by themselves, boiled or fried. If serving fried franks - heat them through in water and then quickly fry in butter or oil. Pile garnish into a mound on a plate and put hot franks on top of garnish.

Bratwurst

Ingredients:
500 g bratwurst
500 g potatoes
1 tbsp butter
1/2 cup milk (for potato puree)

Put bratwurst into a pot with boiling water, bring water back to boil, and simmer 10-15 minutes until they are heated through. Serve bratwurst by itself, boiled of fried, or with garnish. To fry - cut brats lengthwise into 2 halves and fry on oil or butter. When serving - dress garnish with oil used to fry brats.

Ham with Peas

Ingredients:
500 g smoked ham
1 carrot
1 parsnip
1 onion
1 can (400 g) green peas or 100 g dried peas
1/2 tbsp sugar
1 tbsp butter

Wash smoked ham with cold water and cook following instructions of "Boiled Salt Beef" recipe. Just before serving remove the skin from the ham, slice meat thinly, put it on a plate and pour 2-3 tbsp of strained cooking liquid over it. Garnish with green peas dressed with butter.

Boiled ham can also be used in this recipe. About 3-5 minutes before serving put slices of ham into hot water or meat broth and warm though without bringing to boil. Besides green peas, boiled ham can also be garnished with spinach, sorrel, or potato puree, braised cabbage or canned corn.

Tongue with White Sauce and Raisins

Ingredients:
1 beef tongue
1 carrot
1 parsnip
1 onion
100 g raisins
1 tbsp flour
2 tbsp butter

Put thoroughly washed tongue into a pot, add peeled and washed roots and onion, season with salt. Cover contents of the pot with hot water and put it on a stove. Cook for 2-3 hours.   Take tongue out of the pot, dip into iced water and remove the skin. Make sauce from the tongue cooking liquid. Slightly fry 1 tbsp in the same quantity of butter, add strained broth (1 1/4 cups), bring to simmer, add picked over and washed raisins and cook 5-10 minutes. Remove sauce from the heat, season with salt, add lemon juice, piece of butter, and mix well.

Just before serving slice tongue into thin slices, put on a plate, add garnish (green peas, pasta, braised cabbage, potato or pea puree), and dress tongue slices with sauce.

Sauce could be made without adding raisins, or tongue could be served without sauce, just drizzled with broth.

Pork tongue could be used instead of beef, but then the cooking time has to be 1-2 hours.

Boiled Tripe

Scald fresh, thoroughly washed tripe, clean with a knife and wash again with cold water. Cut prepared tripe into squares or tie it into a roll with a kitchen string , put into a pot, cover with cold water, season with salt, pepper, and bay leaf, 1 carrot, 1 parsnip, 1 onion and cook 4-5 hours.

Cut boiled tripe into noodle shape and dress with white sauce made with tripe cooking liquid. If desired - add tomato paste to the white sauce. Boiled tripe could also be served cold, cut into thin slices or small pieces. Serve horseradish and vinegar sauce, cucumbers, tomato salad, or green cabbage salad on a side.

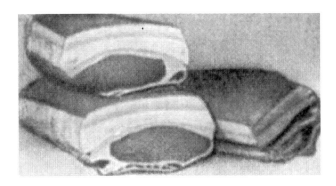

BRAISED MEAT

Braised Beef with Pasta

Ingredients:
500 g boneless meat
200 g pasta
1 tbsp tomato puree
1 carrot
1 onion
1 parsnip
1 tbsp flour
2 tbsp butter

Wash meat (rump, top round roast, sirloin), season with salt, put the whole cut on a skillet and fry on all sides until caramelized crust forms. Put fried meat in a pan, add tomato puree, 3-4 cups broth or hot water, peeled, washed and sliced root vegetables and onions, 2-3 bay leaves, 8-10 peppercorns (or 1/10 chili pepper). Cover with lid and braise for 2-3 hours. Approximately 30-40 minutes before the end of braising add one tablespoon of flour, fried until dark-brown, in one tablespoon of butter. In order to prevent flour from clumping, it should be diluted with a small amount of broth. After that mix and keep braising on low heat until meat is ready.

When serving, remove meat from sauce, slice, put on a plate; serve pasta with butter as garnish; add salt to sauce, strain and pour over the meat.

Instead of pasta, other garnishes may be served, such as potato coquettes, fried potatoes, braised cabbage. Separately serve cucumbers, lettuce or marinated fruits and berries.

Braised Beef with Onions and Potatoes

Ingredients:
500 g meat
800 g potatoes
2-3 onions
1 tbsp flour
2 tbsp butter

Wash boneless meat (rump, top round roast), cut into pieces 80-150 g, add salt and pepper, coat in flour and fry on a skillet from all sides until caramelized crust forms. Then put meat in a pan; pour 1 cup of water in a skillet where meat was frying, boil and strain through a sieve into pan with meat. Add 2 more cups of hot water, cover pan with lid and braise for 2-2 1/2 hours. After braising, add separately fried, finely chopped onions, fried potatoes (whole or sliced into 2-4 parts), 1 bay leaf, 2 cloves, 5-6 peppercorns (or 1/10 chili pepper) and braise for another half hour. When serving, sprinkle with finely chopped parsley or dill.

Separately serve cucumbers, green salad or tomato salad.

Beef Goulash

Ingredients:
500 g boneless meat
1 kg potatoes
2 onions
1 tbsp flour
3 tbsp tomato paste
3 tbsp butter

Wash meat (rump, sirloin, chuck), cut it into cubes, season with salt, pepper, and brown in oil in a skillet. When meat is browned, add diced onions, sprinkle meat with flour, and fry everything together. Put contents of the skillet into a pot, add 2-3 cups of stock or water, add tomato paste, 2-3 bay leaves, cover the pot and braise 1-1 1/2 hours. Serve goulash with fried or boiled potatoes, sprinkled with finely chopped dill or parsley leaves.

Georgian-Style Solyanka

Ingredients:
400-500 g boneless meat
2 onions
2 pickles
2 tbsp tomato paste
1/4 cup dry red wine
2-3 tbsp oil

Wash meat (sirloin, ribeye or rump), remove sinews, cut into small pieces, add diced onions and brown everything in oil in a heated skillet.
Put browned meat into a shallow pot, add tomato paste, peeled and diced pickles, a clove of

garlic, season with salt, pour in wine, 2-3 cups of beef stock, cover the pot and braise meat 30-40 minutes.

Sprinkle with finely chopped parsley leaves before serving.

Meat with Quince

Ingredients:
400 g boneless meat
400 g quince
1 onion
2 tbsp butter

Wash meat (sirloin, rump, top round roast), cut into small pieces (3-4 pieces per serving), put in shallow pan and fry in heated butter.

Pour over with water just so it covers the meat and braise for about an hour.

Slice quince, peel and remove insides, put in pan with meat, add fried onions, salt, pepper and continue braising until meat is fully ready.

When serving, put meat with quince on a heated plate and sprinkle with parsley or dill.

Veal Zrazi (Stuffed Veal Roll)

Ingredients:
500 g boneless veal
1 onion
100 g stale crustless white bread
1/2 cup milk
3 tbsp butter or oil
1 cup meat stock
2 tbsp tomato paste

Cut veal into thin, palm-sized slices, and pound them carefully. Prepare stuffing - dice onion and brown it in oil, soak bread in milk, squeeze extra liquid, and mix with onions, season with salt and pepper, and lightly fry on low heat. Put 1 tbsp of stuffing on each slice of meat and roll up each slice to enclose the filling, tie rolls with a string and season with salt. Sear each roll in a hot skillet on all sides until nicely browned, then lower the heat, add 1 cup of meat stock, 2 tbsp tomato paste, and braise 40-50 minutes. Just before serving remove strings and pour cooking liquid over rolls. Serve with spicy tomato sauce on a side.

Lamb Ragout

Ingredients:
500 g lamb
600 g potatoes
2 carrots
1 parsnip
1 turnip
1 onion
2 tbsp tomato paste
2 tbsp oil

Wash lamb (breast or shoulder), remove marrow bones, chop into pieces, season with salt and brown in a skillet. Just before the end of browning sprinkle meat with 1 tbsp of flour. Put browned lamb into a pot, add tomato paste, 2-3 cups hot stock or water, cover the pot, and braise on low heat. Put lamb into a shallow pan after 1 1/2 - 2 hours (40 - 50 minutes for young lamb) of braising, add washed, peeled, sliced, and lightly fried vegetables - carrots, parsnip, onion, parsnip, and potatoes. Add 1-2 bay leaves, 6-8 black peppercorns, and strained lamb cooking liquid, and braise for another 30 minutes. Put finished ragout on a serving plate and sprinkle with finely chopped dill or parsley leaves.

Lamb Braised with Vegetables

Ingredients:
500 g lamb
600 g potatoes
2 carrots
1 onion
1 turnip
200 g white cabbage

Wash lamb and cut into small pieces. Put meat into a pot and add 2-3 cups of hot water. Cover the pot and bring to boil. Add 2-3 potatoes to the pot when water comes to boil, season with salt, lower the heat and cook for 1 hour. Move lamb into a shallow pan. Put vegetables on top of lamb in the following order - washed and cleaned cabbage, diced carrots, onion, turnip, sliced potatoes, 1-2 bay leaves, 5-8 black peppercorns, and 4-5 cloves. Take boiled potatoes from the broth, rub it through a sieve, mix with strained broth, and pour this mixture over vegetables. Continue cooking on low heat 30-40 minutes.

Sprinkle with finely chopped dill or parsley leaves before serving.

Chanahi

Ingredients:
500 g lamb
750 g potatoes
200 g tomatoes
300 g eggplants
200 g green beans
1 onion
parsley or cilantro

Cut washed lamb into small pieces (2-3 pieces per serving), put meat into a 2-3 qt pot (preferably clay one). Add thinly sliced onions, peeled and slice potatoes, cut in half tomatoes, cleaned from strings and cut into small pieces green beans, diced eggplants, parsley or cilantro, season with salt and pepper, add 2 cups water. Cover the pot and put into preheated oven to braise for 1 1/2 - 2 hours.

Serve chanahi in the same pot in which it was cooked.

Lamb with Green Beans

Ingredients:
500 g lamb
400 g green beans
1 onion
2-3 tbsp oil

Cut washed lamb into small pieces (3-4

pieces per serving), put into a shallow pan and brown in oil. Cover lamb with water and braise in covered pot 30-40 minutes, then add browned diced onion, cleaned from strings and cut into small pieces green beans, season with salt and pepper, and continue cooking until lamb is done.

To serve - put lamb and beans on a heated serving plate and sprinkle with finely chopped dill or parsley leaves.

Veal or Lamb Kidneys in Wine Sauce

Ingredients:
500 g veal or lamb kidneys
200 g ceps or champignons
1 tbsp flour
1/4 cup Madeira
1 cup meat stock
2 tbsp butter

Clean kidneys from fat and film, cut in half lengthwise and then slice thinly crosswise. Boil mushrooms and slice thinly. Mix together sliced kidneys and mushrooms, season with salt and pepper, and sauté on a heated skillet, then add flour and fry for 1-2 minutes longer. Add Madeira and meat stock to the skillet, bring to boil and cook 3-4 minutes.

To serve - put kidneys on a heated serving plate, and sprinkle with finely chopped parsley leaves. Serve boiled potatoes dressed with butter on a side.

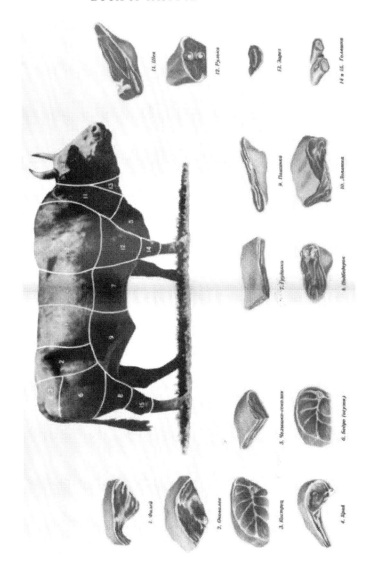

Beef Kidneys in Sauce with Onions

Ingredients:
500 g beef kidneys
600 g potatoes
1 onion
3-4 pickles
1 tbsp flour
2-3 tbsp oil or butter

Remove fat and film from kidneys, put into a pot, cover with water and bring to boil. Drain, wash kidneys again, cover with fresh water and cook until ready (approximately 1 - 1 1/2 hours). Make sauce from the kidney broth. Fry flour in the same quantity of butter until dark brown, add 1 1/2 cups hot broth and simmer 5-10 minutes. Thinly slice boiled kidneys, mix with diced browned onions, and fry together for 2-3 minutes, then move them to a shallow pot and add sliced, fried potatoes, peeled and sliced pickles, 1-2 bay leaves, 5-8 black peppercorns, top with strained sauce, cover the pot and braise 25-30 minutes. To serve - put kidneys with garnish on a heated serving plate and sprinkle with finely chopped dill or parsley leaves.

Pork kidneys can also be used in this recipe; however, they do not need to be boiled. Slice raw pork kidneys and start with frying step.

Braised Beef Heart

Ingredients:
500 g beef heart
1 tbsp flour
1 onion
2 tbsp tomato paste
2 tbsp distilled vinegar
1 tsp sugar
2 tbsp butter

Wash beef heart and dry it with paper towels, cut into small pieces, season with salt and brown in oil in a heated skillet. When meat is browned - sprinkle flour over it and fry for 1-2 minutes longer. Put heart into a shallow pan and deglaze the skillet with stock or water.

Strain liquid from the skillet into a pan with heart, add 1 1/2 cups of stock or water, cover the pot, bring to boil, lower the heat and cook 2-3 hours.

Brown diced onions in a skillet add tomato paste, vinegar, sugar, 2 bay leaves, bring to simmer and add to the pot with beef hart 20-30 minutes before the end of cooking. Season everything with salt.

Serve with garnish of buckwheat porridge, boiled rice, pasta, fried or boiled potatoes.
In addition to this recipe, beef heart can be cooked following instructions of "Braised Beef" recipe.

Beef Lung Goulash

Ingredients:
500 g beef lungs
1 onion
1 tbsp tomato paste
1 tbsp flour
1 tbsp butter

Put washed beef lungs into hot water and simmer 1 1/2 - 2 hours. Cut cooked lungs into pieces about 30-40 g each, season with salt, pepper, and fry in a skillet with hot oil.

Sprinkle fried lungs with flour, add diced onion and continue frying a couple of minutes longer.

Put browned lungs into a pot add 2-2 1/2 cups of broth from the first stage of cooking, tomato paste, bay leaf, cover the pot and cook for 10-15 minutes. Serve goulash with boiled or fried potatoes.

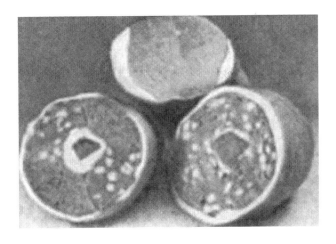

Beef Heart or Udder Goulash

Ingredients:
500 g beef heart or udder
1 tbsp flour
1 tbsp butter
1 tbsp tomato paste

Cut washed heart or udder, cut into pieces 30-40 g each and wash again, season with salt and pepper and brown together with diced onion in oil on a preheated skillet. Sprinkle with flour and fry a couple of minutes longer. Put contents of the skillet into a pot, cover with hot water, add tomato paste, bay leaf, cover the pot and braise on low heat 1-1 1/2 hours.

Server with fried or boiled potatoes.

Meat Holubtsi

Ingredients:
300 g boneless meat
800 g white cabbage
1/2 cup grain (rice, barley, millet)
1 onion
1 tbsp flour
2 tbsp tomato paste
2 tbsp sour cream
2 tbsp butter

Pass meat through a meat grinder, cook and cool grain, and mix everything together with slightly browned diced onions, season with salt and pepper. Separate head of cabbage into leaves and parboil them for 5-7 minutes. Remove cabbage leaves from water and accurately pound thick stalks to the thickness of the leaf. Put stuffing in the middle of each leaf and roll it to enclose the filling. Lightly fry rolled cabbage leaves in a skillet and put into a pot. Make a sauce by simmering sour cream, tomato paste, cup of water, and flour in that same skillet. Pour the sauce over holubtsi, cover the pot and braise on low heat for 30-40 minutes (or cook in the oven in the uncovered pot). Serve in the same sauce in which holubtsi cooked, sprinkled with finely chopped dill or parsley leaves.

Sauce for holubtsi can be made without sour cream - in which case use more tomato paste.

Dolma (Stuffed Grape Leaves)

Ingredients:
500 g boneless lamb
1/2 cup rice
1 onion
400 g grape leaves
1 tbsp oil
cilantro or parsley

Pass lamb meat through a meat grinder, add cooked rice, finely diced onion, herbs, season with salt and pepper.

Wash grape leaves, remove tough stem side, put leaves on a board (1-2 leaves), put stuffing on top of leaves and roll leaves to enclose stuffing - just like holubtsi. Season stuffed grape leaves with salt and put into a shallow pan in tight rows, pour oil over, add cup of stock cooked from lamb bones, cover the pot and braise on low heat for about an hour.

Just before serving, put dolma on serving plate. Serve sour milk mixed with grated garlic and season with salt, and ground cinnamon mixed with powdered sugar.

FRIED MEAT

Meat (beef, veal, lamb, pork) can be fried in large or small (portion) pieces. Meat fried in a large piece is used for hot and cold dishes, in small pieces - only for hot dishes. Other meat products such as suckling pig, rabbit, liver, kidneys, calves feet, pigs feet can also be fried as well.

If large piece of meat is fried, it needs to be washed, tendons removed, dried with a towel and salted. Then put meat (beef) on a skillet with heated butter and from on all sides until caramelized crust forms. Once the thin crust forms, put it in the oven, add a little broth or water and fry until meat is fully ready.

Pork, veal and lamb are not fried on a skillet; they are placed in oven immediately.

Each 10-15 minutes, remove meat from oven and pour it over with juice that forms during frying. If there is not enough juice, add a little broth or water. Juice obtained during frying can be used as gravy for meat or for sauce preparation.

Large piece of meat takes 1 1/2 - 2 1 /2 hours to prepare, depending on type and size. Meat is checked for readiness by poking it with fork and pressing on it. If the juice is red, meat is not yet ready, if the juice is light in color - meat is ready.

Some people prefer their meat "bloody", but this is allowed only for beef and lam, while pork and veal must be well-done.

When frying small (portion-sized) pieces of meat, they are placed on well-heated skillet with butter. There should be some spacing between the meat pieces, 1 1/2 - 2 cm / 0.6 - .8 in. If the pieces are fried with no spacing left between them, butter on the skillet gets cooled, crust on the meat is not formed and meat tastes like boiled meat, not fried meat.

Fried meat (especially portion-sized pieces) should be cooked immediately prior to serving, in order for it to keep all its taste qualities.

Roast Beef

Wash meat (sirloin, ribeye, tenderloin), remove tendons, add salt, place the whole piece on a heated skilled with butter and fry a little. Then put it in the oven and cook until ready. Every 10-15 minutes, pour meat over with juice that is forming. If there is not enough juice, add broth or water. Frying time depends on desired state of roast beef - well-done, medium or bloody.

When roast beef is ready, remove it from skillet, slice and put on a plate. Carrots and sweet peas with butter, potatoes (boiled, fried, in milk or mashed), horseradish can be served as garnish. Pour meat over with strained frying juice and melted butter.

Separately serve cucumbers and green salad.

Fried Meat with Sour Cream and Onions

Ingredients:
500 g meat
1 kg potatoes
1/2 cup sour cream
1 onion
1 tbsp flour
1 tbsp "Yuzhni" sauce
3 tbsp butter

Wash meat (sirloin), remove tendons, cut into one or two slices per serving, pound with meat mallet, sprinkle with salt and ground pepper. Fry on a hot skillet with butter, turning meat from side to side until caramelized. Separately fry finely chopped onions. When onions are fried, sprinkle it with flour, fry a bit more; add 1/2 cup sour cream and juice obtained during frying.

Boil prepared sauce for 3-5 minutes, add sauce "Yuzhni" and salt to it. When serving, put meat on a plate and pour over with sauce.

Serve fried potatoes as garnish.

Fried Breaded Beef (Rump Steak)

Wash meat (ribeye), remove tendons, slice into portion sizes and pound with meat mallet. Sprinkle with salt and pepper, moisten with whipped eggs and coat with breadcrumbs on both sides. After that, put on a very hot skillet with butter and fry until fully ready (10-12 minutes). As garnish, serve fried potatoes and boiled, sliced, buttered sweat peas, corn and carrots. Pour meat over with butter.

Beef Stroganoff

Ingredients:
500 g meat
1 kg potatoes
3/4 cup sour cream
1 tbsp "Yuzhni" sauce
2 onions
1 tbsp flour
3 tbsp butter

Wash meat (sirloin, ribeye, top round roast), remove tendons, slice into small pieces, pound with a meat mallet, then julienne. Peel and wash onions, slice and fry in butter. When onions are fried, add meat, salt and pepper, fry for 5-6 minutes while stirring with a fork.

Sprinkle meat with flour, mix and fry for another 2-3 minutes. Then add sour cream, mix and fry yet another 2-3 minutes, add "Yuzhni" sauce and salt.

Serve fried potatoes as garnish. Sprinkle meat and potatoes with finely chopped dill or parsley.

Beefsteak with Potatoes

Wash meat (tenderloin), remove tendons, cut across fibers into slices weighing approximately 100 - 150 g, pound with meat mallet, sprinkle with salt, pepper, put on a very hot skillet with butter and fry on both sides until fully ready (10-15 minutes).

When steak is ready, put it on a plate, pour over with juice and butter. Serve fried potatoes and peeled, washed and planed horseradish. Cucumbers or salad may be served separately.

Beefsteak with Onions

Prepare tenderloin just like in the recipe "Beefsteak with Potatoes", with only difference being - meat slices should be pounded to make them thinner and wider. Caramelize washed peeled and sliced into rings onions (1/2 onion per serving) in oil. When serving - put caramelized onions over fried beefsteak and pour pan juices or oil over. Garnish with fried potatoes.

Beefsteak with Egg

Cook meat following instructions of the recipe "Beefsteak with Potatoes". Just before serving put egg fried sunny side up over meat. Garnish with potatoes.

Fried Rib-eye with Potatoes

Wash and trim beef rib-eye, cut into serving pieces and pound slightly. Slightly pound it, season with salt and pepper, cook on both sides in oil on a very hot skillet or shallow pan until nicely browned.

Put cooked beefsteak on a plate and pour pan juices or melted butter over it. Garnish with fried potatoes (or potatoes mashed with milk) and grated horseradish. Sprinkle finely chopped dill or parsley leaves over potatoes.

Languette with Garnish

Wash and trim tenderloin, and slice across the grain (2 slices per serving). Pound slices of meat until very thin, season with salt and pepper and fry in oil on very hot skillet. Put meat on a plate and deglaze the skillet with couple of tablespoons of water or stock. Pour pan sauce over meat.

Garnish meat with green peas with butter, sliced carrots, and fried potatoes.

Tenderloin Kebabs

Ingredients:
500 g beef tenderloin
2 onions
1 tbsp red wine vinegar
100 g scallions
200 g tomatoes
1/2 lemon

Wash and trim beef tenderloin. Cut into pieces 40-50 g each, put into a ceramic or other non-reactive container, season with salt and pepper, add vinegar and finely chopped onion mix everything well. Cover container and leave 2-3 hours in cool place to marinate.

Thread marinated meat on skewers and cook over glowing coals approximately 8-10 minutes, rotating skewers to insure that meat cooks evenly on all sides.

To serve - remove grilled meat from skewers, put on a heated plate, garnish with tomatoes, thinly sliced onions, scallions, and lemons.

Roast Veal

Wash veal (rump roast, loin roast, shoulder roast, breast roast), season with salt, drizzle with 2-3 tbsp melted butter, put into a roasting pan and roast in preheated oven, basting it from time to time with pan juices.

Cut cooked veal into servings, put on a serving dish and dress with strained pan juices. Garnish with fried potatoes or vegetables - peas, carrots, cauliflower, green beans. Serve red cabbage or salad on a side.

Roast Lamb

Wash lamb (leg roast, loin roast), season with salt, drizzle with 2-3 tbsp melted butter, put into a roasting pan and roast in a preheated oven until desired doneness, basting it from time to time with pan juices.

Cut roast lamb into servings, put on a serving plate, garnish with boiled potatoes with butter or fried potatoes, beans in tomato sauce or with butter. Sprinkle with finely chopped dill or parsley leaves, and pour strained pan juices over the meat.

Roast Pork

Prepare a piece of pork (top leg roast) and cook until well done just like "Roast Veal" recipe, fat side up. Garnish with fried or boiled potatoes, mashed potatoes, or braised cabbage. Cut cooked pork into slices; pour strained pan juices over meat. Serve pickled apples, red cabbage, cucumbers, or pickles on a side.

Fried Breaded Lamb Rib Roast

Wash lamb rib roast, cut the films on lungs, put in a pot in whole piece, add salt, pro over with hot water and boil. When ready, remove the ribs, put meat on dripping pan, and cool under press, so that the rib roast is straightened. After this slice diagonally into wide pieces, add salt, pepper, coat in flour, moisten with egg, coat with breadcrumbs and fry on a heated skillet with butter.

Put prepared rib roast on a plate and pour over with several spoons of melted butter.

Serve fried potatoes or mashed potatoes as garnish.

Separately serve red cabbage and cucumbers.

Breaded Chops and Regular Chops

Ingredients:
500 g pork or veal loin
1 egg
1/2 cup breadcrumbs
2 tbsp butter

Wash pork, lamb or veal loin, and cut into cops (with rib bone). Pound each chop a little with meat mallet, salt, sprinkle with pepper, moisten with whipped egg and coat in breadcrumbs.
Put prepared chops on a heated skillet with butter and fry on both sides until caramelized crust forms (approximately 15-20 minutes).
Once chops are ready, put them on a plate and pour over with melted butter. For garnish you may serve fried potatoes, mashed potatoes or assorted vegetables with butter (carrots, corn, cauliflower, sweet peas, etc.)
Regular chops are prepared the same way, except they are not coated in breadcrumbs. In this case pour chops over with juice that forms during frying.

Schnitzel

Ingredients:
500 g pork or veal

1 egg
1/2 cup breadcrumbs
1/2 tbsp capers
1/2 lemon
2 tbsp butter

Wash pork or veal (kidney part of loin or flesh of the hind leg), remove tendons, cut into chops, but without bone. Pound each piece with meat mallet, salt, sprinkle with pepper, moisten with whipped egg and coat with breadcrumbs. Put prepared pieces on a heated skillet with butter and fry on both sides until caramelized crust forms; then put on a plate and pour over with butter that was used to lightly fry finely chopped and scalded lemon zest and capers.

Put a slice of lemon sprinkled with parsley or dill on each piece. Garnish can be fried potatoes or vegetables with oil. Serve green or vegetable salad separately.

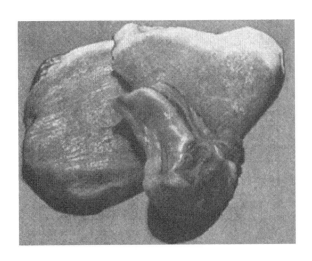

Slices of Veal, Pork, Lamb with Mushrooms and Tomatoes

Wash veal, pork, lamb - kidney part of loin or flesh of the hind leg. Remove tendons, slice into portion slices (2 per serving) and pound with a meat mallet. Sprinkle with salt and put on a skillet with heated butter and fry on both sides until ready (8-10 minutes).

Peel fresh cepes (porcini) or champignons, wash with cold water, slice and fry in butter. Wash tomatoes in cold water, cut in halves, sprinkle with salt and pepper and fry in butter as well. When serving, put meat on a plate, place mushrooms on tomatoes on top and pour over with tomato sauce with a little chopped garlic. Serve boiled potatoes as garnish.

Shashlik (Shish Kebab)

Ingredients:
500 g lamb
2 onions
100 g scallions
200 g tomatoes
1/2 lemon
1 tbsp vinegar
1 tbsp butter

Wash lamb (loin part or flesh of the hind leg), cut into small pieces, put in a pan, sprinkle with salt and ground pepper, add finely chopped onions, vinegar or teaspoon of lemon juice and mix. Cover with lid and put in a cold place for 2-3 hours, so that lamb gets marinated.

Before frying, thread marinated pieces of lamb on a metal skewer, in between sliced onions. Fry shashlik over coals (no flame) for approximately 15-20 minutes while turning the skewer so that the meat fries uniformly.

If roaster is not available, shashlik can be fired on a skillet.

When shashlik is ready, remove it from skewer, put on a plate, pour over with butter and garnish with scallions, sliced tomatoes and pieces of lemon. Boiled rice can also be served as garnish, as well as dried ground berberis or pomegranate juice.

Shashlik can also be prepared with pork, same recipe applies.

Karsky-Style Shashlik (Ancient Armenian Shish Kebab)

Ingredients:
500 g lamb
2 kidneys
1 onion
100 g scallions
1 tbsp vinegar
1/2 lemon

Wash loin part of lamb, remove tendons, make cuts in the meat so it doesn't get tightened when fried, and cut into serving sizes of 250 g. Wash kidneys and cut them in half.

Put prepared lamb mean and kidneys into a bowl, sprinkle with salt and pepper, finely chopped onion and parsley, add vinegar or lemon juice and leave for 2-3 hours to marinade.

Thread each piece of lamb on a metal skewer, adding half a kidney on each side, and fry over coals (no flame). Turn the skewer so lamb fries uniformly from all sides. Meat can also be fried on a skillet.

Once shashlik is ready, remove it from skewer and put on a plate with kidneys and a piece of lemon. Sprinkle with scallions and parsley. Serve sauce "Yuzhni" separately.

Fried Veal Kidneys on Skillet

Wash veal kidneys and dry them with a napkin. Cut into thin circular slices (across the kidney). Sprinkle each piece with salt and ground pepper and coat in flour. Put kidneys on hot skillet with butter and fry on both sides for 5-6 minutes.

When kidneys are ready, sprinkle with finely chopped parsley pour over with lemon juice and serve on a skillet.

Separately, as vanish, serve fried julienned potatoes and a lemon cut in four pieces.

Liver in Sour Cream

Ingredients:
500 g liver
1/2 cup sour cream

1 tbsp flour
1 onion
2 tbsp butter

Wash liver (beef, lamb or pork), remove film and gall ducts, slice, sprinkle with salt and pepper, coat in flour and fry in skillet with butter. Put in a shallow pot; add finely chopped fried onions, sour cream, juice from skillet where liver was frying and one cup of meat broth or water. Close lid and braise on low heat for 25-40 minutes. When liver is ready, serve it on a plate, pour over with sauce obtained while braising and sprinkle with parsley. For garnish you may serve fried potatoes or boiled potatoes or pasta.

Fried Veal Liver

Ingredients:
500 g veal liver
2 tbsp flour
2 tbsp oil

Wash and clean liver, removing all film and bile ducts, cut into slices about 1 cm, season with salt and pepper, coat in flour and fry in oil on a preheated skillet 10-12 minutes. Transfer cooked liver to a serving plate and pour oil and juices from the skillet over it. If desired - top each slice of fried liver with slice of fried smoked pork bacon.

Liver can also be served with onions, sliced and slowly caramelized in oil. Put onions over slices of liver, or make a sour cream and onion sauce.

Serve with fried, boiled, or mashed potatoes.

Fried Brains

Ingredients:
1 set of brains
1 tbsp flour
1/2 lemon
2 tbsp oil

Soak brains in cold water for 30-40 minutes, drain and remove film and membrane. Put brains into a pot, cover with cold water, add 1-2 tbsp of vinegar, salt, 2-3 bay leaves, and 5-6 black peppercorns, and bring to boil. Lower the heat when water comes to boil and simmer for 25-30 minutes. Take cooked brains out of the pot and let it dry slightly. Cut each half of the brain into 2 parts, season with salt and pepper, coat in flour and fry in oil in a hot skillet. Transfer cooked brains to a serving plate, drizzle with oil it was cooked in and lemon juice, and sprinkle with finely chopped dill or parsley leaves. Serve with fried, boiled, or mashed potatoes, green peas, green beans, or carrots.

Fried Breaded Brains

Ingredients:
1 set of brains
1/2 cup breadcrumbs
1 egg
1 tbsp flour
3 tbsp oil

Boil brains following instructions in the recipe "Fried Brains". Cut each half of the brain into 2 parts, season with salt and pepper, coat in flour, then dip into beaten egg and coat with breadcrumbs. Fry in well-heated oil until nicely browned for 7-8 minutes. Transfer cooked brains to a serving plate and pour cooking oil over. Sprinkle with finely chopped dill or parsley leaves.

Serve with fried or mashed potatoes, green peas, carrots, or green beans. If desired - serve tomato sauce on a side.

Fried Calf's or Pig's Feet

Ingredients:
4 feet
2 eggs
1/2 cup flour
1 cup breadcrumbs
1 carrot
1 parsnip
1 onion
3-4 tbsp oil

Scald calf's or pig's feet, clear the stubble, rub with flour and singe to remove any remaining hair. Wash feet and cut them along into 2 halves. Put feet into a pot, cover with cold water, add carrots, parsnip, onion, salt, and cook approximately 3-4 hours.

Take boiled feet out of the pot and separate meat from bones, season with salt and pepper, coat with flour, dip into beaten egg, coat with breadcrumbs and fry in a skillet with well-heated oil.

Serve with mashed potatoes, green peas, or cucumbers. Feet can also be served boiled, in which case serve them with boiled potatoes or rice.

Broth from cooking could be used in making soups or sauces.

Fried Sausage

Ingredients:
500 g sausage
2 tbsp oil

Peel smoked or half-smoked sausage, slice it, and fry in oil in a preheated skillet. Transfer fried sausage to a serving plate and pour oil it was cooked in over. Serve with braised cabbage, mashed potatoes, or fried potatoes.

Fried Ham with Tomatoes

Ingredients:
500 g ham
400 g tomatoes
1 tsp lemon juice
3 tbsp oil

Fry sliced ham in oil in a preheated skillet. In a separate pot or skillet fried washed, cut across in half, seasoned with salt and pepper tomatoes. Put fried tomatoes on top of slices of fried ham, sprinkle with finely chopped dill or parsley leaves, and serve in a skillet ham was fried in. Drizzle with lemon juice just before serving.

Suckling Pig

Wipe scalded pig with a towel, rub with flour where there is still bristle remaining, and singe those areas. Cut belly from tail towards the head and remove innards. Remove large intestine by chopping hip bones. Thoroughly wash pig in cold water. Cut along the vertebrae in the neck area. Season inside of pig with salt, put into a roasting pan, baste with sour cream, drizzle with melted butter, add 1/4 cup water to the pan and put into a preheated oven. Roast for 1-1 1/2 hours.

To insure nice brown skin baste pig from

time to time with fat drippings. Pig can be roasted whole or cut into 2 halves lengthwise.

Take cooked pig out of the roasting pan and prepare sauce. Put pan on fire and boil all the liquid out, drain all the fat from the pan, then add 1 cup of hot stock or water, deglaze the pan and strain the sauce.

When serving put buckwheat porridge on a heated serving plate and sprinkle it with chopped hardboiled eggs. Cut pig head off, and then cut the carcass in half. Cut each half across into servings, and put them over buckwheat in a shape of whole pig, including head. Pour fat from the pan over meat. Serve sauce on a side.

Fried Tripe with Buckwheat Porridge

Ingredients:
500 g tripe
1 onion
1 cup hulled buckwheat
3 tbsp oil

Pass cleaned and boiled tripe through a meat grinder, season with salt and pepper, and fry in oil in a preheated skillet. Add to the skillet previously fried diced onion, cooked buckwheat, mix everything and fry together 3-5 minutes.

CHOPPED MEAT PRODUCTS

To make dishes from chopped meat, beef, pork, lamb and veal may be used. Noisettes, rolls, zrazi, schnitzels are mainly made from beef (rump, top round roast).

Meat for chopped meat dishes should be washed, tendons removed, cut into pieces and passed through a meat grinder. Add salt, mix, add white bread soaked in cold water or milk, and pass through meat grinder once or twice.

Bread gives croquettes additional volume and juiciness because he juice that is released by the meat when fried, accumulates inside the bread. Stale bread is better, with crust removed. Fatty meat should be used, it makes croquettes juicier. Ground pepper can be added to the meat and also fresh or fried onions.

A lot of dishes that follow are easier prepared if prepared ground meat is purchased ion a store.

Croquettes and Chops

Ingredients:
500 g boneless meat
125 g white bread
1/2 cup breadcrumbs
3/4 cup milk or water
2 tbsp butter

Prepare ground meat, shape it into oval croquettes or round chops, coat in breadcrumbs. Put croquettes or chops on a hot skillet with butter, fry on both sides until ready for 8-10 minutes.

As garnish, serve boiled, fried or mashed potatoes, porridge, pasta, noodles, and also vegetables.

Pour over croquettes or chops with butter, sour cream, red or tomato sauce, and also separately serve hot tomato sauce, "Yuzhni" or "Lyubitelski" sauce.

Meatballs in Tomato Sauce

Ingredients:
500 g boneless meat
100 g scallions
1 onion
1/2 cup tomato puree
100 g white bread
2 tbsp flour
2 tbsp butter

Prepare ground meat, add finely chopped washed scallions or grated onion and mix well. Out of this mix, make balls that weigh 20-30 g each, coat them with flour and fry in butter on heated skillet. Put fried meatballs in a shallow pan, add tomato puree, cup of meat broth, 1-2 bay leaves, 5-6 peppercorns (or 1/10 chili pepper), 2-3 garlic cloves rubbed in salt. Cover with lid and braise on low heat for 10-20 minutes, then add salt, spoon of hot tomato sauce. When serving, sprinkle with parsley.

As garnish, serve boiled rice, buckwheat porridge, fried potatoes or mashed potatoes.

Meat Roll with Pasta

Ingredients:
500 g boneless meat
100 g white bread
150 g pasta
1 egg
1 tbsp breadcrumbs
1 cup red sauce
2 tbsp butter

Prepare ground meat, lay it out on a napkin soaked in cold water, and even out with a knife so that a uniform oblong layer is formed, about 1 1/2 cm thick. Put boiled and cooled pasta with butter in the middle of the ground beef, covering the whole length. Then connect the edges of the ground meat. Carefully remove the formed meat roll off the napkin and place it seam down on a greased skillet.

Moisten top of the roll with egg, sprinkle with breadcrumbs, pour over with butter, make several punctures with fork and put into oven for 30-40 minutes to bake. When meat roll is ready, cut in into portion pieces and pour over with red sauce.

Instead of pasta, meat roll can be stuffed with rice or buckwheat porridge with fried onions and boiled eggs.

Croquettes with Milk Sauce

Ingredients:
500 g boneless meat
125 g white bread
2 tbsp grated cheese
1 tbsp flour
1/2 cup milk
3 tbsp butter

Make croquettes out of ground meat and put them on a skillet greased with butter. On top of each croquette lengthwise, make a small cavity with a teaspoon. Fill it with thick milk sauce, sprinkle with grated cheese, butter and put into oven to bake for 10-20 minutes. For garnish serve boiled green beans or sweat peas, mashed potatoes, Brussels sprouts or asparagus in milk sauce. Pour croquettes over with butter and juice obtained while baking or use red sauce.

Chopped Schnitzel

Ingredients:
500 g meat
1/2 cup breadcrumbs
2 tbsp butter

Wash meat and remove tendons. Pass through a meat grinder or chop with knife, add salt pepper and make 5-6 oval-shaped schnitzels about 1/2 cm thick.

Coat prepared schnitzels in breadcrumbs and fry on hot skillet with butter for 5-6 minutes. Serve fried potatoes, mashed potatoes or vegetables for garnish. Pour over schnitzel with butter.

Siberian Pelmeni (Dumplings)

Ingredients:
1 1/2 cup wheat flour
300-400 g meat (half beef, half pork)
1 egg
1 onion
1/4 cup sour cream or 1-2 tbsp butter

Prepared quality pelmeni are always available to purchase in stores.

Purchased or home-made pelmeni (see pelmeni recipe) are submerged into boiling salted water and cooked for 5-6 minutes. Remove pelmeni, put them on a plate, pour over with butter or sour cream and serve right away.

Many people prefer pelmeni Siberian-style, pouring them over with hot sauce (mustard mixed with vinegar, especially grape).

Fried pelmeni are very tasty: purchased or home-made pelmeni should be boiled in salted water (in this case only cook for 2-3 minutes). Remove pelmeni and fry them on a skillet on both sides.

BAKED MEAT

Meat Casserole

Ingredients:
300 g boneless beef
500 g potatoes
3 eggs
1-2 onions
1 tbsp tomato paste
1/4 cup milk
2 tbsp oil

Pass washed meat through a meat grinder and lightly brown it in a skillet; add diced fried onion, tomato paste, season with salt and pepper, pour in a little stock or water, cover the skillet, and braise on low heat 15-20 minutes. Fry peeled, washed, and sliced potatoes. Put fried potatoes in a layer on the bottom of a skillet, top potatoes with meat mixture, smooth the top, add eggs beaten with milk and put to bake into a preheated oven for 5-10 minutes.

Just before serving sprinkle casserole with finely chopped dill or parsley leaves.

Zucchini Stuffed with Meat

Ingredients:
2 medium zucchini
200 g boneless meat
1/2 cup rice or millet
1 onion
2 tbsp sour cream
2 tbsp tomato paste
1 tbsp flour
1 tbsp butter

Make stuffing just like for "Holubtsi". Peel and cut each zucchini into 4-5 pieces across. Remove seeds with a teaspoon, put prepared zucchini into a well-oiled baking pan or a skillet, and stuff with stuffing. Slightly sauté tomato paste, then add sour cream mixed with flour and a cup of water. Season zucchini with salt, add prepared tomato and sour cream sauce and bake in a preheated oven 30-40 minutes. Sprinkle with chopped dill just before serving.

Meat Solyanka

Ingredients:
200 g meat products
1 kg sauerkraut

2 pickles
2 onions
3 tbsp tomato puree
1 tbsp flour
1 tbsp capers
2-3 tbsp butter

Put sauerkraut in a pan, add one tablespoon of butter, 1/2 cup water or meat broth, cover with lid and braise for 40 mites. Add fried onions, tomato pure, vinegar, sugar, salt, bay leaf, pepper and braise until ready - for approximately 10 minutes. When sauerkraut is ready, add fried flour to the pan, mix and boil. At the same time, slice meat products (boiled meat, canned meat, sausage, hot dogs), fry with onions, add sliced cucumbers, capers, 2-3 tablespoons of broth, cover with lid and boil for several minutes.

Lay out half of sauerkraut in an even layer on a skillet, put prepared meat with garnish on top, cover with the rest of the cabbage, even out, sprinkle with breadcrumbs, add butter and bake in oven for 10-15 minutes. When serving, decorate with parsley, olives, red bilberry, etc.

SAUCES FOR MEAT DISHES

Meat Juice Sauce (for Fried Meat)

Put meat that has been fried in portion sizes on a plate. Add a little meat stock or water on a skillet where meat was fried and boil; strain juice and pour over the meat on the plate.

If the meat was fried in one big piece (veal, lamb, pork or poultry), pour out the juice for skilled, add to it some stock or water and boil for 1-2 minutes. Strain and pour over meat or poultry placed on a plate.

Red Sauce (for Chopped Meat, Meat Roll, Tongue with Peas, etc.)

Ingredients:
1 tbsp flour
1 carrot
1 parsnip
1 onion
1 tbsp tomato puree
1 1/2 tbsp butter

Fry one tablespoon of flour with same amount of butter until it is dark-brown. Mix with tomato puree and dilute with 2 cups meat stock. Add fried chopped root vegetables and onions and cook on low heat for 20-30 minutes. When finished, add salt, 1-2 tablespoons of wine (madeira or port) and strain.

Tomato Sauce (for Fried Meat, Chopped Meat, Brains, etc.)

Ingredients:
1/2 cup tomato puree
1 tbsp flour

1 carrot

1 parsnip

1 onion

1 tbsp spicy tomato sauce

1 tbsp butter

Peel root vegetables and onions, slice and fry in one tablespoon of flour, then add tomato puree, mix, dilute with one cup of meat stock and cook for 8-10 minutes. When finished, add salt, tablespoon of spicy tomato sauce, butter and thoroughly mix until uniform, then strain.

Spicy Onion Sauce (for Fried and Braised Meat, Liver, Chopped Meat, etc.)

Fry one tablespoon of flour with same amount of butter and dilute with 2 cups of meat stock. Peel 2 onions, finely chop and fry in butter. Add 2 tablespoons of tomato puree, salt, pepper and fry again; then add 2-3 tablespoons of vinegar, cook until thickness of sour cream is achieved. Add chopped gherkins, mix with sauce and boil for 5 minutes.

White Sauce (for Boiled Rabbit, Veal, Lamb and Poultry)

Ingredients:

1 tbsp flour

1 1/2 cup broth

1 egg yolk

2 tbsp butter

Fry one tablespoon of flour with same amount of butter, dilute with strained broth obtained while boiling rabbit, poultry, lamb or veal and cook on low heat for 5-10 minutes. After that remove from heat, add egg yolk mixed in a glass with a small amount of sauce, add salt, butter and mix.

White Sauce with Capers (for Boiled Veal, Lamb, Rabbit, Poultry)

Prepare white sauce (see appropriate recipe), and add 1 1/2 tablespoon of small capers.

Horseradish Sauce (for Boiled Beef, Corned Beef, Lamb, Pork, Tongue)

Ingredients:
1 tbsp flour
2 tbsp grated horseradish
1/2 cup sour cream
2 tbsp vinegar
2 tbsp butter

Fry one tablespoon of flour in the same amount of butter, dilute with cup of hot broth obtained while boiling meat products, add sour cream and boil on low heat for 5-10 minutes. At the same time, prepare horseradish: in a small pan or skillet put 2 tablespoons of butter and grated horseradish and fry it a little. Then add 1-2 tablespoons of vinegar (depending on its strength) and same amount of water or broth, add 1 bay leaf, 5-8 peppercorns (or 1/10 chili pepper) and bring to boil in order to evaporate liquid.

Put boiled horseradish into prepared sauce, boil, remove from fire, salt, add butter and mix.

Sour Cream Sauce (for Chops, Croquettes, Liver, Fried Game)

Ingredients:
1/2 cup sour cream
1 tbsp flour
1 tbsp butter

Fry one tablespoon of flour in same amount of butter, dilute with 1 cup of hot meat or vegetable broth, add sour cream and cook on low heat for 5-10 minutes. When finished, add salt, butter and mix.

Sour Cream Sauce with Onions (for Liver, Croquettes and Chops)

Ingredients:
1/2 cup sour cream
1 tbsp flour
1 onion
1/2 tbsp "Yuzhni" sauce
1 1/2 tbsp butter

Fry one tablespoon of flour with same

amount of butter until color turns light-yellow. Dilute with one cup of hot meat broth, add sour cream and boil on low heat for 5-10 minutes. At the same time fry finely chopped onions on a skillet. Put onions in the sauce jus before the end of boiling. Remove from heat; add salt and "Yuzhni" or "Lyubitelski" sauces.

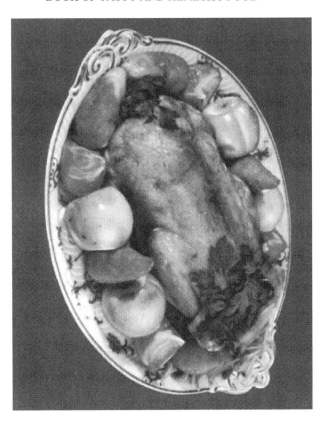

POULTRY AND GAME

Poultry dishes mostly include chicken, duck, goose and turkey and game dishes - grouse, quail, black grouse, wood grouse, and pheasant.

Poultry is mostly sold frozen and plucked, but not gutted; unfrozen birds are sold either gutted or partially gutted. Game such as grouse, quail, black grouse, pheasant are sold with feathers.

Chickens for frying should be young; old ones can be used for boiling or making croquettes.

Pluck birds starting with neck. Stretch the skin with fingers of your left hand as much as possible to prevent damaging the skin while plucking: torn skin spoils the bird's appearance and will make it too dry when frying.

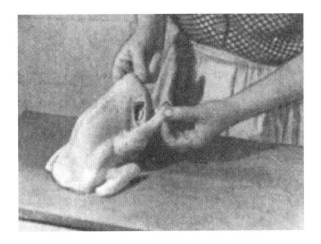

Singe the plucked bird to remove remaining down; prior to that stretch the bird out so that there are no skin folds, dry it with a towel and rub with flour. Attention needs to be paid so that the bird doesn't get smoked.

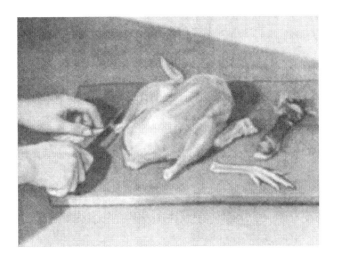

After you singe, chop off the neck and feet and carefully gut, trying not to crush the gallbladder. Wash the gutted bird, not leaving any blood clots inside. Also remove the feather roots, which can be especially numerous in goose and duck.

Birds can be fried on a frying pan, in a shallow pot or in an oval Dutch oven with heated butter. Length of frying varies depending on the age and size of the bird. In order for brown caramelized crust to form, it is advisable to smear chicken with sour cream prior to frying.

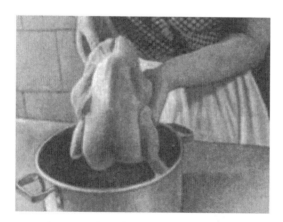

Before serving, prepared bird is chopped

into serving pieces. Separate it into quarters. These quarters can be divided into even smaller serving pieces.

To make hot chicken dishes, canned chicken can be used.

In cases when old chicken needs to be fried, it should be boiled first. Boiled chicken is fried in bread crumbs or without. To fry in breadcrumbs, chicken is chopped to pieces and each piece is coated in flour first and then, after moistening with beaten egg, in breadcrumbs. If not using breadcrumbs, the skin is smeared with sour cream and chicken is fried using well-heated cooking fat, which allows the formation of caramelized crust.

Poached Chicken or Spring Chicken

Ingredients:
1 chicken or spring chicken
1 1/2 tbsp flour
1 carrot
1 parsnip
1 onion
2 tbsp butter

Put prepared raw chicken or spring chicken in a pot, add cleaned and washed root vegetables and onion, pour over meat broth or water so that 3/4 of bird is covered by it. Add salt, close lid and bring to boil. Cook chicken for 1 - 1 1/2 hours and spring chicken for 30-40 minutes.

Prepare sauce once chicken or spring chicken are finished cooking. To make sauce, fry 1 1/2 tbsp of flour in the same amount of butter, dilute with 1 1/2 - 2 cups of broth obtained when boiling bird. Mix and boil for 5-10 minutes. If the spring chicken is small, use less flour and butter. Strain sauce; add a teaspoon of lemon juice (or lemon acid), salt, small piece of butter. Mix thoroughly until uniform consistency is achieved. Sauce will taste even better if 1/2 cup of white grape wine is added during boiling.

When serving, chop chicken or spring chicken into pieces, put on a heated plate and pour over with prepared sauce. Green beans with butter, boiled rice or boiled potatoes can serve as garnish.

Boiled and sliced cepes (porcini) or

champignons can be added to the sauce as well.

Chicken with White Sauce

Ingredients:
1 chicken
2 tbsp flour
2 tbsp butter

Chop boiled chicken into pieces, put on a plate and pour over with white sauce. Serve boiled rice with butter as garnish.

This dish is prepared in those cases when chicken broth is prepared, which is used as first course; part of the broth is used for sauce. Lemon acid is not added to this broth, and it needs to be thick.

Boiled Chicken with Cornelian Cherry Gravy

Ingredients:

1/2 chicken, 500-600 g
100g fresh cornelian cherry
50g raisins
1 tbsp sugar

Boil prepared and washed chicken, strain broth, cut chicken into serving portions.

Wash raisins and pitted cornelian cherries, put them in a pot and pour over hot strained broth so that it cover the berries, add sugar, cover and cook for 5-10 minutes.

When serving, put chicken in the middle of the bowl and pour over cornelian cherry gravy.

Fried Spring Chicken

Ingredients:
1 Spring Chicken
2 tbsp butter

Prepare spring chicken carcasses, salt and fry on all sides in heated frying pan or shallow pot with butter. After frying, place spring chickens in oven.

If oven is not available, add 1-2 tbsp of water to the frying pan, cover and fry on low heat for another 20-30 minutes.

Ready spring chickens are chopped into pieces and placed on a plate. Pour over with the juice that was obtained when frying and decorate with parsley and lettuce. Salad can be served separately - greens or vegetable/fruit, potato salad or celery.

Young chicken can be prepared in the same manner.

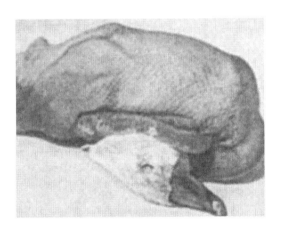

Fried Breaded Spring Chicken

Ingredients:
1 averaged-sized spring chicken
5 tbsp cooking fat (enough to have the bird submerged in it, but no more than indicated)
1.2 cup breadcrumbs
2 tbsp flour

1 egg

Put prepared spring chickens in salted boiling water and cook until ready. Remove, drain water, chop into 2-4 pieces, salt, coat with flour, moisten with egg, and coat with breadcrumbs.

Fry until caramelized crust forms, submerging into cooking fat for 8-10 minutes.

Remove fried spring chickens from fat, put on a plate with paper napkin and decorate with parley.

Separately you may serve green salad, cucumbers, red cabbage or salad made from fresh or frozen vegetables and fruit.

Spring Chicken on Skewer

Take prepared, gutted, averaged-sized spring chicken. Wash, sprinkle with salt, pepper, put on a metal skewer (from leg to wing), fry over hot coals (no flames) for 20-30 minutes. During frying, keep smearing the bird with butter and rotating the skewer, so that the spring chicken is fried uniformly on all sides.

When serving, remove from skewer, put on a heated plate, garnish with lettuce, fresh cucumbers or dills and fresh or canned tomatoes.

You can serve "Tkemali" sauce separately (see next recipe).

Quail, partridge and other small game birds can also be prepared in the same manner. Cut game birds along the chest, without cutting the back.

"Tkemali" Sauce (Plum Sauce)

Wash sour dried plums and boil in water. Strain the broth and rub pitted plums through a sieve. Mix with broth until consistency is similar to fluid sour-cream, add crushed garlic, salt, ground pepper, finely chopped fennel, boil and cool.

"Tkemali" sauce can be served with spring chicken on skewer, shish kebab, filet, etc.

Fried Breaded Chicken

Ingredients:
1 chicken
1/2 cup breadcrumbs
2 tbsp flour
1 egg
4-5 tbsp butter

Boil chicken and chop into pieces. Salt each piece, coat in flower, moisten with whipped egg, coat in breadcrumbs. Fry with butter for 8-10 minutes. When caramelized crust forms evenly on the surface, put on a plate, pour over with butter and decorate with parsley. Separately serve green salad, cucumbers or vegetable salad with slices of lemon.

Chicken Chahohbili

Ingredients:
1 chicken or 500 g lamb
2 onions
2 tbsp tomato puree
1 tbsp vinegar
2 tbsp wine (port, Madeira)
2-3 tbsp butter

Wash and chop prepared chicken into small pieces and fry them in shallow pot with heated butter. After that add finely chopped onion, tomato puree, add vinegar, wine, 1/2 cup meat broth, salt, pepper; close lid and braise 1 1/2 hours on low heat. Before finishing cooking, add sliced tomatoes.

When serving, put a slice of lemon on each piece of chicken and sprinkle with greens.

Similarly you can make chahohbili with lamb, which is chopped into 3-4 pieces per serving.

Fried Turkey

Sprinkle prepared turkey with salt on all sides, put on a frying pan with back facing up, pour over with melted butter, add 1/2 cup water and place into an oven that is not too hot. During frying, keep pouring the juice that is dripping from turkey with spoon over the bird and keep rotating it, so that it is evenly cooked on all sides (frying time for turkey is 1 to 2 1/2 hours, depending on size).

When finished frying, take turkey out, drain fat, add a cup of meat broth or water, boil and strain.

In case turkey is not prepared whole, but in halves, before and after preparation it is fried on a frying pan.

When serving, chop into halves, and then chop each half into 4-8 pieces. Place on heated plate, pour over with juice and decorate with parsley and lettuce. Baked apples or fried potatoes can serve as garnish. Separately serve green salad, cucumbers, marinated fruit and berries.

Chicken is prepared the same way. Frying for chicken lasts 1 - 1 1/2 hours, depending on size.

Fried Goose or Duck with Apples

Ingredients:
1 goose or 1 duck
1- 1 1/2 kg apples (if cooking goose)

750 g apples (if cooking duck)
2 tbsp butter

Stuff prepared goose with apples that have had their core removed and sliced. Sew the belly with thread. Place the goose on frying pan, add 1/2 cup water and put in the oven. Pour the goose over with fat and juice that has been forming several times. Cook for 1 1/2 - 2 hours.

Once goose is ready, remove the thread, take out the apples with spoon, place them on a plate. Chop goose into pieces and place on top on apples.

Duck with apples is made the same way. Goose and duck not stuffed with apples can also be prepared in same fashion. Baked apples, braised cabbage, buckwheat or potatoes can be served as garnish.

Ragout from Giblets

Ingredients:
500 g giblets
600 g potatoes
2 carrots
1 parsnip
1 onion
1/2 cup tomato puree
1 tbsp flour
2 tbsp butter

Salt well-cleaned and washed poultry

giblets and lightly fry them on a frying pan. Sprinkle with flour and fry for another few minutes. Put fried giblets into a shallow pot, pour over 2 cups of broth or water, add tomato puree, cover with lid and braise on low heat.

1/2 hour after braising starts add cleaned, sliced and fried potatoes and vegetables (carrot, parsnip, onion), pepper and bay leaf. Carefully mix and continue braising for another 1/2 hour.

"Pozharskie" Croquettes

Ingredients:
1 chicken, approximately 1 kg
100g white bread
1/2 cup milk
2 tbsp breadcrumbs
4-5 tbsp butter

Singe, gut and wash chicken. Remove meat together with skin from bones and pass it through a meat grinder. Add white bread soaked in milk, pass through a meat grinder one more time, add some heated butter, salt and mix. Divide this force meat into croquettes and coat them in breadcrumbs. Fry croquettes in butter on both sides in a frying pan for 4-5 minutes, until caramelized crust forms. Then put frying pan with croquettes in oven for 5 minutes or cover with lid and leave on low heat for some time.

When serving, place croquettes on a plate

and pour over with melted butter. Different
vegetables can be served as garnish: sweat peas,
beans, cauliflower - boiled and buttered, and also
fried potatoes.

Remaining bones and giblets can be used to
make broth.

Fried Hazel Grouse, Partridge, Black Grouse

Ingredients:
1 hazel grouse, partridge, black grouse
1-2 tbsp butter

Take prepared hazel grouse, partridge, or
black grouse. Salt it, and put it in a pot with
melted butter. Fry until caramelized crust forms
on all sides evenly. Turn the bird on its back and
place into oven for 15-25 minutes (35-45 minutes
for black grouse). During frying, keep pouring
butter over the bird using a spoon. When finished,
remove from oven and chop in halves lengthwise.
Black grouse is chopped into 4-6 pieces. For
garnish, serve fried potatoes, or assorted
vegetables, lettuce, red cabbage, marinated fruit
and berries.

Fried Woodcock, Snipe, Garganey, Quail

Salt prepared game, put in shallow pot or
frying pan with heated butter. Fry until
caramelized crust forms on all sides evenly. After
that, place pot in the oven or cover with lid and

keep frying on low heat, pouring the bird over with butter in which it is frying. Frying time for woodcock, snipe and garganey is 20-25 minutes. Quail is fried for 10-15 minutes. When game is ready, remove from pot and put and heated plate, on top of sliced bread fried in butter (sliced into squares 1 - 1 1/2 cm thick, with a dent in the middle). Cover game with strips of fried bacon and pour over with strained juice obtained while frying and melted butter. Decorate with parsley. Separately serve green salad, fruit or celery salad.

Fried Rabbit

Wash rabbit; chop it into pieces, salt. Put pieces in shallow pot or skillet; add 2-3 tbsp butter. Fry a little on all sides. Put pot in oven and fry until fully ready, pouring rabbit over with juice every 10-15 minutes and turning it from side to side. Fry for 30-40 minutes. When rabbit is ready, chop it into serving sized pieces, put on a plate. Add several spoons of broth or water to the pot and boil. Strain this juice and pour over rabbit. For garnish, serve fried potatoes, mashed potatoes, boiled rice or buckwheat.

Rabbit in White Sauce

Ingredients:
1 rabbit
1 carrot
1 parsnip
1 onion

Wash rabbit, chop into pieces, put in a pot, pour over with hot water just so it covers rabbit. When water boils, remove foam, add salt and washed carrot, parsnip, onion. Also add 5-8 peppercorns and 1-2 bay leaves. Cook 40-60 minutes on low heat. Remove finished rabbit from pot, chop into serving pieces, put on a plate and pour over with white sauce that was prepared using the broth obtained from boiling rabbit.

Serve boiled potatoes, mashed potatoes or rice with butter as garnish.

Hare Braised in Sour Cream

Ingredients:

1 hare, about 3 kg

2 carrots

2 parsnips

2 onions

1 cup vinegar

2 cup sour cream

2 tbsp flour

3 tbsp butter

Chop hare into parts (kidney, leg, shoulder blade), cut off membranes, wash, put in a pot, pour over cold water with vinegar (cup vinegar per 1 l of water) and leave for 2-3 hours to marinade. After this, remove pieces of rabbit from marinade, put in a frying pan, salt, add chopped root vegetables and onions, pour over with butter and put into hot oven until caramelized crust forms. During frying, periodically pour over with forming juice using spoon. When done, chop hare into serving pieces, put in a shallow pot, pour over with sauce made from sour cream and juice, cover with lid and put into oven for 25-30 minutes for braising.

Another method is also used. Parts of rabbit are chopped into serving pieces, held in marinade for 1 - 1 1/2 hours, then fried on skillet with butter, and then placed in a pot.

To make sauce, take sour cream and juice from frying hare, pour into pot, salt, bring to boil. Once it boils, add 2 tbsp of flour that has previously been fried with butter and diluted with

1 cup of water or broth. Constantly stir while cooking for 3-4 minutes. Strain into dish with hare. When serving, put hare on a plate together with sauce and sprinkle with chopped parsley or dill. Serve boiled or fried potatoes as garnish.

Hare becomes especially delicious if it is stuffed with bacon before frying. To do this, chop bacon into pieces of 4-5 cm long and 0.5 cm thick. In hare's flesh, make punctures with a wooden peg and place bacon pieces into these punctures.

VEGETABLES AND MUSHROOMS

VEGETABLES AND MUSHROOMS

Vegetables contain necessary nutrients for the human body: carbohydrates, proteins, mineral salts and vitamins. While vegetables don't contain as much protein as animal products, and mostly don't contain any fat, they are very rich in mineral salts and vitamins.

Acids, attars and oils in vegetables also have a very pleasant taste, enlivening food.

Some vegetables, such as lettuce, radish, tomatoes, and cucumbers are eaten raw, but most vegetables are cooked - boiled, steamed, braised, fried or baked. There are great numbers of delicious and nutritious dishes that can be prepared from vegetables.

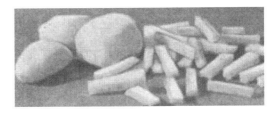

Vegetables have to be thoroughly washed first and then peeled. Potatoes, carrots, beets and other root vegetables are peeled with sharp knife, which removes only the top layer. It is recommended to use a special grooved knife to peel vegetables.

Vegetables should be peeled immediately

prior to cooking, since peeled vegetables quickly lose their aroma and wither; peeled potato not submerged in cold water quickly turns dark.

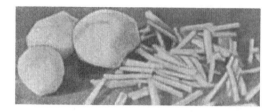

After peeling, wash vegetables again in cold water, and then cut into different shapes (tourne, dice, brunoise, rondelle, paysanne, batonnet, julienne, etc.)

Vegetables, especially boiled or steamed should be served with some kind of sauce. Sauces make vegetables taste better.

BOILED VEGETABLES

Vegetables can be boiled or steamed. For boiling, use jus enough water to cover the vegetables. Size of the container should be appropriate for amount of vegetables cooked.

For steaming, a pot with removable mesh/grid is recommended. If it is not available, use a regular pot and put a strainer inside. When steaming, pour some water into the pot, from which steam will form when heated. Steaming vs. boiling has its own pluses and minuses. Steaming removes less minerals from vegetables compared to boiling, and steamed vegetables are closer to fresh vegetables in terms of aroma and taste than boiled vegetables. However, steaming takes longer than boiling and steaming also destroys more vitamins than boiling.

Boiled Potatoes

Peel, wash potatoes, pour over with hot water and bring to boil. Once it boils, add salt and cook for another 20 minutes, until potatoes become soft.

At the same time, ensure that potatoes don't get over boiled. As soon as it is ready, pour water out, cover with lid and leave on low heat for 5-10 minutes for drying. Put prepared potatoes on a heated plate.

Butter is served separately.

Boiled Potatoes with Butter and Greens

Boil potatoes the same way as in "Boiled Potatoes" recipe. After drying, put butter and parsley or dill into the pot with potatoes. Mix by shaking and put on a plate.

Young Potatoes with Sour Cream

Ingredients:
1 kg potatoes
1/2 cup sour cream
1 tbsp butter

Boil peeled young potatoes in salted water,

drain, add sour cream, butter and mix by shaking. Sprinkle with dill or parsley.

Steamed Potatoes

Pour 3-4 cups of water into a pot with removable mesh/grid. Put in peeled potatoes - whole or chopped into 2-4 pieces, salt, close lid tightly and bring to boil. As soon as water boils, reduce heat and continue cooking on low heat for about 25-30 minutes. Steamed potatoes are especially good for making mashed potatoes and croquettes.

Potatoes in Milk

Ingredients:
1 kg potatoes
2 cup milk
2 tbsp butter

Peel and wash potatoes, dice it, boil in water for 10 minutes, drain. Pour over with hot milk and boil for another 20-30 minutes. Make sure potatoes don't burn, use low heat for cooking.

Put in butter, shake and sprinkle with parsley and dill.

Mashed Potatoes

Ingredients:
1 kg potatoes
1 cup milk
2 tbsp butter

Peel and wash potatoes, drain. Leave pot with potatoes on low heat or in oven for some time, so that the remainder of water also evaporates. After this, not allowing potatoes to cool, rub it through a sieve or crush with mallet. Add butter, salt, and while stirring, gradually pour hot milk. Mashed potatoes are served as a separate dish or as garnish for beef, tongue, croquettes, hot dogs and other meat dishes.

Vegetables in Milk Sauce

Different vegetables can be prepared in

milk sauce: potatoes, carrots, sweet peas, green beans, asparagus, etc. Vegetable dish with milk sauce can consist of one or several kinds of vegetables.

Vegetables have to be peeled, washed, sliced or diced, boiled in salted water and drained. Then put vegetables into a pot, pour over with hot milk sauce and mix. Thickness of milk sauce for vegetables should resemble sour cream. To prepare it, take one tablespoon of wheat flour, 25 g butter per 1 kg of vegetables. Fry flour with butter, dilute with 1 1/4 cups hot milk, add salt and cook for 10-15 minutes.

Cauliflower

Remove outer leaves and thick stalk from head of cauliflower. Put cleaned cauliflower into salted cold water for 30 minutes, then drain and rinse it, put into a pot and cover with boiling water, season with salt, cover the pot and cook. Depending on the size of the cauliflower it should be cooked anywhere from 20 to 30 minutes.

To check if cauliflower is cooked test it with a tip of a sharp knife - if it goes easy into the stem then cauliflower then it is cooked. Remove cauliflower from the pot and drain in a strainer.

Put cauliflower onto a serving plate stem side down. Decorate with parsley sprigs. Serve meted butter or sauce (breadcrumb, egg-and-butter, or egg-and-wine) on a side in a sauce boat.

Braised Carrots

Ingredients:
1 kg carrots
1/2 tbsp sugar
2 tbsp butter

Slice peeled and washed carrots, put into a pot, add a little bit of water - to cover vegetables halfway, season with salt, add sugar and 1/2 tbsp of butter, cover the pot and cook carrots for 20-30 minutes. Season carrots with remaining butter and move to a serving plate, sprinkle with finely chopped parsley leaves and top with white bread toasts.

This method of cooking can be used to cook kohlrabi, rutabaga, or turnip. Scald turnip with boiling water prior to cooking.

Carrots with Milk Sauce

Ingredients:
500 g carrots

1/2 tbsp flour
2/3 cups milk
1 tsp sugar
1 tbsp butter

Slice peeled and washed carrots and put into a pot, add a little of stock or water, add 1/2 tbsp of butter, season with salt and sugar, cover and braise 20-30 minutes. Mix cooked carrots with hot milk sauce and stir accurately. If desired use turnips, green peas, string beans, or asparagus instead of carrots in this recipe. Turnips should be sliced and scalded with hot water before braising. Cut string beans on a bias, while asparagus should be cut into battonets before cooking.

Green Peas in Butter

Ingredients:
500 g green peas
1 tsp sugar
2 tbsp butter

Shuck green peas from pods and cook in salted boiling water. Cook on high heat for 10-15 minutes. Strain cooked peas, put into a pot together with butter and sugar and shake until well mixed. Pile peas in a middle of a warmed serving bowl and serve.

If using canned peas for this recipe - warm peas in a pot together with liquid from the can, then strain and mix with butter.

Frozen peas should be cooked in boiling water for 5-7 minutes, then strained and mixed with butter.

This dish could be served with soft-boiled eggs and toasts. Cook and peel eggs and put them on top of seasoned peas. Make toasts from slices of white bread cut into triangles. Soak bread in milk mixed with eggs and sugar and fry in butter.

Green Beans or Snow Peas in Butter

Remove string from pods of snow peas and cook in boiling salted water. To preserve bright green color of the peas cook in a large, wide pot, maintaining rapid boil. Drain cooked peas in a strainer, add to a pot with butter, and, if desired, some sugar and warm through.

Clean green beans by removing both ends and the string. Cut beans lengthwise or crosswise on a bias. Cook just like snow peas and season with butter, salt, and pepper.

Boiled Pumpkin

Peel pumpkin and remove the seeds, cut into pieces and put into a pot. Add salted boiling water, cover the pot and cook pumpkin 15-20 minutes. Serve with butter, sour cream, or breadcrumb sauce.

Boiled Corn on the Cob

Use only young (so-called milk) corn to cook on the cob. Shuck the corn, remove the silk, and boil in salted water. Put cooked corn onto a serving plate. Serve butter on the side.   Corn on the cob can also be cooked without removing outer leaves. Remove them from the cobs before serving.

Canned Corn with Butter

Ingredients:
1 can corn
2 tbsp butter

Put canned corn into a pot together with

liquid from the can and bring to boil. Drain corn before serving, put into a warmed salad plate or deep bowl and top with butter.

Canned Corn in Tomato Sauce

Ingredients:
1 can corn
1 onion
2 tbsp tomato paste
1 tsp sugar
2 tbsp butter

Drain corn in a strainer, then add to a skillet together with diced and lightly browned onions, tomato paste, salt, and sugar. Mix everything well and sauté for 5 minutes.

Just before serving pile corn on a plate and sprinkle with finely chopped scallions, parsley leaves, or dill.

Canned Corn with Apples and Toasts

Ingredients:
1 can corn
1 onion
2 tbsp tomato paste
2 apples
1 tsp sugar
10-12 white bread toasts
2 tbsp butter

Drain corn in a strainer and add to a skillet together with diced and lightly browned onion, tomato paste, salt, and sugar. Mix well and sauté for 5 minutes. Wash, core, and slice apples, and bake them in the oven. Make toasts with white bread.

To serve - pile corn in a middle of a serving plate. Surround corn with slices of apples alternating them with toasts. Decorate with sprigs of parsley.

Spinach with Toasts

Ingredients:
1 kg spinach
1 tbsp flour
1 1/4 cups milk (for sauce)
1-2 tbsp butter

Pick over leaves of spinach and wash in cold water, put into a pot, add a little water, cover the pot and cook over high heat.

Rub cooked spinach through a sieve. Cook milk sauce (1 tbsp flour, 1 tbsp butter, milk), mix with spinach, season with salt, pepper, and nutmeg, and warm through.

Make toasts - soak slices of white bread in milk mixed with egg and sugar. Fry in butter until browned.

To serve - put spinach in the middle of a serving plate or deep bowl and surround with toasts. If desired - top spinach with peeled soft-boiled eggs.

Brussels Sprouts with Celery in Milk Sauce

Ingredients:
500 g Brussels sprouts
25 g celery
1 tbsp flour
1/2 cup milk
2 tbsp butter

Cook washed Brussels sprouts in boiling salted water for 10 minutes. In a separate pot make sauce -- melt butter and add finely sliced celery stalk. Sauté for 2-3 minutes then add flour and saute a little bit longer. Little by little add hot milk and 1/2 cup of cooking liquid continuously mixing. Simmer sauce for couple of minutes, then add Brussels sprouts and season with salt.

If desired -- top Brussels sprouts with breadcrumbs, sprinkle with melted butter and brown in the preheated oven.

Boiled Artichokes

Only artichoke hearts and leaf bases are edible, leaf tips are not. Artichokes need to be prepared as follows: cut off the stems just underneath the base and cut off hard parts of leaves. Rub the bottom of the artichoke heart with lemon, to prevent the part where the stem has been cut off from turning dark. Remove the core of the artichoke with a handle of a tablespoon. Wash prepared artichokes, put in a pot in on row, pour over with enough hot water just to cover the artichokes, salt and boil for 10-15 minutes with lid closed. Readiness of artichokes can be tested with a knife blade tip: if the knife easily passes through the artichoke, it is ready. Put ready artichokes into a sieve with bottoms facing up, drain, and then put artichokes on a plate with an envelope-folded napkin.

Put artichokes in one row, decorating with greens

Egg sauce with wine or egg-butter sauce should be served with artichokes.

Boiled Asparagus

Pick asparagus that is straight, if possible. Peel it with sharp knife, while trying not to break the head, which is the tastiest part of asparagus. Wash asparagus, tie into a bundle (8-10), cut evenly and boil in salted water on high heat for 20-25 minutes (ed. note - This time seems a bit excessive, 5 minutes should be enough). Asparagus is only good when it's not overcooked; otherwise it loses its aroma and becomes watery. Once the heads become soft, asparagus is ready. Drain it and put on a plate that's covered with a napkin. Untie the bundle of asparagus, cover it with napkin's edges and serve. Separately serve egg sauce with wine, or egg-butter sauce or breadcrumb sauce.

FRIED VEGETABLES

Vegetables can be fried two ways: on a regular skillet with small amount of fat or in a deep pan, submerging vegetables into heated fat.

In order for crust to quickly form during frying, vegetables should be well-dried on a napkin. This applies especially to potatoes.

Fried Potatoes

Potatoes can be fried raw or previously boiled. Raw fried potatoes are juicier and tastier, although they require somewhat longer preparation time than previously boiled potatoes.

Cut boiled potatoes into slices, put on a heated skillet with butter, add salt. Fry on high heat while stirring for 5-10 minutes. Sprinkle potatoes with parsley or dill when potatoes are ready.

Raw potatoes are fried the same way as boiled potatoes, but they can also be deep-fried. In this case, they are cut into slices, buttonets or julienned. After that wash and dry potatoes on a napkin. Fry them, submerging into hot cooking fat, while stirring for 10-12 minutes, until caramelized crust forms. Remove potatoes, drain them and salt.

Potatoes fried in butter can be served for breakfast or dinner with cucumbers, tomatoes or use as garnish for fried meat, croquettes, or fried fish.

Fried Potatoes with Eggs

Ingredients:
1 kg potatoes
3 eggs
1 cup milk
2 tbsp butter

Peeled and boiled potatoes are sliced and fried in butter. Break eggs into the pot, add milk, salt and stir well. Pour potatoes over with eggs and bake.

Potato Croquettes

Ingredients:
1 kg potatoes
2 eggs
1/2 cup flour
4 tbsp butter

Boil and drain peeled potatoes. Let stand for 10 minutes to dry. Mash boiled potatoes while still hot.

Add 1 tbsp of butter and egg yolks to mashed potatoes, mix well and form croquettes. Coat croquettes in flour or breadcrumbs and fry in butter on all sides. Serve with mushroom sauce on the side.

Potato Pirozhki with Mushrooms

Ingredients:
1 kg potatoes
100 g dried mushrooms
2 onions
2 eggs
1/2 cup breadcrumbs
4 tbsp butter

Cook potatoes just like in recipe "Potato Croquettes". Prepare stuffing. Wash and cook dried mushrooms, drain and preserve the cooking liquid. Finely chop cooked mushrooms and fry in butter. Add diced, browned onions, season with salt and pepper, and mix well. Form mashed potatoes into patties, put mushroom stuffing in the middle of a patty, fold the sides together into a half-moon shape and pinch them shut. Dip pirozhki into beaten eggs, coat with breadcrumbs and fry in butter on all sides. Serve with mushroom sauce. Make sauce using mushroom broth, adding sour cream or tomato paste to it. These pirozhki can be made with vegetable stuffing.

Potato Pancakes

Ingredients:
500 g potatoes
1/2 cup flour
25 g fresh yeast
2 tbsp butter

Quickly (to prevent discoloration) grate

peeled potatoes into a pot or a mixing bowl. Add yeast dissolved in 1/4 cup of warm water, season with salt, add flour (add 1 egg if desired). Mix everything well and put into a warm place to rise. Cook pancakes in butter on a hot skillet. Serve hot with sour cream or butter.

Fried Cauliflower with Breadcrumbs

Cook cauliflower in water, when cooked - separate into florets and fry in butter on a hot skillet. Just before serving sprinkle with fried in butter breadcrumbs and shake well to distribute.

Cabbage Croquettes

Ingredients:
1 kg white cabbage
1/2 cup farina
1/2 cup milk
3 eggs, separated
1/2 cup breadcrumbs
3 tbsp butter

Wash cabbage, remove core and outer leaves, and finely shred it. Put shredded cabbage into a pot, add hot milk, cover the pot and braise until cooked, approximately 30-40 minutes. Gradually add farina constantly mixing to avoid lumps and continue to cook for 5-10 minutes. Remove pot from the heat, add egg yolks, season with salt and mix well. Let the mixture cool. Form croquettes from cooled cabbage, dip in egg whites, coat with breadcrumbs, and fry on all sides. Serve with milk or sour cream sauce.

Carrot Croquettes

Ingredients:
1 kg carrots
1/2 cup farina
1/2 cup milk
3 eggs, separated
1/2 cup breadcrumbs
1 tsp sugar
3 tbsp butter

Slice or julienne washed and peeled carrots, add to a pot with hot milk, sugar, and 1 tbsp of butter. Cover the pot and braise carrots on medium heat until cooked, stirring from time to time to prevent burning. Add farina to cooked carrots and continue cooking on low heat for 8-10 minutes stirring frequently. Remove pot from the heat, add egg yolks and mix well to incorporate and let the mixture cool. Form croquettes from cooled carrots, dip into egg whites, coat with breadcrumbs, and fry in butter on a heated skillet. Serve with sour cream sauce or milk sauce.

Vegetable Croquettes

Ingredients:
1 kg vegetables:

(200 g carrots
200 g rutabaga
300 g pumpkin or squash
300 g cabbage)
1 1/2 cups milk
1/2 cup farina
3 eggs, separated
1/2 cup breadcrumbs
1 tsp sugar
3 tbsp butter

Julienne peeled and washed carrots and rutabaga, put into a pot, add hot milk, 1 tbsp of butter, sugar, and salt, cover the pot braise. After 15 minutes of cooking, add finely shredded cabbage and peeled and sliced pumpkin. Continue braising until cooked through for 15 -20 minutes. When vegetables are cooked add farina to the pot and cook for 8-10 minutes mixing all the time to prevent lumps. Remove pot from the heat, add egg yolks, season with salt, mix well and let the mixture cool. To finish cooking - follow the steps from the recipe "Carrot Croquettes".

Cabbage Schnitzel

Ingredients:
1 kg cabbage
1/2 cup flour
2 eggs
1/2 cup breadcrumbs
3 tbsp butter

Remove outer leaves and core of the cabbage and cook it in salted water until cooked through. Put cabbage into a strainer and let all the water drain, then separate into separate leaves, and either flatten thick ribs with a mallet or cut them off with a knife. Fold each leaf in a shape of an envelope, coat with flour, dip in beaten eggs, coat with breadcrumbs, and fry in butter on all sides. To serve - put cabbage on a serving plate. Serve sour cream or sour cream sauce on a side.

Fried Tomatoes

Select ripe whole tomatoes, what them in cold water, and cut across into halves. Season each half with salt and pepper. Fry in butter with cut side up. When outside is cooked through - flip the tomatoes over and slightly fry on the cut side.

Fried Zucchini

Select medium zucchini with small seeds for frying. Peel zucchini and slice into slices 1 cm thick, season with salt, coat with flour and fry in butter on both sides until nicely browned.

If fried zucchini are still not cooked through, cover the skillet and cook on low heat for 5-10 minutes.

If desired - add sour cream to zucchini in the skillet and bring to simmer, or just serve sour cream on a side.

Fried Pumpkin

Slice peeled and cleaned pumpkin into slices, season with salt, coat with flour and fry in butter until cooked through. Serve with sour cream or butter.

Pumpkin in Milk Sauce (Pumpkin Gratin)

Ingredients:
1 kg pumpkin
1 cup milk
1 tbsp flour
2 tsp breadcrumbs
2 tbsp butter

Fry slices of pumpkin until cooked through. Add milk sauce to the skillet, top with breadcrumbs, sprinkle with butter and brown in the preheated oven.

Eggplants Fried with Onions

Ingredients:
2 eggplants
2 onions
3 tbsp flour
1/2 cup sour cream
1 tbsp tomato paste
3 tbsp butter

Wash eggplants, cut the stem off, scald with boiling water, and slice into thin slices. Season eggplant slices with salt, coat with flour and fry in butter on both sides. Peel and slice onions and also fry in butter. Put cooked eggplant slices on a plate alternating them with slices of onions. Add sour cream and tomato paste to the skillet that was used to cook eggplants, mix everything well and bring to simmer, and then pour the sauce over eggplants.

Fried Onions

Slice onions into thin slices, separate those slices into rings and fry in butter, mixing frequently, until onions become brown. Drain cooked onions in a strainer and season with salt. Fried onions are usually served as a garnish to fried meat.

BAKED VEGETABLES

Potato Casserole

Ingredients:
1 kg potatoes
2 eggs
3 onions
1 cup milk
3 tbsp butter

Add hot milk, eggs, melted butter, and salt, into hot boiled and grated potatoes and mix well. Put half of the mix onto a buttered ovenproof skillet, smooth the top, put a layer of caramelized onions on top and cover with remaining potato mix. Smooth the top again, top with sour cream or sprinkle with melted butter and put into preheated oven for 20-25 minutes. Serve with milk, sour cream, or mushroom sauce on a side.

Potato Casserole with Meat

Cook potato puree just like in the recipe "Potato Casserole". Put half of the potato puree into a buttered and sprinkled with breadcrumbs ovenproof skillet. Put stuffing on top of the puree and cover meat with the remaining puree, brush with egg wash and bake in preheated oven for 20-30 minutes. Stuffing can be made from beef, veal, pork, or poultry, or with sub-products like liver, lungs, or heart. Pass boiled or roasted meat through a meat grinder, or chop finely, add browned onions, season with salt and pepper, and mix well. Use broth or juice from cooking of the meat to make red sauce which could be poured over the casserole or served on a side.

Potato Roll with Vegetables

Prepare potatoes just like in the recipe "Potato Casserole". Julienne vegetables for stuffing and sauté until cooked. Remove vegetables from the heat, add raw eggs, season with salt, and mix well. Spread potato puree on a dump kitchen towel into an approximately 2 cm thick layer. Put prepared vegetables in the middle of potatoes. With the help of the towel form potato layer into a roll, put the roll onto a buttered baking sheet with its seam down. Brush the top of the roll with eggs or sour cream, top with bread crumbs and sprinkle with melted butter. Bake in the preheated oven for 25-30 minutes until it is nicely browned.

Slice cooked roll into servings, set on a serving plate and pour melted butter over it. If desired - serve with sour cream or milk sauce.

This roll could be stuffed with meat and onions or eggs, or rice with mushrooms and onions.

Cauliflower with Milk Sauce (Cauliflower Gratin)

Ingredients:
1 head of cauliflower
1 cup milk
1 tbsp flour
1 tbsp grated cheese
1-2 tbsp butter

Cook prepared cauliflower in water until cooked, approximately 20-30 minutes, then put into a strainer and let drain. Put cauliflower with its stalk down onto an ovenproof skillet, pour milk sauce over it, sprinkle with grated cheese and melted butter, and put into a preheated oven for 10-15 minutes.

White Cabbage with Milk Sauce (Cabbage Gratin)

Ingredients:
1 kg white cabbage
1 cup milk

1 tbsp flour
1 tbsp grated cheese
3 tbsp butter

Separate head of cabbage into individual leaves and cook them in salted water for 30 minutes. Drain cooked cabbage, squeeze each leaf to extract more water, and then fold it into a shape of an envelope. Fry prepared cabbage in butter, pour milk sauce over it, top with grated cheese and sprinkle with melted butter, bake in the preheated oven for 10-15 minutes until nicely browned.

Spinach Baked with Egg

Ingredients:
500 g fresh spinach
1/3 cup milk
3-4 eggs
2 tbsp butter

Wash and cut spinach, boil it in salted water, then drain. Put spinach on a skillet with heated butter, fry it a little, pour over with eggs whipped with milk, and bake in oven. When serving, sprinkle with parsley or dill.

BRAISED VEGETABLES

Braised Potatoes with Fresh Mushrooms

Ingredients:
750 g potatoes
500 g fresh mushrooms
1-2 onions
1/3 cup sour cream
3 tbsp butter

Peel, wash fresh mushrooms, scald, slice and fry on a skillet together with sliced onions. Slice peeled potatoes, fry and put in a pot together with fried onions. Cover with water all the way to top layer, add salt, bay leaf, pepper, 1-2 parsley branches, cover with lid and braise for 25-30 minutes. 1 - 2 tbsp of sour cream may be added to potatoes. When serving, remove parsley and bay leaf, sprinkle potatoes with chopped greens.

Potatoes can be prepared with dried mushrooms also. In this case mushrooms are boiled, sliced and then fried with onions. Use part of the broth to braise potatoes, the rest for soup.

Braised Potatoes with Smoked Brisket

Ingredients:
500 g potatoes
100 g smoked brisket
1 onion
1 tbsp tomato puree
1 tbsp butter

Dice or slice peeled potatoes. Fry chopped onions in butter. Cut smoked brisket into small slices. Put all these products in a pot, pour over with water so that everything is covered, add tomato puree, salt, pepper, bay leaf, cover with lid and braise for 40-50 minutes.

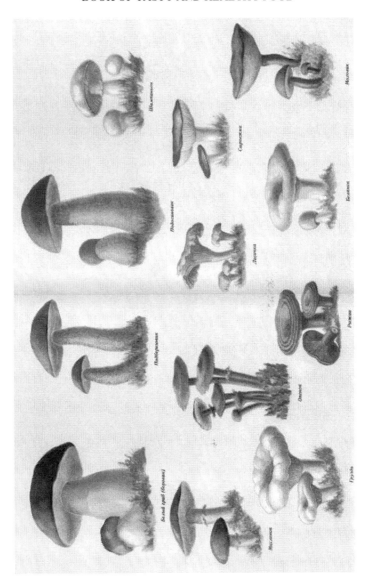

Braised Cabbage

Ingredients:
1 kg cabbage
2 onions
2 tbsp tomato puree
1 tbsp distilled vinegar
1 tbsp sugar
1 tbsp flour
3 tbsp butter

Remove outer leaves and core of the cabbage and finely shred it, put into a pot, add one tablespoon of butter, 1/2 cup water or meat broth, cover with lid and braise for 40 minutes. Then add fried onions, tomato puree, vinegar, sugar, salt, bay leaf, pepper and continue braising until ready, approximately 10 minutes. When cabbage is cooked, add flour that has been fried with butter, mix and bring to simmer.

Fresh cabbage can be replaced with sauerkraut, but in this case don't add any vinegar.

Braised Beets in Sour Cream

Ingredients:
500 g beets
1 carrot
1 parsnip or 1 celery
1 tsp vinegar
1 tsp sugar
1 cup sour cream
1 tbsp flour
2 tbsp butter

Peel and wash beets, carrot, parsnip or celery, julienne them, put in a pot, add butter, vinegar and some water, mix and braise with close lid until ready, making sure vegetables don't burn. When vegetables are ready (usually 45-60 minutes), add flour, mix well, add sour cream, salt, sugar, bay leaf, mix again and cook for another 10 minutes.

Braised Carrots

Ingredients:
1 kg carrots
2 tsp flour
2 tbsp butter

Peel carrots and slice them. Put carrots in a pot, cover half-way with water, salt, add 1 tablespoon of butter, cover with lid and braise for 20-30 minutes. Add flower, sour cream with the rest of the butter, and braise for another 5-10 minutes.

Braised Carrots with Rice

Ingredients:
1 kg carrots
1 1/3 - 2 tbsp rice
2 tbsp butter

Put sliced carrots in a pot, add washed rice, 1 tbsp butter, pour over with water or milk, cover with lid and braise until ready. When serving, sprinkle with parsley.

Vegetable Ragout

Ingredients:
500 g potatoes

3 carrots

2 turnips

2 onions

2 tomatoes or 2 tbsp tomato puree

3 tbsp butter

1 tbsp flour

2 cups meat stock

Depending on the season different vegetables can be used for this dish - carrots, turnips, rutabaga, green cabbage, cauliflower, green beans, leeks, and potatoes. Dice or slice peeled vegetables, leave small onions whole. Braise carrots, turnips, and rutabaga, boil green beans and cabbage in water. Sauté flour on a skillet, add liquid from braised or boiled vegetables and diced tomatoes or tomato paste, and boil thoroughly. Add sauce to pot with all prepared vegetables, season with salt add pepper, add 3-4 cloves, a piece of cinnamon, cover the pot and braise 15-20 minutes. Sprinkle with finely chopped parsley leaves before serving.

Vegetable Ragout with Beans

Ingredients:

800 g vegetables and potatoes

1 cup dry beans

1 tbsp flour

2 tbsp butter

Cook just like recipe "Vegetable Ragout",

adding cooked beans before final braising.

Braised Kohlrabi

Ingredients:
500 g kohlrabi
1 tbsp flour
1 cup sour cream
2 tbsp tomato paste
2 tbsp butter

Peel and slice kohlrabi, season with salt, coat with flour and slightly fry in butter. Put kohlrabi into a pot, season with salt and add sour cream mixed with tomato paste. Braise on low heat for 40 minutes. Sprinkle with finely chopped dill or parsley leaves before serving.

Eggplants Braised in Sour Cream

Ingredients:
2 eggplants
1 tbsp flour
1 cup sour cream
2 tbsp butter

Wash, peel, and slice eggplants, put into hot salted water for 5 minutes, drain well in colander, coat with flour and brown in skillet. Add eggplant to a pot together with sour cream, cover the pot and braise on low heat for 30-40 minutes. Sprinkle with finely chopped dill or parsley leaves just before serving.

Stuffed Vegetables

Different vegetables can be used for stuffing: squash, eggplant, tomatoes, turnips, peppers, etc. Different stuffing can be used for prepared vegetables: meat, grain, mushroom and vegetable. Stuffed vegetables are placed on a skillet and braised or baked in oven. Ready vegetables can be served poured over with butter, sour cream or sauce (milk, sour-cream or tomato).

Stuffing for Vegetables
(Amount of ingredients corresponds to stuffing approximately 1 kg of vegetables)

Meat stuffing. Wash and cut meat, pass it through a meat grinder. Fry on a skillet with butter, then pass through a meat grinder once more. Add finely chopped fried onions and juice that was obtained while frying the meat, and also salt, pepper, parsley or dill and mix everything well. To prepare meat stuffing, boiled meat may also be used, which also needs to go through a meat grinder. In this case fry onions separately, add a teaspoon of flour, fry again, dilute with 2-3 tablespoons of broth, let it boil, mix with the meat, add salt, pepper, parsley or dill.
For 500 g of meat, use 1 - 2 onions, 3 tbsp butter.
Meat and rice stuffing. Wash and cut meat, pass it through a meat grinder. Mix with boiled

rice and finely chopped fried onions, also adding salt and pepper.

For 500 g of meat, use 1/2 cup rice, 1 onion and 3 tbsp butter.

Rice and mushrooms stuffing. Wash, cook and drain rice. Put peeled and washed fresh mushrooms in boiling water for 5 minutes, then drain. Finely chop them and fry in butter. If dried mushrooms are used instead of fresh ones, they need to be cooked first, then chopped and fried. Mix boiled rice with mushrooms; add fried onions, salt and pepper.

For 1 cup of rice, use 2 onions, 500 g fresh mushrooms (or 50 g dried mushrooms) and 3 tbsp butter.

Mushroom stuffing. Peel and wash mushrooms. Pour over with boiling water, leave for 5 minutes. Put on a sieve and rinse. Chop and fry mushrooms in oil, add tomato puree, boil and mix with finely chopped fried onions, salt and pepper.

For 500 g fresh mushrooms, use 2 onions, 2 tbsp tomato puree and 3 tbsp butter.

Vegetable stuffing. Julienne peeled and washed vegetables and fry in butter. Add sliced tomatoes and fry for another 5 minutes. Add salt, pepper, finely chopped parsley.

For 5 carrots, use 3 onions, 1 parsnip or celery, 2 tomatoes, 3 tbsp butter.

Stuffed Cabbage

Ingredients:
1 head green cabbage
500 g meat
125 g white bread
3/4 cups milk
1 cup sour cream
3 tbsp vegetable oil

Take a medium-sized head of cabbage, remove outer leaves and core and put into salted boiling water. Cook until leaves become pliable and would not break when handled, remove cabbage from the water and drain well. To make stuffing wash meat and pass it through a meat grinder, mix it with bread soaked in milk, and pass the mixture through the meat grinder once more. Season stuffing with salt and add some oil, mix well to incorporate. When cabbage is cool enough to handle - separate leaves, lightly season with salt and put stuffing between them, then push leaves back together into the shape of the whole head of cabbage. Put stuffed cabbage into an oven-proof skillet, drizzle with oil, add stock or water to the skillet, and put it into preheated oven for an hour.

Approximately 15-20 minutes before finish pour sour cream over cabbage. Move cooked cabbage into a serving plate, cut into servings and pour strained sauce from cooking over it.

If desired - replace meat stuffing with stuffing made from rice, mushroom, and onions, in which case add 2-3 eggs to the stuffing.

Stuffed Bell Peppers

Wash green bell peppers, remove top together with stem, and clear all the seeds. Parboil prepared peppers in salted boiling water for 2-3 minutes, and then drain in a strainer. Fill with prepared stuffing (meat, rice, or vegetable), put into a pot in one or two layers, cover with broth, add butter and tomato paste, and braise covered in a preheated oven or on top of the stove for 30-40 minutes. Top with sour cream sauce just before serving.

Peppers can be served hot or cold. If serving cold - use vegetable oil instead of butter in this recipe.

Stuffed Beets

Wash beets, bake until cooked through, then peel and remove insides with a teaspoon. Stuff prepared beets with meat and rice stuffing, put on well oiled ovenproof skillet and bake in a preheated oven 15-20 minutes. Just before serving pour sour cream over stuffed beets, put them back into the oven for couple of minutes, then move beets to a serving plate and pour the sauce from the skillet on top.

Stuffed Zucchini

Use medium-sized zucchini for stuffing.

Cut off the ends and peel zucchini, remove seeds with a spoon. Wash them inside and out, stuff with stuffing (meat, grain, mushroom, or vegetable), and fry in oil on all sides. Put zucchini into a pot, add stock or sour cream, cover and braise 30-40 minutes. When serving put zucchini on a serving plate, cut into servings and pour the sauce obtained from cooking on top.

Vegetable Holubtsi (Cabbage Rolls)

Ingredients:
1 kg green cabbage
3-4 carrots
2-3 onions
1 parsnip
1 rib celery
2 tomatoes
1 cup sour cream
2 tbsp tomato paste
2 tbsp oil

Remove outer leaves and core from a head of green cabbage, put it into a pot with salted boiling water and boil for 10-20 minutes. Put cabbage into a colander and let it drain, then separate into leaves. Soften large cores of leaves with a meat mallet, or cut them off with a knife. Working with one leaf at a time put vegetable stuffing into the middle of the leaf and roll it into an oblong shape. Lightly fry holubtsi in a skillet with oil, put them into a pot, add sour cream, tomato paste, cover the pot and braise on low heat or in the preheated oven for 30-40 minutes. Baste rolls with cooking liquid a couple of times during cooking. Put cooked holubtsi on a serving plate and pour braising liquid on top.

Stuffed Eggplants

Wash and cut off both ends of an eggplant, make a small cut along the fruit and remove its seeds with a teaspoon. Parboil prepared eggplant for 5 minutes in salted water, drain, and stuff with vegetable or mushroom stuffing, put into an oiled ovenproof skillet or baking sheet, cover with sour cream and bake in a preheated oven for about 1 hour.

Turnips Stuffed with Farina

Ingredients:
10 medium turnips
1/4 cup farina
1 cup milk
1 tbsp sugar
25 g cheese
3 tbsp butter

Peel and wash turnips and add them to a pot with hot water. Cook until half-cooked. Scoop out the insides of the turnips and finish cooking it, then mash through a sieve, and mix with farina cooked in milk, sugar, and butter. Stuff turnips with prepared stuffing; put them into a well-oiled skillet, sprinkle with grated cheese, brush with melted butter and bake in the preheated oven for 20-25 minutes.

Turnips can also be stuffed with meat stuffing.

Tomatoes Stuffed with Meat

Ingredients:
8 tomatoes
200 g meat
1/4 cup rice
1 onion
2-3 tbsp oil

Use medium-sized tomatoes in this recipe. Wash tomatoes in cold water, cut off the stem side and remove seeds and flesh, being careful not to break the walls.

Season prepared tomatoes with salt and pepper and fill with stuffing.

Make stuffing from finely chopped or ground meat mixed with cooked rice, diced browned onions, salt, and pepper.

Put tomatoes into an oiled skillet, top with grated cheese if desired, sprinkle with oil and bake in a preheated oven for 15-20 minutes. To serve put cooked tomatoes on a serving plate and pour sour cream sauce on top. Sprinkle with finely chopped dill or parsley leaves.

SAUCES FOR VEGETABLE DISHES

Milk Sauce (for Cabbage or Carrot Croquettes, etc.)

Ingredients:
1 tbsp flour
1 tbsp butter
1 1/2 cup milk

Sauté flour in butter until lightly brown. Gradually add hot milk whisking all the time. Simmer the sauce for 10 minutes. Season with salt to taste.

Sour Cream Sauce (for Potato, Cabbage, Carrot Croquettes and Casseroles)

Ingredients:
1 tbsp flour
1 tbsp butter
1 cup sour cream

Sauté flour with butter until lightly brown and add 1/2 cup of vegetable stock and 1 cup sour cream. Simmer for 5 minutes, season with salt and pepper and strain.

Mushroom Sauce (for Potato Croquettes and Casseroles)

Ingredients:
50 g dried mushrooms
1 tbsp flour
1 onion
2 tbsp butter

Wash dried mushrooms in warm water and soak in 3 cups of cold water for 2-3 hours, then cook in the same water without adding salt.

Sauté flour in 1 tbsp of butter until lightly brown and gradually add 2 cups of hot strained mushroom broth. Simmer sauce for 15-20 minutes. Brown diced onion in butter, add chopped cooked mushrooms and fry everything together a little longer, then add to the sauce, season with salt and bring to boil again before taking off the heat.

Tomato Sauce (for Potato Pirozhki, Stuffed Vegetables, etc.)

Ingredients:
1/2 cup tomato paste
1/2 tbsp flour
1/2 carrot
1/2 parsnip
1/2 onion
1 tbsp butter

Peel and finely chop carrot, parsnip, and onion. Sauté them in butter, adding flour when vegetables are soft. Add tomato paste, mix and add a cup of water (or meat stock), simmer for 5-10 minutes. Season sauce with salt, mash it through a sieve, add a small piece of butter and mix to incorporate.

Egg Sauce (for Potato Rolls and Cabbage Croquettes)

Ingredients:
1 tbsp flour
1 egg yolk
1 tbsp butter

Slightly fry flour in butter until lightly brown, add hot broth or stock and let simmer for 10-15 minutes. Blend egg yolk with 1/4 cup of stock or milk, add to the sauce and mix well.

Use chopped hardboiled egg instead of egg yolk if desired.

Egg-Butter Sauce (Hollandaise - for Cauliflower, Asparagus, Artichokes)

Ingredients:
2 eggs, separated
150 g butter

Add 2 tbsp of cold water to a pot or a mixing bowl. Blend in 2 egg yolks, season with salt. Put the pot on a very low heat or on water bath, making sure that bottom of the pot does not touch simmering water. Whisk in butter, one small piece at a time, making sure to incorporate it before adding the next piece. When sauce becomes thick - dilute it lemon juice to taste.

Egg Sauce with Wine (for Cauliflower, Asparagus, Artichokes)

Ingredients:
3 egg yolks
3 tbsp powdered sugar
3/4 cup white table wine
1/4 lemon

Mash egg yolks with powdered sugar, add lemon zest and whip while pouring over with wine. Put this mixture on low heat or in water bath and keep whipping until it thickens, but do not allow it to boil. When done cooking, remove lemon zest and add lemon juice to taste.

Breadcrumb Sauce (for Cauliflower and Asparagus)

Ingredients:
2 tbsp breadcrumbs
3-4 tbsp butter

Add finely crushed breadcrumbs into a skillet with melted butter; put the skillet on heat and brown breadcrumbs. Alternatively, brown breadcrumbs on a dry skillet and then add melted butter.

MUSHROOMS

Use ceps (porcini), birch bolete, aspen mushroom, champignons, morels, slippery jack mushrooms, chanterelles, honey mushrooms in mushroom dishes. If preparing ceps (porcini), aspen mushrooms and birch bolete, clean the stalk and peel it, separate cap from stalk, then wash and scald.

When preparing champignons, clean the stalks and remove thin film from caps; then put champignons in a pot with cold water, add some lemon acid to prevent mushrooms from turning dark. Then put champignons into another clean pot, pour over with hot water, add lemon acid and boil for 20 minutes.

If preparing morels or chanterelles, clean the stalks; wash and boil for 10 minutes. Then wash again, slice and then fry. For slippery jack mushrooms, clean the stalk; remove thin film from caps, then wash, slice and fry.

Mushrooms in Sour Cream

Ingredients:

500 g fresh mushrooms
1/2 cup sour cream
25 g cheese
1 tsp flour
2 tbsp butter

Clean, wash and scald mushrooms. Drain, slice, salt and fry them. Before finishing frying, add one teaspoon of flour and mix; then add sour cream, boil, sprinkle with grated cheese and bake.

When serving, sprinkle with parsley or dill.

Canned mushrooms can also be baked in sour cream. Drain the brine, then wash, slice and fry mushrooms. Continue preparing the same way as fresh mushrooms.

Morels in Sour Cream

Ingredients:
500 g morels
1 cup sour cream
25 g cheese
1 tsp flour
2 tbsp butter

Clean the roots or morels, wash the mushrooms and put in boiling water for 10 minutes, then wash again in cold water. Slice prepared mushrooms, add salt, put in a skillet and fry in butter; then sprinkle with flour, fry again, add sour cream, boil, sprinkle with grated cheese and butter, then bake in oven. Sprinkle morels with parsley when finished cooking.

Fried Mushrooms

Ingredients:
500 g fresh mushrooms
3-4 tbsp flour
2-3 tbsp butter

Clean, wash, scald and dry mushrooms (ceps, champignons, saffron milk caps). Slice, salt and fry on a pre-heated skillet with butter. Sprinkle with flour and fry again. Serve on the same skillet while hot, after sprinkling with parsley or dill.

Fried Mushrooms with Onions

Ingredients:
500 g fresh mushrooms
1 onion
3 tbsp butter

Clean, wash, scald and thinly slice mushrooms. Add salt, fry and mix with separately fried onions. When serving, sprinkle with parsley or dill. Fried potatoes can be served together with mushrooms, if desired.

Braised Mushrooms

Ingredients:

500 g fresh mushrooms
3 tbsp butter

Clean, wash and boil mushrooms (chanterelles, honey mushrooms, russula) in salted water. Drain them, then put in a pot with pre-heated oil, add 2-3 tbsp meat broth, cover with lid and braise approximately 30 minutes. When serving, add chopped greens and mix.

Braised Mushrooms in Cream

Ingredients:
500 g mushrooms
1 cup cream
1 tbsp butter

Clean, wash, scald, slice, salt and lightly fry fresh mushrooms (ceps, birch bolete, aspen mushrooms). Put them in a pot or pan and pour over with boiled cream. Tie together springs of parsley or dill, inserting some cinnamon, cloves, pepper, bay leaf in the middle of the batch, and put it in the pot with mushrooms. Salt, cover with lid and put into moderately hot oven to braise for 1 hour. When mushrooms are ready, remove the tied greens, and serve mushrooms in the same pot if was cooking in.

Baked Mushrooms

Many types of mushrooms can be baked, but morels are especially delicious. Clean and wash mushrooms, then put in boiling water for 5-10 minutes, drain and wash in cold water again (broth is not suitable for consumption).

Slice and fry on a pre-heated skillet with butter. Before finishing frying, add some flour, mix, add sour cream, boil, add butter (also grated cheese, if desired) and bake in oven.

Serve baked mushrooms on the same skillet while still hot.

Mushroom Solyanka

Ingredients:
500 g fresh mushrooms
1 kg fresh cabbage
1 pickle
1 onion
2 tbsp tomato puree
1-2 tsp sugar
2 tbsp butter

Chop cabbage, put in a pot, add butter, some water, vinegar and braise for about an hour. 15-20 minutes before finishing braising, add tomato puree, sliced pickles, sugar, salt, pepper, bay leaf.

Clean, wash and put mushrooms (ceps, birch bolete, saffron milk caps) in boiling water for 10-15 minutes, slice and fry in butter. Put mushrooms in a bowl, then on the same skillet, fry onions and then mix with mushrooms, adding sliced pickle, salt, and pepper.

Put half of braised cabbage on a skillet, put prepared mushrooms on top, and cover with layer of remaining cabbage. Sprinkle with breadcrumbs and butter, and put skillet in the oven.

When serving, put slices of lemon or olives in solyanka.

Mushroom solyanka can also be prepared with sauerkraut, not adding vinegar. Fresh mushrooms can be replaced with pickled or dry ones.

GRAIN AND FLOUR DISHES

GRAIN AND FLOUR DISHES

Different types of porridges, croquettes, casseroles can be prepared from grains.

Porridge is usually prepared either crispy or viscous. Crispy porridge is prepared from whole unground grain (rice, barley, buckwheat) or coarsely ground grains. Viscous porridge (mostly with milk) can be prepared from any grains.

When cooking porridge, the ratio of grain and liquid is very important. For crispy porridge, the ratio is fixed, and for viscous porridge it can be varied depending on the desired level of thickness.

Before cooking, grain (millet, rice and barley) is washed two or three times in cold water.

Millet needs to be washed especially thoroughly, since it contains hulling bran that gives it bitter taste.

If the grain contains too many impurities, it should be sifted through a sieve or hand-picked. Peeled grain is washed if it contains dust. Peeled grain can be fried lightly first.

Barley should be soaked for 3-4 hours in order to speed up its cooking time.

To prepare crispy porridges enough water should be used for the grain to swell. Too little water will result in porridge that's dry; too much water will make it viscous.

As a general rule of making porridge, put grain into boiling salted water and boil on low heat, occasionally stirring, until it thickens. To make porridge sweat, cover tightly with lid and put in water bath or oven. Sweating time is different for various grains. If the oven is too hot, porridge may burn, so put the pot into a skillet with water to prevent this from happening.

When making porridges with milk, salt is added to the milk before the grain, and lesser amount of salt is used than for porridge with water. For sweet porridges, minimal amounts of salt are used, depending on taste.

PORRIDGES

Buckwheat Porridge with Butter

Ingredients:
2 cups buckwheat
1 tsp salt
3 cup water
2 tbsp butter

Pour water in a pot, add salt and bring to boil. Add buckwheat to boiling salted water; boil while stirring for 15-20 minutes, until it thickens. Cover tightly with lid and arrange for buckwheat to sweat for 3-4 hours.

Fried Buckwheat Porridge with Butter

Ingredients:
2 1/2 cups hulled buckwheat
1 tsp salt
2-3 tbsp butter

Put 1 tablespoon of butter on a skillet, melt it and add buckwheat. Put skillet on low heat or in oven. Cook buckwheat, while frequently stirring it, until it becomes caramelized. Pour 3 1/2 cups of water in a pot, add salt and bring to boil. When water boils, add buckwheat and occasionally stirring, cook until it thickens. Tightly cover with lid and arrange for it to sweat for 1 - 1 1/2 hours.

Porridge is prepared somewhat differently in a Russian stove.

Put buckwheat in a pot without frying it, pour in 3 cups of boiling water, add salt, 1 tablespoon of butter and put in closed Russian stove to sweat for 3-5 hours. Mix hot porridge well before serving, and add 1-2 tablespoons of butter.

Buckwheat Porridge with Milk

Ingredients:
2 1/2 cup hulled buckwheat
2 l milk
1 tsp salt

Cook crispy buckwheat porridge and cool it. Serve on plates and pour over with milk.

Buckwheat Porridge with Fatback and Onions

Dice fatback and fry with sliced onions. Put fried fatback in prepared buckwheat porridge and mix.

Buckwheat Porridge with Brains

Ingredients:
2 1/2 cup hulled buckwheat
300 g brains
1 1/2 tsp salt
1 tsp vinegar
2-3 tbsp butter

Cook crispy buckwheat porridge. Put brains in cold water for 15 minutes, then take out, remove film, put in a pot and pour over with cold water just to cover brains. Add salt, bay leaf, pepper, vinegar and bring to boil. As soon as water boils, remove from heat and leave in the same pot for 10-15 minutes. Remove brains from water, thinly slice and fry on skillet with butter. Mix with porridge and fry for another few minutes.

Buckwheat Porridge with Eggs

Ingredients:
2 1/2 cups hulled buckwheat
2 eggs
1 tsp salt
2-3 tbsp butter

Cook crispy buckwheat porridge. Hard boil the eggs, peel them, cut in halves and then thinly slice each half. Put sliced eggs together with butter in prepared buckwheat porridge and mix.

Buckwheat Porridge with Beef Lung

Ingredients:

2 1/2 cup hulled buckwheat
300 g lung
1-2 onions
1 tsp salt
2-3 tbsp butter

Cook crispy buckwheat porridge. Wash lung, put it in a pot, pour over with water, add salt and boil on low heat for 1 - 1 1/2 hours, until it softens. Cool boiled lung and pass it through a meat grinder or finely chop it with knife. Slice onions and fry on skillet with butter. Add another 1-2 tbsp butter and chopped lung, salt and pepper. When fried lung and onions are fried, mix it with prepared hot buckwheat porridge.

Buckwheat Porridge with Mushrooms and Onions

Ingredients:
2 1/2 cup hulled buckwheat
50 mushrooms (dried ceps)
2 onions
1 tsp salt

2-3 tbsp butter

Wash dried mushrooms, put them in a pot, pour over with 3 cups of cold water and leave for 1 - 1 1/2 hours. When mushrooms swell, remove them from water, finely chop, put back in same water, salt and bring to boil. Once water boils, add fried buckwheat and mix. When porridge thickens, arrange for it to sweat for 1 - 1 1/2 hours. Finely slice onions and fry on skillet with butter. Mix fried onions with porridge.

For this porridge, vegetable oil can be substituted for butter.

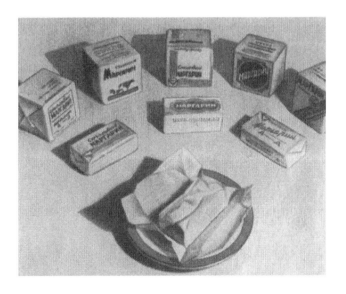

Millet Porridge with Butter

Ingredients:
2 cups millet
1 tsp salt
2-3 tbsp of butter

Add 4 cups of water, 1 tbsp of butter, and salt to a pot and bring it to boil. Add washed millet to boiling water and cook until thickened. Cover the pot and leave porridge to sweat for 50-60 minutes. Add remaining butter to the porridge and mix it well.

Another way of cooking millet porridge is boiling grain in 7-8 cups of salted boiling water for 10-15 minutes, and then draining it. Put drained millet back into the pot, add 1 tbsp of butter and let it sweat for 40-50 minutes.

Millet Porridge with Pumpkin

Ingredients:
1 1/2 cups millet
750 g pumpkin
3 cups water
1 tsp salt

Peel and remove seeds from pumpkin, cut into small pieces, put into a pot with 3 cups of water, bring to boil and cook 10-15 minutes. Add washed millet to the pot and continue cooking on low heat 15-20 minutes more stirring frequently. Cover pot with thickened porridge and let it sweat for 20-30 minutes. This porridge can also be cooked with milk. Serve with butter on a side.

Cracked Wheat Porridge

Ingredients:
2 cups cracked wheat
4 cups water (for loose porridge) or 5 cups water
(for thick porridge)
1 tsp salt

Add previously washed grain to the boiling salted water (finely cracked wheat does not have to be washed). Cook 15-20 minutes stirring frequently. When porridge becomes thicker cover the pot and let it sweat for 40-50 minutes. Serve with butter or sweetened condensed milk.

Wheat Porridge

Ingredients:
2 cups wheat (whole grain)
5-6 cups water

Whole grain wheat should be used to cook thick porridge. Pick over and wash wheat and add it to boiling salted water, cover the pot and cook 25-30 minutes stirring from time to time. Leave the pot to sweat for 1 1/2-2 hours after cooking. When finished - pass this porridge through a meat grinder, add butter and warm through, or make a casserole. After this porridge was passed through a meat grinder it can be used to make croquettes.

Barley or Cracked Oats Porridge

Ingredients:
2 1/2 cups grains
1 tsp salt
2-3 tbsp butter

Put 4 1/2 cup of water, 1 tbsp butter, and salt into a pot and bring to boil. Add grains to the pot when water start boiling and cook until thickened. Leave porridge to sweat for 30-40 minutes. Stir finished porridge, put it into bowls and pour melted butter on top.

Barley Porridge with Pork Fat or Lamb Fat

Ingredients:
2 1/2 cups barley

100 g pork or lamb (inner) fat
1 tsp salt

Cook barley porridge. Finely chop fat or it pass through a meat grinder, put into a skillet and render all the fat. Add rendered fat together with cracklings to the porridge, mix it, cover the pot and let porridge sweat for 30-40 minutes.

Pearl Barley Porridge with Butter

Ingredients:
2 cup pearl barley
1 tsp salt
2-3 tbsp butter

Put grain into boiling water and let it boil for 5 minutes. Drain barley in a colander. Put 3 1/2 cups of water into a pot, add 1 tbsp of butter and salt. Bring pot to boil and add prepared grain, cook until thickened. Seat porridge for 1 1/2 hours. Add remaining butter to the porridge and mix it in.

Sago Porridge with Butter

Ingredients:
1 1/2 cups sago
3/4 tsp salt
2 tbsp butter

Add 5 cups of water and salt to a pot and

bring to boil. Add sago to the boiling water and cook on low heat until it thickens. Leave porridge to sweat for 20-30 minutes. Add butter to the finished porridge and mix it in.

Rice Porridge with Butter

Ingredients:
2 cups rice
1 tsp salt
2-3 tbsp butter

Add 4 cups of water, salt, and butter to a pot and bring to boil. Add washed rice to the boiling water and cook on low heat until thickens. Sweat the porridge for 50 minutes.

Rice Porridge with Tomato Sauce and Cheese

Ingredients:
1 cup rice
1/2 cup tomato sauce
30 g grated cheese
3 tbsp butter

Wash rice, cook it in salted water and drain in

a colander. Put drained rice into a skillet with melted butter and fry, carefully stirring, until it browns slightly. Add hot tomato sauce and grated cheese and mix well.

MILK PORRIDGES

Milk porridge can be prepared from all kinds of grains, except for peeled barley.

Use either whole or skim milk (add butter if using skim milk). Powdered and condensed milk may also be used.

Condensed milk is recommended for making sweet porridge.

Milk porridge is cooked thick, viscous.

Butter and sugar may be added to prepared milk porridge, if desired.

Rice Milk Porridge

Ingredients:
1 cup rice
4 cups milk
1 tbsp sugar
1/4 tsp salt

Wash rice, put in boiling water and cook for 5-8 minutes, then drain. Put rice in a pot with hot milk, and cook on low heat for 15 minutes while stirring. Add sugar and salt, mix, cover with lid and put in water bath for 10-15 minutes to sweat.

When serving, add butter.

Cream of Wheat Porridge

Ingredients:
1 cup cream of wheat (farina)
5 cups milk
1 tbsp sugar
1/2 tsp salt

Pour grain into pot of boiling milk in a slow, steady stream. Cook for 10-15 minutes, constantly stirring, until it thickens. Add sugar, salt and mix.
1-2 tablespoons of butter may be added.

Cracked Oats Milk Porridge

Ingredients:
2 cups cracked oats
4 cups milk
1 tsp salt
2-3 tbsp butter

Add cracked oats and salt to boiling milk and cook, frequently stirring, on low heat 20-30 minutes, until thickened.

Oatmeal ("Hercules")

Ingredients:
2 cups rolled oats
5 cups milk
1/2 tsp salt

Add oats to boiling milk and cook 10-15 minutes until thickened. Season with salt and mix well.

Add 2 tablespoons of butter to prepared porridge.

Barley or Oats Milk Porridge

Ingredients:
1 cup grains
5 cups milk
1/2 tsp salt

Add grain into boiling milk in a thin stream, mixing all the time. Cook 10-15 minutes on low heat until porridge thickens, add salt and mix well.

Add 1-2 tbsp of butter to the porridge if desired.

Pearl Barley Milk Porridge

Ingredients:
1 cup pearl barley
4 cups milk
1/2 tbsp sugar
1/4 tsp salt

Add washed barley into boiling water. Parboil for 10-12 minutes, then strain in a colander. Add strained barley to boiling milk and cook 15 minutes on low heat, stirring frequently. Add sugar and salt, mix well and sweat 10-15 minutes on water bath.

When serving add butter to the porridge if desired.

.

Millet Milk Porridge

Ingredients:
1 cup millet
4 cups milk
1 tbsp sugar
1/4 tsp salt

Add thoroughly washed millet to boiling milk and cook on low heat 30 minutes, stirring frequently. Add sugar, salt, cover the pot and sweat porridge for 15-20 minutes.

Millet Milk Porridge with Pumpkin

Ingredients:
1 cup millet
3 cups milk
500 g pumpkin
1 tsp sugar
1/2 tsp salt

Put peeled and cut into small pieces pumpkin into boiling milk and cook 10-15 minutes, then add thoroughly washed millet, salt, mix everything and continue cooking 15-20 minutes longer until it thickens. Cover the pot and leave porridge to sweat in a warm oven or on a water bath for 25-30 minutes.

GRAIN CASSEROLES, PUDDINGS AND PATTIES

Casseroles are mostly made from millet, rice and cream of wheat.

Thick, viscous porridge is required to make casseroles. For 1 cup of grain, 3 cups of milk or water should be used.

Prepared porridge is fried on a skillet greased with butter. Sprinkle the bottom and edges of the skillet with breadcrumbs so that casserole doesn't get burned. Sprinkle porridge on the skillet with breadcrumbs, pour over with butter and put in oven for 15-20 minutes until caramelized crust forms.

Cream of Wheat Pudding with Fruit

Ingredients:
1 cup cream of wheat
4 cups milk
1/2 tsp salt
2-3 tbsp sugar
100 g various fruit
2 eggs
 2-3 tbsp butter

Cook cream of wheat porridge with milk. Add

sugar, eggs, salt, butter to the cooked porridge, mix well and put it into a well-buttered ovenproof skillet. Smooth the top of the porridge, sprinkle with sugar and bake until caramelized crust forms.

Just before serving top pudding with freshly cooked or canned fruits and pour sweet fruit or berry sauce over the fruit.

Millet, Rice, Barley, or Oat Porridge Pudding

Ingredients:
1 cup grains
3 cups milk
1 tbsp sugar
1 tbsp breadcrumbs
1/4 tsp salt
2 tbsp butter

Add grain to boiling milk and cook until thickened. Add salt and sugar, mix well, put into a well-buttered and sprinkled with breadcrumbs ovenproof skillet and bake in the oven until done.

Separate finished pudding from the skillet and put it on a serving plate. Cut pudding into 5-6 servings. Just before serving pour melted butter over it. If desired - substitute butter with hot kissel and sprinkle pudding with sugar or top with sour cream.

Millet Pudding with Raisins

Cook thick millet porridge with milk or water. Add 1 egg and picked over and washed raisins into the porridge. Mix well and put into a well-buttered and sprinkled with breadcrumbs ovenproof skillet. Bake until done.

Buckwheat Krupenik (Grain Pie)

Ingredients:
1 cup buckwheat
2 cups milk
200 g farmers cheese
1/2 cup sour cream
2 eggs
1/2 tsp salt
2 tbsp sugar
2 tbsp butter

Add buckwheat to boiling milk and cook until thickened. Pass farmers cheese through a sieve and add it to the porridge together with sour cream, mix well, then add eggs, salt, and sugar and mix to incorporate. Put mixture into a buttered and sprinkled with breadcrumbs shallow pot or ovenproof skillet, smooth the top, top with sour cream, and drizzle 1 tbsp of melted butter over sour cream. Bake in a preheated oven 40-50 minutes. Sprinkle finished krupenik with remaining melted butter, or, if desired, replace butter with sour cream.

Rice Pudding

Ingredients:
1 cup rice
2 cups milk
2 eggs
2-3 tbsp sugar
50g raisins
1/2 tsp salt
1-2 tbsp butter

Parboil washed rice for 10 minutes. Drain water and add hot milk to rice, add salt and cook 25-30 minutes, stirring from time to time. Add sugar, eggs, raisins, mix well and put mixture into a buttered and coated with breadcrumbs skillet and bake until done. Unmold pudding to a serving plate, cut into servings and serve with fruit-and-berry sauce.

Rice Patties

Ingredients:
2 cups rice
5 cups water
1 tbsp sugar
1 tsp salt
1/2 cup breadcrumbs
2 tbsp butter or vegetable oil

Add washed rice to salted boiling water and cook 20-25 minutes, stirring from time to time. Cover the pot and leave thickened porridge to sweat/cool. Add sugar, and, if desired, eggs, mix well and form patties, coat in breadcrumbs and fry in butter. Serve rice patties with either sweet or mushroom sauce.

Millet Patties

Ingredients:
2 cups millet
5 cups water or milk
1 tbsp sugar
1 tsp salt
1/2 cup crushed breadcrumbs
2-3 tbsp butter or vegetable oil

Add salt, sugar, and finely washed millet to boiling water and cook 15-20 minutes, stirring frequently. Cover the pot and leave to sweat for 25-30 minutes.

Cool porridge and form patties with hands dipped in cold water. Coat patties in four or breadcrumbs and fry in butter. Serve with kissel, sour cream, butter, or milk sauce.

Buckwheat Patties

Ingredients:
1 cup buckwheat
100 g farmers cheese
2 eggs
1 tsp sugar
1/2 cup crushed breadcrumbs

1/2 tsp salt
2 tbsp butter or vegetable oil

Add buckwheat to 1 1/2 cup of boiling salted water and cook 30-35 minutes. When porridge is thickened, add passed through a sieve or meat grinder farmers cheese, eggs, and sugar and mix well. Form patties from the mix, coat them in breadcrumbs and fry on all sides until nicely browned.

Put sour cream on top of each patty when serving. These patties can be served with borscht or rassolnik.

PILAFS

Pilafs are rice dishes cooked in a special way. Pilaf is made with fried or boiled lamb, poultry, fish, eggs, boiled or dried fruit, nuts and vegetables.

To make most pilafs, rice is washed before cooking and soaked in warm water for an hour to swell, after which it is drained and cooked according to the following two methods.

First method. Add washed rice to salted boiling water and cook until grains of rice on the outside become soft, and the grains of the rice in the middle are still somewhat stiff. Drain it and pour over with cold water to cool. Melt some cooking fat in the bottom of a deep pot, put in boiled rice, pour over with melted fat, close the lid and heat for 40-45 minutes.

To prevent rice from sticking to the bottom of the pan, put a very thin plain dough flatbread on the bottom of the pan. Serve this flatbread together with pilaf.

Second method. Add some butter or melted fatback to boiling salted water (2 cups), add 1 cup of washed rice and boil on low heat, without mixing. When rice absorbs all water, pour in the rest of the cooking fat, close lid and continue cooking for another 30-40 minutes.

Lamb Pilaf

Ingredients:
1 1/2 cup rice
500 g lamb
2 onions
2 medium pomegranates
1/2 cup clarified butter

Chop lamb into small pieces, sprinkle with salt and pepper, fry in butter or fatback with finely chopped onions. As soon as onions and lambs are fries, pour them over with just enough water to cover them; add pomegranate grains, close lid and braise until meat becomes soft.

When serving, put pieces of lamb with juice on plates, cover them with hot pilaf made according to first method.

Guriski Pilaf

Ingredients:
2 cups rice
150 g raisins
150 g honey
1/2 cup clarified butter

Prepare pilaf according to first method. Before serving, pour it over with sweet gravy. To make gravy, mix honey with equal amount of water, add washed raisins and boil for 10 minutes.

Uzbek Pilaf

Ingredients:
400 g fatty lamb
2-3 cups rice
200 - 300 g carrots
150 - 200 g onions
200 g fatback (lamb, beef) or vegetable oil

Cut lamb in small pieces and fry in a cast iron pot, in preheated cooking fat. Add julienned onions and carrots, and fry them with lamb; then pour over with 4 cups water, add salt, pepper and boil.

Thoroughly wash rice, draining tree-four times, put in a pot with meat, evenly.

When water evaporates, make several cavities (to the bottom of the pot) on the surface of the rice with a clean wooden stick; to prevent pilaf from burning, pour 1-2 tablespoons of water into the cavities, then tightly close with lid and leave on very low heat for 25 - 30 minutes.

When serving, serve pilaf on a plate, shaping rice in a form of a hill. Put pieces of lamb on top and sprinkle with julienned raw onions.

Pilaf with Pumpkin and Fruit

Ingredients:
1 1/2 cup rice
500g pumpkin
200 g fresh apples
100 g quince
100 g raisins
1/2 cup butter

Peel fresh apples and quince, remove seeds, dice and mix with washed raisins.

Melt some butter in a pan, cover the bottom of the pan with julienned pumpkin (peeled and with seeds removed). Sift 1/2 of washed rice on top of pumpkin, add a layer of fruit mix, sift more rice on top, add another layer of fruit and cover with remaining rice. Pour over with remaining butter and just enough salted water to cover the top layer of rice. Cover with lid and cook on low heat for one hour.

Pilaf with Raisins

Ingredients:
2 cups rice
100 g raisins

1/2 cup clarified butter
2 tbsp butter

Wash rice, pour over with boiling water for 10 - 15 minutes. Then put rice in a pan with boiling water and cook until ready. Drain rice.

In another pot, melt the butter, add boiled rice, pour over with clarified butter, tightly cover with lid, put on low heat for 25-30 minutes.

Separately, in butter, fry raisins that have been washed and swollen in water.

When serving, add a small piece of butter in each plate with pilaf, covering butter with rice. Place raisins on top of rice.

DISHES MADE WITH FLOUR PRODUCTS

Dumplings

Dumplings are made from wheat flour, farina (cream of wheat), or oat flour.

To form dumplings, take dough with a tablespoon and press it against a side of the pan. With a teaspoon dipped into hot water separate pieces of dough from the contents of the tablespoon and put them into boiling salted water. Dumplings should have somewhat oblong shape and be of somewhat uniform size.

Dumplings in butter, breadcrumbs, and sour cream are served as a stand-alone dish, or can be served as a garnish to meat dishes. Dumplings in milk could be served as a second course or as a dessert.

Wheat Flour or Farina Dumplings in Butter

Ingredients:
1 cup farina or wheat flour
5 eggs
1/2 tsp salt (for dough)
4 tbsp butter

Bring 3 1/2 cup of water to boil, add salt and 1 tbsp of butter, then add farina or flour and cook for 6-8 minutes constantly stirring. Remove dough from heat and add eggs, one at a time, mixing well to incorporate.

Make dumpling from the dough and cook in boiling, lightly salted water, for 5-7 minutes. Remove dumpling from the pot with a skimmer and put into colander to drain. Put drained dumpling on a serving plate, drizzle with melted butter and serve.

Instead of butter dumplings could be dressed with sour cream. If using sour cream - take 1 tbsp of butter to make the dough and 1/2 cup of sour cream for serving.

Oat Dumplings in Milk

Ingredients:
2 cups oat flour
2 eggs
4 cups milk

1/2 tsp salt (for dough)

Put out flour into a pot; add 2 cups of cold water and mix well to avoid lumps. Add eggs and salt to the dough and mix to incorporate. Make dumpling from the dough and cook in boiling milk 8-10 minutes. Serve in the milk in which dumplings were cooked.

Pelmeni in Butter

Ingredients:
1 1/2 cup wheat flour
1 egg
2 tbsp butter
1/2 cup sour cream
400 g boneless meat
1 onion

Prepare pelmeni following instructions in the recipe "Broth with Pelmeni". Put pelmeni into boiling salted water and cook 10 minutes. Remove pelmeni from the pot with a skimmer, put on a serving plate and dress with melted butter or sour cream.

Chiburekki

Ingredients:
3 cups flour
400 g boneless lamb
100 g lamb fat

1 egg
3/4 cups water (for dough)
50 g rice
pepper to taste
200 g clarified butter (for frying)

Pass lamb meat together with lamb fat (preferably fat tail) and onion through a meat grinder or finely chop with a knife. Season ground meat with salt, pepper, finely chopped parsley leaves, and, while mixing, add 2-3 tbsp cold water. Mix prepared stuffing with cooled cooked rice.

Make dough with flour, water, egg, and 1/2 tsp salt just like noodle dough. Roll the dough 1 mm thick and cut out circles approximately 5" in diameter. Put some stuffing in the middle of the circle, moisten the edges with beaten egg, and pinch edges together forming half-moon shape. Just before serving fry chiburekki in a deep skillet.

Ukrainian Halushky

Ingredients:
2 1/2 cups wheat flour
2 eggs
1/2 cup sour cream
100 g butter or clarified butter

Make a well in the middle of a mound of sifted flour and add 1/2 cup water, 2 tbsp of melted butter, and 2 eggs beaten with less than a teaspoon of salt. Mix with flour until you get smooth dough, but do not knead.

Roll the dough 1/2 cm and cut into small pieces of any shape.

Put pieces of dough (halushky) into a pot with boiling salted water, lower the heat and simmer approximately 10 minutes. When cooked halushky float to the top take them out with a skimmer and put into a strainer to drain. Meanwhile, heat butter in a pot or in a skillet, add halushky and sauté until slightly browned. Serve immediately.

If desired - add sour cream to finished halushky.

PASTA

Making dishes from pasta (noodles and vermicelli) is relatively easy, doesn't require much time and effort. Pasta products are placed in salted boiling water. Use 2 cups of water and 1/2 tsp of salt for 100 g of pasta. Cook pasta for 20-30 minutes, noodles for 12-15 minutes. Drain cooked pasta. Once drained, add butter or sauce to pasta, before it gets cool.

Use broth from pasta for soups, pureed soups and sauces.

Pasta can be made without draining. In this case less water is used, just so it gets absorbed into pasta. Use 1 cup of water for 100 g of pasta. Put pasta in salted boiling water, cook while stirring for 20 minutes, then close lid and put on low heat to sweat for 15-20 minutes. Then add butter, mix and serve.

Pasta, Noodles and Vermicelli in Butter

Ingredients:
250 g pasta, noodles or vermicelli
2 tbsp butter

Cook pasta, vermicelli or noodles according to the introduction recipe, drain, add butter and mix.

Pasta with Cheese

Ingredients:
250 g pasta
50 g cheese
2 tbsp butter

Put butter and half the cheese into hot boiled pasta and mix it well. When serving, sprinkle with remaining cheese.

Pasta with Tomatoes, Mushrooms and Ham

Ingredients:
250 g pasta
100 g boiled ham
200 g ceps (porcini) or champignons
4 tbsp tomato puree
2 tbsp butter

Cook pasta. Julienne ham and boiled mushrooms and fry in butter. Add tomato puree and boil, mix with pasta and serve.

Makaronnik or Lapshevik (Noodle Pie) with Eggs

Ingredients:
250 g pasta or noodles
1 egg
1 cup milk
2 tbsp sugar
2 tbsp breadcrumbs
1/2 tsp salt
1 tbsp butter

Cook pasta or noodles, drain. Pour cold milk into another pan; add raw eggs, sugar and salt. Mix well. Put pasta or noodles into a skilled greased with butter, pour over with milk and sprinkle with breadcrumbs, add butter and cook in oven for 15-20 minutes, until caramelized crust forms. When serving, sift with sugar or pour over with butter.

Makaronnik or Lapshevik (Noodle Pie) with Farmers Cheese

Ingredients:
250 g pasta
2 eggs
1 cup farmer cheese
2 tbsp sugar
2 tbsp breadcrumbs
1/2 tsp salt
1 tbsp butter

Cook pasta or noodles and mix with raw eggs, salt and sugar. Rub farmer cheese through a sieve or pass through a meat grinder. Mix it well with pasta or noodles, put on a greased skillet, sprinkle with breadcrumbs and butter and put skillet in oven for 15-20 minutes. When serving, sift with sugar.

Makaronnik or Lapshevik (Noodle Pie) with Meat

Ingredients:
250 g pasta or noodles

250 g boneless meat
1 egg
1/2 tsp salt
2 tbsp breadcrumbs
1 tbsp butter

Cook pasta or noodles. Pass meat (beef, lamb, pork) through a meat grinder, sprinkle with salt and pepper, put on a skillet with heated butter and brown on low heat. When meat is ready, pass it through a meat grinder again, add 2 tablespoons of broth or water where noodles were boiled in and mix. Fried onions may also be added to meat. Raw meat can be substituted with boiled or fried meat.

Add raw egg to noodles, sprinkle with salt, mix and put half of it on a greased skillet evenly. On top, add a layer of prepared meat, and cover with a layer of remaining pasta or noodles. Sprinkle with breadcrumbs and butter. Put skillet in oven for 15-20 minutes.

BREAKFAST CEREALS

Breakfast cereals are ready to eat products from grains of corn, wheat and rice.

Breakfast cereals such as "Corn Flakes", "Wheat Flakes", "Air Rice", "Air Corn", "Air Wheat" contain many nutrients such as proteins, carbohydrates, minerals and fats.

"These products, - Comrade Mikoyan said - are ready to eat". Since they don't require any culinary processing, according to Comrade Mikoyan this makes it "very convenient for any housewife who doesn't have much time to spend in the kitchen, and very useful for kindergartens or schools that can not afford large kitchens and numerous kitchen staff".

For example, this is how "Corn Flakes" are made.

These flakes are made from top grades of corn. Corn grain is cleaned and boiled for 2 to 2 1/2 hours in syrup (sugar, salt, water) in spinning apparatus. Then they are cooled, dried and flattened by a special machine. After that they are fried, cooled and packaged.

During the entire processing and packaging cycle, no human hands come in contact with the product; everything is done by machines and fully automated. People just oversee the operation.

After this advanced processing, very thin and fine flakes of corn are produced, delicious and nutritious. The advantages of corn flakes over corn grain are twofold: first, they are much better absorbed and digested and second, they are ready to eat.

Corn flakes don't require any heating, cooking, they are eaten cold with milk, cream, sour cream, curdled milk, farmer cheese, coffee, fruit/vegetable/berry juice, compote, kissel, honey, jam.

During eating, flakes are gradually added to the bowl, so they don't become too moist. "Wheat Flakes" are thin, caramelized petals obtained from specially processed (flattened) top grade wheat; they are consumed the same way as "Corn Flakes".

Popped grains of corn, rice and wheat are called "Air Rice", "Air Corn" and "Air Wheat".

Processing of this type of breakfast cereals involves placing the grain into special canon-shaped apparatus, where the grain is gradually heated. When pressure reaches a certain high point, an opening is created and vapor inside each grain suddenly expands, exploding it. Explosion increases the volume of the grain (for example, wheat and rice by as much as 10 times)

These popped grains are ready to eat. They are nutritious, have pleasant taste and are well-digested.

Popped grains are eaten the same way as flakes.

DISHES WITH LEGUMES

Beans, peas and lentils are legumes. They are very nutritious because lentils have a high protein content.

Adding butter, fatback, smoked ham to legumes allows many nutritious and delicious meals to be prepared. Beans are usually tastier than peas and lentils. Beans can be white or colored, and comes in different sizes. Quality beans are not damaged, shiny and uniform in color and size.

Quality peas are large, almost the same size, and color is white, yellow or green. Split peas are also sold; they contain less fiber and are cooked quicker.

For lentils, just like for beans and peas, size and uniformity are important, as well as green color.

Prepared legumes can be served as a separate dish or as garnish for meat or fish.

Before cooking, legumes should be picked and thoroughly washed. In order to ensure that legumes boil quicker and more uniformly, soak them in cold water for 3 - 4 hours.

Legumes should not be soaked for too long, especially in a warm room, or they might turn sour.

Water acquires an unpleasant taste after legumes, especially bean, have been soaked in it, so pour the water out. Boil soaked beans in fresh unsalted water. Salt is added towards the end of cooking, since legumes take longer to prepare in salted water. Hardness of water also affects preparation time: beans are cooked considerably longer in hard water than in soft water.

Included are several recipes for legume dishes.

Recipes for soups and appetizers made with legumes are found in corresponding sections of the book.

Beans with Onions

Ingredients:
1 cup dry beans
1/2 tsp salt
1 onion
1 tbsp butter

Wash and soak beans in cold water for 3-4 hours, then drain, add fresh water and cook until done. Drain cooked beans and add fried onion, season with salt and mix everything well.

If desired - substitute peas for beans.

Beans in Tomato Sauce

Ingredients:
1 cup beans
2 tbsp tomato paste
1 onion
1 tbsp butter

Cook beans just like in the recipe "Beans with Onions", drain, add fried in oil onion, tomato paste, season with salt, mix and heat through.

Beans with Potatoes

Ingredients:
1 cup beans
500 g potatoes
2 onions
2 tbsp sour cream
2 tbsp tomato paste
2 tbsp butter

Boil beans and potatoes separately. Cut boiled potatoes into slices, brown in oil and mix with beans. To the pot with potatoes and beans add sour cream, diced browned onions, tomato paste, season with salt and pepper, mix, cover the pot and warm through in an oven or on a low heat.

Beans with Walnuts

Ingredients:
1 cup dry beans
50 g shelled walnuts
1 onion or 75g scallions

Pick beans over, wash, and soak in cold water. Drain soaked beans, cover with cold water and bring to boil. Cook until done, then add sliced leek and bring back to boil.

Crush walnuts; add to drained beans, season with salt and pepper.

Put prepared beans into a salad or other deep bowl. Sprinkle with chopped herbs just before serving. This dish could be served hot or cold.

Green Beans with Walnut Sauce

Ingredients:
(for the sauce)
100 g shelled walnuts
100 g scallions
50 g cilantro or parsley
1/4 cup distilled vinegar
1 clove garlic

Remove strings from green beans, wash beans in cold water, cut into pieces and cook in boiling salted water, approximately 15-20 minutes.

Drain cooked beans in a strainer, then put into a salad or other deep bowl and top with Walnut Sauce. Sprinkle with finely chopped dill or parsley leaves just before serving.

To make sauce, crash walnuts in a mortar together with garlic, add salt, ground red pepper (cayenne, paprika, and chili powder), finely chopped scallions and cilantro (or parsley). Mix everything well and then add vinegar.

Bean Croquettes with Mushroom Sauce

Ingredients:
2 cups cooked beans

50 g white bread
1/4 cup milk
2 eggs
20 g dried mushrooms
1/2 tbsp flour
2 tbsp breadcrumbs
3 tbsp butter or vegetable oil

Mix cooked beans with bread soaked in milk. Pass the mixture through a meat grinder, add eggs, season with salt and mix well. Shape croquettes from the ground beans, coat with breadcrumbs and fry in a skillet.

Serve with mushroom sauce. (ed. note - Presumably dried mushrooms and flour in this recipe should be cooked into mushroom sauce; however, this recipe stops right after this sentence.)

Bean and Potato Casserole

Ingredients:
2 cups beans
500 g potatoes
2 onions
2 tbsp butter

Pass boiled potatoes and beans through a meat grinder, season with salt and mix well. Put half of the mix on a well-oiled ovenproof skillet, smooth the top, put a layer of caramelized onions, and cover with the remaining bean and potato mix. Smooth the top again, sprinkle with oil and bake until browned on top.

Pea or Lentil Puree

Ingredients:
1 cup peas or lentils
1 onion
2 tbsp butter

Pick over and wash peas, then cover with water cook on low heat. When peas are cooked, drain the remaining water, season with salt, then mash and rub through a sieve or pass through a meat grinder. Add diced browned onion and mix well.

Same procedure is used for making puree with lentils.

Lentils with Butter, Tomato Paste, and Onion

Ingredients:
1 cup lentils
2 tbsp butter

Pick lentils over, wash, add 2 cups of cold water and soak for 3-4 hours. Drain soaking water, cover lentils with fresh water and bring to boil. Season with salt just before the end of cooking. Lentils are cooked when its grains are soft. Drain all remaining water and dress lentils with butter.

Lentils could be dressed with browned onions. Finely slice 1 medium onion and brown it in a small quantity of butter (oil), remaining butter add directly to lentils.

Lentils with tomato paste and onions are cooked according to above instructions, just add 3-4 tbsp of tomato paste to fried onions and fry a little bit longer. For lentils with sour cream and onions add 1/2 cup of sour cream to onions and bring to simmer.

Lentils Braised with Smoked Brisket

Ingredients:
1 cup lentils
150 g brisket
2 onions
1 tbsp tomato paste

Soaked washed lentils in cold water for 3-4 hours, drain. Scald brisket with boiling water and slice thinly. Thinly slice onions and brown them on a skillet together with brisket. Put drained lentils into a pot, add brisket with onions, tomato paste, salt, pepper, bay leaf, 1 cup of water or broth, cover the pot and cook on low heat for 30 minutes. Just before serving pile lentils into a mound on a serving plate and sprinkle with finely chopped dill or parsley leaves.

Lentils with Dried Apricots

Ingredients:
1 cup lentils
50 g/2 oz dried apricots
1-2 onions
25 g shelled walnuts
2-3 tbsp vegetable oil

Wash picked over lentils, cover with 2 1/2 cups of cold water and boil 1-1 1/2 hours. Fry thinly sliced onions together with dried apricots, soaked for about 15 minutes in warm water, in oil, season with salt and pepper and add it to a pot with lentils. Add crashed or passed through a meat grinder walnuts and cook for another 10-15 minutes.

Sprinkle with finely chopped cilantro leaves just before serving.

DAIRY AND EGG DISHES

DAIRY AND EGG DISHES

The most common ways of cooking eggs is boiling them - soft-boiled, medium-boiled (ed. note - We spent some time trying to figure out how better to translate the name of this stage of boiling an egg since it has a specific name in Russian - "v meshochke" which literally translates as "in the bag'), hard-boiled. Before boiling, eggs should be washed in cold water. If they are served in a shell, any spots on them should be rubbed off with salt.

Eggs should be submerged into boiling water all at once, not one by one.

Soft-boiled and medium-boiled eggs should be served on a plate with a napkin. Porcelain or plastic shot glasses should also be placed on the table. They will be used as stands for eggs while eating.

Soft-Boiled Eggs

Wash eggs, put them in boiling water and cook for 3-4 minutes. Soft-boiled eggs may be cooked without boiling them. Put eggs in a pan and pour over with boiling water just so the eggs are covered. Keep eggs in water for 10 minutes, pour the water out, and pour eggs over with boiling water once again. After 2-3 minutes, take the eggs out. The egg white doesn't become hard, just becomes thicker, while the yolk remains semi-liquid.

Medium-Boiled Eggs

Put eggs in boiling water. After submerging the eggs, water needs to boil fast again, so use high heat and enough boiling water. Take the eggs out after 5-6 minutes after putting them in, pour over with cold water and serve while they are still hot.

Hard Boiled Eggs

It takes 8-10 minutes to hard boil eggs, counting from the moment the water begins to boil. If eggs are boiled longer, egg whites become too hard and yolks lose their bright-yellow color. Hard boiled eggs should be submerged in cold water immediately; otherwise they will be hard to peel.

If boiled eggs are cooked to be an ingredient of any dish, they should be submerged in cold water and peeled. Correctly boiled egg peels easily, solidified egg white coats the semi-liquid yolk.

Eggs Sunny Side Up

Heat butter on a skillet. Break eggs into the skillet, trying not to rupture the membrane of the yolks. Add salt and fry for 1-2 minutes, then put in oven for 3-4 minutes. As soon as the egg white turns milky-white, serve eggs on same skillet or heated plate.

If oven is not available, cover skillet with lid or plate during frying.

Eggs Sunny Side Up with Garnish

In order to make eggs sunny side up with garnish, first fry slices of black bread, fatback, ham, hot dogs, sausage, champignons or other fresh mushrooms, tomatoes, squash, etc. Champignons and other mushrooms should be fried until ready. Then break eggs into the skillet on top of the garnish, add salt, and fry the same way as described in Eggs Sunny Side Up recipe.

Scrambled Eggs

Melt butter in a small pan, break eggs into the pan, pour over with milk (for 3 eggs, use 1 tbsp of butter and 2 tbsp of milk), add salt and whip. Cook on medium heat, constantly stirring with wooden spoon. When eggs reach the consistency of thin porridge, remove from heat and continue stirring for a short while, than serve on a plate or cup, placing white bread croutons (fried in butter) around scrambled eggs.

Scrambled eggs may also be served with vegetables and also meat products, for example with boiled ham, smoked brisket, hot dogs. These meat products should be diced, fried on skillet with butter and mixed with scrambled eggs. Products such as fried mushrooms in sour cream, fried fresh tomatoes, boiled green beans, sweet peas with oil are usually placed on top of scrambled eggs once they are ready.

Fried Eggs with Green Beans

Ingredients:
5 eggs
200 g green beans
1 tbsp butter

Remove strings, cut green beans and cook in boiling salted water. Drain, fry on skillet with butter. Pour over with eggs, salt and fry until eggs are ready. Serve on the same skillet.

Fried Eggs with Herring

Take one small herring; remove skin and bones, cut into 8-10 pieces. Put pieces of herring on a hot skillet with butter, break 4-5 eggs into skillet and fry for several minutes. When serving, sprinkle with parsley and finely chopped leeks.

OMELETS

Omelet is cooked with just eggs, or with addition of meat, fish, or dairy ingredients, or different vegetables, herbs, fruits, and berries. These ingredients are either mixed with beaten eggs or added as a filling and wrapped in an omelet.

Omelets are served with a sauce that is suitable for the filling - tomato, red wine, milk, or egg-and-butter.

Plain Omelet

Ingredients:
3 eggs
1 tbsp milk
1 tbsp butter

Break eggs into a mixing bowl, season with salt, add milk and whip with a spoon or a fork. Pour beaten eggs into a hot skillet with oil and fry on high heat, lightly shaking the skillet to make sure that eggs are cooked uniformly. When eggs start to thicken, wrap the omelet from 2 sides to the middle with a spatula to form an oblong shape, and put it onto a plate with a seam side down. Smear with a small piece of butter and serve immediately.

Omelet with Cheese

Ingredients:
3 eggs
50 g cheese
50 g white bread
3 tbsp milk
1 tbsp butter

Soak crustless white bread in milk and mash it, add eggs and beat with a spoon or a fork, add grated cheese, season with salt, and pour the mixture into a hot skillet with butter and cook according to instructions from "Plain Omelet" recipe. This omelet can be cooked in the oven - immediately after egg mixture was added to the hot skillet, put the skillet into preheated oven.

Omelet will be more voluminous if half of the egg whites are separated, whipped into a foam, and added back to a mixture right before cooking.

Omelet with Scallions

Ingredients:

3 eggs
1 tbsp scallions
1 tbsp milk
1 tbsp butter

Break eggs into a mixing bowl and slightly beat them. Add finely chopped scallions, season with salt, mix and cook just like "Plain Omelet".

Omelet with Zucchini, Pumpkin, or Cepes

Peel and dice vegetables, slice mushrooms thinly, season with salt and fry until cooked, then add beaten eggs. These omelets are very good when dressed with hot thick sour cream sauce and sprinkled with finely chopped dill or parsley leaves.

Omelet with Apples

Ingredients:
3 eggs
100 g apples
1 tbsp butter

Peel and core fresh and not very sour apples, slice thinly and sauté in butter in a frying pan. Pour beaten eggs over sautéed apples and cook until done.

Omelet with Spinach

Omelet with spinach is cooked just like omelet with onions, the only difference being - you should take twice as much fresh spinach (2 tbsp) as onions.

Omelet with Potatoes

Ingredients:
3 eggs
100 g potatoes
1 tbsp milk
1 tbsp butter

Peel and dice potatoes, and fry them in butter on a skillet. When potatoes are cooked through - add eggs beaten with milk, mix everything and cook just like "Plain Omelet".

Omelet with Salmon

Ingredients:
3 eggs
50 g salmon
1 tbsp butter

Remove skin and bones from a piece of salmon and cut it into small pieces, mix with milk and eggs and fry just like plain omelet. When serving dress with egg-and-butter sauce or melted butter.

Stuffed Eggs

Ingredients:
5 eggs
25 g cheese
50 g ham
50 g white bread
1/2 onion
2 tbsp milk (for stuffing)
1/2 cup milk for puree
500 g potatoes
2 tbsp butter

Peel hard-boiled eggs, cut in half lengthwise, remove egg yolks and cut some of egg white out to enlarge the hole from the yolk. Rub egg yolks through a sieve, add finely chopped pieces of egg white that were removed, ham, parsley leaves, fried in butter onion, soaked in milk bread, salt, pepper, little bit of milk and a raw egg. Mix everything well and stuff one half of the egg with a mixture, cover with the second half of the egg.

Put potato puree into a skillet, lay eggs in symmetrical pattern, top with grated cheese, sprinkle with melted butter and bake in a preheated oven.

Other ingredients can be used in stuffing instead of ham - finely chopped and fried ceps, champignons, fried meat, fried veal, poultry, or game.

DAIRY DISHES

In order to make dairy dishes such as syrniki (cheese pancakes), vareniki (dumplings), puddings, tvorozhniki (cheese fritters), dry pressed farmers cheese or prepared flavored cheese (sweet or savory) is needed. Moist farmers cheese should be put under press. To do this, wrap farmers cheese in gauze that has been washed in boiling water, wrung out, and folded in half. You may also use cloth napkin. Put wrapped farmers cheese in between two cleaned, scalded boards. Put heavy weight on top and leave for 2-3 hours.

Tvorozhniki (Cheese Fritters)

Ingredients:
500 g farmers cheese
1/2 cup sour cream
1 egg
2 tbsp butter
2 tbsp sugar
1/2 cup flour
1/2 tsp vanilla extract

Pass cheese through a meat grinder or through a sieve, put into a mixing bowl, add 1/4 cup of sifted flour, sugar, salt, vanilla extract, egg. Mix everything well, then put onto a table sprinkled with flour ad roll cheese mix into a thick log. Cut log across into 10 equal size patties. Coat each patty in flour, and fry in an oil in a hot skillet in batches until nicely browned on each side. Put finished tvorozhniki on a serving plate. If desired - sprinkle with powdered sugar. Serve hot with sour cream of fruit syrup.

Tvorozhniki with Carrots (Cheese and Carrots Fritters)

Ingredients:
300 g farmers cheese
500 g carrots
2 tbsp sugar
1/2 cup flour
1 egg

2 tbsp butter

Thinly cut washed and peeled carrots, put into a pot with 1/2 cup of water and 1/2 tbsp of butter. Cover the pot and braise carrots checking from time to time to prevent burning. If all water boils out but the carrots are still hard, add 1-2 tbsp of water to the pot. All the water should be gone by the time carrots are cooked.

Rub carrots through a sieve, mix with creamed cheese, add 1/2 cup flour or farina, egg, sugar, salt, and mix well. Continue cooking following instructions in the "Tvorozhniki" recipe.

Syrniki with Potatoes (Cheese and Potato Pancakes)

Ingredients:
500 g farmers cheese
800 g potatoes
1 egg
3 tbsp sugar
1/2 cup sour cream
1 cup flour
3 tbsp butter

Peel potatoes and cook them whole in salted water. Drain cooked potatoes in a colander, put them into a bowl and mash thoroughly. Mix mashed potatoes with cheese; add egg, 1/2 cup flour, sugar, salt. Mix everything well, put on a table sprinkled with flour, form patties, coat them in flour and brown on both sides in hot oil. Serve hot with cold sour cream.

Syrniki can also be cooked with raisins. Add 50 g picked over and washed raisins to the cheese mix.

Vareniki with Farmers Cheese (Dumplings with Cheese)

Ingredients:
500 g farmers cheese
3/4 cup sour cream
2 eggs
2 cups all-purpose flour
2 tbsp sugar
2 tbsp butter

Add 1 egg and 3/4 tsp salt to 1/2 cup of cold water or milk and mix everything together. Add 2 cups of sifted flour and make stiff dough. Pass cheese through a meat grinder, add sugar, egg yolk, 1 tbsp melted butter, 1/2 tsp salt and mix everything well. Roll the dough thinly, cut circular shapes using a glass or a cookie cutter, moisten circles of dough with beaten egg white, put 1 tsp of cheese stuffing in a middle of a circle and crimp sides together.

10 minutes before serving put dumplings into salted boiling water and cook until they float to the top. Take them out with a skimmer, put into a serving bowl, pour melted butter over and serve with sour cream or fruit sauce.

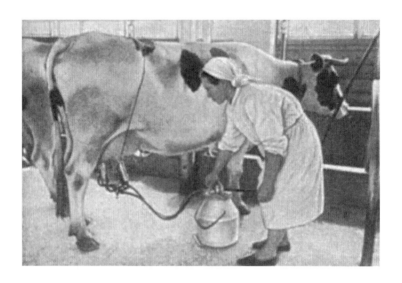

Cheese Croquettes

Ingredients:
200 g spreadable cheese
2 egg whites
1 egg yolk
2-3 tbsp breadcrumbs
1 cup sour cream
cooking fat (for frying)

Whip egg whites to foam. Grate cheese and add it to whipped eggs. Shape small balls from the mix and put into refrigerator to harden. Finely crush breadcrumbs. Lightly beat egg yolk with 1 tbsp of water. Roll chilled cheese balls in breadcrumbs, then in egg yolk, then in breadcrumbs again, deep fry for 1-2 minutes. Serve with sour cream and green bean garnish.

Nalistniki with Cheese

Prepare dough and farmer cheese stuffing the same was as for blini (crepes) with cheese. Cook very thin blini on small frying pans. Wrap farmers cheese in blini, molding them into hot dog shape. Moisten prepared blini in raw eggs, coat in breadcrumbs and fry on a skillet in butter. Serve hot with sour cream or jam.

Farmers Cheese with Fresh Greens

Ingredients:
500 g farmers cheese
1 cup sour cream
100 g lettuce or spinach
2 tbsp sugar

Wash and drain salad or spinach leaves. Dry with clean towel and finely chop. Add salt and sugar to farmers cheese, mix and pass through meat grinder or rub through sieve. Mix cheese with chopped greens and serve on big plate or serving plates, in a shape of a mound. In the center of the mound, make a cavity and fill it with cold sour cream. Decorate edges of the plate with lettuce leaves or parsley.

Instead of lettuce, finely chopped dill, parsley or radish leaves may be used. Use no more than 50g of greens.

Blini with Cheese (Crepes with Cheese)

Ingredients:
2 cups wheat flour
500 g farmers cheese
3/4 cup sour cream
3/4 cup sugar
3 cups milk
2 eggs
2 tbsp butter

Break 1 egg into a mixing bowl, add 1 tbsp sugar, 1/2 tsp salt, 1 cup cold milk and mix well. Add flour, little at a time, mixing to incorporate, and then add remaining milk to the batter, also little at a time.

Heat a frying pan or a crepe pan over a medium heat. When the pan is hot - butter it and add enough batter to cover the bottom of the pan in a thin layer. Cook on medium heat. Take blin out of the pan when the bottom is nicely browned and repeat the process until no batter is remaining.

Blini should be very thin. If they come out too thick - thin the batter with a little bit more milk.

Rub farmers cheese through a sieve, add egg yolk, sugar, 1/2 tsp salt, lemon or orange zest, 1 tbsp melted butter and mix everything well (if desired - add picked over and washed raisins to the cheese mixture). Put 1 tbsp of cheese mixture on the cooked side of the blin and wrap it into an envelope shape. To insure that it does not unwrap during frying - moisten the final fold with egg white. Fry in butter on a preheated skillet, until nicely brown on all sides. Sprinkle stuffed blini with powdered sugar and serve hot. Serve sour cream on a side.

Cheese Galushki

Ingredients:
500 g farmers cheese
1/2 cup sour cream
2 eggs
3 tbsp sugar
1 cup wheat flour
2 tbsp breadcrumbs
3 tbsp butter

Pass cheese through a meat grinder or rub it through a sieve, add 2 eggs, sugar, 1 tbsp melted butter, 1/2 tsp salt and mix everything well. Add sifted flour to the cheese mixture and mix to incorporate. Put cheese dough on table sprinkled with flour, cut it into 4 equal parts and roll each into a thin log, slightly flatten it, and cut into small pieces on a bias. Put galushki in a pot with a boiling salted water until they float to the top.

Take cooked galushki out of the pot with a skimmer; put them on a serving plate. Pour melted butter over galushki and sprinkle with golden fried breadcrumbs.

Cooked galushki could be finished in the oven. Put galushki into an oven-proof skillet, top with sour cream and sprinkle with melted butter.

Put skillet into a baking pan filled with a bit of hot water and bake in a preheated oven until they are browned on top.

Cheese Casserole

Ingredients:
500 g farmers cheese
1 egg
3 tbsp sour cream
3 tbsp sugar
2 tbsp farina
100 g raisins
1/2 tsp vanilla extract
1 cup fruit or berry sauce
3 tbsp butter

Pass cheese through a meat grinder and add 2 tbsp melted butter, egg beaten with sugar, farina, 1/2 tsp salt, vanilla extract, and raisins. Mix everything well. Put cheese mixture into a well-buttered and sprinkled with breadcrumbs ovenproof skillet, smooth the top, cover with sour cream, sprinkle with more melted butter and bake in a preheated oven 25-30 minutes. Serve hot with a fruit or berry sauce or sour cream.

Cheese Pudding with Spinach

Ingredients:
500 g farmers cheese
1 cup sour cream
3 eggs
1 tbsp sugar
1 tbsp farina
1 tbsp butter
250 g spinach
25 g cheese

Pass cheese through a meat grinder or run it through a sieve. Add egg yolks, 2 tbsp melted butter, sugar, salt, farina to the creamed cheese. Mix everything well. Pick spinach over, remove stems and wash in 2-3 changes of water, then put into a strainer and let it drain. Finley chop drained spinach and mix it with cheese.

Whip egg whites to stiff peaks and add to the cheese mixture. Put it into a well buttered and sprinkled with breadcrumbs ovenproof skillet, smooth the top and spread sour cream over it, sprinkle with grated cheese and melted butter and bake in a preheated oven for 25-30 minutes. Put hot pudding onto a serving plate, pout melted butter over it, and serve with sour cream.

Cheese Pudding with Candied Fruit

Ingredients:
500 g farmers cheese
4 eggs
1/2 cup sugar
2 tbsp farina
100 g candied fruit
50 g raisins
zest from 1 orange
3 tbsp butter

Rub cheese through a sieve and add egg yolks, sugar, 1/4 tsp salt, orange zest, farina and melted butter. Mix everything well.

To the cheese mixture add raisins, diced

candied fruit, and whipped to stiff peaks egg whites. Put everything into a buttered and sprinkled with sugar pan and steam it or bake in a preheated oven (if baking - sprinkle the pan with breadcrumbs instead of sugar). Serve hot with fruit sauce or jam.

Sweet Cheese Spread

Ingredients:
500 g farmers cheese
3 tbsp sour cream
1 cup sugar
1/2 tsp vanilla extract
100 g butter

High-quality sweet cheese spread is produced for sale by dairy industry; however, when necessary, it can also be made at home.

Cut softened butter into small pieces and put them into a mixing bowl. Whip with a wooden spoon until it is white and fluffy. Add sugar, vanilla extract, 1/4 tsp salt and mix well. Add cheese, rubbed through a sieve, and sour cream, a little at a time, mixing to incorporate before new additions.

Pile finished cheese spread into a mound on a plate and smooth the sides with a knife. Decorate with fresh or frozen berries, chopped toasted almonds, almond cookies, or chopped pistachios. Store in a cold place until serving.

Another flavoring options are 1 tbsp of

cacao powder or grated chocolate, 1 tsp of cinnamon, finely chopped candied fruit, raisins and nuts.

Feta Cheese Dumplings

Ingredients:
1 cup wheat flour
100 g feta cheese
1 egg
1/3 cups milk
1/2 cup sour cream
2 tbsp butter

Rub fresh and not very salty feta cheese through a sieve, put into a mixing bowl, add milk, flour, 1 tbsp melted butter, egg, and mix everything together. Continue mixing until the dough is smooth, at which moment cover it with a moist towel and leave to rest for 1 hour. Roll the dough out on a surface sprinkled with flour to 1/2 cm thickness, cut it into strips 2 cm wide, and cut each strip into small pieces.

Cook dumplings in a boiling salted water until they float to the top. Remove from a pot with a skimmer and let drain. Lightly fry dumplings in butter in a hot skillet. Serve hot with sour cream or butter on a side.

Cheese Pudding with Walnuts

Ingredients:

500 g farmers cheese
5 eggs
1/2 cup sugar
4 tbsp breadcrumbs
100 g raisins
50 g walnuts or almonds
3 tbsp butter
zest from 1 lemon or orange

Sift crushed breadcrumbs though a sieve. Toast chopped walnuts (or blanched almonds) in a preheated oven and mash them in a mortar with 2 tbsp of sugar. Pick raisins over for stems and wash in the warm water. Rub cheese through a sieve, add sugar, 3 tbsp melted butter, egg yolks, 1/2 tsp salt, lemon zest and mix thoroughly. Mix in sifted breadcrumbs, walnuts, raisins, and then add whipped egg whites.

Butter pudding mold inside and sprinkle with sugar. Fill the mold 3/4 high with mixture, cover it and put into a large pot with water (water should reach 1/2 way up the sides of the mold). Put thick piece of paper or folded in half cheesecloth on the bottom of the pot. Cover the pot and cook pudding approximately an hour, adding water from time to time as it evaporates.

Uniform elasticity of raised and slightly separated from the sides of the mold cheese mixture indicates the doneness of the pudding. Take finished pudding out of the mold onto a plate and serve hot, with fruit sauce or sour cream.

PASTRY

PASTRY

YEAST DOUGH

Yeast, or so called sour dough is used in baking different pastries - pirozhky, pies, kulebyak, buns, vatrushki, ponchiki (donuts).

Yeast added to the dough ferments sugars contained in the flour, breaking it down into carbon dioxide and alcohol. Carbon dioxide created as bubbles in dough raises the dough and makes it loose.

Use 20-50 g of yeast for each kilogram of flour. The more shortening (eggs, butter) is added to the dough, the more yeast should be used. Yeast should be fresh, soft, with pleasant alcohol aroma.

When making dough yeast should be dissolved in warm water or warm milk. The most favorable temperature for yeast growth is 25-30 deg. Celsius. Cold milk or water slow down the normal development of yeast and prevent normal fermentation and rising of the dough. At the same time, very hot water or milk can completely kill yeast.

Container with just mixed dough should be covered with a clean towel or napkin and put into a warm place for fermentation. Raised dough should be punched down and then should be left to rise again. This process of punching down the dough releases some of the carbon dioxide and replaces it with air, which in turn improves fermentation providing for better rising.

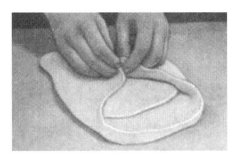

Before making dough flour should be sifted to remove any lumps and insure good aeration.

Any of the following shortening can be used - butter, clarified butter, margarine, lard, or vegetable oil.

Dough can be made using either straight

dough method or sponge method. Sponge method is recommended when dough will contain a lot of shortening.

In straight dough method dough is mixed all at one, then it is allowed to rise, pushed down and left to rise the second time.

In the sponge method initially a sponge (batter) is made by combining full quantity of liquid (water or milk) with yeast and only half of the flour. This sponge is left in a warm place to develop for 45-60 minutes. During this time the sponge develops a flavor and increases in size 1.5-2 times. Shortening with salt is added to the dough when the fermentation of the sponge stops and it starts somewhat loosing its volume. Then the remaining flour is added and the dough should be developed until it does not stick to hands or sides of the mixing bowl. Only then this dough is left in a warm place for second rising for 1 1/2 - 2 hours. Second rising ends when the dough starts losing its volume, just like sponge.

Neither the sponge not the dough should be allowed to stand too long since it decreases the quality of the dough. Leaving the dough to stand too long allows development of the sour milk bacteria which convert sugars into milk acid, giving the dough and pastries made from it characteristic sour taste.

Therefore, it is absolutely not necessary to make dough in the evening to let it rise overnight. 2 1/2 - 3 hours are enough for development of dough.

It is necessary to maintain proportion of ingredients (flour, shortening, water) in the dough. When the quantity of the main ingredient (flour) changes, quantity or volume of other ingredients should be adjusted accordingly.

Ingredients for making of dough should be carefully measured and weighted. To make dough for 1 kg of flour use 30-40 g yeast, 2 cups water or milk, 2-4 tbsp shortening, 2-3 eggs, 1 tbsp sugar and 1 tsp of salt.

Baked Pirozhki with Yeast Dough

Make straight or sponge dough. Put finished dough on a table or a bench sprinkled with flour, cut into pieces and roll them into balls, leave the dough balls to rise for 5-10 minutes. Roll the balls out to circles about 1 cm thickness and put stuffing in the middle of each circle. Bring the sides of a circle together and pinch them shut, making oval-shaped pirozhki.

Put finished pirozhki seam side down into

an oiled baking sheet or skillet 1 1/2 - 2 cm away from each other and put into a warm place for 15-20 minutes to rise. Brush pirozhki with egg wash and bake in a preheated oven 15-20 minutes.

Take baked pirozhki out of the baking sheet, brush the top with melted butter and cover with clean towel.

Pie Baked with Yeast Dough

Just like pirozhki, a pie can be stuffed with any stuffing - meat, offal, fish with rice, cabbage, rice with eggs, porridge, mushrooms.

Divide prepared dough (straight or sponge) into 2 equal pieces and roll each one into an approximately 3/4 cm thick rectangular shape. Put one sheet of dough into an oiled baking sheet, put stuffing in an even layer on top of this sheet of dough, cover with the second sheet of dough and pinch sides together. Cut any extra dough off to give pie its correct rectangular shape. Another way to prepare a pie is to roll the dough into 1 sheet, then, before adding any stuffing sprinkle the dough with flour, fold it in half and move to the baking sheet.

Pie can be decorated with different shapes. Roll the remaining dough thinly and cut out with a knife or cookie cutters shapes like diamonds, stars, circles, brush the bottom side with beaten egg and attach it to the pie. Leave the pie to rise in a warm place, brush with a beaten egg, make 2-3 pricks with a tip of a knife to allow steam to escape during baking, and bake in a preheated oven 25-30 minutes.

Pie should be served hot, cut along into 2-3 parts (depending on the size of the pie), and across into pieces 4-5 cm wide. Serve butter on the side, or caviar with a pie with fish stuffing. If the pie is not served hot - put it on top of clean paper and cover with a towel, to insure that it cools down gradually, to preserve soft and tender crust.

Fried Pirozhki with Yeast Dough

Ingredients:
1 kg wheat flour
21/2 cup milk or water
2-3 tbsp butter

1 tbsp sugar

2 eggs

1 tsp salt

30 g yeast

Prepare sponge, for which you'll need to dilute yeast in warm water (or milk), put in half the flour and thoroughly knead, so that there are no lumps. Put bowl with sponge in warm place to rise. When dough rises, put in melted butter, eggs, sugar, salt, mix well, put in the rest of the flour and knead until dough doesn't start separating from the walls of the bowl. Then put dough in warm place again for 1 1/2 hours. When dough rises, it needs to be punched down and allowed to rise again, then placed on a table or board covered with flour for cutting.

Same dough can be prepared without sponge. Dilute yeast in water or milk, add butter, eggs, sugar and salt, put in all the flour, knead well and let the dough rise twice.

While dough rises, prepare stuffing so that as soon as dough is ready, you may begin making pirozhki.

Prepared sponge or straight dough for pirozhki should be cut into pieces of 40-50 g each, roll them into a ball, letting the dough rise a little. Then flatten each ball, making it 0.5 - 1 cm, place stuffing in the middle, connect edges and pinch shut. Put pirozhki on a board or baking sheet sprinkled with flour, allowing them to rise in a warm place.

Then fry pirozhki on a skillet with butter or oil, turning them from side to side so that they get caramelized. Doughnuts with jam, preserve, apples, etc., can be prepared the same way.

Vatrushki with Yeast Dough

Divide prepared dough into small pieces, roll them into little balls, lay them out on a baking sheet greased with butter, leaving 2 - 3 cm of space in between and put in warm place. When dough rises, make a cavity in each one with a bottom of a shot glass and fill it with farmers cheese stuffing. Moisten vatrushki with egg and put in hot oven for 10-15 minutes.

Stuffing for vatrushki can be made from fresh berries, jams or preserve. Put fresh berries - strawberries, wild strawberries, raspberries - into the cavity in the dough, sprinkle with sugar and moisten edges of the dough with whipped egg.

Sweet Pie with Yeast Dough

Sweet pie is made with jam, preserve and apple stuffing.

Roll out prepared dough so that it is about 0.5 cm thick, put on a baking sheet or round skillet, cut off extra dough, place stuffing and fold edges by 1 1/2 - 2 cm.

Take remaining dough, cut it into narrow strips and put them on top of stuffing, forming a grid or mesh. Attach strips of dough to the edges with egg. Put pie in a warm place to rise. When it rises, moisten the top with whipped egg and put in hot oven for 20-30 minutes.

When pie is ready, remove from baking sheet, put on a paper. Sprinkle with powdered sugar mixed with vanilla, cut, and serve on a plate.

Milk or fruit juice may be served together with pie.

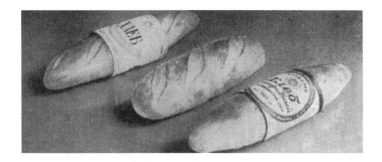

Sweet Pie with Fresh Berries

Cut prepared dough the same way as indicated in "Sweet Pie with Yeast Dough" recipe, place on a cast iron skillet or baking sheet, then put in stuffing of fresh berries (strawberries, wild strawberries, raspberries, blueberries) and sprinkle with sugar. Bake the same way as in "Sweet Pie with Yeast Dough" recipe.

Kulebyaka with Yeast Dough

Ingredients:
1 kg flour
1 3/4 cup milk
50 g yeast
100-125 g butter
4-5 egg yolks
2 tbsp sugar
1 tsp salt
stuffing

Kulebyaka differs from pie by its shape -- it should be more narrow and taller then a pie which is usually made wide and flat. In addition to that, kulebyaka is usually made with two or three different fillings positioned in layers, for example -- a layer of cooked rice topped with a layer of meat, followed by layer of sliced hardboiled eggs. To insure that the bottom layer of the dough on the inside would not become too soggy, the first layer of filling should be drier, such as rice, loose porridge, and only on top of that layer goes a layer of juicy and moist meat or fish stuffing.

Roll straight or sponge method dough into a strip as long as the baking sheet it will be baked on, 1 cm thick and about 20 cm wide. Put the dough on top of a clean towel sprinkled with flour, set the narrow strip of stuffing in the middle of the dough throughout its entire length, pinch the opposite sides of the dough shut, and with a help of the towel put kulebyaka into an oiled baking sheet with a seam side down. Kulebyaka could be decorated with thin strips of dough positioned across some distance from each other. To insure that strips of dough stay on kulebyaka, their ends and middle on the underside should be brushed with beaten egg. Leave kulebyaka in warm place to rise a little, then brush with an egg, make two-three small holes with a tip of a knife to let steam to escape during baking and put into a preheated oven to bake for 35-45 minutes. If during baking one side of kulebyak browns faster than the other - turn the baking sheet around, and if the top browns too much - cover it with moist paper towel. To test kulebyaka for readiness prick it with a toothpick. If toothpick comes out dry and there is no dough on it then kulebyaka is done. Remove kulebyaka from the baking sheet and cover with clean towel to insure that it retains its soft crust while cooling down. It could be served with meat or chicken broth.

Belyash (Vatrushka with Meat)

Ingredients:
500 g flour
1 cup milk or water

15 g yeast
1/2 tsp salt

Stuffing:
400 g boneless meat
2-3 onions
100 g fat (for frying)
salt

Make yeast dough, cut into pieces and roll each piece into small circles about 0.5 cm thick.

Make meat filling. Cut meat into small pieces - chop it or pass it through a meat grinder, and mix it with finely chopped onions, season with salt and pepper.

Put 1 tbsp of stuffing in the middle of dough circle and pinch sides of the dough in a shape of vatrushka (Danish).

Fry prepared belyashi (ed. note - plural from belyash) on both sides in a heated oil, starting with open side. Transfer to a serving plate.

Carrot Babka

Ingredients:
500 g flour
250 g carrot puree
100-125 g butter
1 cup sugar
3 eggs
20 g yeast

1/2 tsp salt

Dissolve yeast in 1/2 cup of warm water in a mixing bowl, add grated carrots, eggs, 1 cup of sifted flour, mix and put into a warm place to rise.

Add remaining flour to the risen sponge, then add butter, sugar, vanilla extract, orange zest, salt, mix everything well and leave for the second rising. When dough doubles in size, put it into a well-buttered mold and bake in a preheated oven approximately 1 hour.

Finished carrot babka should have bright saffron color, pleasant smell, and good flavor.

UNLEAVENED DOUGH

Unleavened dough is made primarily with sour cream with following proportion of ingredients: for 500 g of flour use 1 cup of sour cream, 2 tbsp of butter or margarine, 2 eggs, 1 tbsp of sugar and 1/2 tsp of salt.

If dough is made without sour cream, for 500 g of flour use 200 g of butter or margarine, 1 tbsp sugar, 2 tbsp vodka or cognac, 1/2 tsp salt.

These recipes will produce enough dough for 20-25 pirozhki or vatrushki.

Pirozhki with Unleavened Dough

Ingredients:
500 g flour
1 cup sour cream

2 eggs
1 tbsp sugar
1/2 tsp salt
2 tbsp butter

Sift flour into a mound on a work surface, make a well in the flour and add sour cream, butter, salt, sugar. Break eggs into the well and mix everything together. Roll the dough into a ball, put it on a plate, cover with a towel and put in a cold place for 30-40 minutes. Roll the dough 0.5 cm thick, cut out circles with a cookie cutter, brush circles of dough with beaten egg, put filling in the middle of the circle and pinch sides together. Put pirozhki on baking sheet 1 1/2 - 2 cm away from each other, brush the tops with beaten eggs and bake in a preheated oven 10-15 minutes.

Vatrushka with Unleavened Dough

Make unleavened dough according to the steps in the recipe "Unleavened Dough", roll it out 1/2 cm (1/5 in) thick and cut out circles using a cookie cutter. Gather remaining dough together, roll it out again and cut circles. Put farmers cheese or berries in the middle of circle and fold in sides of circles. Put vatrushki on a baking sheet, brush with beaten egg and bake in a preheated oven for 10-15 minutes.

Puff Pastry

Ingredients:
500 g flour
400 g butter
1/2 lemon
1/2 cup water
1 tsp salt

Take half of the sifted flour, mix it with butter and roll it out into a square 1 1/2 - 2 cm, transfer to a plate and keep in cool place. Add 1/2 cup of water and juice of 1/2 lemon to the remaining flour, add salt and make a dough.

Roll the dough into a ball, cover it with a towel and let it stand 20-30 minutes, then roll this dough out into a rectangle twice as wide and slightly longer then the square of the dough with butter.

Put prepared dough with butter in the middle of the rolled out dough, wrap the sides around the butter dough and pinch the seams together. This way the dough with the butter ends up enclosed in an "envelope".

Sprinkle a table with flour and roll the dough out into a rectangle approximately 20-25 cm wide and 1 cm thick. Fold the dough twice to get 4 layers, transfer to a baking sheet and put into a cold place for 30-40 minutes.

Roll chilled dough out and again fold twice and let it cool. Repeat this operation one more time. After final cooling, roll out the dough and make pies or pirozhki. Cuts of the dough should not be kneaded, instead just put them together, let it cool and roll out again.

Pirozhki with Puff Pastry

Prepare puff pastry as indicated in "Puff Pastry" recipe; roll it out in a shape of rectangle approximately 1/2 cm thick. Cut out circles with a glass or a cookie cutter.

Moisten circles of dough with water and put a ball of filling in the middle.

Cover the filling with another circle of dough.

Press around the filling with hands or smaller cutting shape.

Transfer pirozhki to a baking sheet moistened with water, brush tops with beaten egg and bake in a preheated oven 10-15 minutes.

Puff Pastry Kulebyaka with Vyaziga and Fish

Roll two strips from puff pastry, about 1/2 cm thick, 15 - 30 cm long. Make one strip 10 cm and one strip 20 cm wide. Ends of the strips should be made oval or straight. Put the narrow strip in the middle of a baking sheet and cover it with thin blini so that the stuffing doesn't make the dough soggy.

Put stuffing made from vyaziga (dried spinal cord of sturgeon) about 6-7 cm wide on top of blini. On top of vyaziga put pieces of boiled sturgeon, salmon and then cover with another layer of vyaziga. Cover stuffing with blini, moisten with beaten eggs on the sides, bind them with edges of blini on the bottom, moisten edges of puff dough around stuffing with beaten egg, cover with wider strip of dough and press edges of strips together.

Kulebyaka can be decorated with a decoration or with narrow strips made from leftover puff pastry. Moisten one side of decorations with whipped eggs and attach them to the kulebyaka. Edges of kulebyaka can be covered with a dough strip. Trim, moisten with whipped egg, make punctures on ends with a knife to let steam escape and place in hot oven for 40-50 minutes. If kulebyaka is browned on top but is not ready on the sides, cover the browned part with paper, moistened with water on the outer side. If the bottom of kulebyaka is not ready yet, place baking sheet on a stove that's not very hot.

Kulebyaka with rice and fish, meat, offal, cabbage, etc., can be prepared the same way.

Serve kulebyaka with caviar, butter and ukha.

Quick Puff Pastry

Ingredients:
500 g flour
300 g butter
1 egg
4/5 cups water
1/2 tsp salt
1 tsp lemon juice or vinegar

Sift flour, add cut into small pieces butter, and chop everything with a knife. Make a well in the flour mixed with butter and pour into this well water mixed with salt, egg, lemon juice or vinegar and mix the dough. Roll the dough into a ball, cover it with a towel and leave in a cool place for 30-40 minutes. Roll the dough out and use it to bake vatrushki, pirozhki and cookies.

STUFFING FOR PIES, PIROZHKI, KULEBYAKI AND VATRUSHKI
(for Dough Prepared with 1 kg Flour)

Beef Stuffing

Ingredients:
800 g boneless beef
2-3 tbsp oil
3 eggs, hardboiled
1-2 onions

Pass meat through a meat grinder, brown it in oil in a preheated skillet, and pass it through the meat grinder again. Separately brown diced onions and mix it with ground meat, add chopped eggs, finely chopped dill or parsley leaves, and season with salt and pepper.

Meat stuffing can also be made with boiled beef cut into small pieces and passed through a meat grinder or copped with knives. Brown diced onions in a skillet, add meat to the onions and fry

for 3-4 minutes. Add chopped eggs to the meat
and onion mixture, season with salt and pepper,
add dill, 1-2 tbsp of vegetable oil, and, if the
stuffing is too dry - 1-2 tbsp of beef broth.

Offal (Liver, Lung, Heart) Stuffing

Ingredients:
1 kg offal (liver, lungs, hearts)
2-3 tbsp butter
3 eggs, hardboiled
2 onions

Wash beef, veal, lamb, or pork offal in

warm water, put into a pot, cover with water and put to boil. Cut boiled offal into small pieces and pass it through a meat grinder, add to a skillet with browned onions and lightly fry the mixture. Add chopped eggs, dill or parsley leaves, season with salt and pepper and mix everything well.

Buckwheat and Liver Stuffing

Ingredients:
300 g liver
1 cup hulled buckwheat
2-3 tbsp oil
3 eggs, hardboiled
1-2 onions

Wash and trim veal, lamb, or pork liver, removing all film and bile ducts, cut it into small pieces and fry in oil together with sliced onions. Finely chop prepared liver, mix it with cooked buckwheat, chopped eggs, and season with salt and pepper.

Fish Stuffing

Ingredients:
750 g fish or 500 g fish fillet
2 tbsp oil
1-2 onions

Scale and gut fish (pike, walleye, catfish, or carp) and wash it in cold water. Separate flesh from the bones, cut into small pieces, season with salt and pepper and fry in oil. Add fried onions, dill, mix everything well. If desired - add chopped hardboiled eggs.

Fish and Rice Stuffing

Ingredients:
300 g fish fillet
3/4 cup cooked rice
2-3 tbsp oil or butter

Wash and cut fish fillet into small pieces and fry in 1-1 1/2 tbsp of oil. Mix with cooked rice, add melted butter, finely chopped dill or parsley leaves, and season with salt and pepper.

Boiled fish can be used in this stuffing. Cut boiled fillet into small pieces and mix it with rice. If desired - add diced browned onion to this stuffing.

Vyaziga Stuffing for Pie

Ingredients:
100 g vyaziga (dried spinal cord of sturgeon)
2-3 tbsp butter
3-4 eggs, hardboiled

Soak vyaziga in cold water for 2-3 hours, rinse it, cover with fresh water and simmer for 3-3 1/2 hours. Drain cooked until soft vyaziga in a colander, pass it through a meat grinder or chop with a knife, add chopped eggs, dill or parsley leaves, melted butter, season with salt and pepper. If desired this stuffing can be mixed with cooked rice, finely chopped boiled fish, and onions browned in oil.

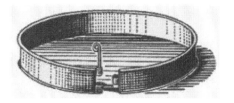

Rice and Eggs Stuffing

Ingredients:
1 1/4 cups rice
3-4 eggs, hardboiled
2-3 tbsp butter or oil

Wash rice in a couple of changes of warm water and then cook in salted boiling water (10-12 cups). Drain cooked rice in a colander. Transfer rice into a mixing bowl, add finely chopped eggs, melted butter, dill, season with salt and mix well.

Buckwheat Stuffing

Ingredients:
2 cups hulled buckwheat
3-4 eggs, hardboiled
2-3 tbsp butter or clarified butter

Cook loose buckwheat porridge; mix it with chopped eggs and butter. Fried onions and 50 g of boiled and chopped dried mushrooms can be substituted instead of eggs.

Fresh Ceps Stuffing

Ingredients:
1 kg ceps (porcini) mushrooms
1-2 tbsp butter
1 onion
1/4 cup sour cream

Boil trimmed and washed mushrooms, then cut them into small pieces and fry in butter on a skillet.

Add sour cream and diced browned onions to the skillet with mushrooms, cover it and braise 10-15 minutes. Add finely chopped dill or parsley leaves, mix and let cool.

Pickled Mushroom Stuffing

Ingredients:
1 kg pickled mushrooms
2-3 tbsp oil or clarified butter
1-2 onions

Rinse pickled mushrooms. If they are still spicy - soak them in cold water for 1-2 hours and then drain in a colander. Chop mushrooms finely and fry in oil. Fry diced onions separately and add it to mushrooms, season with pepper.

Dried Mushroom and Rice Stuffing

Ingredients:
50 g dried mushrooms
1 cup rice
1-2 onions
2-3 tbsp butter or oil

Finely chop boiled dried mushrooms, add diced browned onion, mix it together and fry for 2-3 minutes. Mix in cooked rice and season with salt and pepper.

Sago Stuffing

Ingredients:
1 cup sago
2 eggs
2-3 tbsp butter

Wash sago in cold water, put into salted boiling water (10-12 cups) and cook 20-25 minutes stirring from time to time, until it becomes transparent. Drained cooked sago in a colander. When the grain is dried transfer it to a mixing bowl, add melted bitter, chopped eggs, finely chopped dill or parsley leaves, season with salt and mix well.

Rice or Millet with Raisins Stuffing

Ingredients:
1 cup rice or millet
200 g raisins
2-3 tbsp sugar
1 1/2 tbsp butter

Pick raisins over, wash in warm water 2-3 times, drain in a colander, dry with a towel or a paper towel, and mix with cooked rice (or loose millet porridge), sugar and melted butter.

White Cabbage Stuffing

Ingredients:
1 head (1 1/2 - 2kg) white cabbage
3-4 eggs, hardboiled
2-3 tbsp oil

Shred clean and cored cabbage and scald it with boiling water, then pour cold water over it and squeeze all the water out. Put cabbage into a pot with hot oil and fry 10-15 minutes stirring frequently to prevent cabbage from burning. Add chopped eggs, sugar and season with salt.

Sauerkraut and Mushroom Stuffing for Pie

Ingredients:
1 kg sauerkraut
3-4 tbsp butter or oil

2-3 onions
50 g dried mushrooms

Pick sauerkraut over, and, if it is too sour, wash it and scald with boiling water, then chop it finely, put into a pot together with oil or melted butter and braise, covered, until cooked. Fry diced onions until browned, add finely chopped boiled mushrooms, salt, pepper, and fry 3-4 minutes longer. Mix with cooked sauerkraut.

Scallion and Egg Stuffing

Ingredients:
400 g scallions
4 eggs, hardboiled
3-4 tbsp oil

Clean and wash scallions, slice them (not too thin) and lightly fry in oil. Mix with chopped eggs, season with salt and pepper.

Carrot Stuffing

Ingredients:
1 - 1 1/2 kg carrots
3-4 eggs, hardboiled
2-3 tbsp butter or oil
1 tsp sugar

Thinly slice peeled and washed carrots and put them into a pot. Add 1/2 cup of water and 1 tbsp oil. Cover the pot and braise carrots until cooked. Chop cooked carrots, season with salt; add 1 tsp sugar, remaining oil and mix well. Add chopped eggs and stir to combine.

Farmers Cheese Stuffing

Ingredients:
500 g farmers cheese
1 egg
1/2 cup sugar
1 tbsp butter

Rub farmers cheese through a sieve or pass it through a meat grinder, add egg, sugar, a little bit of salt, melted butter and mix well.

If desired - add vanilla extract, raisins, finely chopped candied fruit. If farmers cheese is too moist - wrap it into cheesecloth and let it drain.

Apple Stuffing

Ingredients:
1 kg apples
1 cup sugar

Thinly slice peeled and cored apples, put into a pot with sugar, add 2-3 tbsp water and cook on low heat until apples are cooked into thick jam.

This filling could be used in pies from yeast or unleavened dough, or puff pastry, apple turnovers or apple donuts.

This filling could be made with fresh apples as well. If using fresh apples - mix peeled and sliced apples with sugar and use in baking.

Dried Apricot Stiffing

Ingredients:
400 g dried apricots
1/2 cup sugar

Pick dried apricots over and wash with warm water. Put apricots into a pot and cover with boiling water, simmer 10-15 minutes. Drain apricots in a colander, then put on prepared dough and sprinkle with sugar.

Cooking liquid from apricots could be used to make kissel or sweet sauce.

BLINI

In order to make thin juicy blini, small skillets need to be used - whether cast iron or other metal, but the bottom must be thick. Before pouring the dough on the skillet, it must be heated and well greased, otherwise blini will get burned.

New skillets used for the first time should be heated for 10-15 minutes with cooking fat. Then drain the fat, and rub the skillet with salt immediately. Ancient Russian proverb states: "First blin comes out as a lump". There is a lot of truth to that - first blin is lumpy - pale, thick, unappetizing. First blini give an indication as to how much dough to use in order for blini to come out straight and thin.

In a Russian stove blini are baked from both top and bottom.

Good blini can be made on a regular stove, primus stove or kerosene stove. To ensure that blin doesn't get burned, it should be turned from one side to another.

Wheat flour as well as buckwheat flour can be used to prepare blini.

Blini can be made with different seasonings: scallions, chopped boiled eggs, herring, pieces of salmon, smelt and other fish.

Blini with seasoning are made as follows: grease the skillet, sprinkle with scallions or chopped eggs, or put pieces of salmon, pour dough and bake as regular blini.

Blini can be served with melted butter or vegetable oil, sour cream, herring, lamprey, balyk, sprat, anchovies, salmon and caviar.

Blini are served hot. Put blini on a heated plate in a stack, covered with a napkin, or keep them in oven. It is even better to serve blini right after they are done, from a skillet.

Sponge Dough Blini

Ingredients:
1 kg wheat flour
4-5 cups milk
3 tbsp butter

2 eggs
2 tbsp sugar
1 1/2 tsp salt
40 g fresh yeast

Make sponge - in a mixing bowl dissolve yeast in 2 cups of warm water, add 500 g of flour, mix well, cover the bowl and leave in warm place for about an hour.

When sponge is ready - add salt, sugar, egg yolks, melted butter, mix and then add remaining flour, mixing the dough until smooth.

Add warm milk to the dough - 1 cup at a time, mixing well before each addition. Cover the bowl again and leave in a warm place to rise. When the dough has risen - mix it until it settles down and leave to rise again. Settle the dough again by mixing whipped egg whites into it.

Blini should be baked immediately after final rising. Blini are very good if the dough was allowed to rise two-three times.

If you like your blini to be drier - replace half of the flour with buckwheat flour in the recipe. Make sponge with wheat flour and 1 tbsp of buckwheat flour. Remaining buckwheat flour should be added together with shortening. All the other steps of the recipe remain unchanged.

Quick-Ripened Blini

Ingredients:
500 g flour

3 cups water
2-3 eggs
1 tbsp sugar
1/2 tsp salt
1/2 tsp baking soda
1/2 tsp lemon acid

Mix eggs with 3 cups of warm water, add salt, sugar and baking soda, add flour and whip so that the dough is uniform, with no lumps. Dilute acid in a cup of water, add to prepared dough, mix and start making blini immediately.

If there is no acid available, the dough for blini can be prepared as follows: flour, eggs, sugar, salt are mixed with soured milk. Soda is diluted in a cup of water and added to the dough and mixed before baking blini.

Ukrainian Blini

Ingredients:
300 g millet
300 g buckwheat flour
3-4 tbsp butter
2 eggs
2 tbsp sugar
1 cup sour cream
2 cup milk
15 g yeast

Pick and wash millet, cook thick porridge, let it cool and rub through a sieve.

Pour 1/2 cup of milk in a pan, add 1 tbsp butter and boil. Add 1 cup of buckwheat flour, boil until thick mixture forms and let it cool to room temperature. Then pour in yeast diluted in warm water, mix and let the dough rise. Then add prepared millet, rest of the flour, raw yolks beaten with sugar, salt. Pour in warm milk, thoroughly mix and let dough rise again. Add whipped egg whites and bake blini.

Before serving, pour blini over with butter. Serve sour cream separately.

PANCAKES

Ingredients:
500 g flour
2 cups milk or water
2 eggs
1 1/2 tbsp sugar
3-4 tbsp shortening (butter or vegetable oil)
1/2 tsp salt
25 g fresh yeast

Dissolve yeast in warm milk, add flour and make dough. let it rise in a warm place, then add eggs, salt, sugar and 1 tbsp of shortening, mix well, then leave to rise for the second time. Without mixing it after the second rise, take portions of dough with a spoon dipped in water and fry on both sides in butter in a preheated skillet.

Serve with sugar, honey, preserves, jam, or

farmers cheese with sour cream and sugar.

Pancakes can be made with apples or raisins. Instructions for making pancakes with apples will be described in a separate recipe. For pancakes with raisins - pick raisins carefully over, thoroughly wash, and add to the dough.

Pancakes with Pumpkin, Squash or Carrots

Ingredients:
1 kg flour
1 kg vegetables
2 eggs
1-2 tbsp sugar
2 tbsp vinegar
1 1/2 tsp salt
1/2 tsp baking soda
2 tbsp butter

Peel fresh vegetables (pumpkin, squash or carrots), slice and boil in a small quantity of water; pass boiled vegetables through a meat grinder or rub through a sieve. Break eggs into this vegetable puree without letting it cool, add salt, vinegar, flour mixed with soda, punch it down. Bake pancakes on a hot skillet.

Pancakes with Apples

Ingredients:
500 g flour
2 cups milk or water

2 eggs
2 tbsp butter
1 tbsp sugar
1/2 tsp salt
25 g yeast
3-4 apples

Dilute yeast in warm milk or warm water, add butter, eggs, sugar, salt, thoroughly mix and gradually pour in flour. Cover with towel and put in a warm place to rise.

Peel apples and remove the core, then thinly slice. Before baking, put apple slices in prepared dough that has risen. Mix and fry pancakes on a skillet with heated butter, adding dough with a spoon moistened in water.

BLINCHIKI (CREPES) AND BLINCHIKI PIE

Blinchiki are made from thin batter made with milk, eggs, and sugar.

Blinchki are served with honey or sugar, or filled with farmers cheese, apples, or preserves.

Blinchiki with Honey or Sugar

Ingredients:
250 g flour
2 1/2 cups milk
3 eggs
2 tbsp butter
2 tbsp clarified butter

1/4 tsp salt

Mix 3 egg yolks with 1/2 cup of milk, add salt, sugar in a mixing bowl, then pour in flour mixing all the time. Add 2 tbsp of melted butter and mix to incorporate (to prevent lumps), then add remaining milk, a little at a time. Finally, add egg whites whipped into foam.

Bake thin blinchiki on a preheated skillet brushed with clarified butter.

Fold each blinchik in half, and then in half again, without taking it out of the skillet, then transfer to a preheated serving plate and cover with a napkin.

Serve with honey or sugar.

(ed. note - blinchiki should not be flipped during cooking, i.e. they are cooked only on one side.)

Blinchiki with Farmers Cheese, Apples and Other Fillings

Ingredients:
250 g flour
2 1/2 cup milk
3 eggs
1/2 tbsp sugar
1/4 tsp salt
1 tbsp clarified butter or margarine (for frying)

Mix eggs with salt, sugar, 1/2 cup of milk, add flour and make a batter without lumps. Thin the batter with remaining milk.

Brush well-heated medium-sized skillet with clarified butter or a piece of fatback; pour some batter into the skillet tilting the skillet so that batter spreads thinly and evenly over the bottom of the skillet. Take browned on one side blinchiki out of the skillet and stack into a pile on a plate.

Take each blinchik with its browned side up and put 1 tbsp of farmers cheese or apples stuffing, or a thick jam or preserves in the middle. Wrap the sides to enclose the filling and quickly fry on all sides in a skillet.

Sprinkle with powdered sugar just before serving. Blinchiki can also be filled with meat, in which case they should be served with sour cream and tomato sauce.

Blinchiki Pie

Bake blinchiki following instructions in the recipe "Blinchiki with Stuffing". Butter and sprinkle with breadcrumbs a round mold or a shallow pan. Layer blinchiki on the bottom and the sides of the mold, browned side in, put a layer of filling, cover with blinchik, put another layer of filling, and cover with another blinchik. Repeat the process until the mold if filled. Cover the top layer of filling with blinchik, brush with beaten egg, sprinkle with breadcrumbs and melted butter and bake in a preheated oven 30-40 minutes.

Unmold the pie onto a serving plate and serve hot.

Serve butter, meat or chicken broth in a cup.

Blinchiki pie could be made with any filling - one or different. Some of the possible fillings are chopped chicken meat dressed with white sauce.

BUNS, KRENDELKI (SWEET PRETZELS), KULICHI (EASTER CAKES) AND OTHER PRODUCTS

Buns

Ingredients:
1 kg flour
2 1/2 cup milk
150-200 g butter or margarine
2 eggs
3/4 cup sugar
3/4 tsp salt
30 g yeast

Pour 2 1/2 cups of warm milk (or water) into bowl that will be used to make dough. Add yeast and half of flour, mix well. Punch down dough so that there are no lumps, cover bowl with towel or napkin and put in a warm place.

When sponge rises, add salt, sugar, heated butter or margarine (you may also add 2-3 eggs, vanilla or powdered cardamom), mix, add the rest of the flour and punch down dough until it starts separating from the edges of the bowl.

Cover bowl again and leave it in a warm

place to rise. When volume increases to twice the original, lay dough out on a board sprinkled with flour and divide dough into small balls weighing approximately 50-60 g each. Put buns on a baking sheet, grease them with a little butter, let dough rise in a warm place, then moisten buns with whipped egg and put in hot oven for 12-15 minutes for baking.

"Shanezhki" Buns

Ingredients:
1 kg flour
1 1/2 cup milk
5 egg yolks
1 1/2 cup sugar
300 g butter or margarine
1/2 tsp salt
40 g yeast

For glaze:
1 tbsp sour cream
1 tbsp flour
1 tbsp butter
1 - 1 1/2 tbsp sugar

Dilute yeast in warm milk, pour in half of flour and let it rise. When volume increases approximately two times, add salt and egg yolks whipped with sugar, mix, pour in the remainder of the flour and punch down the dough. Then add melted butter or margarine, and punch down the dough so that it separates from the walls of the bowl. Sprinkle with flour, cover and put in a warm place to rise. When volume increases by twofold, lay dough out on a board and make small buns. Put buns on baking sheet that has been greased with butter and let them rise in a warm place. To glaze buns, mix one tablespoon of sour cream with same amount of flour and one tablespoon of melted butter. Glaze the surface of the buns with resulting mixture, sprinkle with sugar and put in oven to bake for 12-15 minutes.

Krendelki (Sweet Pretzels) for Tea or Coffee

Ingredients:
1 kg flour
1 1/2 cups milk
5 eggs
1 cup sugar
100-125 g butter or margarine
3/4 tsp salt
30 g yeast
zest from 1/2 lemon

Make the dough just like in the recipe "Shanezki buns". When adding sugar and eggs - add finely grated lemon zest. When dough is ready put it on a work surface, sprinkle with flour and shape small krendelki. Brush krendelki with butter, sprinkle with sugar and bake in a preheated oven 10-15 minutes.

Roll with Poppy Seeds

Ingredients:
1 kg flour
1 1/2 cup milk
5 eggs
1 cup sugar
100 - 125 g butter or margarine
3/4 tsp salt
30 g yeast

For stuffing:
300 g poppy seeds
150 g honey
3/4 cup sugar

Make dough the same way as for "Shanezhki" buns. Prepare poppy seeds separately: out it in a pan, pour over with boiling water, cover and let it stand for 30-40 minutes. Then drain water, squeeze poppy slightly, then crush it in a mortar, gradually adding honey and then sugar, so that the mixture resembles thick preserve.

Roll out the dough into thickness of about 1 cm, place a layer of prepared poppy on top, even out and roll dough into a tube. Place the roll on a baking sheet greased with butter and put in a warm place to rise; then moisten roll with egg and place in a hot oven to bake for 20-30 minutes.

For aroma, you may add some vanilla or lemon peel to the dough. When serving, slice roll and sprinkle with powdered sugar.

Rusks

Ingredients:
1 kg flour
1 1/2 cups milk (for the dough)
4 eggs
200 g butter or margarine
1 - 1 1/2 cups sugar
3/4 tsp salt
vanilla, cardamom, saffron or zest from 1/2 lemon
1 cup milk
100 g almonds

Make the dough just like in the "Buns" recipe, but a bit denser. Put the dough on work surface and cut into baguettes as long as a baking sheet. Transfer baguettes to a lightly buttered sheet. With a dull side of a knife make shallow cuts across the tops of the baguettes and leave in a warm place to rise. Brush the top of the dough with beaten egg and bake in a preheated oven 15-20 minutes.

Slice cooled baguettes across, put slices on a baking sheet, drizzle them with milk and sprinkle with sugar, crushed almonds, or crashed almonds mixed with sugar. Dry on low heat in the oven.

Kulich (Easter Cake)

Ingredients:

1 kg flour

1 1/2 cups milk

6 eggs

300 g butter or margarine

1 1/2 - 2 cups sugar

40-50 g yeast

3/4 tsp salt

150 g raisins

50 g candied fruit

50 g almonds

1 tsp vanilla extract or 5-6 cardamom seeds, ground

Dough for kulich could be made two different ways.

First method. Dissolve yeast in 1 1/2 cups of warm milk in a mixing bowl, add half of the flour, mix to break all the lumps, cover and leave sponge in a warm place. When the volume of sponge doubles, add salt, 5 egg yolks mixed with sugar and vanilla extract, butter. Mix everything well, then add whipped into foam egg whites and remaining flour. The dough should not be too stiff, but mixed well and should easily pull away from the sides of the mixing bowl.

Cover the dough and leave in a warm place. When the dough doubles in volume add raisins (washed and dried), diced candied fruit, blanched and chopped almonds. Mix everything together and then divide the dough among prepared molds. To get lighter kulich - fill the mold only 1/3 of way up, to get denser kulich - fill the mold 1/2 way up.

To prepare mold cover the bottom with buttered on both sides circle of paper, butter the sides and sprinkle them with flour or crushed breadcrumbs. Put filled with dough molds into a warm place and cover with towel. When the dough reaches 3/4 of the way up, brush the top with beaten egg and put into a preheated (not very hot) oven for 50-60 minutes. To insure even baking carefully turn the mold around without shaking it.

To prevent burning of the top of kulich cover it with a circle of dump paper once it is nicely browned. To check if kulich is done stick a bamboo skewer into it -- if the skewer comes out dry then kulich is ready, if there is some dough on the skewer -- it needs more time to bake.

Once cooled kulich could be covered with glaze and decorated with candied fruit, berries from preserves, chocolate shapes.

Second method. Dissolve yeast in 1 1/2 cups of warm milk in a mixing bowl, add 4 cups of flour and mix to combine, then add salt, egg yolks beaten with sugar until they are white, melted butter or margarine, egg whites beaten into foam, and mix everything well. Sprinkle the dough with flour, cover the bowl and leave in a warm, draftless place overnight. Following morning add remaining flour, sugar, vanilla extract; mix the dough and leave to rise. Once it doubles in volume, continue the process following the steps of the first method - i.e. add raisins, candied fruit, put dough into molds.

Almond Kulich (Easter Cake)

Ingredients:
1 kg flour
1 1/2 cup milk
6 eggs
300 g butter or margarine
1 1/2 - 2 cup sugar
3/4 tsp salt
300 g sweet almonds
40 - 50 g yeast
1 tsp vanilla extract

Prepare dough the same way as in Kulich recipe; punch down cake, add blanched, peeled, thinly sliced or finely chopped, dried almonds (250 g). Follow Kulich recipe for the rest of the preparation. Before putting kulich in oven, sprinkle it with almonds.

Rum Baba

Ingredients:
1 kg flour
2 cups milk
7 eggs
1 1/4 cup sugar
300 g butter or margarine
3/4 tsp salt
200 g dried currants
1 tsp vanilla

50 g yeast

For syrup:
1/2 cup sugar
1 3/4 cup water
4-6 tbsp grape wine, liqueur or 1 tsp rum essence

Dilute yeast in one cup of warm milk, add 3 cups of flour and knead thick dough. Roll it into a ball, on one side make 5-6 shallow cuts and place dough in a pan with warm water (2 - 2 1/2 l), cover with lid and put in warm place.

After 40-50 minutes, when dough rises and its volume increases by twofold, remove it, put in a bowl for kneading. Add a cup of warm milk, salt, egg yolks whipped with sugar and vanilla, whipped egg whites, mix everything, then add the rest of the flour and knead dough. After that add whipped butter (or margarine) and knead dough again (it shouldn't be too thick), cover and put in warm place. When volume of the dough becomes twice the original, add dried currants, mix and pour dough into molds (fill the mold 1/3 of way up), that have been prepared the same way as molds for kulich, cover and put in warm place to rise. When dough rises to 3/4 of the height of the mold, then carefully, without shaking, put it in an oven that's not too hot for 45-60 minutes.

During baking turn the form very carefully, since even a little push may result the dough to cave and the middle to empty. When rum baba is ready (use same method of determination as for kulich), remove it from the mold and put on a plate on its side. When it cools, pour it over with syrup with wine, carefully turning it on the plate so that syrup soaks in on all sides of rum baba. Put it upright on the plate, let it dry a little, then put on another plate, cover with paper napkin and serve.

Krendel (Pretzel) with Almonds

Ingredients:
1 kg flour
1 1/2 cups milk
12 egg yolks
1 1/2 cup sugar
300 g butter or margarine
3/4 tsp salt
200 g raisins
100 g sweet almonds
40-50 g yeast
1 tsp vanilla extract
1-2 tbsp powdered sugar

Make a sponge by mixing warm milk, yeast, and half of the flour in a mixing bowl, and let it rise in a warm place. Separately beat egg yolks with sugar and vanilla extract until white; add softened and whipped butter or margarine, mix and then add to the prepared sponge. Add salt, remaining flour and mix the dough until it pulls away from the walls of the bowl. Add washed and dried raisins, mix, cover the bowl and put into a warm place to rise. The dough should be fairly dense. When the dough has risen transfer it to a work surface, sprinkle with flour, knead, and roll with your hands into a shape of a cord - thinner at the ends, fold the ends in a shape of a pretzel, put on a baking sheet and leave in a warm place for a couple of minutes. Brush the top with beaten egg yolk, sprinkle with sliced or crushed blanched almonds and bake in a preheated oven 40-50 minutes. Transfer finished krendel from baking sheet to a sheet of paper folded a couple of times to make sure that the bottom does not become soggy.

Just before serving sprinkle krendel with powdered sugars and transfer to a serving plate covered with a napkin.

COOKIES

Home Cookies

Ingredients:
3 cups flour
2-3 eggs
250 g butter or margarine
1 - 1 1/4 cup sugar
1/2 tsp baking soda
1 tsp vanilla

Whip eggs with sugar; add melted butter or margarine, baking soda, vanilla and mix. Add flour and knead very thick dough (as for pasta).

Pass prepared dough through a meat grinder. Shape strands of dough that have come out into cookies. Put cookies on baking sheet greased with butter and put into oven for baking. When cookies are ready, sprinkle them with powdered sugar.

Shortbread Cookies

Ingredients:
2 cups flour
1/2 cup sour cream
1 cup sugar (powdered or granulated)
100 - 125 g butter or margarine
1/2 tsp baking soda
1 tsp vanilla

Add sugar, soda, vanilla to dough and mix well. Then add sour cream, butter or margarine in pieces and knead dough. Roll dough in a ball, cover with napkin and leave in cold place for 20-30 minutes and then roll dough out so that the thickness is about 1/2 cm. On the surface of the dough, make dimples with fork and cut out little shapes: circles 3-4 cm in diameter, crescents, diamonds, rectangles, etc. and lay them out on a baking sheet. You can also decorate some of these shapes by placing a raisin or a berry on top in the middle.

Wash shapes with whipped egg and put in oven to bake for 10-12 minutes.

Pryanichki (Spice Cookies)

Ingredients:
1 cup flour
3 eggs
1 cup sugar
5 grains of cardamom or 1/2 tsp vanilla extract or
lemon zest

Beat eggs with sugar until the mixture is
white; add ground cardamom or any other spice
being used. Add flour and mix well. Take a
teaspoon of dough at a time and with a help of
another teaspoon put it on a buttered baking pan.

Put pieces of dough about 4 cm away from
each other. Bake in a preheated oven 7-10 minutes.

Take finished pryanichki out of the oven
and transfer to a serving plate.

(ed. note - the name pryanichki came from
the word pryanost - spice)

Almond Cookies

Ingredients:
200 g almonds
1 3/4 cups sugar
6 egg whites
1/2 cup flour

Almonds for these cookies should be
blanched, skinned, and left to dry in a warm place.
Dried almonds should be finely pounded in a
mortar while slowly adding egg whites (1-3) and

sugar.

Add remaining egg whites to the almond paste, mix well and warm through, then cool slightly, add flour and mix to incorporate. Transfer the mix to a piping bag and pipe small circles onto a sheet of parchment paper on top of a baking sheet.

Put baking sheet into a not very hot oven. During baking cookies should brown slightly and dry out. When cookies are ready - put parchment paper with cookies on top of a dump napkin (towel).

Once the cookies could be separated from the parchment paper they could be transferred to a vase.

Almond cookies could be sandwiched together. Brush the flat side of cookies with hot marmalade, jam, or melted chocolate and join them together.

Whipped cookies (Meringues)

Ingredients:
4 egg whites
1 cup powdered sugar or fine granulated sugar

Whip egg whites with a whisk until stiff picks form, and, continuing whipping, ass powdered sugar or fine granulated sugar. Shape cookies by taking whipped egg whites with a tablespoon and putting them on a parchment paper on top of a baking sheet. Meringue could also be piped out of the piping bag into some decorative shapes. Meringues are baked in a not very hot oven.

Cookies should be well-dried; therefore, they could be left to dry overnight in the oven after it was turned off. Keep cookies in dry place.

Biscuit Cookies

Break 2-3 eggs into a pot, add 1/2 cup sugar and whip over low heat until sugar completely dissolves. Remove from heat and continue whipping until the mixture is white. Add 1 - 1 1/4 cups flour, vanilla extract and mix to incorporate. Batter should not be too thick. Shape cookies with a help of a teaspoon or pipe different shapes with a piping bag on a buttered and sprinkled with flour baking sheet. Bake cookies in a not very hot oven for 5-7 minutes.

Similar-shaped cookies could be sandwiched together with a help of thick jelly or jam.

Honey-Cakes

Ingredients:
2 cups flour
1/2 cup sugar
150 g honey
1 egg
1/2 tsp baking soda
50 g almonds or walnuts

ground cinnamon
ground cloves

Break an egg into a bowl, add sugar and mix to combine; then add honey, ground cinnamon and cloves, baking soda and mix again. Add flour and mix dough with a beater 5-10 minutes. To make sure that the dough has the dark color - caramelize 1-2 teaspoons of sugar in a small skillet, dissolve it with 1 1/2 - 2 tbsp of water, bring to simmer and add together with honey. Transfer dough to a buttered and sprinkled with flour baking sheet, smooth the top, sprinkle chopped almonds or walnuts and but into a not very hot oven for 15-20 minutes. Cool finished cake, cut into servings and transfer to a serving plate.

Cake could be cut into 2 layers, spread jam between layers, and top with a glaze, then cut it into servings.

Moscow-Style Donuts

Ingredients:
1 1/2 cups flour
2 tbsp sugar
1 tbsp butter
1 egg
1/2 cups milk
1/2 tsp baking soda
100 g fat (for frying)
ground cinnamon

Add baking soda and ground cinnamon to flour; mix it in, and sift the flour. Mix together sugar, butter, and eggs, dilute with milk; then add flour and mix to incorporate.

Roll the finished dough out 1/2 cm thick and cut out donuts with a circular cutter. Cut holes in the middle of circles with a smaller cutter. Fry donuts in hot oil or fat. Sprinkle finished donuts with powdered sugar.

Molasses Poppy Seed Candies

Ingredients:
1 cup treacle
1 1/2 cups poppy seeds
1 tsp clarified butter
1/2 cups chopped walnuts

Add poppy seeds, chopped walnuts, and butter to warmed up treacle, mix everything well and cook it down constantly stirring for about 1 hour. Pour boiled down mixture onto a wet work surface, smooth it with wet hands to about 1/2 cm thickness, and, before it completely cools down, cut into diamonds or triangles. Let the candies cool.

Rye Cookies

Ingredients:
2 cup rye flour

3 tbsp sugar
2 eggs
2 tbsp sour cream
1/2 tsp baking soda

Break eggs into a bowl, add sugar and mix together with a wooden spoon while pouring in melted butter (ed. note - the list of ingredients does not mention butter at all. Apparently editors missed this problem in the book), then mix in cold sour cream. Add baking soda mixed with a small quantity of flour, then add remaining flour and make stiff dough.

Roll the dough into a thin layer, brush with beaten egg and make wavy line decorations with a fork. Cut out different shapes using cookie cutters - circles, diamonds, transfer them to buttered baking sheet. Bake in a preheated oven.

Corn Flake Biscuits

Ingredients:
2 cups corn flakes
2 eggs
4/3 cups sugar
1/2 cups raisins
1 tsp vanilla extract
1 tbsp butter (for baking sheet)

Whip egg whites to stiff peaks, then continue whipping while adding sugar mixed with vanilla extract. Mix corn flakes and raisins with whipped egg whites, and shape cookies with a spoon, preferably a round one, on a warmed buttered baking sheet. Put baking sheet into a not very hot oven for 30-40 minutes, let biscuits brown a little and dry out. Once biscuits are done - transfer them to a bowl.

Cruller

Ingredients:
2 1/2 cups flour
3 egg yolks
1 tbsp sugar
2 tbsp cognac
1 tbsp sour cream
1/4 tsp salt
1/2 cup milk
1 cup clarified butter or fat (for frying)

Mix milk, sour cream, egg yolks, powdered sugar, salt, and cognac, mix everything well, then mix a stiff dough by adding flour, a little at a time.

Roll the dough out thinly, cut it into thin strips about 10-12 cm and braid 2-3 strips together at a time and join the ends with egg whites. If desired - make roses from the dough - cut out circles of different sizes, put them on top of each other, squeeze in the middle and make cuts on the sides.

Put prepared dough into hot fat and fry until done. Take crullers out with a fork and let it drain on a wire screen or paper towels, sprinkle with granulated sugar mixed with vanilla, lemon zest, or cinnamon.

Korzhiki

Ingredients:
2 cups flour
2 tbsp butter
2/3 cup sour cream
1 egg
3 tbsp sugar
1/2 tsp baking soda

Sift flour into a mound on a work surface, make a well in the middle of the mound and put sour cream, egg, sugar, salt (to taste), softened butter and make dough.

Roll the dough out into a layer approximately 1/2 cm and cut out circles using a cookie cutter. Transfer circles of dough to a baking sheet and brush it with beaten egg, make several pricks with a fork to prevent dough from rising during baking, and bake in preheated oven for 10-15 minutes.

PASTRIES, CAKES and KEKSI (QUICK BREADS)

Puff Pastry with Apples

Ingredients:
2 cups flour

250 g butter
1 egg
1/4 tsp salt
3/4 cups water
1/4 lemon or a little bit of dissolved lemon acid
1 kg apples
1 1/2 cups sugar

Make the dough according to instructions of the "Puff Pastry" recipe. Roll the dough to 1/2 cm thickness as long as the sheet on which it will be baked. Cut the dough into the strips of 7-8 cm, put on a lightly moistened sheet, brush strips with beaten egg and decorate with drawings using a fork or a tip of a knife. Bake in a preheated oven 20-25 minutes. Baked pastry should be 4-5 cm thick. Make apple filling following the recipe "Apple Stuffing". Cut baked strips of pastry along into two layers. Put some apple filing on top of the bottom layer, smooth the top of the filling and cover with the top layer of the pastry. Cut each pastry into servings, sprinkle with powdered sugar and transfer onto a plate covered with paper napkin.

Puff Pastry with Cream

Ingredients:
2 cups flour
250 g butter
1 egg
3/4 cups water

1/4 tsp salt
1/4 lemon or a little bit of dissolved lemon acid

For meringue:
4 egg yolks
1 cup fine granulated sugar

Make the dough according to instructions of the "Puff Pastry" recipe. Roll the dough out thinly to the size of the baking sheet. Transfer the dough to the baking sheet and prick with fork in a number of places and bake in a preheated oven 12-15 minutes. Make a number layers following this procedure. Transfer baked sheets to a work surface, straighten the edges. Finely chop the trimmings and put them aside. Put a layer of cream (pastry or butter cream) on top of one of the layers of puff pastry, smooth and cover with another layer of puff pastry. Make 3-5 layers following this process. Sprinkle the top layer with cream with chopped trimmings. Cut the cake into strips 6-7 cm wide and then cut each strip into pastries. Sprinkle the top with powdered sugar, transfer pastries to a serving plate and serve.

When the cake is cut into strips it could be topped with a layer of meringue, about 1 cm thick, smooth the top, sprinkle with chopped trimming and put into the hot oven for 2-3 minutes, remove from the oven, cut each strip into individual pastries and transfer to a serving plate.

Shortbread Pastry with Almonds

Ingredients:
2 cups of flour
150 g butter or margarine
3/4 cups sugar
2 eggs
1/2 tsp vanilla extract or zest from 1/2 lemon
100 g almonds

Mix together flour and sugar, add butter or margarine cut into pieces, eggs (leave one egg white for brushing), vanilla or finely grated zest and make dough. Roll the dough into a ball, cover and leave it in a cool place anywhere from 30 minutes to 1 hour. Roll the dough out 1/2 cm thick, cut our circles with a cookie cutter and cut a smaller circle from the middle of the bigger circle. Transfer the dough circles to a baking sheet and brush with egg white, sprinkle with chopped almonds or walnuts and bake in a preheated oven 10-15 minutes. Sprinkle finished pastries with powdered sugar, transfer to a plate covered with napkin and serve.

Sour Cream Sponge Pastry

Ingredients:
2 cups flour
1 1/2 cups sour cream
6 eggs
1 cup sugar
1 tsp vanilla extract

Beat sugar with egg yolks until white in color, add vanilla extract, sour cream, mix well, add flour, and after it has been incorporated - add whipped into a foam egg whites. Carefully mix them in, pour the batter into a buttered mold and put into a note very hot oven 20-25 minutes to bake.

Transfer baked cake to a plate covered with a napkin; sprinkle it with powdered sugar.

Sponge Pastry with Jam

Ingredients:
100 g wheat flour
100 g potato flour
1 cup sugar
10 eggs
1/2 tsp vanilla

Separate egg whites from yolks. Put egg whites in cold place or cold water. Whip yolks with sugar (you may add vanilla), then add flour, mix and add whipped egg whites, mixing them with dough from bottom to top. Put dough into a mold that has been greased with butter and sprinkled with flour. Fill the mold 3/4 of the way and put into medium-hot oven for baking. A cake that is ready easily comes off from the edges of the mold and a thin wooden stick will remain dry, if you test the cake with it by inserting it. Remove cake from mold and let it cool, then cut it into two layers. Wash each layer with jam and then return cake into its original shape. You may also glaze the pastry; decorate it with berries, citron and nuts. Put cake on a plate with a napkin and slice with a thin sharp knife.

Pastry with Whipped Cream or Custard

Ingredients:
1 cup flour
100 - 125 g butter or margarine
4-5 eggs
1 cup water
1/4 tsp salt
1 cup cream
2 - 2 1/2 tbsp sugar
1/2 tsp vanilla or 1-2 spoon liqueur

Pour one cup of water into a pan, add butter, salt and bring to boil. As soon as the water boils, add all the flour, stir and cook on low heat for 2-3 minutes while stirring. Then remove from heat and add eggs, one by one, thoroughly mixing. As soon as dough starts stretching, stop adding eggs. Make small buns out of the dough, place them on a baking sheet about 3 1/2 - 4 cm apart. Put in a hot oven for 15-20 minutes. As soon as buns become caramelized and increase in volume, reduce heat and bake until buns are ready.

Cut prepared buns lengthwise, crack them open and fill the inside with cream that has been whipped with sugar, vanilla or liqueur. You may also fill them with custard or cream filling (see appropriate recipe). Then sprinkle with powdered sugar, put on a plate and serve.

Berry Baskets

Ingredients:
2 cup flour
150 g butter or margarine
3/4 cup flour
2 eggs
1 tsp vanilla or lemon peel

Prepare dough the same way as for shortbread pastry. Roll out dough so that it is 1/2 cm thick. Cut out circles that are a bit larger than metal molds for baskets. Put dough circles on top of molds and press them in, evening out the edges. Place molds with dough on skillet or on baking sheet and put in oven for 12-15 minutes to bake. When they are ready, remove baskets from molds by turning them over. Then fill the baskets with berries - strawberries, raspberries or grapes and then pour them over (using a spoon) with hot marmalade (see marmalade recipe). Baskets can be decorated with chopped nuts or fried almonds.

Sponge Cake Roll

Prepare sponge cake dough (see recipe), pour it out on a baking sheet (greased with butter and sprinkled with flour) in thickness of 1 cm. Put sheet in medium-hot oven. As soon as sponge cake becomes caramelized and will start separating from baking sheet, immediately put in on a table and wash with a thin layer of jam or preserve (250 g), then fold it into a roll and sprinkle with powdered sugar.

When the roll cools, slice it diagonally, place on a plate and serve.

You may add vanilla to the dough for aroma and flavor.

Dry Sponge Cake

Ingredients:
1 1/4 cup flour
1 cup sugar
8 eggs

Whip egg yolks with sugar until white. (you may also add grated peel from one lemon or orange). After that, mix with flour and carefully add egg whites whipped to stiff peaks. Place resulting mix into a mold and bake in oven for 15-20 minutes.

Almond Cake

Ingredients:
450 g almonds
10 fresh eggs
2 cups sugar
1/2 cup breadcrumbs

1/2 tbsp butter

For cream paste:
1/2 l cream
1 cup sugar
1/2 tsp vanilla

Whip eggs with sugar. Prepare almonds separately - take 400 g almonds and wash, dry, crush in a mortar or pass through a meat grinder. Mix this almond dough with eggs and sugar continuously for 10-20 minutes. Bake two flat cakes out of this mix; in order to do this pour dough into two skillets of the same size, greased with butter and sprinkled with breadcrumbs and put in oven for 12-15 minutes.

Prepare cream paste separately. Pour 1/2 l of cream into a pan, add a cup of sugar and a little vanilla, bring to boil and cook until paste thickens (color should be light-brown). Then remove cream paste from heat, cool it and whip it.

Put one flat bread on a plate, put a layer of cream paste on it, cover with another flat bread, cover with cream paste, and sprinkle with chopped almonds that have been caramelized in oven.

Shortbread Cake

Ingredients:
2 cup flour
150 g butter or margarine

3/4 cup sugar
2 eggs
1 tsp vanilla
400 g jam or preserve

Prepare dough the same way as for shortbread pastry (see appropriate recipe). Divide dough into three parts; roll them out into a circle or a square of equal size, with a thickness of about 1 cm / 0.4 in. Put these flat breads on a baking sheet and bake in oven. Once they are ready, let them cool. Place one flat bread on a plate, cover with layer of jam or preserve, cover with second flat bread and then another layer of jam or preserve. Glaze the top of the third flat bread, decorate with berries from jam, marmalade, etc.

You may also wash one flat bread with whipped egg and sprinkle with chopped almonds. This flat bread would be placed on top and sprinkled with powdered sugar.

Shortbread Pie with Berries

Ingredients:
2 cups flour
150 g butter or margarine
3 tbsp sugar
2 eggs
500 g strawberries
1/2 tsp vanilla extract

For jam:

250 g apples or apricots

200 g sugar

Sift flour through a fine sieve, pile into a mound on a work surface, make a well in the middle of the mound and put into the well sour cream (ed. note - ingredient not mentioned in any shortbread pastry recipe, including this one.), egg, sugar, softened butter, vanilla extract, make the dough and leave it for some time in cold place. Roll the dough out on a work surface sprinkled with flour 1/2 cm thick and transfer to a baking sheet. Put large plate over the dough and cut around the plate using a knife, then remove the plate leaving the dough on the sheet. Gather trimmed dough into a ball and roll it out again, then cut into strips 2 cm wide. Put these strips along the edge of the circle, brushed with egg, and pinch them to shape ridges.

Brush the dough with beaten egg yolk and put into a preheated oven for 15-20 minutes.

When the dough becomes lightly brown - lower the heat and continue to bake for 5-7 minutes and then take it out of the oven. Cool the pie shell without taking it off the baking sheet. Fill the shell with strawberries and pour apple or apricot jam over berries. Transfer pie to a serving plate, sprinkle the edges of the pie with powdered sugar and serve. Pie can also be made with other different fresh and canned berries and fruits.

Lemon Keks (Quick Bread)

Ingredients:
2 cups sugar
150 g butter or margarine
1 cup sugar
5-6 eggs
75 g raisins or candied fruits
zest of 1/2 lemon
1 tsp vanilla extract

Beat butter with sugar until all the sugar is dissolved and the mixture is fluffy, add egg yolks, a couple at a time, and beat until the mixture is white, then add lemon zest, flour, raisins or dried currants or candied fruit, and mix well. Finally, fold in gently egg whites whipped into foam. Transfer batter into a buttered and sprinkled with flour or breadcrumbs and put into a preheated oven to bake for 30-50 minutes (depending on the thickness of batter).

Keks can be baked in small molds (for 15-20 minutes) - metal or paper.

Sprinkled baked keks with powdered sugar.

Vanilla Keks (Quick Bread)

Ingredients:
2 cups flour
1/2 cup milk
30 g yeast
1/2 cup sugar

100 g butter or margarine
2 eggs
50 g raisins
50 g walnuts or almonds
1/4 tsp salt
1/2 tsp vanilla extract

Dissolve yeast in warm milk in a mixing bowl, add salt and flour and mix stiff dough, collect it into a ball, make a cut on the top, put the dough into a pot with warm water (2 - 2 1/2 l), cover the pot and leave in a warm place to rise. Beat egg with sugar and vanilla until the mixture becomes white, add softened butter and beat everything together until it is fluffy. When the dough doubles in volume take it out of the water with a skimmer, put into some other bowl and knead it, then add egg and butter mixture, knew it again until it becomes smooth and pulls away from the walls of the bowl, mix in raisins, and, if desired, walnuts or almonds. Put the dough into a mold (it should reach 1/2 up the walls of the mold), cover with a napkin and leave in warm place to rise. When the dough rises 3/4 up the walls of the mold, put it into a preheated oven for 30-50 minutes.

Take baked keys out of the mold, sprinkle with powdered sugar and transfer to a plate covered with a paper napkin.

CREAMS AND FRUIT FILLINGS FOR PASTRIES AND CAKES

Custard

Ingredients:
1/2 l milk
4 eggs or 5 egg yolks
1 cup sugar
2 tbsp flour
1/2 tsp vanilla extract

Mash eggs or egg yolks with sugar, add
flour, mix to incorporate, add cold milk, then put
everything on a stove and cook mixing all the
time. When the cream comes to boil - remove it
from heat and add vanilla extract. If custard is not
used instantly, transfer it to a ceramic bowl,
smooth the top and put pieces of butter (to
prevent forming of crust) or sprinkle with sugar.

Butter Cream

Ingredients:
200 g unsalted butter
1/2 cups milk
1 cup sugar
1 egg
1/2 tsp vanilla extract or 2-3 tbsp liqueur

Mash sugar with eggs, add milk, and cook
until on the stove until the mixture almost comes
to boil, mixing all the time. Remove from heat and
cool the mixture down. Whip butter until white,

and while whipping, add cooled milk mixture to the butter. Add vanilla or liqueur to the cream.

Butter Cream with Condensed Milk

Ingredients:
200 g butter
300 g condensed milk
1/2 tsp vanilla or 2-3 tbsp liqueur

Whip softened butter until it is white in color, then while whipping, add condensed milk until incorporated. Add vanilla or liqueur to the finished cream. To make chocolate cream add 3 tsp of cocoa powder.

Apple Jam

Wash 500 g of apples, cut each apple in half, core it, and bake in the oven. Rub baked apples through a sieve. Add 400 g of sugar to the apple puree, mix and cook on the stove stirring all the time until the jam thickens (5-10 minutes). Remove from heat and cover pastries or cake whit jam while it is still hot.

Apricot Jam

Wash 500 g of apricots, remove pits, put into a pot with 1 cup of water, cover the pot, and put it on the stove to cook. When apricots are cooked - mash them through a sieve. Add 400 g of sugar to

the apricot puree, mix and return to the stove.
Cook stirring all the time until jam thickens.

SWEETS

KISSELS

Kissel can be prepared from berries or fruit - fresh, frozen, dried, from rhubarb and milk. Preparing kissel is much easier if instead of berries and fruits, berry/fruit syrups or juices are used. The easiest way to make kissel is from dry kissel concentrate that is available in stores. Dry kissel contains fruit or berry extract, sugar, potato starch and lemon acid. Dry kissel is diluted with cold water (100 g kissel per 1 cup). Pour it into boiling water (1 1/2 cup), mix, boil and cool.

Using more or less potato flour results in berry and fruit kissels of different thickness. Usually medium-thick kissel is prepared. Use 2 tbsp of potato starch per 4 cups of kissel. If 3 tbsp of potato starch is used per 4 cups, thick kissel will come out. When preparing kissel, dilute potato starch in cooled boiled water (2 tbsp potato starch per 1 cup water). Dilute starch while making syrup, because if it is diluted ahead of time, it will form residue on the bottom.

Strain diluted potato starch, pour into hot syrup at once, and quickly mix. Don't boil kissel for too long, because it will become too thin.

Kissels are served cold; medium-thick kissel can also be served hot. Thick kissel should be poured into molds and cooled well. The mold should be moistened with cold water from the inside first; this way kissel will easily separate from it. To prevent film from forming on top of kissel, it should be sprinkled with a thin layer of sugar. Kissel can be served with sugar, cold milk or cream.

Cranberry or Currant Kissel

Ingredients:
1 cup cranberries or currants
3/4 cup sugar
2 tbsp potato starch

Wash berries in hot water, crush with mallet or spoon, add 1/2 cup cold boiled water, rub through a sieve and dry with gauze. Pour over with 2 cups of water, bring to boil. Boil for 5 minutes, then strain. Put sugar in the strained broth, boil, pour into diluted potato starch, mix and boil again. Put pressed juice into prepared kissel and mix well.

Kissel with Strawberries, Wild Strawberries and Other Berries

Ingredients:
1 cup strawberries
3/4 cup sugar
2 tbsp potato starch

Wash strawberries, clean and rub through a sieve. Pour 2 1/2 cups of hot water into a pan, add sugar and mix. Boil this syrup, add diluted potato starch and boil again. Put berry puree into hot kissel and mix well.

You may also prepare kissel from wild strawberries, raspberries, blueberries.

Cherry Kissel

Ingredients:

1 cup cherries
3/4 cup sugar
2 tbsp potato starch

Wash cherries in cold water and pit them. Cover them in sugar and leave for half an hour. During this time, mix it several times so that more juice is formed. This juice should be drained and then added to prepared kissel. Crush pits; pour over with 2 1/2 cups hot water, boil and strain. Pour over this broth over cherries and boil again. Add diluted potato starch to boiling broth with cherries, return to boil, remove from heat, add cherry juice and mix.

Apple Kissel

Ingredients:
500 g apples
3/4 cups sugar
1 1/2 tbsp potato starch

Slice washed apples thinly, put into a pot with 2 cups of water and bring to boil. Pass the contents of the pot through a sieve when apples are completely cooked. Add sugar, bring to boil and add potato starch mixed with water.

Dried Apple or Dried Apricot Kissel

Ingredients:
100 g dried apples
3/4 cup sugar
2 tbsp potato starch

Put picked over and washed dried apples into a pot, cover with 3 1/2 cups boiling water and leave to soak for 2-3 hours. Put the pot on a stove. Bring to simmer and cook for 30 minutes. Pass the contents of the pot through a sieve, mashing the solids through, add sugar, and bring to simmer. Add potato starch dissolved in water.

Kissel with dried apricots is cooked the same way, just use 1/2 cup of sugar.

Dried Blueberries or Rose Hip Kissel

Ingredients:
50 g dried blueberries or dried rose hip berries
3/4 cup sugar
2 tbsp potato starch

Cover washed in hot water dried blueberry (or dried rose hip berries) with 2 cups of water, bring to boil, and cook 15-20 minutes. When blueberry becomes soft, strain the cooking liquid into a different pot, mash berries with a pestle or a spoon, add 1 cup of cold water, bring to boil, and strain again into the pot with cooking liquid, pressing on solids to extract as much liquid as possible. Add sugar to strained cooking liquid, bring to boil and add potato starch dissolved in water.

Milk Kissel

Ingredients:
4 cup milk
1/2 cup sugar
2 tbsp corn starch

Put 3 cups of milk into a pot, bring to boil and then add sugar. Mix corn or potato starch with a cup of cold milk or boiled water, add to the boiling milk, and simmer 5 minutes stirring at all times.

To flavor milk kissel - while it is still hot add a little bit of vanilla or almond extract, or finely grated orange or lemon zest and mix well. Pour hot kissel into cups and cool it down. Just before serving, kissel can be transferred from cups to small plates. Soy milk can be used instead of regular to make this kissel.

This kissel can be made with dry milk. Dissolve 1 cup of dry milk with 2 cups of water and leave for 30 minutes to soak. Add 2 more cups of water, mix well and bring to boil. Add sugar to the boiling milk, then add starch mixed with water, and return to boil.

Cherry Syrup Kissel

Ingredients:
1 cup cherry syrup
2 tbsp sugar
2 tbsp potato starch

Add cherry syrup to 2 cups of hot water together with sugar and a small crystal of lemon acid dissolved with a little bit of water. Mix everything well, bring to boil, add potato starch mixed with 1 cup of water and bring back to boil. Any other berry syrup can be used to make this kissel.

COMPOTES

Compote can be made from one or several types of fruit. Fresh, frozen or dried fruit may be used.

A variety of prepared compotes is available for purchase. They are made from quality fruit (apples, pears, quince, apricots, peaches, cherries, tangerines, etc.), which are poured over with clear syrup made with pure sugar.

Fresh Apple or Pear Compote

Ingredients:
500 g apples or pears
3/4 cups sugar

Cut peeled apples into 6-8 slices and remove the core. To make sure that peeled apples do not become dark - put them into water slightly acidulated with lemon acid. Add sugar to a pot, then add 2 cups of hot water, add apples, bring to boil, and simmer 10-15 minutes (depending on the breed of apples), until apples become soft.

If desired - add lemon or orange zest, or some cinnamon to compote.

Fresh pear compote is cooked using the same procedure; however, use less sugar (depending on sweetness of pears). Cook compote 10-15 minutes. If pears are too ripe - it is sufficient to just bring compote to boil. Cool compote before serving.

Compote with Fresh Apricots or Plums

Ingredients:
500 g apricots or plums
3/4 cups sugar

Wash apricots or plums in cold water, make

a cut along the fruit and remove pits. Add sugar and 2 cups of hot water into a pot, mix to dissolve sugar, add fruit and bring to boil.

Peach Compote

Ingredients:
500 g peaches
3/4 cups sugar

Put peaches into boiling water for 2-3 minutes. Take peaches out of the water, peel, and take out the pit. Add sugar and 2 cups of hot water to a pot, mix to dissolve sugar. Add peaches and bring to a boil. Remove pot from the heat and add vanilla extract to taste.

Fresh Apple and Cherry Compote

Ingredients:
300 g apples
200 g cherries
3/4 cups sugar

Wash and pit cherries and put them aside. Cover cherry pits with 2 cups of hot water, bring to boil, and strain into another pot. Add sugar to the strained liquid, mix to dissolve, add peeled, cored, and sliced apples and simmer 10 minutes, until apples become soft. Add set aside cherries, return to boil and take compote off the heat.

Fresh Apple and Plum Compote

Ingredients:
300 g apples
200 g plums
3/4 cup sugar

Add sugar and 2 cups of hot water into a pot and mix to dissolve, then add peeled, cored, and sliced apples, bring to boil and simmer 10 minutes, until apples become soft. Add washed and pitted plums to the boiling compote, return to boil and take off the heat.

Fresh Apple and Mandarin Orange Compote

Ingredients:
250 g apples
4 mandarin oranges
3/4 cups sugar

Peel and separate mandarins into segments, set aside. Remove white pith from the peeled skins of mandarins, julienne zest and parboil it in 1 cup of water. In a pot mix sugar with 2 cups of hot water, add parboiled zest, peeled, cored, and sliced apples and cook on low heat for 10 minutes, until apples become soft.

Put cooled apples and mandarin segments into dessert bowls and pour syrup over.

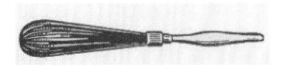

Canned Fruit Compote

Canned fruit compote with apples, pears, peaches, apricots, cherries, etc should be transferred to dessert bowls before serving. Large fruit, for example apples or pears, should be cut into smaller slices before being covered with syrup. To improve taste of canned compote - drain syrup from fruit into a pot, add sugar to taste, and, if necessary, add a little lemon juice or lemon acid, bring the pot to boil and take off heat. Cool before serving. To flavor the syrup - add lemon or orange zest while it is still hot, or a little bit of wine (Port wine, Madeira, or Muscat) or liqueur when it is cool.

Canned compote from different fruit can be mixed together before serving - make following combinations - peaches and greengage, apples and plums, apricots and cherries.

Dried Fruit Compote

Ingredients:
200 g dried fruits (mix)
1/2 cup sugar

Wash dried fruits in 2-3 changes of warm water, put apples and pears into a pot with 4 cups of cold water, bring to boil, lower the heat, and simmer 25-30 minutes. Add all remaining fruits and berries, sugar, and cook 5 minutes longer.

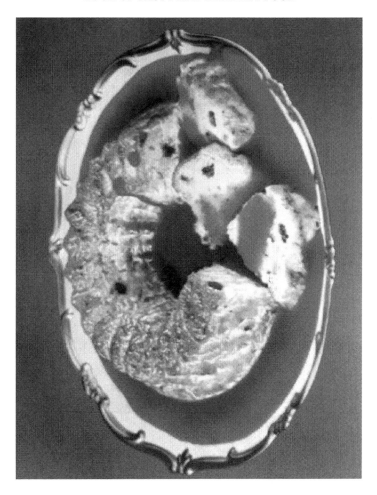

Compote with Frozen Fruit and Berries

Ingredients:
500 g frozen fruits
3/4 cup sugar

Frozen fruits or berries (plums, cherries, strawberries and raspberries) could be used to make compote just like fresh fruits; however, they do not have to be cooked.

Rinse frozen fruits with cooled boiled water, put
into dessert bowls, together with berries, and
cover with previously cooked and cooled syrup.
To make syrup - dissolve sugar with 1 1/2 - 2 cups
of water and bring to boil. To improve taste, add a
little bit of wine (Port Wine, Muscat) liqueur, or
cognac to syrup.

Prune Compote

Ingredients:
200 g prunes
1/2 cup sugar

Wash prunes in 2-3 changes of warm water.
Mix sugar with 2 1/2 cups of hot water in a pot,
add prunes, bring to boil, lower the heat and
simmer until prunes are soft (15-20 minutes).
Dried apricot compote is made following the same
procedure; however, it is sufficient just to bring

this compote to boil. Simmering is not required.

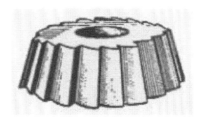

Prune, Raisins, and Dried Apricot Compote

Ingredients:
50 g dried apricots
100 g prunes
50 g raisins
1/2 cup sugar

Wash prunes, raisins, and dried apricots in 2-3 changes of warm water. Mix sugar with 3 cups of hot water in a pot, add prunes, bring to boil, lower the heat and simmer for 15 minutes. Add dried apricots, raisins, and cook 5 minutes longer. If prunes are too dry - soak them in warm water before cooking.

GELATIN DESSERTS AND MOUSSES

Gelatin desserts and mousses are made from fresh or freshly frozen berries and fruit, from fruit-berry juices, syrups, from all kinds of jams and preserves, and also from red wine.
For mousse preparation purees and sauces from different fruit are also used. It is better to use

prepared purees and fruit sauces - they are made from ripe, top-quality fruit - apples, apricots, plums, etc.

Gelatin is used to make gelatin desserts and mousses, and gelatin desserts also use agar-agar (plant-based gelatin), the amount of which should be half of regular gelatin.

In order for gelatin and agar-agar to dissolve quickly and evenly, they need to be soaked in cold water for 25-30 minutes. When leaves swell, squeeze the water out of them.

To make gelatin desserts tastier, different types of wine (Cherry, Muscat and Madeira), liqueurs, orange and lemon peel, vanilla, lemon juice or lemon acid may be added.

Gelatin desserts and mousses may be prepared in special molds or little bowls. Before serving submerge the mold with hardened gelatin dessert in hot water for several seconds, so that gelatin dessert may be easily separated and removed from the mold.

Preparation method for gelatin desserts and mousses is almost exactly the same, except that mousses are whipped. To whip mousse, you will need a deep bowl, because the volume of whipped mouse increases 2 - 2 1/2 times. Whipping should only be done on ice or in cold water. Mousse is ready when it is foams and thickens. Quickly pour prepared mousse into molds or little bowls and put it in cold place. Separately serve berry syrup or fruit/berry juices.

Mousse may be prepared by using farina

instead of gelatin. Cook farina with sugar and fruit juice or puree and then cool. When the temperature of prepared mousse goes down to 40 degrees C, whip it, pour it into molds and cool.

Lemon Gelatin Dessert

Ingredients:
1 lemon
1 cup sugar
25 g gelatin

Pour 3 cups of water into a pan; add sugar, mix and boil. Put lemon peel from half a lemon into hot syrup, and also add soaked and pressed gelatin. Boil again while continuously stirring and pour in lemon juice.

Strain hot syrup, cool and pour into molds or little bowls.

Lemon Gelatin Dessert with Fruit

Ingredients:
1 lemon
1 cup sugar
25 g gelatin
300 g fresh fruit or 200 g canned fruit

Prepare lemon gelatin dessert following instructions of the preceding recipe, slightly cool it, and pour it into dessert bowls or molds 1-2 cm high and let it set. Put fruits on top of the set layer of gelatin dessert and cover it by pouring more on top. Cool until set.

Orange Gelatin Dessert

Ingredients:
1 orange
1/2 cup sugar
15 g gelatin

Peel oranges and slice them across into circles, remove seeds, sprinkle with 1/4 cup of sugar and leave for 30 minutes to macerate. Put 1/4 cup of sugar into a pot together with 1 1/2 cups of water and bring to boil.

Add soaked and squeezed gelatin and orange zest to the syrup, bring syrup back to boil, stirring at all times, then remove it from heat and add juice released by oranges. Add dissolved lemon acid to taste.

Strain hot syrup, lightly cool it and pour into dessert bowls or molds a layer 1 cm (2/5 in) thick and put into a cold place. Put orange slices on top of the set layer and pour the remaining gelatin dessert over it. Cool again.

Mandarin orange gelatin dessert can be made following instructions in this recipe.

Berry Preserves Gelatin Dessert

Ingredients:
1 cup preserves
1/2 cup sugar

25 g gelatin
2 tbsp liqueur

Dissolve berry preserves with 2 1/2 cups of boiling water, mix and strain, set berries aside. Put strained liquid into a pot together with sugar and gelatin, bring to boil stirring all the time, add liqueur, strain and slightly cool. Put berries into dessert bowls or molds, cover with gelatin dessert and cool.

Red Wine Gelatin Dessert

Ingredients:
1 cup red wine
25 g gelatin
3/4 cup sugar

Put sugar into a pot, add 2 cups of hot water, soaked and squeezed gelatin. Bring the pot to boil stirring all the time, add wine, a little vanilla extract, and, if desired, dissolved lemon acid to taste. Strain hot syrup, slightly cool it, and pour into molds. Just before serving, gelatin dessert could be decorated with fresh or frozen berries - strawberries, raspberries, cherries, sour cherries, or slices of orange.

Fresh Apple Mousse

Ingredients:
250 g apples

3/4 cup sugar
15 g gelatin

Thinly slice washed, peeled, and cored apples. Put apples into a pot, add 2 1/2 cups hot water, and cook until apples are soft. Strain cooking liquid and rub apples through a sieve. Add sugar and soaked gelatin to cooking liquid, bring it to boil stirring all the time, take off the heat and cool. Transfer cooled syrup together with apple puree and a little vanilla extract into a mixing bowl and whip with a whisk until the mixture foams. When the foam will start thickening - quickly transfer it into dessert bowls or molds and cool.

Lemon Mousse

Ingredients:
1 lemon
15 g gelatin
3/4 cups sugar
2 cups water

Prepare mixture just like in "Lemon Gelatin Dessert" recipe, transfer to a bowl, put the bowl into an ice bath and whip with a whisk until you get homogeneous foam.

When foam starts thickening quickly transfer it into molds and chill. Serve berry or red wine sauce on a side.

Berry Mousse

Ingredients:
1 cup berries
3/4 cup sugar
15 g gelatin

Pick over fresh or frozen berries, wash them with cold water, mash with a spoon or a wooden pestle in a ceramic dish, and rub through a sieve. Add 2 cups of hot water to the remnants of berries, bring to boil and strain. Add sugar and soaked gelatin to the strained liquid and return it to boil, stirring all the time. Remove syrup from heat and let it cool. Add berry puree to the cooled syrup and whip it with a whisk until it turns into foam. When the foam starts thickening - transfer it into molds or dessert bowls and chill.

Cranberry Mousse with Farina

Ingredients:
1 cup cranberries
1 cup sugar
3 tbsp farina

Mash picked over and washed cranberries with a wooden pestle, add 1/2 cups boiled water and squeeze berries through a cheese cloth. Leave squeezed juice in a cold place. Put squeezed cranberries into a pot with 3 cups of water, bring to boil, lower the heat and simmer 5 minutes.

Strain cooking liquid into another pot and cook farina in it - steadily adding it to the boiling liquid while stirring.

After 20 minutes of simmering add sugar to farina, return it to boil and take it off the heat. Add squeezed juice to cooked farina and whip it with a whisk until thick foam forms. When the volume of foam doubles transfer it into dessert bowls and store in a cool place. Serve cranberry mousse with cold milk.

Honey Mousse

Ingredients:
1 cup honey
4 eggs

Separate yolks from egg whites. Mash egg yolks gradually adding honey and then continue mixing it over low heat until the mixture thickens. Remove egg yolks from heat and let cool. Whip egg whites until the stiff peaks form, fold into egg yolk mixture, transfer into dessert bowls and cool.

If desired - use 3/4 cups of whipped cream instead of whipped egg whites in this mousse.

WHIPPED CREAM DESSERT

Whipped cream dessert is made with dairy cream with fat content not lower than 20%, or sour cream, whipped into thick foam. Whipped cream, just like gelatin dessert or mousse, can be prepared in molds or dessert bowls. Just before serving whipped cream should be unmolded into dessert plates.

If desired - serve sweet sauce from berries, red wine, chocolate, coffee, or fruit and berry syrups with this dessert.

Whipped Cream

Ingredients:
1 cup heavy cream
1/2 cup powdered sugar
10 g gelatin
1/2 tsp vanilla extract

Soak gelatin for 20-25 minutes in cold water, then squeeze it out, and dissolve in 1/4 cup of boiling water. Meanwhile, pour heavy cream into a pot and put the pot into an ice bath. Whip the cream with a whisk until thick foam forms - it should hold its shape. Gradually add powdered sugar to the whipped cream, mixing all the time, add vanilla extract, and then pour in dissolved warm gelatin.

Whipped Sour Cream

Ingredients:
1 cup sour cream
1/2 cup powdered sugar
10 g gelatin
1/2 tsp vanilla extract

Put sour cream into a pot, add sugar and vanilla extract, put the pot into an ice bath and whip it with a whisk until it doubles in volume. Gradually add dissolved gelatin to the whipped sour cream, mixing all the time, instantly transfer into molds or dessert bowls and chill.
Whipped sour cream can be flavored with fresh berry puree - wild strawberry, strawberry, or raspberry. Pick berries over, wash in cold water and rub through a sieve, then mix with whipped sour cream before adding gelatin.

Vanilla, Chocolate, or Coffee Whipped Cream

Ingredients:
1 cup heavy cream
1/3 cups powdered sugar
10 g gelatin
1/2 tsp vanilla extract

Pour heavy cream into a pot, and put the pot into an ice bath. Whip the cream until stiff peaks are just about to form. Continue whipping while gradually adding powdered sugar until stiff peaks form, add vanilla extract and then, in a thin stream - dissolved gelatin. Transfer whipped cream into molds and chill.
Chocolate and coffee creams are made using the same procedure. Mix 1 tbsp of cocoa powder and powdered sugar for chocolate cream. Mix gelatin with 1/4 cup of strong coffee made

from 2 tsp of ground coffee for coffee cream.

Berry Whipped Cream

Ingredients:
1 cup heavy cream
3/4 cups powdered sugar
1/2 cup berries
10 g gelatin

Pick over fresh or frozen berries (wild strawberries, raspberries), wash in cold water and rub through a sieve. Mix berry puree with powdered sugar. Pour heavy cream into a pot on an ice bath and whip with a whisk until stiff picks hold. Fold berry puree into the whipped cream, then, while mixing all the time, in a thin stream pour in dissolved gelatin. Transfer whipped cream into molds and chill.

Whipped Cream with Sugar

Ingredients:
1 cup heavy cream
3 tbsp powdered sugar

Pour heavy cream into a pot, put the pot into an ice bath and whip cream with a whisk until stiff peaks form. Add powdered sugar and vanilla extract to the whipped cream, mix well and serve instantly; otherwise, cream can break down. Whipped cream can be served with fresh berries, ice cream, or cake.

Sour Cream Whipped with Sugar

Ingredients:
1 cup sour cream
2 1/2 tbsp sugar

Put sour cream into a pot, add sugar, put the pot into an ice bath and whip sour cream with a whisk until thick foam forms. Sour cream is ready when its volume increases 2 - 2 1/2 times. If desired - flavor sour cream with vanilla extract.

Whipped sour cream should be served instantly. Serve with fresh berries or buns.

ICE CREAM

Food industry makes several varieties of high-quality ice cream - vanilla, chocolate, fruit, as well as ice cream cakes.

Ice cream produced by food industry is made by special machines and the manufacturing process complies with strict adherence to sanitary and hygienic standards. It tastes better than home-made ice cream.

Ice cream can also be made at home. It is necessary to have a special vessel with a lid and a pail to fill with a mixture of chopped ice and salt.

Two main types of ice cream can be prepared: vanilla and fruit-berry. Vanilla ice cream is made from milk or cream, sugar and eggs, as well as aromatic and flavoring substances. Fruit-berry ice cream is made from juice and puree of different fruit, berries and sugar. The amount of sugar added needs to be carefully monitored, since too much sugar affects the quality of ice cream as does too little.

When serving ice cream, you may decorate it with various canned fruit, cookies, and pour it over with jam, berry syrup, fruit juice, liqueurs and wines.

Vanilla Ice Cream

Ingredients:
3 cups heavy cream or milk
1 1/4 cups sugar
3 eggs, separated
1 tsp vanilla extract

In a pot beat egg yolks with sugar and vanilla until light in color, gradually add hot cream or milk, mixing all the time. Put the pot on low heat and cook while stirring with wooden spoon until the mixture thickens and coats the back of the spoon. Do not let it boil. Take the pot off the heat, strain the custard and cool it down. Pour cooled custard into a container of ice cream maker, surround it with crushed ice mixed with salt (1 kg of salt for each 6-7 kg of ice) and churn the ice cream.

Add more ice during churning and drain water. Churning takes 30-40 minutes. When ice cream becomes thick, open the cover and remove mixing paddle, smooth the ice cream and let it harden for an hour. Put into dessert bowls to serve.

Berry Sorbet

Ingredients:
500 g berries
1 1/2 cups sugar
2 cups water

Wash picked over berries (fresh or frozen wild strawberries, raspberries) in cold water; rub through a sieve into a ceramic bowl. Put sugar into a pot, add water and bring to boil. Cool the syrup down, mix it with berry puree and put into a bowl of ice cream maker. Freeze berry sorbet following directions from "Vanilla Ice Cream" recipe.

Coffee and Condensed Milk Ice Cream

Ingredients:
1 can of coffee with condensed milk
2 cups water

Transfer condensed milk with coffee out of the can into a pot, dissolve it with hot water, mix, and bring to boil. Cool the mixture and transfer it into an ice-cream maker. To freeze - follow instructions from "Vanilla Ice Cream" recipe.
Cacao and condensed milk recipe can be

made following the same instructions.

PUDDINGS AND OTHER SWEET DISHES

Rice Pudding

Ingredients:
1 cup rice
1 cup sugar
100 g butter
2 cups milk
4 eggs
50 g candied fruit
100 g raisins
1/2 tsp vanilla extract

Put picked over and well washed rice into boiling water and parboil it for 10 minutes, then drain in a strainer. Return parboiled rice back to the pot, add hot milk, return to boil and cook 15 minutes longer. Cool slightly.

Beat egg yolks with sugar, add vanilla, and then add this mixture to cooked rice. Also add to the rice diced candied fruit, washed raisins, butter, chopped walnuts, and, finally, fold in egg whites whipped into a thick foam. Mix everything well and transfer into a well buttered and sprinkled with breadcrumbs mold or oven-proof pan. Put into a preheated oven and bake 30-40 minutes.

Just before serving transfer pudding to a serving plate. Serve fruit or berry sauce on a side.

Vanilla Rusks Pudding

Ingredients:
150 g vanilla rusks
3 eggs
1/2 cup sugar
2 cups milk
50 g candied fruit
100 g raisins
100 g butter

Crush vanilla rusks, put into a pot and add hot milk. Cover the pot and leave for 15-20 minutes. Dice candied fruit, pick over and wash raisins in cold water.

Beat egg yolks with sugar and add to soaked rusks, then add candied fruit, raisins, melted butter, whipped egg whites. Mix everything well and transfer the mixture to a well buttered and sprinkled with breadcrumbs bundt cake mold. The mold would be filled only 3/4 to leave some space for expansion during baking. Put the mold into a preheated oven and bake on medium heat for 30-40 minutes. Pudding is done when it springy, has risen, and pulled away from the sides of the mold.

Transfer finished pudding to a serving plate and serve hot. If desired - glaze the pudding with fruit or berry sauce.

Walnut Pudding

Ingredients:
150 g walnuts
3 eggs
250 g white bread
3/4 cup sugar
1 1/2 cups milk
100 g butter

Soak crustless white bread in milk. Shell walnuts and pass them through a meat grinder. Beat egg yolks with sugar and mix it with ground walnuts, soaked bread, and melted butter. Mix everything well, fold in whipped egg whites, and transfer the mix into a buttered and sprinkled with breadcrumbs baking pan or a skillet.

Bake pudding in a preheated oven on a medium heat for 30-40 minutes. Transfer baked pudding to a serving plate and serve hot. If desired - pour vanilla sauce over pudding or serve it on a side.

Airy Apple Pie (Soufflé)

Ingredients:
6 egg whites
1 cup sugar
300 g apples

Slice cored and washed in cold water apples into 4-6 slices, put into a skillet, add little bit of water and bake in the oven until soft. Rub baked apples through a sieve, transfer apple puree into a pot, add sugar to the pot, and cook the mixture, stirring áll the time, until it thickens so much that it does not drip from the spoon dipped into it.

Put egg whites into a pot and cool them, then whip with a whisk until a thick foam forms. Add hot puree to the whipped egg whites and mix well. Pile the mixture into a mound on a buttered skillet, smooth the top with a blade of a knife and put into an oven for 10-15 minutes until meringue is lightly brown and has risen.

Serve the meringue as soon as it is ready, otherwise it will fall. Sprinkle it with powdered sugar and serve in the same skillet it was cooked in. Serve cold milk or light cream on a side. Apple puree or apple sauce could be used instead of apple in this recipe.

Apples Stuffed with Rice and Walnuts

Ingredients:
10 apples
50 g raisins
1/2 cup rice
1 cup milk
50 g walnuts or almonds
1/2 cup sugar
1 egg
2 tbsp butter

Wash apples and remove the core and some of the flesh without cutting apples all the way through. Shell almonds or walnuts and finely chop the nuts. Pick over and wash raisins. Pick over and wash rice, cook it with milk and sugar. Add raisins, nuts, butter, and egg to the rice porridge. Stuff apples with rice mixture and put into a skillet. Bake in a preheated oven. To make sure that apples do not burn, add 2-3 tbsp of water to the skillet. When apples become soft take them out of the oven and transfer to a serving plate. If desired - pour berry (raspberry or black currant) preserves over apples.

White Bread Babka with Apples

Ingredients:
500 g apples
1 cup milk
300 g white bread
1 egg
3/4 cup sugar
3 tbsp butter
lemon peel or orange peel from 1 fruit

Remove crust from white bread loaf, thinly slice it and partially dice it and dry it. Mix and whip milk, raw egg, and 2 tbsp of sugar.

Peel and pit apples, dice them and pour over with sugar. Grease mold or skillet with a thick layer of butter. Moisten slices of white bread with whipped egg paste and lay them on the bottom and the sides of skillet or mold. Pour dried bread dices over with butter and mix with apples.

Also add some grated lemon peel or vanilla. Put apples mixed with bread dices in the middle of the mold, filling it up to the top. Cover the mold with bread slices that have been moistened with whipped egg paste, and put the mold in medium-hot oven for 40-50 minutes.

Once it is ready, leave babka in the mold for 10 minutes and then put it on a plate. If desired, decorate with canned fruit and pour over with fruit sauce. Serve babka hot.

"Gurievskaya" Porridge

Ingredients:
3/4 cup farina
2 eggs
1/2 cup sugar
2 cups milk
2 tbsp butter
50 g almonds
1 tsp vanilla extract
1/2 can canned fruit

Put sugar and vanilla into boiling milk. Gradually pour in farina, mixing all the time, and cook 10 minutes. Add butter and egg to the porridge, mix everything well, transfer into a buttered and sprinkled with sugar skillet and put into a preheated oven. Porridge is ready when it is lightly brown.

Just before serving decorate porridge with canned fruit, glaze with sweet sauce and sprinkle with rushed almonds.

Baked Apples with Preserves

Ingredients:
10 apples
1/2 cup preserves

Wash apples in cold water, remove the core without cutting apple all the way through, prick apple skin, fill apples with preserves and put them into a skillet. Add 2-3 tbsp of water to the skillet and put skillet into a preheated oven. Bake 15-20 minutes on medium heat. When apples become soft take them out of the oven, let cool slightly, and transfer to a serving plate. Pour syrup from skillet over apples.

Use berry preserves for this recipe - wild strawberry, strawberry, black currant, or cherry (pitted). If desired - add 1/2 cup crushed breadcrumbs or shortbread, chopped almonds or walnuts to preserves.

Apples stuffed with sugar following the same instructions - the only difference being - sugar is sprinkled inside apples instead of preserves.

Apples in Puff Pastry

Ingredients:
500 g puff pastry
6-8 apples

3/4 cup sugar
2 tbsp powdered sugar
1 egg

Make puff pastry. Roll the dough on a work surface sprinkled with flour about 1/2 cm thick and cut into squares large enough to wrap an apple.

Core washed apples, and pour sugar into the holes from cores. Transfer apples to dough squares and wrap the dough around apples, then sprinkle tops with sugar and transfer to a moistened baking sheet. Decorate with a leaf or a star made from dough, brush with a beaten egg, and bake in a preheated oven. 10-15 minutes after start of baking, when the dough on the top becomes lightly brown, lower the heat and bake for 8-10 minutes longer. Carefully remove baked apples with a help of a sharp knife, and transfer to a serving plate, sprinkle with powdered sugar. Apples could be served hot or cold.

Cornets with Whipped Cream

Ingredients:
1 1/4 cups flour
2 eggs
250 g powdered sugar
1/4 cup milk
1 cup heavy cream
50 g almonds or pistachios
1 tsp vanilla extract

Break egg into a mixing bowl; add 200 g of powdered sugar and vanilla extract. Mix everything well until a smooth paste is formed. Add flour and mix the dough, then mix in the milk.

Put 1 tbsp portions of dough onto a slightly waxed preheated baking sheet, spread into a shape of a think pancake, then put into a preheated oven. When the edges of pancakes turn brown, take one pastry at a time (without taking the whole sheet out of the oven) and fold it into a cornet.

Finely chop blanched and peeled pistachios or almonds. Whip heavy cream into a thick foam, and then mix with remaining powdered sugar and vanilla extract. Fill cornets with whipped cream from a piping bag, put filled cornets on a serving plate. Sprinkle cornets with powdered sugar, sprinkle whipped cream with chopped nuts.

Apple Fritters

Ingredients:
500 g apples
2-3 tbsp clarified butter
2 tbsp butter
1/4 cup sugar
1 tbsp powdered sugar
1/2 cup flour
4 eggs
1/3 cup milk

Prepare dough. In order to do this, mix melted butter in a pan with milk yolks, add one tablespoon of milk, pour in flour, one tablespoon sugar, 1/2 teaspoon salt, mix and dilute with remaining milk, add whipped egg whites. Lightly mix from bottom to top so that the egg whites don't get settled.

Peel and pit apples, cut into slices of 1/2 cm thick, pour over with sugar and leave for 25-30 minutes. Then take each apple slice with a fork and dip into prepared dough and put on a skillet with heated butter. Fry on low heat, until apples get caramelized on both sides. Put a skillet with apples in medium-hot oven for 5 minutes. Once apples are ready, put them on a plate, pour over with powdered sugar and serve. Separately serve berry syrup, apricot sauce or sour cream.

Slices of White Bread with Fruit

Ingredients:
300 g bread
2 eggs
1/2 can canned fruit
1/2 cup sugar
1 cup milk
2-3 tbsp butter

Mix milk, eggs and sugar and lightly whip. Remove crust from a loaf of white bread and slice. Dip bread slices into egg paste and fry on a skillet with butter on both sides. Place fried slices of bread on a plate, put heated canned fruit on top, pour over with syrup and serve.

Fried slices of bread can be poured over with jam or compote from apples, peaches, apricots and other fruit.

SWEET SAUCES

Vanilla Sauce

Ingredients:
1 1/2 cup milk
2 eggs
1/2 cup sugar
1/4 tsp vanilla
1 tsp flour

Whip sugar, egg yolks and flour. Dilute this paste with hot milk, and cook this sauce until it boils, continuously stirring it. Once sauce thickens, remove it from heat, strain and add vanilla.

Berry Sauce with Wine

Ingredients:
1 cup berries
1 cup sugar
1/4 cup red or white wine

Wash berries (strawberries, raspberries, wild strawberries, currants) and rub through a sieve. Add sugar into a pan, pour in 1/4 cup water, boil and remove scum. Add wine and berry puree to hot syrup and cook until it boils while stirring. Serve sauce hot or cold.

Red Wine Sauce

Ingredients:
1/2 cup red wine
3/4 cup sugar
1 tsp potato flour

Pour wine and 1/2 cup water into a pan, add lemon peel, boil, then add potato flour diluted with 1/4 cups cold water. Without removing the pan from heat, pour in sugar and stir continuously, until sugar dissolves. Serve sauce hot or cold.

Chocolate Sauce

Ingredients:
1 1/2 cup milk
2 eggs
1/2 cup sugar
1 tbsp cocoa
1 tsp flour

Whip egg yolks with sugar, add cocoa and flour, mix, dilute with hot milk and bring to boil. Cook until it boils, while stirring continuously. As soon as sauce thickens, remove from heat and strain.

Dried Apricot Sauce

Ingredients:
100 g dried apricots
1/4 cup sugar
1/4 cup wine (Muscat or muscatel)

Wash dried apricots in warm water, put in a pan, pour over with a cup of water, and cook until soft. Rub boiled dried apricots through a sieve, put it back into a pan, add sugar and 1/4 cup hot water, mix, bring to boil and cook for 5 minutes. Remove from heat, add wine and mix. Apricot sauce may also be prepared similarly, replacing dried apricots with apricot puree (200 g).

BABY/CHILD FOOD

The following section provides recipes of baby/child food. Every recipe in this section lists ingredients sufficient to feed one child one time.

Cream of Wheat

Ingredients:
3/4 cup milk
3 tsp farina
1/2 tsp sugar
1 tsp butter

Add 1/4 cup water to milk and bring to boil. Gradually pour farina into the boiling milk, stirring all the time, add sugar and salt and cook on low heat 10-15 minutes.
Add butter just before serving.

Rice Porridge (Pureed)

Ingredients:
3/4 cup milk
1 tbsp rice
1 tsp sugar
1 tsp butter

Add picked over and washed rice to 1/2 cup of boiling water and cook until half-done, add some of the milk and continue cooking until rice is completely done.

Rub cooked rice through a sieve, add remaining milk, sugar, salt, and bring to boil again, breaking any lumps with a spoon.

Add butter just before serving.

Potato Soup (Pureed)

Ingredients:
1/2 cup milk
2 potatoes
1 tsp butter
1 egg yolk

     Cut peeled and washed potatoes, put into a pot with 1 cup of water, and cook until they become soft. Strain cooking liquid and rub potatoes through a sieve. Mix mashed potatoes with strained cooking liquid, milk, season with salt and bring to boil. Just before serving add egg yolk beaten with butter.

Carrot juice can be used instead of egg yolk.

Vegetable Soup (Pureed)

Ingredients:
1 potato
1/2 carrot
50 g white cabbage
1 tsp butter
1 tbsp sour cream

Wash and cut peeled potato, carrot, and cabbage. Put vegetables into a pot with 1 1/2 cups of cold water, bring to boil, and simmer until vegetables become soft. Strain and cool vegetable broth. Rub vegetables through a sieve; add cooled broth, season with salt and warm the soup up.

Add butter and sour cream to the soup right before serving.

Rice Soup (Pureed)

Ingredients:
1 tbsp rice
3/4 cup milk
1 tsp sugar
1 tsp butter

Add picked over and washed rice to 1 cup of boiling water and cook until rice is done. Rub cooked rice through a sieve, add milk, sugar, and salt, and bring back to boil breaking any lumps with a spoon.

Add butter to the soup just before serving.

Ground Meat with Potato Puree

Ingredients:
50 g boneless meat
1 tsp butter
1/2 tsp flour
50 g meat broth or stock
3 g onion
200 g potatoes
3 tbsp milk
1/2 tsp butter

Remove fat and sinew from meat, pass it together with onion through a meat grinder, and brown it in a pot. When the meat is browned add a little bit of stock and put the pot into the oven to braise until it becomes soft. Pass braised meat through a meat grinder; them rub it through a sieve, add 1 tbsp white sauce, mix, heat it through and serve with mashed potatoes.

Sausage Patties

Ingredients:
50 g meat
15 g crustless white bread
1/2 tbsp butter

Clean sinew and fat from the meat and pass it through a meat grinder. Add soaked in water and squeezed white bread and mix well. Pass the mixture through a meat grinder again, season with salt, add 1 tsp cold water, 1/2 tsp butter and mix everything again.

Transfer ground meat to a moistened board, separate into 2 parts, coat each part in sifted breadcrumbs, shape into a round or oblong patty and fry oil in a hot frying pan - 5 minutes per side, then transfer into preheated oven and cook for 5 minutes.

Serve patties with mashed potatoes, rutabaga sauce, or with noodles.

Meatballs in Soup

Ingredients:
50 g meat
15 g crustless white bread
1 egg white

Make minced meat just like in recipe "Sausage Patties"; add beaten egg white when adding water. Transfer the meat to a moistened board and shape 3-4 meatballs. Cook meatballs for 5 minutes in a salted boiling water. Take meatballs out with a skimmer, let them drain, and then out into a soup, bring soup to simmer and serve.

Pudding with Beef, Chicken, or Steamed Fish

Ingredients:
50 g beef (or chicken, or steamed fish)
15-20 g crustless white bread
1 egg
1 tsp butter

For potato puree:
200 g potatoes
3 tbsp milk
1/2 tsp butter

Cut meat into pieces and pass it twice through a meat grinder together with bread soaked in milk. Rub ground meat through a sieve, season with salt and dilute with milk to the consistency of thin porridge, then add half of an egg yolk and accurately fold in whipped into thick foam egg white. Transfer the mixture into a well buttered and sprinkled with sifted breadcrumbs small mold, cover on the top with a buttered circle of paper, put the mold into a pot with hot water reaching half-way up the sides of the mold, cover the pot and leave on the stove. Take pudding out of the pot in 40-50 minutes, drizzle with stock or broth, and serve with mashed potatoes.

Meatballs

Ingredients:
50 g boneless meat
15 g crustless white bread
1/2 tbsp butter
1 egg white

Pass meat (beef, veal, chicken, or lean fish) twice through a meat grinder together with bread soaked in cold water and squeezed. Mix ground meat with butter and pass the mixture through a sieve, season with salt and fold in whipped egg white. Shape mixture into balls, put into a skillet; add a small quantity of cold stock or broth, cover with buttered paper and bake in the oven 30 minutes.

Serve with potato or carrot puree.

Zrazi with Rice or Buckwheat Porridge

Ingredients:
50 g boneless meat
20 g crustless white bread
1/2 tbsp butter
2 tbsp grain
5 g onion
1/6 egg

For sauce:
1 tsp flour
1 tsp sour cream
30 g stock

Roll ground meat into a shape of a medium pancake on a moistened board, put stuffing in the middle, wrap meat around stuffing and brown on all sides in oil in a hot skillet, then pour sour cream sauce over and put the skillet into a preheated oven for 10-15 minutes. Make stuffing with cooked rice mixed with browned onions and chopped hardboiled eggs, or with buckwheat porridge mixed with browned onions.

(Ed. note - This recipe assumes that you went through all preceding recipes in this category and know fairly well how to prepare ground meat for baby food. It also assumes some knowledge of cooking grains on your part.)

Holubtsi (Stuffed Cabbage)

Ingredients:
50 g cabbage
30 g boneless meat
1 tbsp rice
5 g onion
1/2 tbsp butter
1/4 egg

For sauce:
1 tsp butter
1 tsp sour cream
1/2 tsp flour
1/2 tsp tomato paste
1/4 tsp sugar

Cut the tough parts off of large cabbage leaves, put leaves into boiling water and parboil them, then take them out and drain. Pass meat through a meat grinder and mix with cooked rice, sautéed onion, and chopped hardboiled egg. Put stuffing in the middle of a cabbage leaf, wrap leaf around the stuffing, coat in breadcrumbs and fry on all sides in a skillet, then transfer into a shallow pot, pour tomato sauce over it and bake in the oven 30-40 minutes. One serving is 2 holubtsi.

To make sauce - melt butter in a skillet, quickly fry tomato paste, add sugar and flour, then light broth or stock and sour cream, and simmer for 10 minutes.

Tvorozhniki

Ingredients:
50 g farmers cheese
1 tsp sugar
5 g candied fruit
vanilla extract to taste

Use farmers cheese prepared from boiled milk. Rub farmers cheese through a sieve, then add syrup made from 1 tsp sugar boiled in water, mix and add vanilla and candied fruit. Serve as dessert or with rusks for breakfast.

Cranberry Kissel

Take 50 g (2 tbsp) of berries to prepare 1 serving of kissel (200 g), pick over and scald with boiling water, then mash berries with a wooden spoon. Transfer mashed berries into a cheese cloth and squeeze 1 tsp of juice. Keep juice in a cool dark place. Put squeezed berries into a pot and add 1 cup of hot water, bring to boil, then strain. Cool 1/4 cup of strained liquid and dissolve 2 tsp of potato starch in it. Add 3 tsp of sugar to the remaining berry broth and bring to boil. When the liquid comes to boil add to it dissolved potato starch and return everything to boil stirring all the time. Immediately transfer to a ceramic cup and continue to mix to prevent forming of a film on top of kissel. When kissel cools down slightly - add juice squeezed from berries to it.

Kissel should be cooked in an enameled pot (without any cracks in the enamel). Potato starch should be dissolved in berry broth, not water.

Any fresh berries could be used to make kissel following these instructions.

Farina Pudding with Apples

Ingredients:
5 tsp farina
3/4 cup milk
1/2 egg
4 tsp sugar
1 apple
2 tsp butter

Slowly pour farina into boiling milk. Add sugar, pinch of salt, and cook until ready. Once porridge is done, add butter, egg yolk and mix well. Whip the egg white and also mix it with cooled porridge.

Cut peeled apples and braise them with sugar on low heat. Grease mold, sprinkle with breadcrumbs, put in a layer of farina, add a layer of apples and cover with another layer of farina. Pour over with butter, sprinkle with breadcrumbs and bake in oven.

Cabbage Pancakes

Ingredients:
200 g cabbage
1/2 egg
1 tsp breadcrumbs
2 tsp butter
1 tbsp sour cream
1/4 cup milk

Wash, cut and braise cabbage in milk (1/4 cup), until it becomes soft. Pass braised cabbage through a meat grinder, add salt, mix with raw egg and breadcrumbs and place in the shape of pancakes onto a hot skillet with butter.

Serve with sour cream.

Carrot-Apple Croquettes

Ingredients:
1 carrot
1 apple
1 tsp farina
1/2 tsp sugar
2 tsp butter

Peel, wash and grate carrots, put them in a pan, pour over with water (1/4 cup) and braise until half-cooked. Then add peeled chopped apples and continue braising until they become soft. Pour in farina, add salt, sugar and cook for 5 minutes while continuously stirring, so that lumps don't form. Cool this paste, shape as croquettes, coat in breadcrumbs and fry with butter.

Beet Croquettes

Ingredients:
1 medium beet
1 tbsp breadcrumbs
1 tsp butter

Peel, wash and grate beet. Shape resulting paste as croquettes, coat in breadcrumbs and fry in butter.

Carrot-Apple Puree

Ingredients:
1 carrot
1 apple
1 tbsp cranberries
2 tsp sugar

Grate peeled carrot and apple; mix with pressed berries and sugar.

Crouton Pancakes

Ingredients:
3 tbsp croutons
3/4 cup water
1/2 tsp yeast
1 tsp butter
1/2 egg

Crush or pass croutons through a meat grinder and pour over with hot water, add yeast, and put in warm place for two hours. When dough rises, add egg and mix; then pour dough onto hot greased skilled with a spoon, and fry like regular dough pancakes.

Crouton Casserole with Carrots

Ingredients:
2 tbsp croutons
1/2 carrot
1/4 cup water
1/2 egg

1/2 tsp sugar
1/2 tsp butter

Peel carrot and braise it lightly in water.
Chop it; add butter and use as stuffing for
casserole. Pour over croutons with hot water, add
egg and butter. Mix this crouton paste well, put
half of it a greased skillet, add carrot stuffing,
cover with the rest of crouton paste and bake in
oven.

SPECIAL DIETS

SPECIAL DIETS

The following section provides recipes for people with special dietary needs. Every recipe in this section lists ingredients for one serving.

DISHES FOR PATIENTS WITH GASTRIC DISEASED

Barley Soup with Milk and Egg

Ingredients:
40 g barley
150 g milk
20 g butter
3 g sugar
1/4 egg yolk
3 cups water

Wash barley, put into a pot and add cold water, cover the pot and cook it on low heat no less than 2-3 hours. Mash contents of the pot through a sieve, return to simmer, strain, mix with warm milk mixed with raw egg yolk and add sugar.

Put butter into the soup just before serving.

Pureed Oat Soup with Milk and Egg

Ingredients:
40 g oats
50 g cream
100 g milk
20 g butter

1/2 egg
2 1/2 cups water

Cook oats in water until done, rub through a sieve, return to boil, add milk and cream mixed with egg and butter.

Pureed soups from other grains can be cooked following the same procedure.

Pureed Potato-Carrot Soup with Rice Broth

Ingredients:
100 g potatoes
75 g carrots
30 g rice
20 g butter
200 g milk
1/2 egg yolk

Cook rice in 1 1/2 cups of water, rub through a sieve, add to boiled and rubbed through a sieve potato and carrot, mix with boiling milk and add egg yolk and butter.

Serve with white bread croutons.

Poached Meatballs

Ingredients:
150 g beef
15 g rice
15 g butter
1/6 egg
1/2 cup water (for rice)

Clean meat from fat and sinew, pass 2-3 times through a meat grinder with fine plate. Cook thick rice porridge and add it to ground meat. Pass the mixture one-two times through a meat grinder, add egg, 5 g (1 tsp) of melted butter, mix well, shape into meatballs and put on a buttered skillet. Cover with cold water, bring to boil and cook for 5 minutes, take meatballs out of the skillet and serve with butter.

Steamed Zrazi Stuffed with Omelet

Ingredients:
150 g beef
20 g crustless white bread
1/3 egg
15 g butter
15 g milk

Make ground meat mixture with meat, bread, and 5 g of butter. Whip egg with a whisk, mix it with milk, pour into a buttered skillet and steam it until cooked, cool omelet and chop it. Mix ground meat with moist hands and shape two rounds about size of a pancake, put omelet in the middle of meat and fold meat around the stuffing. Steam zrazi until cooked, or put them into a pot, add water to reach half way of zrazi, and poach 15 minutes. Serve with butter, or milk sauce.

Steamed Meat Pudding

Ingredients:
120 g beef
20 g butter
10 g farina

1/2 egg
1/3 cup water

Boil meat cleaned from fat and sinew, past it two-three times through a meat grinder and mix with porridge cooked from farina, then add raw egg yolk, whipped egg white, mix carefully, transfer into a buttered mold or skillet, smooth the top, and steam until cooked. Finished pudding should be transferred to a plate and serve with butter or with rice or milk sauce.

Steamed Potato Croquettes with Meat in Omelet

Ingredients:
120 g potatoes
50 g beef
15 g butter
2 eggs
100 g milk

Boil meat and pass it though a meat grind. Boil potatoes and rub through a sieve, add 5 g of butter, 1/2 egg, and 25 g milk, mix well and form 4 patties, put meat in the middle of each patty and fold potato mix around the meat and pinch sides together, then roll it into balls.

Butter one-serving mold or skillet, add croquettes, pour in egg mixed with milk, and steam until done. Serve croquettes with butter.

Walleye Quenelles with Butter

Ingredients:
100 g walleye
10 g crustless white bread
30 g cream
15 g butter

Make forcemeat from fish, bread, and cream, shape quenelles using 2 tablespoons, and put quenelles in a buttered skillet. Cover quenelles with cold water, bring to boil and cook 3-5 minutes. Take quenelles out of the water and serve with butter.

Steamed Walleye Soufflé with Butter

Ingredients:
150 g fish fillet
20 g butter
1 tsp flour
1/2 egg
40 g milk

Skin and remove all the bones from fish fillet, boil half of the fish and pass through a meat grinder with a fine plate twice together with uncooked fish. Make a sauce from milk and flour; add to the ground fish together with egg yolk and 10 g butter and mix everything well. Accurately fold in whipped egg white, transfer into a buttered mold and steam until cooked.

Just before serving pour melted butter over soufflé.

Steamed Carrot-Apple Soufflé

Ingredients:
75 g carrots
75 g apples
20 g butter
1/2 egg
10 g sugar
10 g farina
50 g milk

Thinly slice peeled carrots and braise with milk until cooked. Peel and core apples and pass through a meat grinder together with carrots. Add farina, sugar, egg yolk, and 10 g of butter to the ground apples and carrots and mix well. Fold in whipped egg white, transfer into a buttered mold and steam until cooked. Serve soufflé with butter.

Mixed Vegetable Puree

Ingredients:
60 g carrots
60 g cauliflower
30 g green peas
35 g green beans
60 g milk
25 g butter
1 tsp sugar

Braise carrots with a small quantity of milk; boil all the other vegetables, mix together with carrots and pass through a meat grinder with fine plate. Add hot milk and 10 g of melted butter; then whip the mixture, add sugar, and serve with a piece of butter. This puree can be served with medium-boiled egg.

Steamed Farina Soufflé with Milk

Ingredients:
50 g farina
100 g milk
15 g butter
10 g sugar
1/2 egg
25 g water

Make porridge with water and milk and boil it for 10 minutes, then remove from heat. Add egg yolk, sugar, and 10 g butter and mix well. Then add whipped egg white, put into a greased mold and steam until ready.

Rice Roll with Fruit

Ingredients:
50 g rice
100 g milk
1/2 egg
20 g butter
10 g sugar

50 g apples
20 g dried apricots
25 g water

Wash, dry and grind rice using coffee grinder, and make porridge with water and milk. Then add sugar, eggs and 5 g butter, mix and cool; then lay out a layer of porridge 1 cm thick on gauze moistened with water. Put finely chopped apples and dried apricots in the middle, wrap into a roll, put on a greased skillet and steam until ready. Serve with butter.

Sauce with Omelet

Ingredients:
75 g milk
20 g butter
1/2 egg
3 g flour

Mix eggs with one ounce of milk, pour onto a greased skillet and steam until ready, then cool and chop. Make sauce, similar to kissel from flour and 50 g milk, add butter and chopped omelet.

Steamed Egg Omelet

Ingredients:
2 eggs
60 g milk
10 g butter

Mix eggs with milk, pour into a greased mold and steam until ready. Serve with a piece of butter.

Farmers Cheese Cream

Ingredients:
100 g farmers cheese
10 g butter
1/2 egg yolk
35 g sour cream
15 g sugar
20 g milk
vanilla to taste

Whip egg yolk with 10 g of sugar, add milk

and bring to boil, frequently stirring while cooking, but not allowing it to boil. Then cool, mix with farmers cheese, butter and vanilla and 20 g sour cream. Mix it well and shape it nicely. Mix remaining sour cream with powdered sugar (5 g), whip and cover farmers cheese cream with it.

Steamed Farmers Cheese Soufflé with Cookies

Ingredients:
120 g farmers cheese
20 g cookies
15 g sugar
1/2 egg
20 g milk
10 g butter
30 g sour cream

Crush cookies, mix with sugar, pour over with milk, leave like that for 10-15 minutes, then mix with farmers cheese, egg yolk and 5 g melted butter. Add whipped egg white, put into greased mold and steam until ready.

Snowballs with Fruit Sauce (Floating Islands)

Ingredients:
1/2 egg white
25 g sugar
50 g strawberry
5 g potato flour
100 g water
vanilla as desired

Whip egg white and gradually add 15 g sugar and vanilla, while continuing whipping. With a tablespoon, put whipped egg whites into a deep pan with simmering water. Flip snowballs after 2-3 minutes, cover lid. Leave for 5 minutes, then remove, drain and put on a plate. Pour over with strawberry kissel, made from strawberries, flour and 10 g sugar.

Carrot Juice with Cream

Ingredients:
150 g carrots
50 g cream
25 g water

Peel and grate carrots, add cold boiled water, mix, squeeze through cheese cloth and add cream. Serve cooled, but not cold.

DISHES FOR PATIENTS WITH BOWEL DISORDERS

Meat Bouillon with Toasts

Ingredients:
100 g marrow bones
50 g meat (for clarification process)
10 g vegetables
1/5 egg white
600 g water

Chop bones into smaller pieces, cover with cold water in a pot, quickly bring to boil, lower the heat and simmer 4-5 hours. Pass meat through a meat grinder, mix with an egg white and 50 g cold water, add to the stock and simmer 1 hour. Thinly slice vegetables and brown them in a skillet without any fat. Add vegetables to the stock 40 minutes before the end of cooking. Strain cooked bouillon through a clean kitchen towel, degrease, and serve with toasts from white bread.

Rice Soup with Meat

Ingredients:
50 g rice
5 g butter
150 g meat bouillon
500 g water

Add washed rice to boiling water and cook for 1 hour, then strain and add to hot bouillon. Just before serving add butter to the soup. This soup can be served with white bread toasts.

Blueberry Soup with Rice

Ingredients:
40 g dried blueberries
30 g rice
15 g sugar
1/10 lemon
50 g white bread
750 g water

Wash blueberries, add to a pan with 350 g of water, bring to boil and simmer 10-15 minutes, then take off the heat and let it infuse 30 minutes longer. Strain blueberries and add sugar and lemon juice to the strained liquid, let it cool. Cook rice in the remaining water, then pass rice with its cooking liquid through a sieve and add blueberry infusion to it. Serve with thin white bread toasts. This soup should be served at room temperature.

Steamed Meatballs with Garlic

Ingredients:
100 g meat
15 g rice
10 g butter
2 g garlic

Remove all the fat and sinews from meat, then pass meat through a meat grinder two-three times, then mix it with cooked rice and finely chopped garlic, shape mixture into 3-4 meatballs and steam until done. Serve with a piece of butter.

Garlic Sausage

Ingredients:
150 g boneless beef
15 g rice
10 g butter
2 g garlic

Clean meat from fat and sinews and pass it together with garlic three-four times through a meat grinder together with a fine plate. Mix ground meat with cooked rice and transfer the mixture to damp cheesecloth, wrap cheesecloth to form a sausage, tie the ends, and steam until cooked. Take finished sausage out of the cheesecloth, cut into 2-3 pieces, and drizzle with melted butter.

Steamed Chicken Zrazi with Rice

Ingredients:
120 g boneless chicken
15 g rice
10 g butter
1/2 egg white

Pass chicken meat together with half of thick rice porridge two-three times through a meat grinder and then mix well with damp hands. Separate mixture into two portions and shape each one as a flat patty. Put remaining rice mixed with cooked chopped egg white in the middle of meat patties and wrap meat around the stuffing. Steam until cooked. Serve with butter.

Walleye Quenelles with Garlic

Ingredients:
120 g walleye
15 g rice
15 g butter
2 g garlic
50 g water

Cook thick rice porridge, let it cool. Pass fish, rice porridge, and garlic tow-three times through a meat grinder with a fine plate, add 5 g of melted butter, finely mix it with damp hands, shape 10-12 quenelles and steam them until cooked. Serve with butter.

Rice Balls in Red Wine

Ingredients:
50 g rice
40 g red wine
10 g sugar
3 g potato starch
200 g water

Cook rice in 150 g of water, cool slightly, shape 10-12 balls, put into a bowl and add kissel made from red wine, potato starch, and remaining water.

Steamed Rice Pudding with Meat Stock

Ingredients:
50 g rice
200 g meat stock
10 g butter
1/2 egg

Wash and dry rice, then grind it in a coffee grinder. Add ground dice to the boiling stock and cook until done, then add egg yolk, whipped egg white, and 5 g vegetable oil, mix everything well, then transfer into a buttered mold and steam until cooked. Garnish with a piece of butter and serve.

Rice Porridge with Cocoa

Ingredients:
50 g rice
5 g cacao powder
5 g sugar
10 g butter
250 g water

Make thick rice porridge on water. Mix cacao powder with sugar and add it to porridge, dot with butter and serve.

Rice Sauce with Butter

Ingredients:
15 g rice
100 g water
10 g butter

Cook rice in water, then rub it twice through a sieve, bring back to boil, add butter, and use it as a sauce for different dishes.

Steamed Egg White Omelet

Ingredients:
3 egg whites
5 g butter

Beat egg whites with a whisk, add 50 g of water, pour the mixture into a buttered mold, and steam until cooked. Dot with butter and serve.

Steamed Farmers Cheese Soufflé with Cherry Sauce

Ingredients:
120 g farmers cheese
10 g farina
10 g butter
15 g sugar
1/2 egg
25 g dried cherries
5 g potato starch

Make porridge from farina and 30 g of water and cool it down. Rub farmers cheese through a sieve, add cooked porridge, egg yolk, 5 g sugar and 5 g melted butter. Mix everything well, then accurately fold in whipped egg whites. Transfer mixture into buttered molds, and steam until cooked. Make kissel from cherries, 100 g of water, 10 g of sugar, and potato starch. Pour it over soufflé and serve.

Blueberry Kissel

Ingredients:
30 g blueberries
10 g potato starch
10 g sugar
1/10 lemon
300 g water

Wash blueberries, put into a pan and add water. Bring to boil and simmer 10-15 minutes, then strain, add sugar, return to boil, add potato starch mixed with cold water. Mix well without letting mixture to return to boil, then take off the heat and add lemon juice. Let cool before serving.

Rice-Water Gelatin with Acorn Coffee

Ingredients:
15 g rice
5 g acorn coffee
3 g gelatin
250 g water

Add one cup of water to washed rice, cook

until rice is done, strain; add sugar and strong acorn coffee (1/2 cup), return to boil. Add soaked in cold water and squeezed gelatin and stir until is dissolves completely. Strain the mixture into a mold and let it cool.

Cocoa on Rice-Water

Ingredients:
5 g cocoa powder
10 g rice
10 g sugar
300 g water

Cook rice in water until soft, then strain and add cacao and sugar to the strained liquid; return to boil and strain again. There should be 1 cup of liquid. Add 25 g of cream if directed by doctor.

DISHES FOR PATIENTS WITH LIVER DISEASE

Vegetable Broth with Egg White Omelet

Ingredients:
100 g potatoes
30 g carrots
20 g parsnip
50 g cabbage core
5 g parsley
1 egg white

10 g milk
20 g sour cream
5 g butter

Chop vegetables and boil them in salted water under a lid. Let it infuse for one hour and strain.

Mix egg white with milk, pour on a greased skillet, bake, then cool to room temperature and cut omelet into 5-6 pieces.

Add sour cream and remaining butter to broth; then add omelet and chopped greens.

Cauliflower Soup-Puree

Ingredients:
100 g cauliflower
100 g potatoes
20 g rice
100 g milk
10 g butter
500 g water

Chop potatoes and cabbage, pour over with water (300 g) and add 5 g butter. Cook on low heat with lid closed until ready and then rub though a sieve together with liquid. Put 200 g of washed rice into boiling water, cook for one hour. Rub through a sieve, combine with soup, heat and add milk. Before serving, add a piece of butter.

Cold Svekolnik (Beet Soup)

Ingredients:
150 g beets
50 g our cream
10 g sugar
1 egg white
75 g fresh cucumbers
10 g lettuce
15 g scallions
5 g parsley
5 g dill
300 g beet broth
lemon acid to taste

Wash beets, boil in water with lemon acid until ready, then cool, peel beet and strain the broth. Chop beet and combine with broth, add sugar, chopped boiled egg white, chopped lettuce and scallions, finely chopped cucumbers and sour cream. Before serving, sprinkle with chopped beets.

You may also put diced potatoes into svekolnik as well as peeled fresh apples.

Vegetable Stock Borscht

Ingredients:
100 g cabbage
70 g beets
60 g potatoes
15 g carrots
5 g celery

50 g tomatoes
5 g parsley
10 g butter
30 g sour cream
350 g water
lemon acid to taste (or apples or black currants)

Peel and julienne beets, salt, sprinkle with lemon acid diluted with water and mix. Then add butter and 100 grams of water, close lid and braise for 20-30 minutes on low heat, after which add chopped carrots, celery, 20 g tomatoes and braise for another 10 minutes. Add chopped cabbage to prepared vegetables, pour over with water or vegetable broth, boil, add chopped potatoes and cook until ready. When borsch is done, add the rest of sliced tomatoes. Before serving, add sour cream and sprinkle with chopped greens.

Boiled Meat with Apples Baked in Milk Sauce

Ingredients:
150 g beef
10 g butter
75 g milk
5 g wheat flour
100 g apples

Boil lean meat and cut it into 4-5 thin slices, then prepare sauce from milk and flour (same method of preparation and thickness as kissel). Peel and core apples and thinly slice them. Grease a small skillet, put apple slices on the bottom, then put meat mixed with apples on top, pour over with sauce, sprinkle with melted butter and bake.

Holubtsi (Cabbage Rolls) with Boiled Meat, Rice and Vegetables

Ingredients:
250 g cabbage
100g meat
20 g rice
30 g carrots
5 g parsley
30 g rutabaga
5 g wheat flour
30 g sour cream
10 g butter
75 g vegetable broth

Boil head of cabbage (without the core) in salted water until it is half-done, then divide into separate leaves and remove stalk from each leaf. Dice carrots and turnips, then braise them with butter in a small amount of water. Boil meat, pass it through a meat grinder, combine with braised vegetables, boiled rice, chopped greens and mix well. Divide into 2-3 parts, wrap into cabbage leaves, put in a pan, pour over with sour cream sauce and bake.

To make sour cream sauce, mix flour with sour cream and pour this mix into vegetable broth (75 g); boil for 5 minutes, strain, add a 5 g piece of butter and mix well.

Boiled Chicken and Vegetables Casserole

Ingredients:
100 g chicken meat
10 g wheat flour
50 g milk
15 g butter
40 g carrots
50 g cauliflower
1 egg white

Pass boiled chicken meat twice through a meat grinder, mix with 25 g of "Egg-Butter Sauce (For Poached Fish)" and 5 g of butter and fold in 1/2 of whipped egg white. Transfer the mixture to a small buttered skillet and steam until cooked. Braise carrot and cauliflower in a pot with 5 g of butter until soft, rub cooked vegetables through a sieve, fold in the remaining egg white, cover the steamed chicken with this mixture and bake in a preheated oven. Serve in the skillet it was cooked in.

Baked Walleye Roll with Egg White Omelet

Ingredients:
120 g walleye
20 g white bread
35 g milk
10 g butter

20 g sour cream
3 g white flour
1/2 egg white

Pass boneless and skinless walleye through a meat grinder, mix it with bread soaked in 25 g of milk, and pass it through the meat grinder two more times, then add 5 g of melted butter and mix well. Mix egg white with 10 g of milk, pour it into a buttered skillet and bake in a preheated oven or steam until ready. Spread ground fish mixture on a damp cheese cloth 1 1/2 cm thick, top with omelet, roll it and steam until cooked. Transfer cooked roll out of the cheese cloth into a buttered skillet, pour sour cream mixed with flour on top, and then sprinkle with remaining butter. Bake until browned. Cut into 2 - 3 slices and serve.

Dried Apricots, Rutabaga, and Farmers Cheese Pudding

Ingredients:
75 g rutabaga
50 g dried apricots
50 g farmers cheese
1 egg white
30 g milk
10 g butter
10 g sugar
10 g farina
30 g sour cream

Julienne rutabaga and braise it with 5 g of butter and milk until soft, then add farina, sugar, and soaked and finely diced apricots. Mix everything well and let it cook, then add farmers cheese rubbed through a sieve and whipped egg white, mix again, transfer into a buttered mold, sprinkle with melted butter and bake in a preheated oven. Serve with sour cream.

Zucchini and Apple Pudding

Ingredients:
125 g zucchini
75 g apples
25 g milk
15 g butter
1 egg
10 g sugar
15 g farina
30 g sour cream

Peel, grate, and braise zucchini with milk and 10 g of butter until half-done, add grated apples, sugar, and braise 5 more minutes, then add farina, keep the pot covered on a side of the stove 5-10 minutes, then cool slightly. Add egg yolk, and then carefully fold in whipped egg white, transfer into a buttered mold and bake in a preheated oven. Serve with sour cream.

Baked Carrot-Apple Patties

Ingredients:
100 g carrots
100 g apples
1 egg white
10 g butter
10 g farina
10 g breadcrumbs
5 g sugar
30 g sour cream

Julienne peeled and washed carrots; braise with 10 g of butter and 1/4 cup water until cooked, then add grated apples and sugar, and braise 5 minutes more, add farina, mix everything and let everything stand 5-10 minutes on the side of the stove. Fold in whipped egg white and cool the mixture until cold enough to handle. Form 3-4 patties from the carrot-apple mixture; coat them with breadcrumbs or flour, put into a buttered skillet, sprinkle with melted butter and bake in a preheated oven. Serve with sour cream.

Toasts with Vegetables

Ingredients:
60 g wheat bread
75 g milk
1/4 egg
5 g sugar
15 g butter
30 g sour cream
75 g white cabbage

50 g carrots
50 g zucchini
50 g apples
5 g lettuce leaves
5 g dill

Cut bread into 2 slices; dip in 50 g of milk mixed with sugar and egg, and bake until lightly browned. Meanwhile, shred cabbage and peeled zucchini and braise them with 25 g of milk and 10 g of butter. Separately braise thinly sliced carrots. Mix cooked vegetables with grated apples, finely-chopped lettuce and dill, top toasts with vegetable mixture, smooth the top, drizzle with melted butter and brown in the oven. Serve with sour cream.

Turnip Stuffed with Rice and Apples

Ingredients:
150 g turnips
20 g rice
50 g apples
10 g sugar
1/2 egg
5 g flour
50 g milk
10 g butter

Peel and boil turnip until cooked. Meanwhile make milk sauce with flour, butter, and milk. Remove some of the inside of the turnip to give it a shape of a cup, and stuff with boiled rice mixed with grated apples, sugar, butter, and egg. Pour milk sauce over turnip and bake until browned. Drizzle with butter before serving.

Omelet with Cauliflower

Ingredients:
200 g cauliflower
5 g butter
2 egg whites
50 g milk
30 g sour cream

Blanch cauliflower in salted water, separate into florettes; then put florettes into a small buttered skillet, pour egg whites mixed with milk over them, top with sour cream, and bake until cooked. Serve in the skillet in which it was cooked.

Fresh Cucumbers Stuffed with Raw Vegetables

Ingredients:
100 g cucumbers
50 g tomatoes
30 g white cabbage
1/4 egg, hardboiled
40 g sour cream
5 g dill

Peel cucumbers, cut them in half lengthwise and remove the seeds. Thinly slice tomatoes and insides of the cucumber, finely chop cabbage and hardboiled egg, mix everything with 20 g of sour cream and stuff cucumbers with this mixture. Pour remaining sour cream on top and sprinkle with dill.

Tomato and Apple Salad with Sour Cream Dressing

Ingredients:
100 g tomatoes
100 g apples
40 g sour cream
10 g parsley leaves

Slice ripe and hard tomatoes and peeled and cored apples. Lay alternating slices of apples and tomatoes on a serving plate, pour sour cream over salad and decorate with parsley leaves.

Oatmeal "Hercules" with Preserves

Ingredients:
75 g oats (whole grain)
5 g sugar
150 g milk
5 g butter
30 g preserves
100 g water

Add oats into a pot with boiling milk and water, add sugar and salt, cover the pot, and simmer 1 1/2 - 2 hours, stirring frequently.

Dot oatmeal with butter and pour preserves on top just before serving.

Rice Pilaf with Fruits and Vegetables

Ingredients:
50 g rice
15 g raisins
25 g prunes
30 g carrots
40 g cauliflower
15 g butter
100 g water

Add picked over and washed rice into boiling water, add sugar and butter, return to boil and cook until done on a water bath. Transfer cooked rice to a skillet, add washed raisins, prunes, braised carrots and boiled cauliflower, cover the skillet and cook on low heat for about an hour.

Baked Egg White Omelet with Sour Cream

Ingredients:
3 egg whites
30 g sour cream
20 g milk
3 g butter

Beat egg whites with a whisk, add milk and

20 g of sour cream, mix well and pour into a small buttered skillet, drizzle with remaining sour cream and bake in a preheated oven.

Egg White Omelet with Vegetables

Ingredients:
3 egg whites
30 g sour cream
40 g milk
10 g butter
30 g white cabbage
30 g zucchini
10 g lettuce
5 g parsley leaves

Cook shredded cabbage, zucchini, and lettuce with butter and 20 g of milk until cooked, then transfer the vegetables into a buttered mold, and top with egg whites mixed with 20 g of milk and remaining sour cream. Bake in a preheated oven.

Syrniki (Farmers Cheese Pancakes) with Carrots

Ingredients:
120 g farmers cheese
30 g all-purpose flour
1/2 egg
15 g sugar
15 g dried apricots
20 g carrots

10 g butter

30 g sour cream

Braise grated carrots with 5 g of butter and a small quantity of water until all the water evaporates and then cool them. Finely chop dried apricots. Rub farmers cheese through a sieve and mix with half of the flour, a little of sour cream, sugar, egg, dried apricots, and braised carrots. Mix everything well, shape 3 patties, coat patties in flour and put them in a ovenproof skillet, pour sour cream on top, and bake in a preheated oven until cooked.

Farmers Cheese and Fruit Casserole

Ingredients:

120 g farmers cheese

10 g farina

1 egg white

15 g sugar

40 g milk

40 g white bread

25 g apples

15 g raisins

30 g sour cream

10 g butter

Cut bread into 2 slices and dip in milk with sugar. Rub farmers cheese through a sieve, fold in whipped egg white, add remaining sugar, farina, raisins, diced apple and mix everything well. Put a slice of bread into a buttered mold, then put cheese mixture, and finally top with the second slice of bread. Drizzle with melted butter and bake in a preheated oven. Serve with sour cream on a side.

Gelatin Dessert with Fruit

Ingredients:
25 g lemon
25 g dried apricots
20 g apples
20 g pears
25 g sugar
3 g gelatin

Make "Lemon Gelatin Dessert" following instructions of that recipe, meanwhile, dice fruits, put them into a mold, pour in slightly cooled gelatin dessert and chill.

Take set gelatin dessert out of the mold and pour syrup on top.

Sour Milk Cream

Ingredients:
100 g sour milk
25 g sour cream
25 g sugar
20 g milk
3 g gelatin
1/4 egg yolk

0.1 g cinnamon

Beat egg yolk with sugar, mix in soaked gelatin and boiled milk, and warm the mixture up until gelatin dissolves and it slightly thickens. Strain and add cinnamon to the mixture. Whip sour cream and sour milk into foam and gradually add it to the gelatin mixture, mix well, pour into a mold and chill.

DISHES FOR PATIENTS WITH HEART, KIDNEY DISEASE AND HIGH BLOOD PRESSURE

Okroshka with Fruit Infusion

Ingredients:
100g fresh cucumbers
10 g lettuce
5 g parsley
60 g potatoes
5 g dill
1 egg
50 g sour cream
5 g sugar
5 g lemon juice
400 g fruit infusion

Dice fresh cucumbers and potatoes (boiled with skin, then cooled and peeled). Finely chop lettuce, parsley, dill. Hard boil an egg, chop the white, rub the yolk through a sieve and mix with sour cream. Pour everything over with fruit infusion, add vegetables, greens, sugar and lemon acid.

In order to make fruit infusion, take 100 g apples or 25 g dried fruit, pour over with 2 cups of boiling water, boil and let it infuse under a lid for 3-4 hours.

Instead of fruit 100g rhubarb or 20 g rosehip may be used.

Milk Soup with Pumpkin and Farina

350 g milk
100 g pumpkin
25 g farina
15 g sugar
10 g butter
100 g water

Peel pumpkin, cut into small slices and braise with water until ready, then rub through a sieve together with liquid. At the same time, boil milk and cook farina in it for 10 minutes. Combine with pumpkin and add sugar. Serve with butter.

Apple Soup with Rose Hip Broth

Ingredients:
150 g apples
20 g dried rose hip
25 g sugar
0.1 g cinnamon

50 g white bread
500 g water

Pour over rose hip with boiling water, cover lid and boil for 5 minutes, then let it infuse for 3-5 hours. Strain, add sugar and cinnamon. Boil, add finely chopped or grated apples and cool. Dice bread, dry it in oven and serve with soup.

Dried Apricot Soup with Rice

Ingredients:
80 g dried apricot
20 g rice
15 g sugar
50 g cream
450 g water

Wash and chop dried apricots, add sugar, pour over with boiling water, cover with lid and let it infuse for 2-3 hours, then add boiled rice and cream. Serve cold.

Boiled Meat in Sweet and Sour Sauce

Ingredients:
150 g beef
5 g butter
30 g sour cream
5 g wheat flour
10 g raisins

15 g prunes
25 g apples
5 g dill
100 g vegetable broth

Boil lean and tender mean and cut it in 2
pieces. Make sauce from flour, sour cream and
vegetable broth (see appropriate recipe). Soak
raisins and prunes in cold water.
t the same time, chop apples and prunes. Put
butter into a pan, pour in some water, add meat
and then fruit on top. Cover with lid and braise for
5 minutes, then pour over with sauce and braise
for another 10-15 minutes. Before serving, pour
over with chopped greens.

Beef Steak from Boiled Meat with Onions

Ingredients:
150 g meat (tenderloin)
25 g butter
50 g onions

Remove sinews and fat from meat, pound it
with a meat mallet and shape it as a pancake.
Grease bottom of the skillet with butter, put meat
on skillet and pour it over with water so that meat
is covered half way. Close lid and boil for 5-7
minutes, then remove meat, let it dry a little and
fry it in butter from both sides.

Slice onions, divide them into rings and boil
in water until half-ready. Drain onions then fry

them in butter. Put fried onions on top of beef steak and serve.

For garnish serve fried potatoes or squash, pumpkin, cabbage or cauliflower, lettuce.

Farina Zrazi with Meat

Ingredients:
50 g farina
150 g milk
80 g meat
20 g butter
1/3 egg
10 g wheat flour

Boil milk with 5 g butter. Gradually add farina while quickly stirring with a spoon. Cook on low heat for another 10 minutes; then add raw egg, mix well and divide into 2-3 flat breads.
At the same time boil meat, pass it through a meat grinder twice and put meat on top of flat breads. Join the edges, coat in flour and fry.

Walleye Baked in Milk Sauce

Ingredients:
125 g walleye
20 g butter
75 g milk
5 g wheat flour
10 g crabs or crayfish tails
100 g potatoes

1/4 egg
5 g cheese

Cut walleye fillet into 3-4 pieces and boil. Put some milk sauce (see appropriate recipe) on the bottom of a small greased skillet, then add fish and crabs/craw fish tails on top. Pour over with the rest of the sauce and sprinkle with grated cheese. Make puree from potatoes, egg and 25 g milk. Lay out puree around walleye, sprinkle with grated cheese, sprinkle with melted butter and bake.

Apples Stuffed with Farmers Cheese and Raisins

Ingredients:
200 g apples
30 g raisins
60 g cottage cheese
10 g butter
1 egg yolk
5 g farina
30 g sour cream
15 g sugar

Rub farmers cheese through a sieve, mix it with farina, raisins, 10 g sugar, egg yolk, melted butter and apple cores.
Cut off top portions of apples, remove core without cutting the sides, fill apples with farmers cheese and bake.
Serve with sour cream and powdered sugar

(5 g).   .

Schnitzel with Assorted Vegetables in Milk Sauce

Ingredients:
50 g carrots
75 g cabbage
40 g fresh cucumbers
50 g rutabaga
75 g milk
20 g butter
5 g sugar
1/2 egg
10 gram farina
15 g wheat flour
5 g cheese

Braise finely chopped carrots and rutabaga in a small amount of water and 5 g butter. Also braise chopped cabbage in 20 g of milk until it is ready; then combine with carrots and turnips. Add egg, farina, sugar and grated cucumber. Mix all this; make 2 schnitzels, coat in flour and fry in butter. Make sauce from remaining milk and 5 g flour (see appropriate recipe), pour over schnitzel, sprinkle with grated cheese, spray with butter and bake.

Fruit, Vegetable and Farmers Cheese Casserole

Ingredients:

100 g apples
20 g raisins
20 g fig
50 g farmers cheese
1 egg
15 g butter
10 sugar
5 g farina
35 g carrots
25 g spinach
30 g sour cream

Julienne carrots and braise with 10 g butter and small amount of water until ready, then add chopped spinach and braise for another 5 minutes. Add chopped apples, figs, 1/2 egg and mix.

At the same time, rub farmers cheese through a sieve, mix with farina, sugar, remaining egg and raisins. After that grease a mold, fill it with a layer of farmers cheese, then a layer of fruit, etc., with 4 layers total. Spray with butter and bake. Serve with sour cream.

Holubtsi (Cabbage Rolls) with Fruit and Sour Cream

Ingredients:
150 g cabbage
100 g apples
50 g dried apricots
30 g raisins
20 g spinach

20 g butter

30 g sour cream

Remove core from a solid head of cabbage. Boil cabbage until it is half-ready, then drain. Divide cabbage into separate leaves. Remove thick stems from all leaves, and lay cabbage leaves out on a board.

At the same time chop spinach, put it into a pan, pour in some water, add washed raisins, 5 g butter and braise for 5 minutes; then combine all this with chopped dried apricots and apples, put on top of cabbage leaves, wrap then in envelope shape and fry on both sides in butter.

Serve with sour cream.

Pumpkin-Apple Pudding

Ingredients:

100 g pumpkin

100g apples

50 g milk

15 g farina

10 g sugar

1/2 egg

20 g butter

Peel, chop and braise pumpkin until it is half-ready, then add chopped apples and braise until pumpkin is fully ready. Add farina, mix and cook for another 5 minutes. After that cool, add sugar, egg yolk, whipped egg white, carefully mix, put on a greased skillet and bake. Pour over with butter and serve.

Beet Stuffed with Apples, Rice and Raisins

Ingredients:
150 g beets
75 g apples
15 g rice
25 g raisins
15 g butter
50 g sour cream
5 g sugar
1/4 egg
1/10 g cinnamon

Boil or bake beet, peel and core with a spoon, shaping beet as a cup. Cook rice porridge, mix it with sugar, raisins and finely chopped apples. Add 10 g melted butter and cinnamon, mix, stuff beat. Pour over with 20 g sour cream and bake. Serve with sour cream.

Pumpkin with Dried Apricots in Milk Sauce

Ingredients:
150 g pumpkin
75 g dried apricots
15 g butter
5 g sugar
50 g milk
5 g wheat flour

5 g white croutons

Peel pumpkin, dice and fry in butter. Chop dried apricots, mix with pumpkin and place on a greased skillet in a shape of a mound. Pour over with milk sauce (see appropriate recipe), add sugar, crushed croutons, sprinkle with butter and bake.

Salad with Pumpkin, Melon, Apples and Lemon

Ingredients:
50 g pumpkin
50 g melon
50 g apples
1/4 lemon
20 g honey

Rub peeled pumpkin through a sieve and mix with honey. Thinly slice melon, apples, part of the lemon and put in a bowl together with pumpkin. Lay out thin slices of lemon around the salad.

Salad with Carrots, Apples and Nuts

Ingredients:
75 g carrots
75 g apples
25 g shelled walnuts
25 g honey
10 g parsley

Rub carrots through a sieve, chop apples. Mix everything with honey and put into a bowl, decorate with parsley and sprinkle with fried chopped walnuts.

Salad with Grated Carrots, Jam and Nuts

Ingredients:
150 g carrots
30 g jam
20 g shelled walnuts
20 g cranberry

Rub carrots through a sieve, mix with jam, lay out in a shape of a mound in a bowl, surround with cranberries and sprinkle with fried chopped nuts.

Salad with turnips can be prepared the same way.

Farina Pancakes with Apples and Raisins

Ingredients:
50 g farina
30 g apples
20 g raisins
75 g milk
1/2 egg
20 g butter
5 g sugar

Cook farina porridge with milk, sugar and 5 g butter, let it cool and add an egg. Peel and dice apples and add them to porridge together with washed raisins. Mix well and lay out small pancakes onto a heated greased skillet. Cook pancakes on low heat.

You can serve pancakes with jam, syrup and kissel that is not too thick.

Millet Porridge with Fruit and Honey

Ingredients:
50 g millet
30 g prunes
20 g dried apricots
20 g raisins
100 g milk
20 g butter
5 g sugar
30 g honey

Pour well-washed millet into boiling milk, add sugar, 10 g butter and cook until it thickens; then add washed fruit, mix, tightly close lid and put into oven that is not very hot or on stove for 2-3 hours. Serve with butter. Honey is served separately.

Farmers Cheese Souffle with Dried Apricots and Nuts

Ingredients:

100 g farmers cheese
10 g farina
1/2 egg
15 g sugar
20 g milk
30 g dried apricots
25 g shelled walnuts
10 g butter
30 g sour cream

Crush walnuts until they are dough-like in consistency. Combine with finely chopped dried apricots and with farmers cheese paste (see appropriate recipe). Mix everything, put in a greased mold and bake. Serve with sour cream.

Blinchiki with Carrots, Raisins and Dried Apricots

Ingredients:
50 g flour
100 g milk
1/2 egg
10 g sugar
20 g butter
30 g raisins
30 g dried apricots
30 g sour cream
50 g carrots

Mix flour, milk, 5 g of sugar, strain and bake 2 blinchiki. At the same time chop carrots and braise it with a little bit of butter until ready. Then add raisins, chopped dried apricots, and part of the butter. Put this stuffing on top of blinchiki, wrap them and fry on both sides in butter; serve with sour cream.

Prunes Stuffed with Farmers Cheese and Nuts

Ingredients:
50 g prunes
50 g farmers cheese
1 egg yolk
5 g farina
10 g sugar
25 g shelled walnuts
50 g sour cream
3 g butter

Soak prunes in cold boiled water and remove pits. Rub farmers cheese through a sieve, mix with farina, egg yolk, sugar and finely chopped fried walnuts. Stuff prunes with this paste, put on a greased skillet, add some water and bake in oven. Reduce sour cream by half, pour it over prunes and serve.

Stuffed Apples

Ingredients:
150 g apples
20 g dried apricots
15 g raisins

15 g almonds
20 g sugar
1 g cinnamon

Core apples and fill them with raisins mixed with sugar, chopped dried apricots, peeled, chopped and fried almonds; then bake them in oven on low heat, so that the apples don't fall apart. When serving, sprinkle with powdered sugar mixed with cinnamon.

DISHES FOR PATIENTS SUFFERING FORM OBESITY AND DIABETES

Wheat Bran Bread

Ingredients:
100 g wheat bran
100 g rye flour
5 g butter
5 g yeast
200 g water

Dissolve yeast in 100 g of warm water, add 50 g of flour and mix well, then leave sponge in warm place for 30 minutes. Add remaining flour and wheat bran when the sponge has risen, mix the dough and leave in the warm place for 30-40 minutes, then transfer the dough into a buttered mold, let it rise and bake in a preheated oven.

This bread contains half as much carbohydrates as regular bread; therefore, its serving quantity could be doubled.

Meat Broth with Ham Pudding and Greens

Ingredients:
150 g meat on bone
10 g butter
50 g ham
20 g scallions
20 g spinach
5 g parsley leaves
10 g carrots
5 g parsnip
1/2 egg
20 g milk
5 g cheese

Make broth from meat, carrot, parsnip, and 5 g of onion. Finely chop lean ham or pass it through a meat grinder. Shred scallions and spinach and lightly fry it in oil together with ham, then transfer into a buttered mold. Pour egg mixed with milk over ham mixture, then sprinkle grated hard cheese on top and bake in a preheated oven. Just before serving, transfer pudding into a bowl and pour meat broth over it.

Green Shchi with Egg

Ingredients:
150 g beef
1 egg

40 g sour cream
10 g butter
5 g wheat flour
100 g sorrel
120g spinach
20 g onions
10 g scallions
5 g parsley leaves

Make a broth from meat and water. Finely chop sorrel. Put spinach into a pot, add a little bit of water, cover the pot and braise spinach until soft. Pass cooked spinach through a meat grinder.

Chop onions and lightly fry in oil, add flour and fry a little more. Gradually add strained meat broth and bring to simmer, add spinach and sorrel to the broth and cook 10-15 minutes. Just before serving put meat and hardboiled egg, sliced scallions, parsley leaves, and sour cream into shchi.

Spinach can be replaced with some other edible greens.

Meat Broth with Stuffed Cucumbers

Ingredients:
150 g meat
100 g cucumbers
10 g onions
10 g butter
5 g dill
5 g cheese

1/2 egg
500 g water

Make broth with meat and water. Peel cucumbers, remove seeds, and blanch in salted boiling water for 5 minutes, then take them out and let dry. Cut meat and brown it with onions, then pass it though a meat grinder, mix with chopped greens and egg, stuff cucumbers with this mixture, sprinkle with grated hard cheese, drizzle with melted butter and bake in a preheated oven. Just before serving, put stuffed cucumbers into hot broth.

Borscht with Soaked Beets

Ingredients:
150 g meat
5 g butter
30 g sour cream
100 g beets
150 g white cabbage
15 g onions
10 g celery
20 g parsnip
5 g parsley leaves
10 g tomato paste
400 g water
1 tbsp vinegar

Make broth with meat and water. Julienne peeled beets and soak it in 1-2 liters of cold water and 1 tbsp of vinegar for 2 hours. Change water twice during this time.

Slice peeled onion, parsnip, and celery, and fry in oil together with tomato paste. Add drained beets and 1/2 cup of meat broth to vegetables; cover the skillet and braise everything 20 minutes. Add shredded cabbage and braised vegetables to the strained meat broth, return to boil, and cook until vegetables are done. Serve with meat, sour cream, and parsley leaves.

Beef Braised with Eggplant, Mushrooms, and Tomatoes

Ingredients:
150 g beef
20 g butter
20 g onions
5 g tomato paste
100 g eggplants
100 g fresh mushrooms
75 g tomatoes
10 g green pepper
5 g parsley leaves
1 bay leaf

Quickly sear soft meat in 5 g butter on all sides, then add tomato paste, 1/2 cup water, bay leaf, cover the pot and braise it on low heat until cooked through, then cut it into 3 pieces, add diced and fried onions, mushrooms, and green pepper, and braise for 5-8 minutes. Transfer cooked meat to a serving plate, top with mushroom sauce and sprinkle with parsley leaves. Slice eggplants and tomatoes, fry in butter and serve with put around meat in alternating slices as a garnish.

Tenderloin with Tomatoes and Cauliflower

Ingredients:
150 g tenderloin
15 g butter
75 g tomatoes
25 g scallions
25 g sour cream
200 g cauliflower
5 g parsley leaves

Remove fat and sinew from meat, cut it across the grain in 3 pieces, slightly pound it with meat mallet and sear on all sides in butter. At the same time blanch cauliflower, slice tomatoes and onions and fry them in oil, add sour cream and simmer for 5 minutes, then dress meat with this sauce and sprinkle with chopped parsley leaves. Serve meat garnished with cauliflower dressed with butter.

Cabbage Schnitzel

Ingredients:
250 g white cabbage
1 egg

20 g butter

20 g wheat bran

Blanch cabbage leaves in salted water, cool and squeeze slightly, then cut each leaf into to parts, fold them in a shape of a schnitzel, dip into beaten egg, coat in bran and fry in butter.

Holubtsi with Mushrooms and Eggs

Ingredients:

150 g white cabbage

100 g fresh mushrooms

15 g leeks

1/2 egg

15 g butter

40 g sour cream

5 g parsley leaves

Blanch cabbage leaves. Slice leeks and fry in oil, then add sliced mushrooms and fry 10-12 minutes longer, then add parsley leaves and chopped hardboiled egg. Make holubtsi from mushroom stuffing and cabbage leaves, cover them with sour cream and bake until cooked through.

Tomatoes Stuffed with Veal

Ingredients:

150 g tomatoes

100 g veal

1/2 egg
15 g vegetable oil
10 g scallions
5 g dill
10 g green pepper
20 g sour cream
5 g vinegar

Make mayonnaise from half of egg yolk, vegetable oil, and vinegar, mix it with sour cream, then finely chop hard boiled egg white and thinly slice scallions and green paper. Dice boiled or fried veal and mix with egg whites, greens, and half of the sauce. Cut the top of 2 tomatoes from the stem side, scoop the inside of tomatoes, chop and add to stuffing. Fill tomatoes with stuffing. Just before serving pour remaining sauce over tomatoes and sprinkle with chopped greens.

Carrot Pudding

Ingredients:
150 g carrots
15 g butter
30 g sour cream
50 g milk
50 g farmers cheese
1 egg
5 g wheat bran
saccharine to taste

Grate peeled carrots on fin grater, cover

with 2 liters of cold water and soak 3-4 hours, changing water every hour. Drain carrot through a cheese cloth and squeeze it dry. Put carrots into a pot with 10 g of butter and milk and braise. Add egg yolk mixed with farmers cheese rubbed through a sieve, fold in egg white with saccharine. Mix everything well and transfer to a buttered and sprinkled with wheat bran mold. Bake in a preheated oven. Serve with sour cream.

Farmers Cheese and Almond Cookies

Ingredients:
50 g farmers cheese
50 g shelled almonds
1 egg yolk
2 g butter
saccharine and vanilla extract to taste

Blanch almonds, remove skins, pound in a mortar or chop very finely, mix with farmers cheese rubbed through a sieve and mixed with egg yolk, add saccharine and vanilla, mix everything well, shape small round and bake at a moderate temperature.

Oatmeal with Wheat Bran

Ingredients:
40 g whole oats
40 g wheat bran
10 g butter

100 g milk
200 g water

Put wheat bran into boiling water and simmer under a cover for 10 minutes, then add oats and 10 g butter, mix and simmer for 2 hours. Serve with milk.

Potato and Wheat Bran Croquettes

Ingredients:
200 g potatoes
50 g wheat bran
40 g milk
20 g butter
1/2 egg

Boil finely washed potatoes until cooked, peel and pass them though a meat grinder. Mix 40 g of wheat bran with milk, let is stand 15-20 minutes, mix with ground potatoes; add egg and 10 g of bitter. Mix everything well and shape 3 croquettes, coat them in remaining bran and fry in butter.

Sour Cream and Tomato Juice Sauce

Ingredients:
50 g sour cream
1 egg yolk
40 g tomatoes

Cut ripe tomatoes in half, squeeze seeds out, and then rub through a sieve. Add sour cream to the tomato juice, bring to simmer and reduce by half, then add raw egg yolk, and continue stirring until the sauce thickens.

Serve this sauce with holubtsi, stuffed zucchini or tomatoes, or meat.

Mayonnaise

Ingredients:
25 g vegetable oil
1/4 egg yolk
2 g mustard
vinegar to taste

Blend raw egg yolk, mustard, and salt, and gradually add vegetable oil, quickly mixing everything with a whisk. When mixture starts thickening too much add a little vinegar to dilute. Vegetable oil should be room temperature; otherwise, it will not emulsify properly.

Serve with meat, fish, or vegetable dishes.

Mayonnaise can also be made without mustard. Finished sauce should be kept in a cool place.

Lemon Sauce with Mushrooms and Capers

Ingredients:
50 g cream
2/3 egg

15 g lemon
20 g pickled mushrooms
5 g capers

Blend egg with a whisk, add cream, lemon zest, and continue whipping over a water bath until it thickens, then season it with lemon juice and salt to taste. Chop pickled mushrooms and blanch them together with capers, then drain and mix with sauce.

Pumpkin and Rhubarb Marmalade with Saccharine

Ingredients:
150 g pumpkin
100 g rhubarb
saccharin to taste

Bake pumpkin and rub baked pumpkin through a sieve. Thinly slice peeled rhubarb, mix it with pumpkin puree and braise on low heat, stirring from time to time to prevent scorching. Add saccharine when marmalade thickens. Serve this marmalade hot or cold. Cold marmalade can be served with whipped cream.

Rhubarb and Apple Compote with Saccharine

Ingredients:
75 g rhubarb
75 g apples

1/4 g cinnamon
saccharin to taste
150 g water

Peel rhubarb stalks and cut then into matchsticks. Core and slice apples. Bring water to boil, add cinnamon, apples, and rhubarb, cover the pot and let it steep 5-10 minutes on a side of the stove. Add saccharin to taste and cool before serving.

Lemon Gelatin Dessert with Saccharine

Ingredients:
20 g lemon
3 g gelatin
saccharine to taste
130 g water

Bring water to boil, add lemon zest and let it steep in a covered pot 10-15 minutes, then strain. Add soaked in cold water gelatin to the 100 g of hot infusion, let it dissolve, and then add lemon juice and saccharine. Strain the mixture again, pour it into a mold and cool. Dip bottom of the mold with set gelatin dessert into hot water, transfer to a tea plate and pour remaining syrup over it.

DISHES FOR MALNOURISHED PATIENTS RECOVERING FROM SERIOUS ILLNESS OR SURGERY

Cheese Butter

Ingredients:
25 g butter
15 g soviet cheese

Mix butter with grated cheese, shape as desired, decorate with butter on top, sprinkle with grated cheese and cool.

Eggs Stuffed with Caviar and Mayonnaise

Ingredients:
2 eggs
30 g salmon caviar
100 g tomatoes
20 g oil
1/2 egg yolk
2 g dill
vinegar to taste
10 g scallions

Hard boil eggs and cut them lengthwise in halves. Remove yolks and fill egg whites with caviar and put them on a plate. Decorate with sliced tomatoes, egg yolk that has been rubbed through a sieve, scallions and dill. Pour stuffed eggs over with mayonnaise.

Anchovy Oil

Ingredients:
25 g butter
25 g herring

Remove skin from herring and separate fillet from bones. Soak herring fillet in cold water for 10-12 hours, then pass through a meat grinder or finely chop. Mix with butter, shape as desired and cool. Herring can be decorated with softened butter on top.

Chicken Soup-Puree

Ingredients:
100 g chicken
15 g butter
10 g onions
10 g parsnip
10 g wheat flour
50 g cream
1/2 egg yolk
750 g water

Boil chicken until ready. Fry onions and parsnip in butter with flour until it turns light-yellow. Dilute with broth and boil for 15-20 minutes. After that strain, add chicken meat that has been passed through a meat grinder twice. Mix well and add cream mixed with yolk.

Serve with white bread croutons or pirozhki with any stuffing.

Fish Soup-Puree

Ingredients:
75 g walleye
15 g butter
50 g cream
1/2 egg yolk
10 g wheat flour
10 g onions
10 g parsnip
500 g water

Finely chop onions and parsnip and braise with 10 g butter until ready; then add flour that has been fried until it turned light-yellow. Dilute with one cup of water, add fish and cook for 15-20 minutes. Rub through a sieve, pour over with remaining water, mix, boil, then add cream mixed with egg yolk and butter.

Sweet Peas Soup-Puree

Ingredients:
150 g beef
15 g butter
150 g sweet peas
10 g wheat flour
50 g cream
1/2 egg yolk
50 g white bread
10 g onions
10 g parsnip

Cook broth from meat, root vegetables, water and strain it. Braise sweet peas in a small amount of broth until ready and rub through a sieve while still hot. Fry flour with some of the butter, dilute with broth, combine with sweet peas and boil. Strain, add cream mixed with egg yolk and butter. Serve with cube-shaped croutons.

Chicken Croquettes Stuffed with Chicken Quenelle and Mushrooms

Ingredients:
100 g chicken fillet
15 g goose or chicken liver
10 g marinated mushrooms or champignons
25 g dry white bread
25 g butter
1/4 egg
10 g milk

Make stuffing from 20 g chicken meat and 5 g bread soaked in milk. Add fried or braised finely chopped liver and finely chopped mushrooms. Mix and put on a chicken fillet pounded 1/4 in thick and wrap it into a pear shape. Dip into whipped egg, coat in breadcrumbs and fry in butter. After caramelized crust forms, put into oven for 5-7 minutes. Serve with vegetable garnish.

Chicken Schnitzel in Soft Bread Crumbs

Ingredients:
100 g chicken fillet
25 g cream
15 g butter
20 g clarified butter
25 g soft bread crumbs

Pound chicken fillet with a meat mallet, pour over with cream and smash it with a dull edge of a knife. Once fillet is well-soaked with cream, coat it in soft bread crumbs and fry in butter. Serve schnitzel with vegetable garnish or pasta, pour over with melted butter.

Lamb Pilaf with Fruit

Ingredients:
150 g lamb
25 g butter
60 g rice
20 g prunes
20 g raisins
10 g onions
1 bay leaf

Cut lamb in 3 pieces, fry in butter with finely chopped onions, put into a shallow pot. Pour over with broth or boiling water so that meat is covered half way, add bay leaf and braise with closed lid until half-ready. Then add rice, raisins, prunes, pour everything over with broth and braise with closed lid until rice is ready (braise on low heat or in oven for at least 2 hours).

Soufflé with Cauliflower and Brains

Ingredients:
150 g cauliflower
70 g brains
1 egg
20 g butter
50 g milk
10 g farina
3 g white bread crumbs

Braise cauliflower in milk with some butter, pass through a meat grinder, mix with farina and cook on low heat for 10-12 minutes. Then add egg yolk and boiled, finely chopped brains. Carefully mix with whipped egg white, put in a greased mold that has been sprinkled with bread crumbs. Spray with melted butter and bake. When serving, pour over with melted butter.

Deep Fried Walleye

Ingredients:
100 g walleye
20 g clarified butter
30 g wheat flour
1/2 egg
3 g sugar
25 g sour cream

Mix flour with sugar, sour cream, egg yolk, mix well and combine with whipped egg whites. Cut fish (no bones or skin) into 4-5 thin slices, take each piece with a fork, dip it into dough and submerge in boiling butter.

It is recommended to serve fish with fried potatoes.

Fish Pudding with Egg-Butter Sauce

Ingredients:
150 g walleye
1 egg
5 g wheat flour
50 g milk
60 g butter
10 g lemon
1 egg yolk
3 g cheese
30 g fish broth

Braise fish (no bones or skin) in 10 g butter and 30 g broth (or water); then pass through meat grinder twice. Combine with egg yolk, milk sauce (see appropriate recipe) and whipped egg whites. Mix, put in a greased mold, sprinkle with grated cheese and bake.

In a pan, mix egg yolk with 40 g of melted butter and lemon juice. Put pan in a skillet with boiling water and whip until paste becomes thick. Before serving, pour over pudding with this sauce.

Honey and Farina Pancakes with Jam

Ingredients:
50 g farina
25 g honey
1/2 egg
20 g butter
50 g jam
100 g water

Boil water with honey and 5 g butter, gradually add farina while stirring, close lid and remove from heat for 5 minutes. Then add egg, whip and with a spoon, put 6-8 pancakes on a greased skillet. Fry them on both sides until caramelized crust forms. When serving, pour over with jam.

Canned Corn Croquettes with Sour Cream

Ingredients:
120 g corn
50 g milk
10 g farina
25 g butter
1/2 egg
5 g parsley
15 g wheat bread crumbs
30 g sour cream

Put corn in a pan, pour over with milk and

boil until milk evaporates. Then add farina, 5 g butter and braise for 5-10 minutes. Remove from heat, mix with egg, sugar and chopped parsley. Make 3 croquettes, coat in breadcrumbs and fry. When serving, pour over with butter and serve sour cream separately.

Cookie Pudding with Berry Sauce

Ingredients:
50 g cookies
20 g raisins
100 g milk
1/2 egg
10 g sugar
10 g butter
30 g berry syrup
5 g potato flour
70 g water

Crush cookies and pour over with milk mixed with egg yolk. Let it infuse for 20-30 minutes; then add raisins, sugar, whipped egg whites, mix, put in a greased mold and boil in water bath or bake in oven. Serve pudding with sweet gravy made with syrup, flour and water (resembling kissel).

DISHES WITH HEMATOGEN FOR PATIENTS SUFFERING FROM ANEMIA OR EMACIATION

Omelet with Hematogen and Cauliflower

Ingredients:
30 g hematogen
1 egg
100 g cauliflower
20 g butter
10 g scallions
5 g parsley leaves
120 g water

Cover hematogen with cold water, mash it and let soak for 20-30 minutes, then strain, mix with egg and whip the mixture with a whisk. Cook cauliflower in salt water, separate into florettes, fry in butter with scallions and sprinkle with chopped parsley leaves. Pour egg mixture into a buttered skillet and fry lightly. While omelet is still liquid on top -- add cauliflower to it and put skillet into a preheated oven for a couple of minutes. Fold omelet into a roll and serve with butter.

Vegetable and Hematogen Ragout in Sour Cream

Ingredients:
30 g hematogen
50 g potatoes
30 g carrots
50 g cauliflower
30 g green peas

20 g scallions

30 g zucchini

10 g spinach

5 g parsley leaves

5 g all-purpose flour

15 g butter

30 g sour cream

70 g water

Cover hematogen with cold water, break it up and let soak for 20-30 minutes, then strain, transfer to a buttered skillet and bake in a preheated oven. Cool contents of the skillet and cut it into slivers. Boil young potatoes (or fry old ones), dice carrots and sauté in butter, separate cauliflower into florets and cook in salted boiling water, peel and dice zucchini and sauté in butter together with scallions. Put vegetables and hematogen into a wide pot. Mix sour cream with flour, add 75 g of boiling cauliflower cooking liquid and let it simmer, then pour it over vegetables, add finely chopped spinach, then cover the pot and braise everything for 10 minutes.

Sprinkle with chopped parsley leaves before serving.

Sponge Cake Sticks with Hematogen

Ingredients:

20 g hematogen

1 egg yolk

25 g sugar
20 g all-purpose flour
20 g shelled walnuts
5 g butter
60 g water

Cover hematogen with cold water, mix it with a whisk and let soak for 20-30 minutes, then strain, and whip into a thick foam.

Mash egg yolk with 20 g of sugar, mix with hematogen and flour, but do not over mix. Transfer the batter into a piping bag and pipe sticks on a buttered baking pan. Sprinkle piped sticks with chopped walnuts mixed with remaining sugar, and bake in a medium oven, then let it dry in the oven opened just a crack.

These cookies can be served with hot chocolate or fruit juices.

DISHES WITH RAW LIVER AND MARROW

Chopped Herring with Raw Marrow

Ingredients:
35 g herring (fillet)
25 g marrow
5 g butter

Pass soaked in cold water herring through a meat grinder, mix with rubbed through a sieve raw bone marrow, whip well and shape into patties. Decorate with butter piped from a piping bag and chill before serving.

Vinaigrette with Raw Liver

Ingredients:
50 g potatoes
30 g carrots
30 g beets
30 g white cabbage
30 g cucumbers
20 g onions
40 g tomatoes
50 g liver
10 g vegetable oil
25 g sour cream
5 g parsley leaves
vinegar to taste

Boil potatoes, beets, and carrot separately. Peel boiled vegetables, Shred cabbage and dice onions, thinly slice tomatoes and cucumbers, julienne liver and scald it with boiling water (outside of liver will turn white). Drain liver and let it cool; then mix it with vegetables, dress with oil and vinegar, pile into a mound on a serving plate, sour cream on top and sprinkle with chopped parsley leaves.

Sponge Cake with Walnuts and Raw Liver

Ingredients:
20 g wheat flour

50 g sugar
1 egg
60 g liver
25 g walnuts
50 g dried apricots

Whip egg white into foam, gradually add sugar; carefully fold in egg yolk and flour. Bake in a mold or on a baking sheet. Make puree with dried apricots and 40 g of sugar, cool it and mix with liver rubbed through a sieve.

Cut cooled sponge cake into 3 layers, evenly spread apricot mixture on all layers and put them together. Sprinkle with finely chopped toasted walnuts.

Serve with milk, cream, hot chocolate, coffee, tea, or juices.

PRESERVES, MARINADES, PICKLES

PRESERVES, MARINADES, PICKLES

PRESERVES

Preserves can be made from any berries or fruits.

Berries and fruits for preserves should be selected fresh and not overripe.

For each kilogram of fruits or berries use no less that 1 kg of sugar. This allows obtaining sufficient volume of syrup during cooking in which fruits or berries keep their shape, which improves the quality of preserves. In addition to that, correct proportion of fruits to sugar allows storing preserves longer without spoiling.

Preserves could be cooked with honey instead of sugar, which should be taken in the same quantity as sugar. It is also possible to use half of required amount of honey to the same amount of sugar, or adding some molasses to the sugar to prevent crystallization.

Most of the time making preserves starts

from making syrup. Put required amount of sugar into a copper or aluminum pan, add water indicated in the recipe and boil until sugar is completely dissolved. Once all the sugar is dissolved, take the syrup off the heat; add berries or fruits, quickly return to boil slightly shaking the pan so that berries or fruits submerge in syrup.

Skim the foam while cooking preserves and slightly shake pan from time to time. It is very important to correctly identify when preserves are cooked - because quality and how long preserves will keep depends on it.

Readiness of preserves is determined using the following technique - if a drop of preserves dropped onto a saucer does not spread, but keeps its shape - preserves are ready. Also, fruits and berries do not rise to the top in a cooked preserves, but are rather evenly distributed throughout the syrup, and usually become transparent.

Remove foam from the cooked preserves, let it cool, then transfer to class jars which should be covered with dump parchment paper and tied with a twine.

Keep preserves in a dry, cool place.

Wild Strawberry Preserves

Ingredients:
1 kg wild strawberries
1 kg sugar
1/2 cup water

Carefully pick over wild strawberries making sure not top squish berries, remove sprigs, leaves, and unripe berries. Make syrup, take it off the heat and carefully add berries to it. Slightly shake the pan so that berries would submerge in syrup, return to boil, remove foam and cook on low heat until done.

Strawberry Preserves

Ingredients:
1 kg strawberries
1 kg sugar
1/2 cup water

Pick strawberries over, removing stems and leaves. Make syrup, remove it from heat and add berries to it. Carefully shake the pot so that berries submerge in syrup, return to the stove and cook on low heat until it is done.

If berries are too juicy, before cooking put them into a bowl and pour half of the sugar over berries. Leave for 5-6 hours in a cool place. Drain the released juice, add remaining sugar to it, and make syrup without using water.

Raspberry Preserves

Ingredients:
1 kg raspberries
1 kg sugar

Pick raspberries over and remove stems, put berries into a bowl, add half of the sugar and leave for 5-6 hours in a cold place. Make syrup from the juice and remaining sugar, then lightly cool it.

Add berries into the pan with syrup, shake it a bit to allow berries to submerge in the syrup, then cook until the desired thickness of the syrup.

Sour Cherry Preserves

Ingredients:
1 kg sour cherries
1.5 kg sugar
3/4 cup water

Pick sour cherries over, wash in cold water, and remove pits. Put sugar with water into a pot, mix, and bring to boil. Add berries to the hot syrup and cook until done.

Black Currant Preserves

Ingredients:
1 kg black currants
1.5 kg sugar
1 cup water

Remove stems and leaves from black currants, then cover berries with cold water and remove any remaining stems that float to the top. Drain berries in a sieve. Make thick syrup, add prepared berries to it, return to boil, and cook on low heat 40-50 minutes.

Gooseberry Preserves

Ingredients:
1 kg gooseberries
1.5 kg sugar
3/4 cups water

Remove seeds from green (unripe) gooseberries, wash berries and put them into a bowl. Sprinkle some vodka over berries, shake the bowl a couple of times to mix, and put it into a cold place (preferably over ice) for 5-6 hours. Make syrup, strain berries and add them to the syrup. Cook until done.

Apricot Preserves

Ingredients:
1 kg apricots
1.5 kg sugar
2 cups water

Wash apricots and prickle their skins in a number of places with a wooden toothpick. Make syrup; pour it over prepared apricots and leave to macerate for a day. Following day drain syrup, bring it to boil, and repeat the procedure. On the third day cook apricots in the syrup until they become transparent.

Quince Preserves

Ingredients:
1 kg quince
1.5 kg sugar

Thinly slice peeled and cored quince, then put into a pot, add water just to cover, and cook until quince becomes soft. Take quince out with a skimmer and strain the cooking liquid. Put 1 1/2 cups of strained cooking liquid and sugar into a pot and make syrup. Put quince into the syrup, let it come to boil twice and continue to cook on low heat until quince becomes transparent.

Preserves will be more tasty and aromatic if you first cook washed peeled skin of the quince, and then cook sliced or diced quince in this liquid.

Apple Preserves

Ingredients:
1 kg apples
1 kg sugar
3/4 cup water

Sweet apples are the best to use when making apple preserves. Slice peeled and cored apples. Prepare syrup, add apples to it and cook until apples become transparent. If some of the apple slices become done before others, they should be removed with a spoon into some other bowl.

Apple preserves could be flavored with vanilla extract, orange or lemon zest. If making preserves with very sweet apples - it is recommended to add 1 cup of cranberries for each kilogram of apples.

Rose Petals Preserves

Ingredients:
500 g rose petals
1.5 kg sugar
1/2 lemon
1 cup water

Take petals from red or pink roses (remove white bottom part), finely chop them, mix with 500 g of sugar and leave for 2 days. Make syrup with remaining sugar, water, and juice from 1/2 lemon. Put sugared petals into the hot syrup and cook on low heat until preserves are done.

Cantaloupe Preserves

Ingredients:
1 kg peeled cantaloupe
1.5-2 kg sugar
2 cups water

Remove the skin from unripe cantaloupe, cut the melon in half and scoop out all the seeds. Sprinkle prepared cantaloupe with sugar and put into a cold place for 2 hours. Make syrup from the remaining sugar and pour it over prepared melon. On the following day strain syrup and bring it to boil, and pour it over cantaloupe again. On the third day cook cantaloupe in the syrup until done.

Pear Preserves

Ingredients:
1 kg pears
1.5 kg sugar

Slice peeled and cored hard, not overripe, pears, put them into a pot and just barely cover with cold water. Cook until pears become soft. Put sugar into a pot for cooking preserves, add 2 cups of pear cooking liquid, mix and bring to boil. Put pears into the hot syrup and cook on low heat until ready.

Yellow Plum Preserves

Ingredients:
1 kg plums
1.5 kg sugar
2 cups water

Wash slightly under ripe plums, prickle with a wooden toothpick in a number of places and put into a pot.
In another pot make syrup with sugar and water. Pour hot syrup over plums and leave them

for a day. On the second day drain syrup into another pot and return to boil, then pour it over plums again. On the third day cook plums in syrup until preserves are ready.

Orange Preserves

Ingredients:
1 kg oranges
1.5 kg sugar
2 cups water

Cut washed oranges across in two halves, remove rind, slice each half thinly, and remove seeds which make preserves bitter. Make syrup and put slices of orange into it. Return to boil and cook 1 1/2 - 2 hours on low heat, not letting it to boil too fast.

Peeled Orange Preserves
Ingredients:
1 kg oranges
1 kg sugar
2 cups water

Peel oranges and separate them into segments carefully removing seeds in the process. Make syrup, add orange segments, return to boil, and remove from heat. One hour later drain syrup into a different pot, bring it boil and simmer 10-15 minutes, then return it back to oranges. One hour later repeat the process - drain the syrup and return it to boil, then pour it over oranges, and cook everything together 10-15 minutes until desired consistency. To improve flavor - add 1-2 tbsp of julienned and blanched orange zest.

Lemon Preserves

Ingredients:
1 kg lemons
1.5 kg sugar
2 cups water

Cut rind off lemons, put them into scalding water for 20 minutes, then wash with cold water, slice and remove seeds. In a pot make thick syrup, add prepared lemons to it, return to boil and remove from heat.

Oranges or Lemons in Sugar

Ingredients:
1 kg oranges or lemons
1.5 kg sugar

Cut washed oranges or lemons into thin segments, remove seeds, lay in layers in a glass jar, pouring sugar on each layer. Leave the jar in a warm room for three days to let sugar to dissolve and turn into syrup. Keep oranges or lemons in sugar in a cold place.

Cranberry Preserves

Ingredients:

1 kg cranberries

1 kg sour apples

1 cup shelled walnuts

3 kg honey or 2 1/2 kg sugar

Put picked over and washed cranberries into a pot, add 1/2 cup water and cook under a cover until berries become soft. Mash cranberries and rub them through a sieve. In a pot bring honey to simmer, add pureed cranberries, sliced into segments peeled and cored apples, shelled walnuts, and cook for about an hour.

The same preserve can be made with sugar. Add 1 cup of water to sugar and make thick syrup, then follow the steps described above.

Green Walnuts Preserve

Ingredients:

100 green walnuts

2 kg sugar

10 cloves

1 lemon

Remove green skin from unripe walnuts and soak them for 2 days in cold water, changing water three-four times per day.

Drain water and replace it with lime water for one day, mixing walnuts frequently. Rinse walnuts with cold water, prick every walnut in a number of places with a fork and soak with cold water again for two more days. On the sixth day take walnuts from soaking water, put them into boiling water and parboil for 10 minutes, then drain in a sieve.

Mix sugar with two cups of water, bring to boil and remove the foam. Put walnuts, cloves, and lemon juice into the syrup, bring to boil and remove from heat. When preserves cool down, bring it to boil again. On the third time cook walnuts until preserve is done.

To make lime water for soaking walnuts take 500 g of slaked lime and mix with 5 liters of cold water, mix it well, then let it stand for 3-4 hours, then strain into another pot through a cheese cloth.

Apple Jelly Preserves

Ingredients:
1 kg apples
400 g sugar
2 1/2 cups water

Sour apples are most suitable to for jelly preserves. Wash and core apples and then cut them into segments, put apples into a pot, add water, cover the pot and cook on low heat 20-30 minutes, then transfer the contents of the pot into a strain and let apples drain. Add sugar to the strained liquid, return it to boil and cook on low heat, removing foam from the top from time to time. To determine if preserve is ready take some of it into a teaspoon - if drops of it will hold on the spoon instead of dropping down - jelly is ready.

Immediately transfer finished jelly into heated glass jars, cover with parchment and store just like you would preserves. Use apples that are left from cooking in jams or stuffing.

Apple Jam

Apples left over from making jelly preserves could be used in this recipe. Rub cooked apples through a sieve. Put apple puree into a pot, add 3/4 cup of sugar for every cup of puree, and cook on low heat, stirring frequently. When puree becomes thick, remove from heat and let it cool, then transfer into a glass jar and cover the jar with a parchment paper. Keep jam in a cool, dry place.

Apple and Plum Jam

Ingredients:
1 kg apples
1 kg plums
1 kg sugar
1 cup water

Put slices of cored apples and pitted plums into a pot, add water, and cook until fruits are soft. Without letting the fruit cool, rub it through a sieve. Add sugar to the fruit puree, mix well and cook, frequently stirring, until done, approximately 1 1/2 hours.

Fruit Marmalade

Ingredients:
1 kg apples
1/2 kg sugar

Wash and core apples or other fruit, and bake in an oven until cooked. Rub baked apples through a sieve. Add sugar to apple purée and cook on low heat, stirring frequently, until it thickens to a desired consistency.

Transfer hot marmalade to preheated glass jars, a sprinkle sugar on top. When marmalade cools, cover jars with parchment paper and tie with a twine. Keep marmalade in a cool, dry place.

Fresh Berry Puree

Ingredients:
1 cup purée
300-400 g sugar

Remove stems from ripe strawberries, wild strawberries, raspberries, or black currants, wash berries in cold water, drain well, and then rub them through a sieve into a ceramic bowl or enamel bowl. Add sugar to the purée.

Mix everything well and leave it in a cold place for 5-6 hours, stirring it from time to time to make sure that sugar dissolves faster. Pour purée into clean glass bottles and seal it with stoppers that were sterilized in boiling water. If purée is intended for extended storage cover the stoppers with sealing wax or bees-wax. Keep bottles with purée in a cool place.

Berry purée is used as a filling for donuts, pirozhki, cakes, puddings, or fruits, cooked in syrup.

Lingonberry Preserves

Ingredients:
1 kg lingonberry
500 g sugar or honey

Put picked over lingonberry into a bowl, cover with boiling water and instantly drain in a colander. Transfer lingonberry into a pot, add sugar and 1/2 cups of water (or add honey), add a piece of cinnamon, 3 cloves or a little of lemon zest, and cook until done.

Transfer hot preserves into a bowl, and, when it is cooled, put it into a glass jar, cover with parchment and tie with a twine. Keep in a cool, dry place.

This preserve is served with fried poultry or game, or with fried beef, veal, or lamb.

Lingonberry in Syrup

Ingredients:
1 kg lingonberry

300 g sugar

Pick over ripe lingonberries, was them in cold water, and put into a clean glass or ceramic jar. Make syrup from sugar and 2 cups of water, and lemon zest. Put everything on the stove, bring to boil, strain, and cool. Pour cold syrup over lingonberries, cover the jar with parchment paper and tie it with a twine. Keep lingonberry in a cool place.

Serve with fried meat, poultry, or game.

MARINADES

Different fruits, berries, vegetables, and mushrooms can be marinated. Marinades can serve a perfect snack during winter months, can be served with fried meat, and, finally, can be used in salads and vinaigrettes.

Quality of marinade depends a lot on the quality of vinegar. Especially tasty are marinades made with red wine vinegar, or distilled vinegar infused with herbs. If vinegar is too strong (6%) it should be diluted with water in half, then seasoned with salt, sugar, spices (pepper, cinnamon, cloves, nutmeg, coriander, bay leaves), brought to boil, simmered for a while, and cooled.

Put prepared fruits, berries, and vegetables in glass jars and cover with prepared cooled marinade.

To prevent forming of mold, top marinade with a thin layer of vegetable oil. Cover jars with parchment paper and tie with a twine. Keep marinades in a cool, dry place.

Marinated Cucumbers

Ingredients:
1 kg cucumbers
2 cups vinegar
1 tbsp salt

Take medium, firm cucumbers, wash, then scald with boiling water, stack in layers in a jar, adding tarragon between layers of cucumbers. Add one head of garlic, chopped, and one red pepper. Pour simmered and cooled vinegar, cover the jar with parchment paper and tie with a twine. Add more vinegar when some of it gets absorbed by cucumbers. Store in a cool place.

Marinated Cabbage

Finely shred cabbage, slightly rub it with salt (1 tbsp of salt for 1 kg of cabbage), squeeze, transfer into a jar and pour cooled marinade over it. Cover the jar with parchment paper and put into a cold place. Cabbage will be ready in 5-6 days.

To make marinade take 1 cup of vinegar for 1 kg of cabbage, add 3 cups water, 1 cup sugar, pinch of black pepper, 3 bay leaves, bring everything to boil and then cool.

Marinated Tomatoes

Select not very big tomatoes for marinating (plum tomatoes are most recommended), wash them and lay them in a jar.

To make marinade for each cup of vinegar take 1 cup of water, 1/4 cup of sugar, 1/2 tsp of salt, a little of cinnamon, cloves, pepper, bring everything to boil, the cool it and pour over tomatoes. In 2-3 days vinegar will become cloudy. Drain it into a pot, bring to boil, cool it again, and then pour it back over the tomatoes.

Marinated Beets

Wash beets, cook them in a pot and let cool in cooking liquid. Peel beets and slice or dice them, put into jars and cover with marinade.

To prepare marinade for each cup of vinegar take 1 cup of water, 1 tbsp of sugar, 1/2 tsp salt, a little pepper, cloves, bay leaves, mix everything well, bring to boil, and let it cool.

Marinated Grapes

Wash large bunches of ripe but firm grapes, put into prepared glass jars and cover with cooled marinade. Cover jars with parchment paper, tie with a twine and keep in cool place.

To make marinade for each kilogram of grapes take 1 cup of vinegar, 2 cups of water, 1 tsp of salt, cup of sugar, mix everything, bring to boil, then let it cool.

Marinated Cantaloupe

Wash slightly under ripe cantaloupe, cut it in half, remove seeds, cut off the rind, and cut the melon into cubes.

Put prepared cantaloupe into glass jars, pour cooled marinade over it, cover jars with parchment paper and tie with a twine. Put jars into a large pot lined with thick paper. Add enough water to come up to the top of cantaloupe pieces and simmer for an hour.

Take the pot off the heat and let the jars cool in the water, then take them out of the water and store in a cool place.

To make marinade for each cup of vinegar take 1 cup of water, 3/4 cup of sugar, 2 tbsp honey, 2-3 cloves, a piece of cinnamon, a little whole black pepper and 1/2 tsp salt. Bring everything to boil, cool, and then strain it.

Marinated cantaloupe is served as a salad with fried meat or poultry.

PICKLES

Malosol Cucumbers

Select and wash pickling cucumbers, stack them in layers in a jar, alternating with spices (dill and garlic cloves). Pour cooled brine over cucumbers (2-3 tbsp of salt for each liter of water).

Cucumbers will be ready in 2 days.

Malosol cucumber can also be done in a couple of hours. Cut the ends of the cucumbers and cover them with hot brine.

Pickled Cucumbers

Ingredients:
12 l water
600 g salt
50 g dill
5 g tarragon
1/2 spicy red pepper
1 head of garlic
1/2 horseradish root

Select medium-sized fresh cucumbers with thin skin (preferably the ones picked from the garden on the day of pickling).

Pick cucumbers over, remove yellowish or spoiled, wash them in cold water. Line the bottom of a barrel with washed leaves of oak, black currants, or cherry, then lay dill, horseradish, tarragon, and garlic. On top of that set cucumbers vertically in tight layer. Alternate layers of cucumbers with layers of leaves, spices and herbs. Tightly close the barrel with the top cover, then pour in the brine through a hole in the cover and seal it with a wooden stopper.

Cucumbers can be brined in a cask. To insure that cucumbers do not float up after the brine is added, they should be covered with a tightly sized wooden cover with a weight on top. The cover itself should not press on cucumbers. Brine should top cucumbers no less than 3-4 cm. Cover the cask with a clean cloth and kept in a cool place.

Pickled Cucumbers with Vinegar

Ingredients:
10 l water
500 g salt
1 cup red wine vinegar
3/4 cup vodka

Put prepared cucumbers into a barrel or in a jar, together with aromatics and cover with hot brine to which red wine vinegar and vodka has been added. Following day add necessary volume of cooled brine, seal the barrel (or the jar) and put into a cold place. Cucumbers prepared this way are stored much longer.

Pickled Tomatoes

Ripe or green tomatoes can be used in this recipe; however, they should not be combined.

Carefully prepare the cask - wash it thoroughly and then steam it. Pick tomatoes over, discard spoiled ones, wash in water, and lay in rows in the cask. Alternate the rows of green tomatoes with dill, tarragon, savory, as well as cherry and black currant leaves.

Shake cask from time to time to get tomatoes to settle closer to each other. Fill the cask with tomatoes and then pour brine over it. To make brine dissolve 700-800 g of salt in 12 liters of water cool boiled water. Cover the cask with a wooden circle cover, and top it with a light weight. Tomatoes should be kept in a cool place. They will be ready in 40-50 days.

Malosol Cabbage

Shred fresh cabbage, wash it and then dip into boiling water, drain and pour cold water over it. Sprinkle it with salt and pickle following instructions in the next recipe.

Cabbage will be ready in 5-6 days.

Pickled Cabbage

Cabbage is pickled in strong wooden casks. Small quantity (5-10 kg) could be pickled in glass jars.

Choose healthy, without green leaves, heads of cabbage, shred it or chop it and mix it with salt (approximately 250 g of salt for 10 kg of cabbage).

Cover the bottom of thoroughly washed cask with a thin layer of rye flour, then lay down whole cabbage leaves, then densely fill the cask with shredded cabbage, and cover with whole cabbage leaves again. For taste or flavor add whole or sliced carrots and sour apples, also lingonberries or cranberries. Top cabbage with a wooden circle and put heavy weight (washed stone) on top of the cover. In a couple of days the cabbage will start fermenting and foam will appear on top of the liquid.

Volume of foam will initially increase; however, it will eventually go away. When foam disappears completely - the cabbage is ready. During the fermentation process cabbage should be pierced with a clean birch pole to let gasses to escape. If mold appears on top of the brine it should be carefully removed, while wooden cover, cloth, and stone covering cabbage should be washed with boiling water.

Pickled Apples

Pick over and wash apples, preferably sour. Cover the bottom of the cask for pickling apples with a layer of black currant or cherry leaves. Put a couple of layers of apples on top of leaves (stem side up). Put a layer of leaves on top of apples, and repeat the procedure until the cask is full. Top the last layer of apples with another layer of leaves.

Pour specially prepared mash or sweet water over apples. To make mash cover rye flour with boiling water, season with salt, mix well, let it infuse and strain. For 10 liters of water take 200 g rye flour and 2 tbsp of salt.

To make sweet water take 400 g of sugar or 600 g of honey for 10 liters of water, add 3 tbsp of salt, bring to boil and then cool it.

Put cask with apples in a cold place, add mash or sweet water. Cover apples with a round wooden cover and top it with a weight (washed stone).

First 3-4 days apples will absorb a lot of liquid; therefore, more mash or cold water should be added. The layer of liquid during pickling and storage should be 3-4 cm higher then wooden cover. Apples will be ready in 30-40 days.

Tomato Paste

Select the ripest tomatoes, wash them, cut in half, put into a pot and cook on low heat, stirring from time to time, until a thick, homogenous mass forms. Pass the contents of the pan through a sieve, return to the pot and reduce more, stirring until puree becomes thick.

Season tomato paste with salt (1/2 tbsp of salt for each 1 kg of tomatoes), cool, transfer into a jar and top with a thin layer of grease or vegetable oil. Cover the jar with parchment paper and tie with a twine.

Mushroom Preparation

There are many types of edible mushrooms. The most common are cepes (porcini), aspen mushrooms, birch boletus, slippery jacks, milk mushrooms, orange milky caps, chanterelles, russules, honey fungi.

There are also several other types of lesser-known mushrooms that are also edible. Poisonous mushrooms include pale toadstools, red toadstools, bilious mushrooms, false honey fungi - black, red-orange and brick-red.

It is better to pick mushrooms in the morning. Mushrooms should be cut off with a knife, not ripped out with the root. This preserves mushroom spawn from which mushrooms multiply.

Clean off dirt, leaves and pine needles from the mushrooms and store them in a hard container (such as a basket). In a soft container mushrooms break and crumple.

Mushrooms spoil quickly, so they should be prepared for consumption or long-term storage within 4-5 hours.

Drying. Mushrooms most suitable for drying are cepes (porcini), aspen mushrooms, birch boletus, slippery jacks. Before drying, wipe mushrooms with dry cloth. Do not wash them, because they don't dry well after being washed.

On hot days mushrooms can be dried in the sun, just strung on a string. Mushrooms dry well in Russian ovens or stove ovens. They should be put into the oven when the temperature inside falls down to 80-70 deg Centigrade (160-175 deg Fahrenheit). To insure inflow of fresh air and outflow of moisture from mushrooms during the drying process leave the door of the oven slightly open. Mushrooms dried this way should be finished drying in the sun or over a stove.

Keep dried mushrooms in dry, well ventilated room, far from produce with strong smell. If mushrooms became damp they should be picked over and dried again.

Brining. Take saffron milk cap, milk, coral milky cap, russula mushrooms for cold brining. Put milk, coral milky cap, or russula mushrooms into cold water for 5-6 hours, while saffron milk cap could be just washed.

Put prepared mushrooms in layers in casks, ceramic, or glass jars and sprinkle with salt. Take 50 g of salt for each kg of milk, coral milky cap, or russula mushrooms, or just 40 g for each kg of saffron milk cap mushrooms. Cover mushrooms with a wooden disk smaller then the opening of a cask or a jar and top it with a weight. Add more mushrooms to the brining container when the initial load of mushrooms settles down. Check if mushrooms have enough brine 5-6 days after the container has been filled. If there is not enough brine -- increase the weight on top of the cover. Mushrooms will be ready in 1-1 1/2 months.

Hot brining is done using the following procedure. Wash and sort mushrooms. Remove stems from cepes, orange cap boletus, brown cap boletus - they should be brined separately from caps. Large caps, especially if they are brined together with smaller ones, should be cut into 2-3 parts. Wash prepared mushrooms with cold water.

Use the following spices for hot brine for 1 kg of prepared mushrooms:

2 tbsp of salt

1 bay leaf

3 black peppercorns

3 cloves

5 g dill

2 black currant leaves

Add 1/2 cup of water and salt to a pot and bring to boil. Add mushrooms when water starts boiling. During cooking stir mushrooms carefully to make sure they do not burn. When water returns to boil thoroughly remove foam, then add pepper, bay leaf, other spices and continue cooking cepes, red and brown cap boletus for 25 minutes from the moment when water returns to boil, coral milky cap or russula mushrooms for 15 minutes. Mushrooms are ready when they start settling down on the bottom of the pot, and brine becomes clear. Carefully transfer cooked mushrooms to a shallow bowl to let them cool quickly. Put cooled mushrooms into casks or jars together with brine. There should be no more than 1/5 by weight of brin in relation to the weight of mushrooms. Mushrooms will be ready in 40-45 days.

Marinating. Use cepes, orange, and brown cap boletus, as well as Slippery Jack, and honey mushrooms. Use young, firm mushrooms without a single sign of worm infestation. Every type of mushrooms should be marinated separately.

Clean and sort mushrooms, cut the stems

off, remove skin from Slippery Jack mushrooms, wash them in cold water and drain well in a colander.

Add water (1/2 cup for 1 kg of prepared mushrooms) to a pot, add vinegar and salt, then put in mushrooms and bring to boil. When water comes to boil remove foam that forms on the top and add spices (bay leaf, pepper, cloves, cinnamon and dill) and cook 20-25 minutes, stirring frequently.

When mushrooms are done (settle on the bottom of the pan), remove them from heat and let them cool, then transfer to a glass or ceramic jars. For 1 kg of mushrooms take:

1 1/2 tbsp salt

1/2 cup vinegar

1 bay leaf

0.1 g black pepper

0.1 g cloves

0.1 g cinnamon

2-3 g dill

COLD AND HOT BEVERAGES

Cold Tea

Brew strong tea and strain it through a strainer into a porcelain teapot, add sugar to taste and cool. To serve - pour cooled tea into glasses or cups and add a cube if ice and a slice of lemon or orange.

Cold Tea with Fruit or Berry Juice

Make tea following instructions of the "Cold Tea" recipe. Add 2 tbsp of grape, cherry, or black currant juice, ice cubes, and a slice of lemon into each glass, then pour in cooled tea.

Coffee

Roasted coffee should be ground just before making beverage to insure the best flavor. Ground coffee could be mixed with dried chicory root (4 parts of coffee to 1 part of dried chicory root). In addition to dried chicory root some people like to add dried ground pulled figs.

Regular coffee could be replaced with barley or acorn coffee. It is recommended to add a little of regular coffee to these types of coffee (4 parts of barley or acorn coffee to 1 part of regular coffee).

Coffee should be served with cookies, quick breads, vanilla rusks, or biscuits.

Coffee with Milk or Cream

Put ground coffee (1 tsp for each cup of water) into a coffeemaker equipped with a strainer, pour in water, put the coffeemaker on a stove and bring to boil. When water comes to boil take coffeemaker off heat and pour coffee into glasses or cups, leaving room for cream.

Serve boiled milk or cream, sugar, and biscuits on a side.

Coffee with Whipped Cream

Make coffee following previous recipe, sweeten with sugar and pour into glasses, about 3/4 full.

Top coffee with 1 tbsp of whipped cream. If desired - add powdered sugar to the cream while whipping it.

Coffee and Milk

Brew coffee as described in previous recipe, then pour it into a pot, add equal quantity of milk, sugar, and bring to boil. Pour coffee into coffee cups or glasses, top with hot milk foam, and serve.

Coffee with Condensed Milk

Canned coffee with condensed milk is available for sale, made from the best natural coffee and milk with addition of sugar. In any conditions, especially when traveling, having this product allows preparation of wonderful coffee with milk. Add 2 tsp of coffee with condensed milk into a cup, add a little hot water, mix well, and top with boiling water.

Black Coffee

Brew black coffee just like instructed in previous recipe, but stronger one. Use 1 1/2 tsp of ground coffee for each cup of water.

Pour brewed coffee into glasses or cups. Serve with sugar, slices of lemon, cognac or liquor.

Cold Coffee

Brew black coffee, strain, add sugar, and cool it. When serving - add cold cream and pour into glasses or cups. If desired - serve lemon on a side instead of adding cream.

Cocoa

Put cocoa powder into a pot (1 tsp of powder for each cup of cocoa), add 2 tsp of sugar per cup, mix well, then add a little boiling water or hot milk and blend everything together to prevent any lumps. Gradually add hot milk to blended mixture, stirring all the time, bring it to boil, take off the heat and pour into cups or glasses.

Serve cocoa with cookies, rusks, cake, biscuits, or pastry.

Cocoa with Condensed Milk

Wonderful cocoa can be made with canned product "Cocoa with Condensed Milk". You will need just a couple of minutes to boil water. Put 2-3 tsp of cocoa with condensed milk into a cup or a glass, add a little hot water, mix, and top with boiling water.

Cocoa with Whipped Cream

Make cocoa following instructions of the "Cocoa" recipe, pour it into cups filling the 3/4 full and top with 1 tbsp of cream whipped with powdered sugar.

Cocoa with Egg Yolk

Make cocoa following instructions of the recipe "Cocoa". Beat raw egg yolks (1/2 egg yolk per cup of cocoa) with sugar and dilute with a little of cocoa, the pour blended egg yolk into cocoa and whip with a whisk.

Pour into cups and serve instantly.

Chocolate

Mix unsweetened powdered chocolate (1 tsp per cup) with sugar, add a little boiling water or hot milk and mix thoroughly, to break any lumps. Add hot milk in a thin stream, constantly stirring, and bring to boil.

Pour finished chocolate into cups and serve.

Cold Chocolate with Whipped Cream

Make chocolate following instructions in the "Chocolate" recipe, chill and pour it into glasses or cups with crushed ice. Top with tbsp of whipped cream and serve.

Gogol-Mogol (Eggnog)

There are several ways of preparing gogol-mogol (eggnog), producing a nutritious and delicious beverage.

1. Lightly beat 1 egg, add 1 tbsp sugar, 2 tbsp wine, some salt, mix well, add 3/4 cup milk and strain. Instead of wine you may add some ground nutmeg.
2. Whip 1 egg yolk, add 1 tbsp sugar, some salt, 2 tbsp wine and 2/3 cup milk. Mix, strain and add whipped egg white. Before serving, mix well one more time.
3. Mix 1 egg yolk, 1 tbsp sugar, some salt and vanilla, add 3/4 cup milk, mix again and strain.

If sweet gogol-mogol is desired, egg whites with sugar should be whipped until thick, then added to the mixture with yolk or placed on top in the glass.

Fruit Gogol-Mogol (Eggnog)

Whip 2 egg yolks until thick, lemon-colored

paste forms, add a little salt, 3 tbsp sugar and 1/2 cup wild strawberry or cherry juice. Mix well, pour in 2 cups cold milk and 1/2 cup cold water. Add this mix to whipped egg whites, pour into glasses and sprinkle with powdered nutmeg.

Honey Gogol-Mogol (Eggnog)

Mix and whip egg, 2 cups cold milk, 6 tbsp honey, 2 tbsp lemon or orange juice. Serve chilled.

Lemon Drink

Mash lemon zest with sugar 91/2 cup), add juice squeezed out of 1/2 lemon, 1 cup white wine, 1 cup boiling water and mix. Strain, pour into glasses and serve.

Cranberry Juice Drink

Prepare cranberry juice the same way as for kissel. Mix sugar with equal amount of water and boil for 5 minutes. Pour cranberry juice into this syrup and cool.

For 1 cup of boiling water use 3 tbsp cranberry juice, add 1 tbsp sugar, mix and add water.

Fruit Drink

Spray diced melon and pitted peaches with lemon juice and sprinkle with sugar.

Before serving, put prepared melon and peaches in a crystal bowl or in tumblers, pour over with carbonated water and sprinkle with ginger.

Wine and Fruit Drink

Pour champagne or table white grape wine into crystal or glass pitcher, add lemon water (same amount as wine), a small amount of liqueur or cognac, some sugar and mix well. Then add fresh fruit - wedges of oranges or tangerines, pitted and sliced peaches, or canned fruit - peaches, apricots, apples and others. Serve cold.

Wine and Strawberry Drink

Put 300 g strawberries, 3/4 cup sugar, 1 cup white wine, 1/2 cup red wine into a crystal or glass pitcher, then cover and put in cold place. Before serving, pour into glasses.

Southern Drink

Take 1/2 cup sugar per 1 cup of red wine, a bit of cinnamon and boil for 10 minutes. Then add 2 egg yolks whipped with a small amount of cold wine and heat again in water bath without boiling. Serve hot in glasses or cups.

Feast Drink

Pour a bottle of red table wine into a pan,

add 1 cup sugar, some cinnamon, 5-6 cloves, and lemon zest from 1/2 lemon. Mix then heat for 10 minutes. Strain, add 1/4 cup cognac, pour in glasses and serve hot.

Lemonade

There is a wide variety of carbonated beverages available for purchase. They are based on fruit-berry juices and sugar: lemonade, cream soda, etc.

In order to prepare lemonade yourself at home take 1 tbsp of lemon juice (per cup of lemonade), mix with 1 1/2 tbsp sugar and dilute with carbonated water. Serve cooled, with a wedge of lemon in each glass.

Orange Juice with Cream

Whip 1/2 egg yolk (per 1 cup of drink) with 2 tbsp sugar, add 1/2 cup orange juice, mix, pour in glass and add cream.

Liqueur with Cream

Use coffee liqueur to make this drink. Pour cream in glasses, filling them 3/4 of the way. Add 2 to 5 tsp of liqueur per glass. Serve with cookies, biscuits, Eastern sweets.

Wild Strawberry Drink

Mix 1/4 cup milk, 1 tbsp sugar, 1/4 cup crushed wild strawberries, add a little salt and whip. Serve cooled.

Orange Drink

Mix 3/4 cup milk with 1/4 cup orange juice, add 1 tbsp sugar and whip until uniform. Serve cooled.

Raspberry Drink

Add 2 tbsp raspberry juice and 1/2 tbsp sugar into a glass of milk and mix. Serve cooled.

Cherry Drink

Mix 1/4 cup cherry juice 1/2 tbsp lemon juice, add 3/4 tbsp sugar, a little salt, boil on low heat for 5 minutes, then cool.

Mix this syrup with 3/4 cup milk and whip. Serve cooled.

Milk with Fruit-Berry Syrup

Add 2-3 tbsp fruit syrup or grape juice to a 3/4 full glass of milk, and add water to fill the glass. Mix and serve cold.

Crouton Kvass

Ingredients (for 10-12 bottles of kvass):

1 kg rye bread
25 g yeast
200 g sugar
20 g peppermint
50 g raisins

Dry sliced rye bread in the oven, without burning it. Put croutons in a pan, pour over with boiling water, cover and leave for 3-4 hours. Strain, add yeast, sugar and peppermint. Cover with napkin and leave for 5-6 hours to ferment. When kvass starts foaming, strain it again and pour into bottles with a few raisins, and seal. Soak corks in boiling water prior to sealing, to make them more elastic. Reinforce corks with strings to make the seal more secure. Leave bottles in cold place, on their side. Kvass will be ready in two-three days.

Berry Kvass

Pick berries over and remove twigs and leaves. Put cleaned berries into a sieve and wash under a running water, then let all the water drain. Transfer washed berries into a strong, clean barrel, and add boiled and cooled water (2 buckets of water for 1 bucket of berries). Tightly close the barrel and leave in a root cellar for 3-4 weeks.

Rose Hips Vitamin Beverage

Rose hips have a high content of vitamin C.

Wash dried rose hips with cold water, then slightly crush them to improve extraction of the vitamin C from the berries, and cover with 1 cup of boiling water for 1 tbsp of rose hips. The beverage should be brewed in an enameled pot to avoid loss of vitamin C. Bring everything to boil and simmer no more than 8-10 minutes.

Transfer liquid together with berries into a glass or ceramic container, cover and leave to infuse for a couple of hours (or overnight) in a warm place.

Strain the beverage through a double layer of cheese cloth and squeeze berries to extract as much of liquid as possible. The resulting beverage has pleasant, sour taste, which could be sweetened with sugar. It should be consumed the same day it was brewed to avoid loss of vitamin C.

Healthy adult can consume 1-2 cups of this beverage per day, while children should not drink more than 1 cup.

If you are using just the skin of rose hip berries to make this beverage, take just 1/2 tbsp of rose hips per cup of boiling water.

Bekmes and Nardek

Reduced grape juice is called bekmes. It is a thick, very nutritious, pleasant, and tasty beverage found in grape-growing regions.

On the south of the country, where there are a lot of watermelon farms, nardek (watermelon honey) - reduced watermelon juice can be found.   .

Bekmes or nardek can be successfully used in baking sweet pastry, cookies, and making sweets.

OLD RECIPES

A side bar is printed throughout most of the book, sometimes describing ingredients, sometimes glorifying Soviet industry; however, from time to time old recipes from pre-Soviet time (some from 1800's and even 1700's) also appear there. We are including these old recipes in translation of the book.

Oats and Prunes Soup

Wash 1/2 cups of oats with cold water, transfer to a pan and cover with 2 liters of boiling water, add 1 tbsp of butter and cook until done. Pass oats with cooking liquid through a sieve and add one more tablespoon of butter. Cover 200 g of pitted prunes with water, add 1/4 cup of sugar and cook until soft. Mix cooked prunes with oat soup, heat it up and serve.

Aromatic Vinegar

If you for some reason need to prepare flavored vinegar at home (it is easy and simple to buy it in a nearby store) we can offer the following recipe. Add tarragon, celery, or dill to distilled vinegar (100 g for 1 l of vinegar). Some other possibilities are sliced sour apple, black currants leaves, lime blossoms, or bay leaves. Tightly close container with vinegar and let it infuse for 15 days. Strain vinegar through a cheese cloth and use it to dress vinaigrettes, salads, herring and chopped herring.

Sorrel and Beet Tops Soup

Wash 1 kg of beet tops, put them into a pot and add 2 l of hot water. Bring to boil, lower the heat and simmer 10-15 minutes, then add washed sorrel (200 g) and cook 10 more minutes. Take all greens out of the liquid with a skimmer and pass them through a meat grinder, them mix with strained and cooled cooking liquid. Slice cucumbers, onion, dill, radishes, hardboiled eggs, put everything into a soup tureen, add sour cream, mustard, then pour in soup and mix everything well.

Chanterelles Soup

Wash chanterelles (500 g), finely chop 100 g of bacon and sauté finely diced onions for 10 minutes until it starts softening. Add mushrooms to onions and sauté everything on low heat 45 minutes longer. Add 3 liters of boiling water to the pot, season with salt and simmer for 30 minutes. Mix 1 tsp of flour with sour cream and add it to the soup. Season with pepper to taste.

Cold Tomato Juice Soup

Wash 300-400 g of ripe tomatoes, slice them in half, sprinkle with salt and let them stand for a while, then squeeze juice through a cheese cloth. Grate the same quantity of beets and squeeze juice. In a pot add 2 liters of water to tomato and beets remnants and cook 10-15 minutes, then strain, cool, and add to squeezed tomato and beets juices. Thinly slice boiled potatoes (200 g), fresh peeled cucumbers (400 g), boiled rutabaga (200 g), hardboiled eggs, tarragon and scallions. Roast 4 sweet red peppers, let them cool, then remove skin and seeds, julienne and mix with sour cream. Mix everything and add vegetable broth.

Dried Fruit and Pasta Soup

Wash mix of dried fruits (200 g), put into a pot, cover with 3 liters of cold water, and leave for 2-3 hours, then add 1/3 cup sugar, cinnamon and cloves. Cover the pot, bring to boil and cook on high heat for 10 minutes. When fruits become soft take the pot off the heat and let it cool. Cook 100 g of pasta in salted water, rinse it with water, transfer pasta to a tureen, add 1/3 cups of sour cream and pour in fruit broth.

Lamb with Rice

Cut washed lamb into pieces, remove marrow bones if there are any, season with salt and pepper and brown in a skillet. When lamb is nicely browned - add sliced onions and fry a little longer. Transfer contents of the skillet into a pot, add 2-3 cups of stock or waters, a little of tomato paste, bring to boil and braise. 1 - 1 1/2 hours (40-50 minutes if lamb is young) after the start of braising add 1 cup of washed and parboiled for 10 minutes rice, mix everything well and braise for 30 minutes. Serve in the pot in which the dish was cooking.

Salted Tongue with Garnish

Thoroughly wash beef tongue, put it into a pot, cover with cold water, add roots and onion, and cook 3-3 1/4 hours on low heat. Take cooked tongue out, rinse it with cold water and immediately skin.

Thinly slice peeled tongue, lay on a serving plate and drizzle 2-3 tbsp of broth and melted butter over it. Garnish with green peas dressed with butter.

Instead of green peas the tongue can be garnished with pasta, braised cabbage, mashed potatoes, or pea purée.

Boiled Sausage with Onions

Thinly slice boiled sausage, lay slices on a serving plate and top them with thinly sliced onion rounds, drizzle with dressing made from vegetable oil, mustard and vinegar and sprinkle with finely chopped dill or parsley leaves.

Fried Spring Chickens, with Tomatoes and Zucchini

Cut prepared spring chicken into 4 parts,

cut the tendons in joints of legs and wings, and slightly point the meat. Season chicken with salt and pepper, put skin side down into oil in a preheated skillet and fry until browned. Turn pieces over and fry on the other side, then add 2 tbsp of sour cream and continue braising on low heat 10-15 minutes. Separately fry tomatoes cut in half, and peeled and sliced into circles zucchini. To serve transfer spring chicken to a heated serving plate and garnish with slices of fried zucchini and tomatoes, pour strained juices on top and sprinkle with finely chopped dill or parsley leaves.

Fried Chanterelles with Sour Cream

Clean 500 g of mushrooms from dirt, wash them thoroughly, and drain well in a colander. Put mushrooms into a skillet with melted butter and fry. Slice onion and soften it in butter. Add softened onions to chanterelles and continue sautéing for 40-50 minutes. Add 1/4 cup of sour cream to mushrooms and simmer 10-15 minutes. Season with pepper, sprinkle with dill before serving.

Tenderloin on a Skewer

Wash a piece of beef tenderloin, remove all silver skin, season with salt and pepper, set it on a skewer and cook over red-hot coals for about 10 minutes.

Baste meat with melted butter during

cooking, and rotate the skewer to insure even cooking on all sides.

Take cooked tenderloin from the skewer, set it on a serving plate and garnish with slices of tomatoes, onions, scallions, or lemons.

Potatoes Stuffed with Meat

Wash 1 kg of large potatoes, pour over with boiling water, add salt and boil until half-done. Then peel potatoes, cut one side off and remove the middle. Pass 300 g of meat together with removed potato cores, add a whipped egg, finely chopped dill, salt, ground pepper; mix everything well. Put stuffing inside the potatoes and close the sides that have been cut off. Put potatoes tightly into a pan, pour over with broth or water and braise until ready. Add tomatoes, flour and sour cream.

Potatoes Stuffed with Herring

Prepare 1 kg of potatoes the same way as in "Potatoes Stuffed with Meat" recipe. Pass removed potato cores through a meat grinder together with cleaned herring, add 2 finely chopped onions, pepper, powdered bay leaf, raw egg, sour cream and whip it well. Put this stuffing inside potatoes, fry in butter, pour over with sour cream and bake in hot oven.

Potatoes with Fatback

Fry small pieces of fatback in a pan, add 1/2 spoon flour, let it caramelize; while stirring, add pepper, parsley, cumin, bay leaf; pour over with broth or water and boil for 5 minutes. Then add peeled and sliced raw potatoes. When potatoes are done, remove fat and serve.

Marinated Beets

Wash beets, cook them in water and let cool in the cooking liquid. Peel cooked beets, slice or dice them, put into jars and cover with pickle.

To make marinade for each cup of vinegar take 1 cup of water, 1 tbsp sugar, 1/2 tsp salt, a little bit of pepper, cloves, bring everything to boil and then cool before using.

Rutabaga Sauce

Peel 300 g of rutabaga, cook it in water until done and rub it through a sieve. Add 1 tbsp of sugar and 2 tbsp of butter to the puree and cook until it thickens. Cool rutabaga puree, beat into it one egg whites, then pour in lemon juice, add lemon zest, and whip it again. Serve this sauce with fried or braised meat, game birds or poultry.

Dried Potatoes

Peel, boil and drain potatoes. Slice and put on a baking sheet, put in a warm oven with door slightly open for 10-15 minutes (to allow vapor to escape). After 10-15 minutes flip potato slices and resume drying. It is also possible to dry potatoes ground potatoes, by putting a thin layer of them on a sheet.

Dried Carrots, Parsley, Celery, Rutabaga, Turnip

Wash and chop vegetables (scald turnip to remove bitter taste), spread in a thin layer on a cloth or a board and dry, mixing several times. Place dried vegetables on a baking sheet in a layer of 1-2 cm. Put in oven with temperature of 50-60 degrees C for 5-6 hours; mix several times. First 10-15 minutes of drying the oven door should be slightly opened. It is recommended to dry boiled vegetables. In this condition they preserve their appearance and taste well.

Dried Beets

Wash unpeeled beets, place tightly in a pan, pour over with boiling water and cook until beets become soft. Peel, finely chop, put on baking sheets covered with paper, then put into oven heated to 50-60 degrees C for 10-15 minutes. Flip and put back in oven for another hour. Beets can continue drying in a warm spot in the room.

Dried Herbs

Parsley, dill and celery are most suitable for drying.

Before drying wash herbs, shake off water; put stems separately from leaves for drying. Dry herbs in oven heated to at least 40 degrees C for 3-4 hours. Put dried herbs in to small paper packages and store in dry place.

Add dried leaves into soups, meat and fish sauces. Stems are used for broth.

Carrot Pudding with Breadcrumbs

Was 500 g of carrots, cook in water until soft, peel and rub through a sieve. Add 100 g of crushed and sifted breadcrumbs to the carrot purée. Beat 6 egg yolks, 1/2 cup sugar and 100 g of melted butter until the mixture is light and fluffy, about 30 minutes. Into beaten egg yolks add carrot purée, sliced candied fruit or raisins, mix well, season with salt and fold in whipped egg whites. Carefully transfer mixture into a buttered mold and bake in a preheated oven for 1 1/2 hours.

Rutabaga Stuffed with Cepes

Bake 1 kg of rutabagas, peel them, scoop the flesh from the inside and chop it. Wash 300 g of pickled cepes, chop and fry in butter together with 2 diced onions. Mix fried mushrooms with chopped rutabaga and stuff rutabaga shells with it. Put stuffed rutabagas into an ovenproof pot, drizzle with melted butter, cover the pot and put it into a preheated oven for 30 minutes. Add a cup of thick sour cream and gratin it until lightly browned.

Pumpkin with Rice and Eggs

Cut 1 kg of pumpkin into small pieces, put into a pot with 1/2 cup of water and cook until soft, then add 1 liter of milk, 1/3 cup of washed rice and cook for 30 more minutes. Cool pumpkin with rice, beat in 4 eggs, add 3-4 tbsp of melted butter, 1/2 cup of sugar, transfer into a buttered mold and bake in a preheated oven.

Pumpkin and Noodles Casserole

Cook 200 g of noodles, drain well. Julienne 1 kg of pumpkin, season with salt and sauté in hot butter, then add noodles, beat in 4 eggs, add 1/4 cup sugar, a bit of cinnamon, mix, and bake in a preheated oven.

Fried Porcini with Onion Sauce

Wash 1 kg of fresh, young porcini mushrooms, dry caps, season with salt and sauté in hot oil for 15 minutes, frequently stirring, then take of the heat and leave in a warm place. Put 20 g of diced onions into heated oil, season with salt and fry until soft, then add 1 cup of sour cream to the skillet with onions, bring to simmer and pour the sauce over mushrooms.

Rutabaga Patties

Peel and slice 1 kg of rutabaga; cover it with hot water and leave for 10-15 minutes. Drain rutabaga, put it into a pot, cover with boiling water and cook until soft, then pass it through a meat grinder, season with salt, beat in 4 eggs, add 2 tbsp melted butter, 200 g of crushed breadcrumbs, nutmeg, and whip everything well. Shape patties from this mixture, coat in breadcrumbs and fry in hot oil.

Make a sauce to serve with these patties. Put 1 cup of washed raisins into a pot with 2-3 cups of water, add 2 tbsp of butter, 1/2 cup of sugar, bring to boil, and cook for 15 minutes, then add 1/2 cup of sour cream and 1 tbsp of flour, stir well and return to simmer.

Potatoes with Wine

Put butter, pepper, salt, chopped parsley and onions in a pan. Add some flour; pour over with broth and some wine, one cup or more, depending on the amount of sauce being prepared. Bring to boil, add boiled and sliced potatoes and cook until sauce thickens.

Rice Porridge with Pumpkin

Peel 1 kg pumpkin, slice, pour over with milk (1 l) and cook until half-done. Then add 1 cup of rice washed in warmed water and add salt.

Cover with lid and cook until fully ready. Serve with butter and sugar.

Farina with Carrots

Peel, wash and grate 1/2 kg carrots. Add 1/4 cup sugar, 2 tbsp of butter and braise on low heat for 1 hour. Then pour over with 1 l of milk, boil, add one cup of farina and mix, then put in hot oven for 1/2 hour. Serve with berry juice.

Cabbage with Cream

Boil a white head of cabbage in salted water until it is almost done. Drain and cut into several parts. Put butter, salt, ground white pepper, one spoon of flour, cream and cabbage in a pan, cook until ready.

Buckwheat Porridge with Rutabaga

Peel 500g of young rutabaga, wash, grate, put on a skillet with butter and fry while frequently stirring. Wash 300 g of buckwheat, drain, mix buckwheat with fried rutabaga, put in a pan, pour over with 1.5 l of milk and cook until porridge thickens. Add butter, sugar, salt, then mix, cover with lid and put in oven for 2 hours.

When serving, mix porridge well so there are no lumps of rutabaga, pour over with hot butter.

Buckwheat Casserole with Fresh Mushrooms

Ingredients:
1 cup buckwheat
500 g fresh mushrooms
1/2 cup sour cream
2 tbsp butter

Cook buckwheat porridge, add fried fresh mushrooms, melted butter, sour cream, mix well. Put everything in a pan or skillet and bake in oven for 20-30 minutes.

Squash Pancakes

Put 3 tbsp of butter into hot squash puree (made with 1 kg squash), mix and cool. Add 3 eggs, salt, 1/4 sugar, whip, then add 2 cups flour and 2 g baking soda. Mix dough and whip until bubbles form, then pour dough with a spoon on a hot, greased skillet.

Carrot Blini

Wash 1/2 carrots, pour over with hot water, cover with lid and boil until soft. Peel carrots, rub through a sieve, pour over with 3/4 l milk and boil. Add a cup of flour to boiling puree, mix well so that there is no lumps, add 1/4 l milk or water (pour slowly, while stirring). Then add 4 eggs, cup of flour and whip. Pour in 100g of yeast diluted in 1/4 l of water, mix and let the dough rise.

After 2 hours, add salt, 2 tbsp of warm
butter, 1/2 tbsp sugar and mix. Then add 1/2 cup
flour and whip for 15 minutes in warm place, until
bubbles start forming. Cover and put in warm
place. When dough rises, blini are ready for
baking.

Pumpkin Puree Blini

Peel and slice 1 kg pumpkin, boil until soft
and rub through a sieve, pour over with 1 l of milk
and heat until lukewarm. Add 15 g of yeast
diluted with water, 3 eggs and mix. Then add 2-2
1/2 cups of flour, whip dough and leave in warm
place for 2 hours. Add 1 tbsp of heated butter, 1/2
cup sugar, salt, whip well and put in warm place
so that the dough can rise and bake blini.

Egg Croquettes

Cook 5 eggs to hard-boiled stage, peel and
chop them. Make a thick milk sauce. Mix in 2 raw
egg yolks into the hot sauce, then add chopped
eggs and a tablespoon of finely chopped herbs,
season with salt, mix everything well and transfer
into a buttered bowl. To prevent forming of film
on top of the mixture, pour a little of melted butter
over the mixture. Let it cool. Take 1 tbsp of
mixture at a time and shape it into an egg or a ball,
dip into a beaten egg and then coat in
breadcrumbs. Deep-fry croquettes until done, then

take them out of the oil with a skimmer and put into a sieve to drain. Deep fry sprigs of parsley in the same oil.

Set cooked croquettes into a mound on a serving plate and decorate with fried parsley. Serve hot tomato sauce or with green salad dressed with sour cream, or with mayonnaise and vinegar.

Eggs Baked with Mashed Potatoes

Cook 500 g of peeled potatoes in salted water, drain in a colander, then rub through a sieve, add a little butter, season with salt and mix everything well, gradually adding 1/2 cup of hot milk. Transfer mashed potatoes to a buttered skillet, smooth the top and sprinkle with rated cheese or crushed bread crumbs, and bake in a preheated oven until lightly browned on top. Make 5-6 indentations in the mashed potatoes and accurately break one egg into each hole. Return skillet into the oven for 2-3 minutes. Serve in the skillet it was cooked in.

Rhubarb Kissel

Wash 300 g of rhubarb and remove skin and fibers, dice it, and soak in cold water for 10-15 minutes. Make simple syrup from 3/4 cups sugar and 2 cups of water. Add drained rhubarb into hot syrup, return to boil, and simmer 5-10 minutes. Add 2 tbsp of potato starch mixed with water.

Rhubarb kissel should only be served cold.

Raspberry Gelatin Dessert

Pick over 1 cup of raspberries and wash them in cold water. In a pot add 1 1/2 cups of water to 3/4 cups sugar, mix and bring to boil. Add cleaned raspberries to the hot syrup, bring to boil, turn off the heat, cover the pot and leave to infuse 15-20 minutes. Strain the raspberry infusion, add lemon acid to taste, slightly cool, pour into molds and let it set. If desired – decorate gelatin dessert with whole berries.

Cloudberry Preserves

Wash 1 kg of cloudberries in a bowl, then put into a colander and wash it under a cold running water. Let all the water drain. Add water to 1 kg of sugar, put on the stove and bring to boil mixing from time to time, then add berries and cook 30 minutes. Rub berries through a sieve and cook 10 minutes longer.

Carrot and Lemon Preserves

Peel and wash 1 kg of carrots, thinly slice and sprinkle with 1 kg of sugar. Zest 1 lemon with a sharp knife and blanch zest in boiling water. Julienne blanched zest and put to cook in sugar-water for 1 hour. Thinly slice lemon, add to prepared carrots, then add cooked lemon zest.

Cook everything together until carrots become transparent.

Red Currants Preserves/Gelatin Dessert

Mash 1 kg of red currants, add cup of water, bring to boil, strain through a cheese cloth and squeeze as much juice as possible. Add 1 1/4 kg sugar to currant juice, bring to boil, and cook on high heat for 30 minutes. Test readiness of the preserves - pour 1 tablespoon of juice into a plate - if it thickens in 10 minutes - then the preserves is ready, if the juice is still thin - the preserves should be cooked more. Preserves should be thick just like usual gelatin dessert made with gelatin. Cool finished preserves and transfer it into jars.

Rowan Preserves

Pick over and wash 1 kg of rowan berries picked after the first frost, then cover with cold water and let it stand 24 hours. Drain berries in a colander, then cover with cold water again and let it stand. Repeat this process 2-3 times. Add water to 1 1/2 kg of sugar, make syrup, then pour hot syrup over rowan berries, and keep on ice for 24 hours. Take berries with a skimmer, bring syrup to boil, and cook for 20 minutes. Return berries to boiling syrup and cook on medium flame 20-25 minutes, until syrup thickens and berries become shiny. Do not overcook berries, or they will become dry and unappealing.

Apple and Bread Casserole

Soak 1/2 kg of stale white bread in a mix of 3 eggs and 1/2 liters of milk and transfer them to dish. Slice 1 kg of apples and mix with sugar. Butter an oven-proof pot and sprinkle it with breadcrumbs. Line the bottom and the sides of the pot with soaked bread, and fill the middle with alternating rows of apple slices and remaining slices of bread. Dot rows of bread with a little bit of butter. When the pot is full - smooth the top, drizzle with melted butter and sprinkle with almonds crushed with sugar. Bake in a preheated oven.

CONVERSION

Metric to Imperial Conversion

Weight
10 grams = 1/4 oz
15 grams = 1/2 oz
25 grams = 1 oz (actual 28.35 grams)
450 grams = 1 lb
1 kilogram = 2 1/4 lb

Volume
1 level teaspoon = 5 ml
1 level tablespoon = 15 ml
1 oz = 28.35 grams/ml
1 lb = 450 grams
1 cup = 250 ml
1 pint = 600 ml
1 liter = 1000 ml

Length
1 cm = 1/2 inch
2.5 cm = 1 inch
30 cm = 12 inches = 1 ft

Table of Weight Conversion

Weight in Grams

Ingredient:	Cup(250 cm³)	Tablespoon	Teaspoon	Piece
Flour/Grains				
Wheat flour	160	25	10	–
Potato Starch	200	30	10	–
Crushed breadcrumbs	125	15	5	–
Buckwheat	210	25	–	–
Oats	90	12	–	–
Farina	200	25	8	–
Barley	230	25	–	–
Ground barley	180	20	–	–
Rice	230	25	–	–
Sago	180	20	–	–
Millet	220	25	–	–
Beans	220	–	–	–
Green peas	200	–	–	–
Split peas	230	–	–	–
Lentils	210	–	–	–
Oatmeal	140	–	–	–

Table of Weight Conversion

	Weight in Grams			
Ingredient:	Cup(250 cm^3)	Tablespoon	Teaspoon	Piece
Milk/Dairy				
Butter (melted)	250	20	5	–
Whole milk	250	20	–	–
Dry milk	120	20	5	–
Condensed milk	–	30	12	–
Sour cream	250	25	10	–
Vegetables				
Carrot (medium)	–	–	–	75
Potato (medium)	–	–	–	100
Onion (medium)	–	–	–	75
Cucumber (medium)	–	–	–	100
Tomato-paste	–	30	10	–
Tomato-puree	220	25	8	–
Parsnip	–	–	–	50

Table of Weight Conversion

Weight in Grams

Ingredient:	Cup(250 cm³)	Tablespoon	Teaspoon	Piece
Sugar, salt, etc.				
Sugar	200	25	10	–
Salt	325	30	10	–
Vinegar	250	15	5	–
Gelatin (sheet)	–	–	–	2.5
Gelatin (powdered)	–	15	5	–

Made in the USA
Las Vegas, NV
23 November 2020